The Subject of Documentary

VISIBLE EVIDENCE

Edited by Michael Renov, Faye Ginsburg, and Jane Gaines

The Subject of Documentary

Michael Renov

University of Minnesota Press

Minneapolis

London

Copyright 2004 by the Regents of the University of Minnesota

Published by the University of Minnesota Press
111 Third Avenue South, Suite 290
Minneapolis, MN 55401-2520
http://www.upress.umn.edu

Library of Congress Cataloging-in-Publication Data

Renov, Michael, 1950–
    The subject of documentary / Michael Renov.
        p.   cm. — (Visible evidence ; v. 16)
    Includes bibliographical references and index.
    ISBN 0-8166-3440-8 (alk. paper) — ISBN 0-8166-3441-6 (pbk. : alk. paper)
    1. Documentary films—History and criticism.   I. Title.   II. Series.
    PN1995.9.D6R44 2004
    070.1'8—dc22

                                                                2003028176

Printed in the United States of America on acid-free paper

The University of Minnesota is an equal-opportunity educator and employer.

12 11 10 09 08 07 06 05   10 9 8 7 6 5 4 3 2

For Cathy, Veronica, and Maddie

Contents

Acknowledgments

This book is the result of many years of teaching and writing about documentary film, so it is not surprising that I am indebted to a great many people. My students, first at the University of California–Santa Barbara (where I was teaching when I wrote the first chapters), then, for the past eighteen years, at the University of Southern California, have inspired me to think about the meanings and implications of subjectivity in the realm of nonfiction. I was faced with their subjectivity in response to the films, and it always changed my own understanding. Some of those former students (Mark Williams, Su Scheibler, Abé Markus Nornes, Jim Moran, Valentin Stoilov, Bhaskar Sarkar, Dan Walkup, Christie Milliken, Bobby Simmons, Nithila Peter, Allison deFren, and Brody Fox) are now themselves teachers and makers and writers who are reshaping the documentary domain.

The Visible Evidence conference provided the occasion for writing no less than six of the chapters of this book. Since its inception in 1993, Visible Evidence has become a rallying point for documentary devotees, the place to test ideas, see new films and tapes from around the world, sample the regional variations of documentary culture, and expand the critical vernacular. The conference's increasingly global reach has certainly enriched my understanding of the breadth and vitality of the documentary project, a fact I hope is reflected in these pages. More than anything, Visible Evidence has created an open-ended, if necessarily imagined, audience for all manner of speculation in the realm of nonfiction culture. I am grateful to all those who have organized the annual meetings and whose contributions have made it the conference that I cannot bear to miss.

Thanks are due to the succession of University of Minnesota Press editors with whom I have worked on this book over the years. Owing to its lengthy gestation period, there are many: Janaki Bakhle, Micah Kleit,

Jennifer Moore, Carrie Mullen, and Andrea Kleinhuber. Their patience has been monumental, their insights endlessly valuable.

This book would not have been possible to produce were it not for the intelligence and technological know-how of Valentin Stoilov and Priscilla Ovalle, who transformed ancient computer files and ill-matched software into a manuscript.

Finally, I acknowledge the contributions of my family, the three women who share my life and bring me joy. To Cathy, Veronica, and Maddie, thanks for allowing me to immerse myself in the documentary world and for planning family vacations around the site of the next Visible Evidence conference. You form the radiant center of *my* subjectivity.

Surveying the Subject: An Introduction

"Surveying the Subject" was delivered as a keynote address at the "Crossing Boundaries" film festival organized at the Danish Film Institute in Copenhagen in May 2000, an event that showcased the convergence of documentary and experimental forms in contemporary independent filmmaking. One of the festival's central strands was autobiography and the exploration or problematizing of personal or cultural identity by film- and videomakers from around the world. On this occasion, I hoped to provide a context for the "turn to the subject" in documentary production in the 1990s through a broad survey of the sources, variations, and repressions of subjectivity in a century of documentary film practice.

On more than one occasion, I have attempted to describe this book in a single sentence: it's all about autobiography in film and video. As defined in literary studies, autobiography is a form of personal writing that is referential (that is, imbued with history), mainly retrospective (though the temporality of the telling may be quite complex), and in which the author, the narrator, and the protagonist are identical.[1] Autobiographical practice in the West is as old as the confessional writings of Augustine (the late fifth century), yet as memoir, diary, personal essay, or testimonial, it currently enjoys a popularity and critical prominence never before achieved.

But I have always felt uneasy with such a stand-alone description—autobiography in film and video. It assumes too much and, unless carefully conceptualized and historicized, offers little. To begin with, shouldn't the phrase be posed in the form of a question rather than as a statement of fact? As statement, it implies a simple grafting of one set of media practices (film/video/Internet) onto another (literature) with too little regard for the debates, new social relations, and technological transformations that are the very conditions of existence of these new forms of self-inscription. It posits a relatively nascent cultural form as a fait accompli rather than as a still-unfolding phenomenon.

When I published an essay on new autobiography in film and video in *Afterimage* in 1989,[2] most of the work discussed in these pages was still unproduced; the Internet was years away from realizing its potential as a mass cult autobiographical vehicle. What sense can there be in imagining this dynamic mode of visual culture as an extension of traditional literary practices? On the other hand, autobiography has always been boundary defying. Feminist literary theorists Sidonie Smith and Julia Watson make the case succinctly: "Autobiographical writing surrounds us, but the more it surrounds us, the more it defies generic stabilization, the more its laws are broken, the more it drifts toward other practices, the more formerly 'out-law' practices drift into its domain."[3] But what happens when an outlaw literary practice moves beyond literature?

At least one literary critic has argued that there is no real cinematic equivalent for the autobiographical act; indeed, it is said, cinema's cultural preeminence may be a sure sign of autobiography's demise.[4] Twenty years after this pronouncement, it is clear to me that, quite to the contrary, 16 mm film, consumer-grade video, and the Internet have provided unique and increasingly accessible platforms for self-expression while opening up new audience frontiers. Given cinema's century-long hold on the popular imagination and its by now established niche in the academy, I feel no need to plead the case for film's legitimacy. New cultural forms always build on and reinvent their antecedents. And equally, although this book and others like it may in the end expand the vernacular of autobiographical studies, I want to assert no new orthodoxies. I am less concerned with (re)defining autobiography in the strict sense proposed by Philippe Lejeune and others than with examining a diversity of autobiographical practices that engage with and perform subjectivity. Simply stated, I want to ask how and to what effect viable versions of the self come to be constructed through these late-twentieth-century media practices. But even as I articulate this core question, searching perhaps for a poetics of audio-visual autobiography, I'm struck by the instability of the most basic terms.

The word "autobiography" is composed of three principal parts—"auto," "bio," and "graphy"—which make up the essential ingredients of this representational form: a self, a life, and a writing practice. As we shall see, the self is by no means an uncontested term. But neither is it altogether clear just what is meant by a life. Surely every autobiographical act cannot be held accountable for the entirety of a life, so what tokens of it are deemed worthy as emblematic or at least evocative of the whole?

If the "auto" and the "bio" are at issue for every species of autobiography, it is nevertheless the graphological dimension that must be the recurrent focal point for an examination of the filmic, electronic, or digital autobiography. Self-inscription is necessarily constituted through its signifying practices. As Jerome Bruner has argued, "autobiography is life construction through 'text' construction."[5] Given the availability of these relatively new vehicles for self-expression, it is clear to me that careful attention must be given to the new—indeed, transformative—possibilities of autobiographical text construction.

The most striking contribution of Sidonie Smith and Julia Watson's collection *Getting a Life: Everyday Uses of Autobiography* is its once-and-for-all leveling of the hierarchy that has separated the traditional literary autobiography from all other (presumably corrupt) forms. Now we can see as never before that medical records, curricula vitae, and performance art are autobiographical acts of a most profound sort and arguably more pertinent to our lived experience than their pedigreed literary cousins. This book is also devoted to a range of self-inscriptive practices beyond the borders of literature. Part III, entitled "Modes of Subjectivity," stakes out the specificities of the autobiographical film, the confessional video, the electronic essay, and the personal Web page. But medium specificity is not the sole target of concern here. As discussed in the chapter on domestic ethnography (chapter 14), these modes of autobiographical practice may be defined less by the technological apparatus than by the web of social relations surrounding them. Domestic ethnography, a form of self-portraiture in which the self is bound up with its familial other, takes as its unspoken precept "ethnography begins in the home." Self entails other; the other refracts self.

And it is no singular self, as any declension shows: I, me, the ego, the self, the subject, the individual, the citizen. The trouble with the subject has quite a history. It has, in recent decades, been laid siege to on several fronts. Is the subject merely a bourgeois category that occludes our view of class struggle, the arena that really counts (classical Marxism)? If so, we are misguided in our focus on a dissociated self. Is the subject merely an effect of the system (structuralism and Lacanianism)? If so, we must devote our chief attention to the larger mechanisms (language, ideology, the unconscious) that offer the best hope for understanding and intervention. Has the subject been so decentered, hybridized, and now virtualized that it ceases to support a meaningful sense of a self (poststructuralism, cyber-theory)? Or is this absorption in the self a symptom of narcissism, a massive defense of the ego locatable in the artists or in society at large (psychology)? Is the subject abstract or concrete—a theoretical construct requiring learned allusions to every philosopher since Descartes or a vestige of the everyday properly grounded in the materiality of a gendered, performative body? Are we, as alleged by Neal Gabler in a postmillennial Op-Ed piece, living in the Epoch of Ego, in which the individual occupies center stage, both for better and for worse ("the ego, the self, is either a maw to be fed or a scrim through which to see")?[6] These divergent visions of subjectivity in the late twentieth century collectively limn the contours of contemporary cultural theory.[7]

There are countervailing voices. Not everyone agrees that subjectivity is central. A renowned cultural critic of my acquaintance once announced to me with some pride that he had yet to use the terms "subject" or "subjectivity" in his own writing. Taking up that implicit challenge, shouldn't we begin by asking how useful the category of the subject is for media studies and whether or not our attention to it is ill-advised? Perhaps the autobiographical trend is mostly an American manifestation. (Here it is worth recalling Georges Gusdorf's controversial statement that autobiography "expresses a concern peculiar to Western man," a claim that, more than four decades later, seems wrong on two counts, that of gender and of geography.)[8] Sociologist Arlie Russell Hochschild sees the turn to the personal as a product of recent historical conditions in the United States. In a lengthy piece in the *New York Times* on Americans' obsessive identity questing, Hochschild writes the following:

> Americans who came of age in the 1930s, 40s and 60s have been branded by large events—the Great Depression, World War II, Vietnam—and the collective moods they aroused. But from the 70s through the 90s, history's signal events happened elsewhere. Communism collapsed, but not in the United States. Wars raged in Rwanda, the Balkans and elsewhere, but they had little effect here. The forces in the United States have been social and economic, and they have shifted the focus to personal issues—matters of lifestyle that are shaped by consumerism, the mass media and an increasing sense of impermanence in family and work.[9]

This analysis ignores the inroads made by feminist activism during this era. Increased attention was actively accorded the personal; the time-honored emphasis on "large events," as Hochschild calls them, was shown to be the result of a masculinist bias. Politics now included how individuals, rather than nation-states, conducted themselves in the world.[10]

Moreover, I cannot agree with an exclusively Americanist perspective, a view that argues that the autobiographical impulse has thrived best on American soil in an era of economic success and increased leisure time. At least in the realm of contemporary film and video practices, this seems not to be so, as evidenced by the emergence of exciting first-person work from Canada, Europe, Asia, Australia, and the Middle East. But the question remains: should the matter of subjectivity be a central one for media makers and scholars, or is current interest in the personal a local, short-lived, and inconsequential affair?

My first reply is intuitive, for my years of teaching and writing about the self as expressed in film and video tell me that subjectivity continues to matter a very great deal. I know that it matters to my students, who have, over the years, been confronted by countless personal films and tapes and, more often than not, have responded from their guts with anger and with empathy, but only rarely with indifference. Marlon Riggs's opening incantation from *Tongues Untied* (1989)—"Brother to brother, brother to brother"—continues to mesmerize more than a decade later. Rea Tajiri's evocation of her mother's internment camp experiences during World War II in *History and Memory* (1991) never fails to elicit impassioned response. Alan Berliner's verbal sparring sessions with his father in *Nobody's Business* (1996) get laughs in all the right places.

The quality of the best work of this sort is unquestionable, but so is the quantity: the autobiographical is an ever-expanding category of production at festivals, in the repertory houses, and on broadcast venues such as the PBS series *P.O.V.,* which since the mid-1990s has provided a forum for personal, passionate, and frequently controversial nonfiction work. Nor is the autobiographical a uniquely American preoccupation (although I am admittedly most aware of films and tapes made in the United States). For five years (1994–1999), BBC Two broadcast a series of short first-person pieces produced by a diverse sample of individuals whose disparate identities, perspectives, and everyday experiences were to be the subject matter of occasional "field reports." These brief self-reflections (a succession of autobiographical miniatures) cumulatively evoke the breadth of social life in the new Britain. *Video Nation,* as the program was aptly titled, introduced the life stories of all manner of people (the elderly upper-class gentleman, the very pregnant Asian woman, the painfully isolated gay man) into thousands of British homes, fostering a kind of social contact unlikely to occur under other circumstances. *Video Nation*'s short programs were conceived as interventions in the national broadcast schedule, capsule intrusions of the unrehearsed and the diaristic into the professionally produced image flow.

By now the repertoire of first-person work from which I select texts to be screened for my courses is immense, most of it produced in the 1980s and 1990s. Recently, the production program in the USC School of Cinema-Television has begun offering a course in "personal video," a far cry from the Hollywood model that has prevailed there for seventy-five years. The advanced documentary projects made in the school tend more frequently toward the personal than they did a decade ago. So there appears to be an audience for, and myriad producers of, autobiographical work. But how bona fide are its claims to critical attention? And here the intuitive and anecdotal grounds for my interest receive support from other quarters.

Back when I first began to teach autobiographical films (the early 1980s), Michel Foucault wrote that in the face of institutional and state violence and of massive ideological pressures, the central question of our time remained "Who are we?"[11] Foucault claimed that in previous epochs, the struggle against domination and exploitation had taken center stage. Now, for an increasing number of people, the fight was against subjection, against the submission of subjectivity. In Foucault's hands, this circumstance called for a rigorous and historicizing interrogation of power as exerted and experienced. Subjectivity—that multilayered construction of selfhood imagined, performed, and assigned—was proposed as the current site of struggle that mattered most.

For a cultural critic such as myself, most attuned to the nuances of the cinematic, it was crucial to ask a slightly different set of questions: Just how does subjectivity (as self-assertion or as critique) get expressed on film? What modes of self-inscription have been employed by filmmakers? How indebted are these modes to centuries-old literary autobiographical practices? What differences arise when the autobiographer chooses film, video, or the Internet for her mode of production? What are the ethical issues that autobiography entails? These questions are intellectually compelling but also of substantial political import. The assertion of "who we are," particularly for a citizenry massively separated from the engines of representation—the advertising, news, and entertainment industries—is a vital expression of agency. We are not only what we do in a world of images; we are also what we show ourselves to be. As argued by many feminist and subaltern critics, autobiography has become a crucial medium of resistance and counterdiscourse, "the legitimate space for producing that excess which throws doubt on the coherence and power of an exclusive historiography."[12] Whether it is Alex Rivera's comic rewriting of the history of mestizo identity (with equal time given to his Incan father's emigration to New York and the exploitation of potato products) in *Papapapa* (1997) or Vanalyne Green's staging of the recovery of her personhood as the child of alcoholic parents in *Trick or Drink* (1984), filmic/videographic autobiography has become a tool for coupling liberatory public testimony and private therapy.

It is not at all surprising that much current autobiography has been produced at the margins of commercial culture by feminists, gays, people of color, and mavericks of every stripe. Contrary to critics who view this outpouring as reactionary—the individualist backlash against movement solidarity or the acting out of unbridled solipsism—the work is frequently engaged in community building and is deeply dialogic. In instance after instance, the films and tapes build bridges between a self actively constructed and an inscribed other. This other may be the family as in the case of "domestic ethnography" or members of a community linked by racial memory or elected affinity. Tonally, the work is tremendously diverse—celebratory, elegiac, solemn, delirious—but it is almost always affirmational of a self culturally specific and publicly defined. Public declarations of private selves have come to be defining acts of contemporary life, often imbued with great urgency. These are the social stakes of filmic autobiography, but what of the disciplinary ones? What have media scholars to gain from the study of these new autobiographical modalities?

Documentary studies, a burgeoning and deeply interdisciplinary field of inquiry, may be the greatest benefactor. I am unashamed to say that I am an enthusiast as well as a scholar of documentary. I believe that the autobiographical impetus I am describing has infused the documentary tradition with a much-needed vitality and expanded its vernacular. (This is a claim that I have arrived at inductively; these essays, written over a nearly twenty-year period, will provide the evidence of that enlivening and expansion.) On the scholarly side, subjectivity has long been an issue in the study of filmic narrative, fictions whose structuring of point of view, often via the use of handheld camera and voice-over narration, could produce the sense of a specifiable and embodied agency with whom audience members might be temporarily aligned. But the domain of nonfiction was typically fueled by a concern for objectivity, a belief that what was seen and heard must retain its integrity as a plausible slice of the social world. How else to persuade viewers to invest belief, to produce "visible evidence," and even induce social action? Nowadays there are ample grounds for an active distrust of that hoped-for neutrality. The journalistic standards of objective reportage have been so eroded by the news gatherers and high-profile TV anchors, the emergence of the digital has so undercut our faith in the indexicality of signs, irony as master sensibility of our time has become so pervasive that objectivity has become an empty shell of a construct, kept alive by a vocal minority. Given the waning of objectivity as a compelling social narrative, there appear to be ample grounds for a more sustained examination of the diverse expressions of subjectivity produced in nonfiction texts.

But documentary studies, rooted in the Griersonian tradition of high seriousness, tends still to consider the avowal of subjectivity a slightly suspect act. Bill Nichols has written that the standard tropes of subjective editing familiar from fiction films become, in the realm of documentary, the foundation for "a *social* subjectivity . . . [a] subjectivity dissociated from any single individuated character." Here our identification is with the audience as a collectivity rather than with an individual behind the camera.[13] I share the belief that documentary can be serious business and that much of its power is derived from a shared engagement with the ideas that can move us to action. Indeed, Part I of this book, entitled "Social Subjectivity," examines occasions in which personal concerns are shown to overlap with, or be overtaken by, a kind of political urgency. But is it not also the case that this notion of social subjectivity can conceal even as it reveals? Weren't the classic films of the Grierson group also marked by the class values and sensibilities of the young, Cambridge-educated cineasts? Were there not, as the work of Humphrey Jennings best illustrates, subjectivities on display despite the centrality of the group's avowed "project"? Hasn't American TV coverage of battles fought from Vietnam to Iraq always doubled as nationalist and even personal self-promotion? Private visions and careerist goals have always commingled with the avowed social aims of collective documentary endeavors.

The repression of subjectivity has been a persistent, ideologically driven fact of documentary history; yet subjectivity has never been banished from the documentary ranks. In fact, many of the milestone achievements of documentary filmmaking's first decades were exercises in self-expression. Here I'm thinking of Dziga Vertov's *Man with a Movie Camera* (1929), which catalogs the correspondences between human perception (visual and auditory) and the potentialities of the cinematic apparatus, often in dizzying fashion.[14] In true Communist style, Vertov suborns his own subjectivity to that of his comrades—brother Mikhail, the eponymous cameraman, whose point of view is repeatedly shown to be the source of what we see, and editor/wife Yelizaveta Svilova, whose choices at the editing bench are shown to bring the footage to life. Vertov's wife and brother become the delegates of his projected subjectivity. Jean Vigo's *A propos de Nice* (1930) contains several notable instances of intellectual montage, crosscuts between indolent tourists and crocodiles sunning themselves or between a haughty dowager and an ostrich, sequences in which implicit perspective is displaced by overt commentary.

Joris Ivens's *Rain* (1929) is a cine-poem devoted to replicating the filmmaker's experience of rainfall in Amsterdam. A number of shots evidence an unapologetic first-person sensibility, as Ivens describes in his autobiography:

At that time I lived with and for the rain. I tried to imagine how everything I saw would look in the rain—and on the screen. It was part game, part obsession, part action. . . . I never moved without my camera—it was with me in the office, laboratory, street, train. I lived with it and when I slept it was on my bedside table so that if it was raining when I woke I could film the studio window over my bed. Some of the best shots of raindrops along the slanted studio windows were actually taken from my bed when I woke up.[15]

Ivens's subsequent move away from personal explorations to more politicized frameworks for his filmmaking is exemplary of the historical moment. In 1929 he had been invited to the Soviet Union by the renowned filmmaker Vsevolod Pudovkin, whose film *Mother* (1926) had been one of the inspirations for the founding of the Filmliga, Amsterdam's cine-club, two years before. When asked why he had issued the invitation, Pudovkin replied: "Because your films have qualities which many of our documentary directors lack—qualities of tension and emotion that are very valuable in factual films."[16] Ivens has recounted how the visit to the Soviet Union reoriented his priorities, altering forever the balance between aesthetic and social factors in his own work. With the onset of global economic upheaval and heightened class tensions in the 1930s, Ivens determined that social obligation outweighed personal and expressly artistic concerns.

During the filming of *Borinage* we sometimes had to destroy a certain unwelcome superficial beauty that would occur when we did not want it. When the clean-cut shadow of the barracks window fell on the dirty rags and dishes of a table the pleasant effect of the shadow actually destroyed the effect of the dirtiness we wanted, so we broke the edges of the shadow. Our aim was to prevent agreeable photographic effects distracting the audience from the unpleasant truths we were showing.[17]

Thus did Ivens describe his conscious embrace of a kind of asceticism, a turn away from the personal explorations that had driven him to make *The Bridge* (1928) and *Rain,* as well as the "I" film (an unfinished experiment employing an exclusively subjective camera). It was a turn enforced by history.[18] I am to some extent, then, endorsing Arlie Russell Hochschild's notion of historical determinancy in the formation of culture, her sense that "what makes a generation is its connection to history."[19] In the 1930s, worldwide economic crisis and social upheaval defined a generation.

The Griersonian initiative in Great Britain dates to this moment of epochal social change (Grierson's own *Drifters* was completed in 1929), as do the important efforts of America's depression-era documentarians such as Pare Lorentz, Paul Strand, and Leo Hurwitz. The priorities enforced by the depression and World War II reined in the experimentalism and unabashed subjectivity of expression that had so enlivened documentary practice in the 1920s. In the case of the Americans, there is a degree of stylization apparent in the early work of the documentary Left (e.g., *Pie in the Sky* [1935]), though it tends toward a Soviet-style expressionism more than first-person exploration. But the collaborative documentary efforts of the 1930s—the output of the Workers' Film and Photo League, Nykino, and Frontier Films—best illustrate the collectivist ambitions of the day. Individual subjectivity was to be sacrificed to the greater good, the larger historical imperatives.[20] A similar Soviet- or Maoist-style collectivism arose in post-1968 France: Chris Marker's SLON group, Jean-Luc Godard and Jean-Pierre Gorin's Dziga Vertov Group. Individualism, even the acknowledgment of authorship, was spurned by these distinguished cineasts, just as it was by the editors of *Cahiers du Cinéma,* whose collective texts were at the vanguard of early 1970s film theory.

A parallel development occurred in the United States with Newsreel, the New Left documentary collective founded in New York in December 1967, discussed at length in chapter 1. Newsreel's video equivalents, the guerrilla television collectives of the early 1970s such as Raindance, Top Value Television, Ant Farm, and Video Free America also opted for a collective, rather than individual, creative identity.[21] Owing to the fragmentation or dispersal of the Left in both France and the United States as well as internal dissension, these collectives were in decline or defunct by the mid-1970s.[22] These collaboratively produced films and tapes, while they abjured individualism on political grounds and hence rarely hinted at the autobiographical, were deeply impassioned and far from objective. Energized by the civil rights, student, and antiwar movements, the activist works of this period were at odds with the prevailing journalistic standards that preached neutrality as well as with the documentary format that had, by the late 1960s, become decidedly hegemonic, that is, direct cinema.

Beginning in 1960, practitioners such as Richard Leacock, D. A. Pennebaker, the Maysles, and (somewhat later) Frederick Wiseman had evolved an approach to documentary filmmaking that shunned all traces of the maker's presence. There were to be no voice-overs, no interviews, no direction of the films' subjects. It was, in Stephen Mamber's phrase, "uncontrolled documentary." Gripped by an abiding faith in the spontaneous, these filmmakers refused to re-create events or even control the behavior of their subjects. The filmmaker was to be "a reporter with a camera instead of a notebook."[23] The repression of subjectivity was now a cardinal virtue. That precept is most clearly stated by Robert Drew, the

Grierson of this movement: "The film maker's personality is in no way directly involved in directing the action."[24]

Brian Winston has written incisively of the ideological underpinnings of direct cinema, the ways in which it claimed the high ground of science to support its superiority to its predecessors and competitors.[25] The debates surrounding the filmmaker's presumption of objectivity, the construction of documentary practice as "pure reportage," become deeply mired by the end of the 1960s with Wiseman's provenance. In Winston's persuasive account, Wiseman's claims to making "reality fictions," apt versions of his experience of a "real" institution yet shorn of all markers of the filmmaker's presence, were casuistries, shrewd but disingenuous rebuttals of the critique.

Direct cinema's disparaged predecessor was the dramatic reenactment tradition of Flaherty and Grierson, but its real rival was the work of Jean Rouch, the ethnographer/filmmaker whose cinema verité approach was developed contemporaneously in France. Rejecting the Americans' pretense of invisibility, Rouch believed in the necessity of acknowledging the impact of the filmmaker's presence. He chose to "generate reality" rather than allow it to unfold passively before him.[26] To that end, Rouch pushed participant observation to new levels of interactivity; he saw the camera as a "psychoanalytic stimulant" capable of precipitating action and character revelation. Rouch's role as a key precursor to the confessional effusions of contemporary video practitioners is explored in chapter 13. Here it is most important to recall Rouch's rehabilitation of that most-disparaged documentary device, the voice-over.

As described by countless critics, the voice-over has, in recent decades, been deplored as dictatorial, the Voice of God; it imposes an omniscience bespeaking a position of absolute knowledge. Current notions of knowledge as more properly "partial" or "situated" seem at odds with the authorial voice-over.[27] Yet in the hands of Rouch and others such as Marker, Michael Rubbo, and Ross McElwee, the filmmaker's voice has come to imply not certainty so much as a testimonial presence tinged by self-doubt or bemusement. Instead of doubling the image or certifying its authenticity as fact, this mode of documentary voice-over is as likely to question what is shown as to interpret it authoritatively. Emerging first with Rouch in the 1950s (and more obliquely in the work of Marker in films such as *Letter from Siberia* [1957] and *Koumiko Mystery* [1965]),[28] the signifying potential of the authorial voice gets developed with a subtlety and sophistication previously unknown.[29] Although I would not argue for the participant camera style and first-person voicings of Rouch as autobiographical practice per se, they do forge a crucial historical link between the avant-gardism of the 1920s and the autobiographical out-break of the 1980s and 1990s.

Several of the chapters in Part I of this book help to fill in some of the gaps that separate the effusive subjectivity on display in the avant-garde of the 1920s and the current scene. These are, for the most part, textually based historical analyses of films in which the subjectivity of the individual filmmaker is expressly defined in relation to political struggle or historical trauma. Whether it is the social revolts of the 1960s as in the chapters on Newsreel and Haskell Wexler's *Medium Cool,* the search for diasporic identity in a dynamic postwar New York (chapter 4 on Jonas Mekas's *Lost, Lost, Lost*), or the reclamation of Asian American identity (chapter 3), these filmic or videographic explorations of self require a historical other. Mekas's monumental film offers a notable example. Beginning in 1949, Mekas began shooting footage of his life as a Lithuanian émigré and emerging artist in New York City. By the time of the release of *Lost, Lost, Lost* more than a quarter century later, Mekas had developed a deeply personal filmmaking style to which the film serves as witness and proof. Diaristic though the work may be, it offers a vision of a life complexly grounded in the social and political upheavals of the postwar years. Yet despite the documentary qualities that this work so acutely displays, it has, with some exceptions, been largely discounted within the ranks of nonfiction, by makers and critics alike. Had it not been, the explosion of personal work in the 1990s might have been more easily assimilated to the documentary tradition.

Part II, "The Subject in Theory," features essays that attempt to conceptualize subjectivity within documentary discourse through reference to ideas drawn from psychoanalysis, as well as from certain strands of postmodernist theory and ethical philosophy. While I want to make it clear that I'm not interested in proposing a globalizing theory of the documentary subject applicable in all cases, I do want to pose some questions regarding the underlying dynamics that impel our interest in nonfiction (chapter 5), as well as grapple with some ethical issues that may arise. Until recently, it was rare for documentary to be understood in relation to the unconscious and its processes—desire, fascination, terror, fantasy. Elizabeth Cowie has argued that documentary has had a long-standing vocation for representing the visible signs of psychic life; she mentions British post–World War I documentaries on war neuroses, but John Huston's *Let There Be Light* (1948) or Claude Lanzmann's *Shoah* (1985) are equally apposite.[30] Moreover, visual pleasure, indeed ecstatic looking, ought not to be segregated from the domain of nonfiction as it has been since Metz and Mulvey wrote their groundbreaking treatises of the 1970s. I echo Cowie's sense of the rightness of the fit between psychoanalysis and documentary:

> Documentary films as recorded actuality therefore figure both in the discourse of science, as a means of obtaining the knowable in the world, and in the discourse of desire—that is, the wish to know the truth of the world, represented by the question invariably posed to actuality film, Is this really so, is it true? In that question is another, namely, the question of, finally, Do I exist? A question that is addressed to another from whom we seek and desire a response. This is the questioning that psychoanalysis has sought to understand.[31]

The third and final part of the book is devoted to analyses of the various modes of subjectivity from the electronic essay to the video confession to the autobiographical Web site. Here it is the graphological dimension discussed earlier that comes into play, the ways in which self-inscription is constituted through its concrete signifying practices. In chapter 11 ("New Subjectivities"), I offer a context for the recent turn to filmic autobiography, suggesting that the exploration of subjectivity has been the defining trend of "post-verité" documentary practice from 1970 to 1995. The chapters that follow trace in greater detail the precise practices in their variation. In this portion of the book, it is the "how" rather than the "why" that becomes the focus.

Beyond all attempts at description, analysis, and historical contextualization, I am also interested in celebrating subjectivity in documentary. In his critique of much contemporary theorizing on documentary, Noël Carroll offers illustration of his points through reference to PBS-broadcast works such as *Wings of the Luftwaffe* and *Nova*'s "City of Coral." These he claims are more "statistically significant" than the documentary films that film scholars tend to write about: *The Thin Blue Line, Tongues Untied, Roger and Me, Sherman's March,* even *Man with a Movie Camera* and *Chronique d'un été*.[32] These films he calls "art-documentaries," and their existence (even aesthetic excellence) ought not to sway us from our concern for divining how nonfiction film can satisfy the conditions of verifiable knowledge. The question of the truth or falsity of nonfiction's knowledge claims clearly enlivens Carroll's interests far more than understanding the source of any particular film's appeal. This is a viable position to take in the academy, but it produces rarified argument rather than an invigoration of, or real insight into, film culture. It's not for me. The films he singles out are not in fact art-documentaries (go to any museum to see the authoritative discourses on artists and artworks more properly termed art-documentaries). Rather, they are the films that have helped revitalize documentary practice and exercised considerable fascination over audiences. Their power is derived in no small measure from their mobilization and reinscription of a practitioner-self who shows us the world anew.

> I am kino-eye, I am a mechanical eye. I, a machine, show you the world as only I can see it. Now and forever, I free myself from human immobility, I am in constant motion, I draw near, then away from objects, I crawl under, I climb onto them. I move apace with the muzzle of a galloping horse, I plunge full speed into a crowd, I outstrip running soldiers, I fall on my back, I ascend with an airplane, I plunge and soar together with plunging and soaring bodies. Now I, a camera, fling myself along their resultant path, maneuvering in the chaos of movement, recording movement, starting with movements composed of the most complex combinations.
>
> Freed from the rule of sixteen-seventeen frames per second, free of the limits of time and space, I put together any given points in the universe, no matter where I've recorded them.
>
> My path leads to the creation of a fresh perception of the world. I decipher in a new way a world unknown to you.[33]

So wrote Dziga Vertov in 1923. It is a euphoric statement of the unlimited possibilities open to the documentary filmmaker, who is forcefully identified with the apparatus ("Now I, a camera, fling myself . . . "). Yes, Vertov glories in the infinite perfectibility of the camera eye, as every historian has noted, but not as an end in itself. The kino-eye is revolutionary because it can explode the inherited limits of human subjectivity. The new visions of the self created by film- and videomakers of the 1980s and 1990s that I explore in this book may not, after all, be so new.

And yet, at the beginning of a new century, the return to subjectivity, to the exploration of a seeing, feeling, and even healing self expressed cinematically, is newly charged. Was it only a decade ago that Bill Nichols could write, in his groundbreaking volume *Representing Reality,* "Subjectivity and identification are far less frequently explored in documentary than in fiction. Issues of objectivity, ethics, and ideology have become the hallmark of documentary debate as issues of subjectivity, identification, and gender have of narrative fiction."[34] The time has certainly arrived (as Nichols himself demonstrated in his next book, *Blurred Boundaries*) for a reassessment, for the open acknowledgment that the subject *in* documentary has, to a surprising degree, become the subject *of* documentary.

I Social Subjectivity

Early Newsreel: The Construction of
a Political Imaginary for the New Left

"Early Newsreel," first published in Afterimage *in February 1987, was
delivered as a paper at the conference "Hollywood in Progress: The
Years of Transition," in Ancona, Italy, in November 1984. In contrast
to the conference's focus on the deformations of Hollywood production
in the 1960s, I examined a highly politicized documentary alternative to
the sometimes quirky but decidedly commercial practices of that era of
American film history. Newsreel, a New York–based radical documentary collective in sync with the New Left, spawning chapters around the
country, was a late-1960s manifestation that I had been avidly researching in relation to other countercultural forms including the underground
press, street theater, comix, underground radio, and guerrilla television.
Drawing on film theory's psychoanalytic insights, I argued that Newsreel
films offered their politically engaged audiences a site for projection and
identification that was (at least structurally) analogous to that of their
reviled Hollywood counterparts. Especially pertinent to the central argument of this book, "Early Newsreel" testified to the extent to which standard notions of authorial subjectivity were, for that moment in the late
1960s and early 1970s, deemed politically retrograde. Twenty years later,
the pendulum would begin to swing in the other direction as identity,
rather than movement, politics came to the fore.*

In his introduction to *The Archaeology of Knowledge* (1972), Michel
Foucault explores with customary elegance the epistemological foundations of what (in France in 1969) he termed a "new history"; that is, a
field of discourse, a historical problematic, constituted not by the divina-
tion of continuity, the single horizon line of ideas and traditions, but by
a semiosis of discontinuity and its principal parts—threshold, rupture,
break, mutation, transformation. Indeed, Foucault's own work devotes

itself to the detection and rigorous elaboration of just such interruptions in the surface of a globalized historical narration. For if Foucault's grand project remained the analysis of the regulated and legitimated forms of power, the general mechanisms through which these forms operate, and their continual effects, the locus of analysis was fixed precisely at those points at which power became "capillary" or localized. The object of such microanalysis was the overthrow of history as a distillation of a single will or governing animus in favor of a process of discovery—of a series of subject positions progressively and materially constituted within a concretely differentiated play of psychic and social forces.[1]

To shift the terms of the argument toward the terrain of classical Marxist criticism, Foucault's call for a new history entails a reordering of emphasis from overall determination and the construction of a totalizing model to the play of difference within the historiographic field. The emphasis on rupture and transformation can thus be cast as an act of affirmation, a measured deconstruction of a false metaphysics. He writes:

> Continuous history is the indispensable correlative of the founding function of the subject: the guarantee that everything that has eluded him may be restored to him; the certainty that time will disperse nothing without restoring it in a reconstituted unity; the promise that one day the subject—in the form of historical consciousness—will once again be able to appropriate, to bring back under his sway, all those things that are kept at a distance by difference, and find in them what might be called his abode.[2]

The interrogation of dyadic or rigidly determinist systems of thought, whose structuring and conceptualizing of terms deny their interpenetration and thus their mutually constitutive character, is by no means the exclusive province of the poststructuralist or deconstructive critic. One particularly fruitful direction of such study, generated within a Marxist framework, has developed the Gramscian notion of the hegemonic, that reciprocally confirming yet always contested realm of ideas and values that reinforces the relations of domination and subordination within society. Gramsci's formulation and its elaboration by critics such as Raymond Williams and Stuart Hall, in theorizing a process, a series of articulations within ideology through which class rule becomes internalized while remaining all the while susceptible to contestation, has endowed the traditional Marxist binarism of ruler/ruled with a suppleness and fluidity adequate to the contradictions of social life. Williams, for his part, has urged an adjectival usage—the "hegemonic"—as an active inscription of the transformational character of power relations experienced in cultural terms. Writing in *Marxism and Literature* (1977), Williams seems to echo

Foucault's abjuration of static or seamless modes of analysis in favor of a critical method that "instead of reducing works to finished products, and activities to fixed positions, is capable of discerning, in good faith, the finite but significant openness of many actual initiatives and contributions."[3] If, as Williams maintains, hegemony can never be singular but is instead "a realized complex of experiences, relationships, and activities, with specific and changing pressures and limits,"[4] informed cultural analysis must seek to comprehend the dynamic, ever-shifting conditions of signification without enthroning process itself as a mystifying continuity.

It is within this framework of debate over the appropriate methods for writing the history of culture that I situate the following examination of a particular variant of political filmmaking that spoke a new language of contestation for the American New Left, as characterized by the film production and distribution organization known as Newsreel. Indeed, the outpouring of radical documentary filmmaking during the latter half of the 1960s was only one manifestation of an upsurge of cultural activism in the United States after nearly three decades of retreat. This or any examination of collective efforts to reshape society through cultural intervention during the 1960s must take into account the superheated currents of thought and commitment that animated the decade. Such an inquiry is particularly timely given the resurgence of popular and scholarly interest in a decade grown curiously remote despite its storied volatility.

How many of us educators in U.S. universities have encountered, to our boundless dismay, a sea of empty faces when the lecture topic or classroom discussion has turned to the Vietnam War or the mass demonstrations required to stem the tide of institutionalized racism, events of our recent national past? Despite the erosion of popular memory and the evacuation of meaning attached to sixties activism, the decade remains a watershed of consciousness for the post–World War II United States, as evidenced by the recent publication of an admirable collection of essays and reminiscences entitled *The Sixties Without Apology*.[5] The hermeneutic tension that title invokes—namely, what were the sixties, and why should we apologize for them—is one that should animate this discussion.

The references to the privileging of discursive discontinuity and of the theorizing of the dynamic of contestation within the hegemonic in contemporary criticism serve as the preface for my discussion. Instead of investigating the fertile fields of cultural and textual overdetermination we call Hollywood, I have chosen to test the outermost edges of the hegemonic through an analysis of a constellation of oppositional practices circulating around the name Newsreel.[6] The word "Newsreel," like the logo/image that houses it, is assaultive. Shorn of all qualifiers, it asserts an inaugurating refusal of history or referentiality as its prior, constitutive field. The alternation of logo and black leader, in conjunction with the audible staccato of machine gun fire on the sound track, announces a militancy of filmic intention; the stripped-down trace of authorship—Newsreel—stakes a claim for "truth" as a generic ingredient. It is my intention here to chart the terms of Newsreel's oppositional trajectory during the first two years of its existence, from late 1967 through 1969, by an interrogation of its conditions of existence, a brief analysis of two exemplary texts, and a positioning of its shifting functions within the culture of resistance it helped to forge. For despite the tremendous flux of membership within the groups in question, the geographic separations and the ideological splits that the singular form,[7] Newsreel, masks and elides, I claim that Newsreel, taken as an ensemble of cultural practices and effects, functioned as a consistent source of projective imagination and psychic legitimation for an isolated movement. In a sense that I will demonstrate, Newsreel occupied a crucial position in the largely unconscious construction of a political imaginary for the New Left.[8]

> *The development of the productive forces beyond their capitalist organization suggests the possibility of freedom within the realm of necessity. The quantitative reduction of necessary labor could turn into quality (freedom). . . . But the construction of such a society presupposes a type of man with a different sensitivity as well as consciousness: men who would speak a different language, have different gestures, follow different impulses. . . . The imagination of such men and women would fashion their reason and tend to make the process of production a process of creation.*
> :: Herbert Marcuse, *An Essay on Liberation*

> *Many times the films of Newsreel, the movement's only organized film producers . . . give us a sense of action taking place, involving us rather than forcing us to involve ourselves; these films make viable situations out of last-ditch, too-late efforts.*
> :: John Hunt, in *Leviathan*, September 1969

By 1968, Herbert Marcuse's diligent hopes for the emergence of an "aesthetic ethos"—a new reality principle that would invalidate the historic oppositions between imagination and reason, higher and lower faculties, poetic and scientific thought—had been dramatically renewed. Although *An Essay on Liberation* appeared in print in 1969, the book's preface assures us that this distillation of Marcuse's ruminations on freedom predates the protean events of May 1968. Theorizing from within the precincts of late capitalism, Marcuse had come to distinguish between two fundamentally opposed conditions of the working class as the historical agent of social change: the objective element of Marxist orthodoxy whereby labor remained the potential revolutionary class, and its negation, the subjective element, indicative of labor's imbrication within a system of high productive yield and the concomitant satisfaction of the worker's instinctual needs. Given the conservative dynamic of production and exchange, dependent on the exploitation of a marginalized underclass and the satellite states of the Third World, Marcuse postulated that the sources of that Great Refusal, which alone could diminish the self-sustaining momentum of the one-dimensional society, were the subcultural elements burrowing from within. Now the vanguard of oppositional activity was no longer the industrial working class but rather the militant minorities—the urban black, the white middle-class student activist, the hippie, the radical feminist. For Marcuse, the exigencies of the contemporary conjuncture had necessitated an inversion of the traditional Marxist paradigm: material conditions produce consciousness. In this transitional phase of late capitalism, Marcuse could claim: "Under these circumstances, radical change in consciousness is the beginning, the first step in changing social existence: emergence of the new Subject."[9]

Whether or not these countercultural or oppositional groups were in any way "conscious elements" in the revolutionary scenario envisioned by Marcuse, the construction of the "new Subject" was everywhere apparent.[10] A partial chronology of sixties oppositional culture offers a sense of the snowballing of cultural resistance by middecade through organizational tactics (sit-ins, demonstrations, peace vigils) and emergent expressive forms (the be-in, the happening, guerrilla theater, the underground press, free-form radio). It was through the agency of the latter grouping—the forms of the "new culture" in efflorescence from 1966 to 1972—that an embryonic subjecthood began to form. Such a fictional unity was the fount of identity for a constituency whose cultural dispossession was, for the most part, self-willed. (It has become a sociological commonplace that the leadership of the New Left was composed primarily of the children of privilege. Among the major campuses that experienced occupations, only San Francisco State departed from the model of the elite educational institution falling out of step with the overseers of the future, e.g., Columbia, Berkeley, Harvard, Cornell.) This resistance culture sounded a call to arms; like Newsreel, these avatars of the new consciousness embraced negation. Note, for example, the frequency of conventionally repellent appellations as the stance of militant self-exclusion by the underground newspapers: the *Old Mole*, the *Berkeley Barb*, the *Carbuncle Review*, *Rat*; the New

York anarchist action group Up against the Wall, Motherfuckers; the radical feminist Women's International Terrorist Conspiracy from Hell (WITCH).

Here we can distinguish that sense of joyful self-discovery present

Cover of May 1968 issue of the underground newspaper *Rat*.

in every revolutionary moment's seizure of language and the selective appropriation of preexisting forms. The essential mode of nascent revolutionary discourse remains bricolage, a heterogeneous blend of *Ur-sprache* and linguistic elements recruited through inversion or whimsy. For example, one of WITCH's earliest public pronouncements, appearing in *Rat* (15–28 November 1968), took the form of the conjuration of a sacred matriarchy: "In the Holiest Names of Hecate, Isis, Astarte, Hester Prinn and Bonnie Parker, *we shall return*."[11] A 1969 wall calendar created by the Students for a Democratic Society (SDS), advertised in the pages of *Rat,* evinces nothing less than a reinscription of the historical canon; annotated dates of particular interest included January 1 ("Victory of Cuban Revolution—1959"), February 4 ("Black student sit-in movement began, Greensboro, North Carolina—1960"), April 29 ("Columbia University shutdown—1968"), and October 12 ("Indians discover Columbus—1492"). In the words of the SDS ad: "The rest are a surprise."[12] As advertised in the *Village Voice* in the first half of 1968, the program of Newsreel films to be screened each Saturday night at ten o'clock at the Film-Makers' Cinematheque included guerrilla newsreels and actualities, the latter a term certain to evoke the Lumière brothers and their founding efforts in the predawn of cinema. Again, one detects the impulse toward a transvaluation figured through the reinscription of history and the cultural practices embedded within it.

In her 1965 essay "One Culture and the New Sensibility," Susan Sontag describes the function of all modernist art as "shock therapy for both confounding and unclosing our senses," a corrective to what she calls the "massive sensory anaesthesia" of the postindustrial age.[13] By the late 1960s, significant splits within the new sensibility were evident, with the more politicized factions engaging in confrontational art activities. Some political art-warriors devoted their talents to heightening the implicit contradictions of commercial art beyond the limits of containment. An anonymous art collective known only as the Eyemakers produced a form of political supergraffiti based on the principles of photomontage. By juxtaposing shocking or invasive imagery of ravaged Vietnamese women and children or tear-gas-bearing troops with advertising images familiar from the visual repertoire of consumer culture, the Eyemakers forced the glossy promotional appeals to self-destruct beneath the weight of a viscerally experienced disjunction. This was guerrilla art to suit the Marcusean injunction "Every person an artist!" In a do-it-yourself explanation appearing in a March 1968 *Rat,* the Eyemakers encouraged mass replication of their own art act: "For a couple of cents invested in some old magazines, you have available to you all the resources which cost Madison

Avenue millions of dollars and years of research to produce." Working in clear violation of copyright and trademark laws, the Eyemakers' posters were available only by mail or, for a time, at the New Yorker Bookshop in Manhattan. Never daunted, the Eyemakers expressed in their manifesto the revolutionary zeal and street slyness of the late-1960s cultural guerrilla: "They'd have to stop producing ads, they'd have to stop printing magazines; there'd have to be no scissors left in the land to stop collages."[14] The militant artmaker of the late sixties shared the confrontational rhetoric of the political leadership, choosing to overthrow the structure-in-dominance or self-destruct in the process. In the words of *Rat* editor Jeff Shero, used as a voice-over commentary in Newsreel's film *Summer '68,* "If we do our job right, we're going to either be put out of business by the cops or go under financially. That's what it should be all about. That's guerrilla journalism."

▶

Summing Up the Year 1968

> *February: First screening of newsreels produced by the Newsreel group (organized late in December 1967)—the most important new development in the American cinema.*
> :: Jonas Mekas, December 26, 1968

Acts of cultural intervention such as those of the Eyemakers were active and intended as participatory. For its part, *Rat* printed a special "Chicago" edition (August 1968) intended as a manual for the well-informed street fighter; a year later, its preview of the Woodstock festival included directions on how to transform one's own copy of *Rat* into a rain hat via a few simple folds. I would argue, however, that insofar as representational rather than "live" or face-to-face modes of interaction were concerned, the new subjectivity was most dramatically shaped and galvanized within the visual regime most conducive to the complex plays of projection, introjection, and identification—that is, the cinema. Judging by the prevalence and enthusiasm of film reviews appearing in the major organs of the underground press in these years, the movement population never lost its Hollywood habit, while remaining true to the art cinema of its bourgeois intellectual roots. The same newspaper that featured a column called "Blows against the Empire," chronicling the latest minor victories in the heartlands of America, was perfectly capable of running a serious review of *The Detective* (1968), a Frank Sinatra cops-and-robbers vehicle. It was no simple matter to reeducate the radical intellectual, to

wean her or him from visual pleasure to agitation and propaganda. Thus
the earliest mentions of Newsreel in the underground press are clearly
marked as "hard news" rather than as coverage of the cultural scene.

Indeed, the original statement of purpose published by Newsreel
speaks of the need for a radical news service as an alternative to television news. The founding mandate called for low-profile reportage and
analysis collectively assembled from the fieldwork of committed young
filmmakers. A certain naïveté prevails in early Newsreel's "production
for use" ethos, as evidenced by the pronouncements promising the distribution of films within a week of their completion. In fact, three types of
news films were to be made: short newsreels for weekly release; longer,
more analytic documentaries; and informational or tactical films.[15] Yet
there was from the first an unformulated ambivalence with regard to questions of mediation or principles of filmic construction. Clearly there was
a perceived need for immediate coverage of events from a left perspective,
but the call for an alternative to "the limited and biased coverage" of the
mass media offered no programmatic principles that could contribute to
a reconceptualization of standard film and television practices. The very
effects that broadcast television had traditionally celebrated as its claim
to journalistic superiority over the print media—immediacy, emotional
impact, and accessibility—were to be recycled, in unreconstructed form,
to serve radical aims.

Bill Nichols, a preeminent authority on early Newsreel by virtue
of both a master's thesis and a dissertation on the subject, has posited a
barometric, rather than vanguard, relationship between the film collective
and the movement it served.[16] The New Left in its organizational incarnations tended toward an uneasy vacillation between anarchic pluralism and
ultraleft elitism; in neither climate were normalizing working principles
likely to emerge. Despite its rhetoric, Newsreel remained, at least until
the early to mid-1970s and the emergence of two stable production bases
in New York and San Francisco, subject to the personal and political preoccupations of its ever-changing membership. Indeed, a film shot and edited by Newsreel personnel in 1968 and 1969 received the organizational
imprimatur only upon completion, subject to consensus approval by the
collective. A film, nominally approved yet at odds with prevailing political
sentiments, could languish in distributional limbo with few prints struck.
This was the case with Norm Fruchter and John Douglas's *Summer '68*
(1969), which was judged "too cerebral" by the Newsreel majority in the
summer of 1969.[17]

The political current of the late 1960s dictated a concerted self-
effacement of authorship, which we see in the collectivized anonymity

of sister organizations such as the Eyemakers, the San Francisco Mime Troupe, or Newsreel. Indeed, it is only in recent years that early Newsreel members have acknowledged primary responsibility for films that were intended as "authorless texts," the New Left's mythic equivalents of the emanations of the Lévi-Straussian *pensée sauvage*. But strong rifts appeared within the New York membership, in particular over the uneven distribution of craft skills and experience with previously established independent filmmakers such as Robert Kramer, Marvin Fishman, Norm Fruchter, Robert Machover, John Douglas, David Stone, and Peter Gessner—all well-educated white males finding themselves progressively at odds with a younger, more working-class-inflected faction, often feminist or Third World in composition. By 1970, the first-generation filmmakers had left New York Newsreel and the debates concerning correct political lines to be adopted in the wake of accelerating factionalism within the New Left characterized by the dissolution of SDS, the formation of the Weather Underground, and the heightened militancy of feminists within movement organizations. By this time, the interpersonal dynamic within the Newsreel collectives in New York and San Francisco paralleled the crisis state to be found elsewhere within oppositional cultural groups; *Rat,* always a Newsreel fellow traveler, had, by January 1970, been purged of its original leadership by militant feminists.[18]

A substantive contradiction is discernible, then, between early Newsreel's stated concern for the conditions of reception, the immediacy and political utility of product, and the relative disregard accorded the conscious theorizing of its filmmaking practices, the engendering of a viable aesthetic consistent with the political aims of the group. The early Newsreel self-conception was, instead, embedded within a thoroughgoing "romanticism of the barricades" evident around the world during 1968 and 1969. Here was an exuberant militancy that envisioned cameras as machine guns and Newsreelers as Marvel Comics heroes, slamming celluloid bullets into the belly of the beast. In a legendary turn of phrase appearing in a 1969 *Film Quarterly* interview, Newsreel's Robert Kramer spoke of the need for films that "explode like grenades in people's faces or open minds up like a good can opener."[19]

The Newsreel approach constituted a conscious inversion of the Hollywood paradigm in which millions of dollars are invested in production values with no regard given to establishing a context for informed spectatorship or structured response. The entertainment film, paragon of the disposable culture, was thus the antithesis of Newsreel's socialist utopian vision: "Films made by the Newsreel are not to be seen once and forgotten. Once a print goes out, it becomes a tool to be used by others in their own work, to serve as a basis for their own definition and analysis of the society."[20] But for all the sober talk of the films as tools for analysis, Newsreel and its mythic autoconstruction provided the occasion for forays into revolutionary imagination. From *Rat*'s 1969 coverage of an evening of Newsreel's work at the State University of New York at Buffalo, we read: "At the end of the second film, with no discussion, five hundred members of the audience arose and made their way to the University ROTC building. They proceeded to smash windows, tear up furniture and destroy machines until the office was a total wreck; and then they burned the remaining paper and flammable parts of the structure to charcoal."[21] Newsreel, by this account, was less a tool for analysis than an engine of war, fueled by spontaneous combustion.

Judging from the available evidence, Newsreel was, from the moment of its inception, a site of symbolic condensation, a kind of tabula rasa for projections of diverse character. One early and ardent supporter of the Newsreel project was Jonas Mekas, who was instrumental in providing a structured screening outlet and testing ground for new work via the Saturday late-night slot at the Film-Makers' Cinematheque. Newsreel was, in early 1968, sufficiently embryonic in form and political agenda to support Mekas's own utopian aspirations for an avant-garde newsreel expressed in his "Movie Journal" column in the *Village Voice* (29 February 1968). Mekas's pronouncements are worth quoting at length as proof of Newsreel's hold on a broad spectrum of the late 1960s' creative imagination and of the specifiable overlaps within normally adjacent communities of thought and activity—that of the overtly politicized fabricators of culture and of the artistic avant-garde.

> It is too early to predict where the Newsreel will go. One thing is clear, the newsreel has been for a long time one of the most neglected forms of cinema. Which means that one area of life had been neglected by the filmmakers. I hope that by the time the Newsreel reaches its twentieth issue, it will begin to discover its own contemporary style, technique, form, it will begin to escape the established conceptions of the newsreel—which means, it will begin to escape the established content. I am waiting for the avant-garde newsreel. I see no difference between avant-garde film and avant-garde newsreel, because a real newsreel, a newsreel which could help man to get out of where he is, must be an avant-garde newsreel, must be in the avant-garde of humanity, must contain and be guided by the highest and most advanced dreams of man.[22]

Indeed, the years 1968 and 1969, particularly within the hyperactive confines of New York City, were a moment of cultural fusion, a time for

The power structure media will not tell the truth about oppression, exploitation and people's needs and struggles here in the United States and around the world. For the most part, power structure media function for profit, and always to co-opt and suppress criticism and movement for change.

"The first thing a revolutionary has to understand is that the ruling classes have organized the state so as to dedicate every possible means to maintaining themselves in power. And they use not only arms, not only physical instruments, but all possible instruments to influence, to deceive, to confuse."

–Fidel Castro

The realities of America are moving people toward the movement, and the movement toward revolution. Continuous foreign wars and permanent high taxes, decaying cities, high schools that function as prisons, colleges that train students only to serve and maintain the system of their own and other people's oppression, inhuman factory speedup—all these and more are educating the American people to the hard necessities of Empire, and forcing them toward the alternative of people's power, peace and freedom.

NEWSREEL is among the people's counter-media that confirm their experience of this harsh reality, and our films are part of the struggle for revolutionary change.

NEWSREEL was founded two years ago in New York by several radical independent filmmakers. Since then we have grown into a national organization with bases in 10 cities: Boston, New York, Washington, Detroit, Chicago, Atlanta, Albuquerque, Seattle, San Francisco, and Los Angeles, and in Puerto Rico. We have produced more than 35 films, including several feature films, and imported more than a score of films from Cuba, Vietnam and other countries.

Unlike the power structure media, we make our films within the situations they present, from the point of view of the people. And we screen them—whenever possible with Newsreel members participating in discussion of the actions, ideas and issues they present—not only in theaters and auditoriums, but wherever we find the people: in the streets, in backyards and living-rooms, in bars, coffeeshops, churches and community centers, as well as schools and colleges.

We have produced this catalog of themed film programs as an aid in selecting and using our films and understanding the political nature of our work. Our basic rental fees (about a dollar a minute) apply primarily to institutions and groups that can afford them, and to commercial screenings. We are always ready to negotiate or waive fees to get our films before the people. Don't hesitate to call us for help in arranging screenings, or advice as to the relevance of specific films to your situation.

ALL POWER TO THE PEOPLE!

newsreel

404
media

Newsreelers as New Left superheroes.

reaffirming ties across a range of broadly adversarial idioms of expression. In addition to the Film-Makers' Cinematheque screenings, Newsreel films played at the New Yorker Theater, the New Cinema Playhouse, and the Bleecker Street Cinema during the first half of 1968. The Newsreel logo was visible at venues far and wide, and the films were frequently paired with live music for movement fund-raisers such as a benefit for the New York High School Student Union at the Bitter End Cafe in February 1969, also featuring the Fugs. Newsreel attended Woodstock, with continuous screenings at the campgrounds adjoining the festival site. *Windflower* (1968), Adolfas Mekas's film about a draft dodger, shared billing with Newsreels no. 2 and no. 4 at the Forty-second Street Playhouse in February 1968. The temporary fusion of oppositional forms postulated here is graphically figured in an ad that appeared in the *Village Voice* (21 March 1968) announcing a midnight festival of films at the New Yorker Theater to benefit the community-sponsored radio station WBAI-FM. The publicity referred to the event as a festival of avant-garde and antiwar films, the coordinating conjunction "and" bridging a division all too frequently maintained in less-explosive times.

Such patterns of distribution and exhibition helped reinforce a sense of shared cultural identity, while intensifying political conflicts around the world served to polarize public opinion. The culture of protest was at its confrontational zenith; there could be no middle ground. Louis Althusser, in theorizing the notion of interpellation, has provided us with a valuable tool for analysis; modes of discourse, he tells us, operating within a framing ideological ensemble, mobilize a hailing or beckoning power, a mechanism of psychic identification. The explosion of poster art and related forms of mass image production via the underground press of the period strained toward a culturewide effect of suture, by discursive strategies such as the use of the first person plural, the recovery of certain avatars of revolutionary struggle by an act of joyful historical revisionism, or by an emphatic reiteration of shared gesture or bodily linkage—the embrace of arms, the fist raised in solidarity.

Columbia Revolt, Newsreel no. 14 (1968), was the first authentic success for the film collective; in its first month of release, at least fifty prints were struck of this chronicle of the series of student strikes and building occupations at Columbia University in the spring of 1968.[23] Like so many other Newsreel successes since 1968, *Columbia Revolt* was the right film at the right moment. After repeated viewings, the film still creates the impression of a rapidly assembled, rough-hewn object perfectly suited to its purpose, as though a band of settlers had thrown up a rude battlement in a single night. There is no sync sound in the film's fifty minutes; indeed, the panoply of voice-overs becomes both the axiom of narration and the orchestrator of tonal values. The strength of the film lies in its sense of an urgency forthrightly conveyed and in its heterogeneity. This is a heterogeneity of voice; of human visage, with the faces of angry young

In *Columbia Revolt* (1968), Newsreel films mobilized a powerful mechanism of psychic identification.

men and women, black and white, the formerly anonymous ones, locked in combat with the powerful men who ruled Columbia and dictated public opinion, the Arthur Hay Sulzbergers and the William S. Paleys; and of visual materials—still photographs mingled with variously lit film footage often bearing traces of physical duress.

But *Columbia Revolt* is also a film of celebration capable of evoking the spirit of a utopian communality. Every activity of life is raised to ritual status inside the occupied buildings: sharing the food that has broken through the line of siege, transforming Low Library into a pleasure zone through music and dance. But the quintessence of this transvaluation is the candlelit wedding of two young strikers, Andrea and Richard, who tell us in voice-over that they had "wanted to be married at home with our family." The ceremony culminates with a benediction that binds together all who, in Marcusean terms, share the will to freedom within the realm of necessity: "I now pronounce that Andrea and Richard are children of the New Age." At such moments, *Columbia Revolt* beckons toward an imaginary fullness, a cultural plenitude offered as reward for future struggle and as the visible legitimation of present action.

Columbia Revolt performed a dual function—as a self-generated document of struggle and as a source of inspirational renewal. Without question, it succeeded in reinforcing ties of psychic identification and group solidarity for its movement audience; its power to persuade or re-educate an audience beyond the bounds of its prescribed community remained less evident. Norm Fruchter and John Douglas's *Summer '68,* shot during the anxious months of planning and preparation that culminated in the actions at the Chicago Democratic Convention (August 1968) and released the following summer, is a film of radically divergent intent and formal structure. Unlike *Columbia Revolt*, *Summer '68* never found its audience. An unfavorable response from Newsreel members limited the film's availability, as did the filmmakers' unwillingness or inability to promote the film on their own.[24]

At a time when the collective was accelerating community outreach toward the previously unorganized and unconvinced—high school students, the working class, Third World peoples—*Summer '68*, a demanding, densely organized self-examination of the movement within the realm of ideas, was a political tool ill suited to the moment. During its fifty-plus minutes, the film explores a series of crises endemic to the movement by the summer of 1968—those of political tactics and alliances, as well as those of organizational structure and leadership roles. But the key to *Summer '68* is its unremitting will to self-scrutiny, its need to probe beneath the facade of the New Left, constructed through an uneasy interplay of mass media distortions and movement self-promotion, to begin to deconstruct the imaginary ensemble of images and ideas that had become the movement, arguably to its tangible detriment, and to advance in its stead, through an act of consciousness, a substantive effort toward self-knowledge.

If the film can be deemed a primary text within a New Left discourse titled "the politics of identity," no accusation of solipsism or vain self-indulgence is intended. Rather, *Summer '68* evidences a sophistication of discursive strategy that operates on a principle of separation. Word is often disengaged from image. While a Newsreel-typical blending of participant voices and their multiple perspectives is used to narrate events, black-leadered segments punctuate the image track to underscore the primacy of analysis, that is, to narrate ideas. Moreover, the deployment of narrating voices is a complex one, with at least three distinct levels and usages of voice-over occurring. In the first instance, there are the voices of character-participants within the diegetic frame, the draft resistance organizers and underground-press editors whose activities illustrate the breadth and seriousness of movement goals. Sometimes these voice-overs exposit or elaborate on the profilmic; at other points they offer self-critique or comment on the visual track. When draft resistance organizer Vernon Grizzard is invited to go to North Vietnam with other antiwar activists to facilitate the release of captured American pilots, the decision is made to exploit media attention to enhance the prestige of the movement and to offer public proof of its effectiveness. Instead the role of the movement is effectively annulled by media coverage. Amid the first flush of victory at a bustling JFK Airport upon the pilots' return, press conference organizers choose to exclude Newsreel from the proceedings. The hoped-for bolstering of movement legitimacy is called into question. Grizzard's voice-over offers a critique of a performance we witness in the cinema verité–style footage of a media encounter shortly after his return: "I was afraid to cross the boundaries of legitimacy. There's no way to be both legitimate and outraged today in America in front of news media. To get up and talk about murder and the death of children and young men—you can't say that." As in this instance, voice-over commentaries of diegetic participants repeatedly reexamine actions and strategies, questioning their limits and utility. One effect of such a secondarizing of the profilmic is the dampening of an easy identification.

The second category of vocal narration is composed of the voices of other unseen activists who comment on the choices and actions of the visible protagonists. A contrapuntal effect is achieved as two separate voices interrupt the sync-sound continuity of Grizzard's press conference with intermittent critical salvos as the image track remains continuous. The first voice says: "You came on, I thought, very, very cautious, sort of like, 'I'm a red, white, and blue all-American boy; I'm not very political. I'm just an organizer in a draft resistance group which has a disagreement with American policy at this point.'" A second voice intervenes moments later, disrupting the predictable rhythm of the media event: "Did it ever occur to you that you oughta say, 'Look, motherfuckers, this is what I saw in North Vietnam, and you're gonna have to kill everybody there before they quit?'" These sound elements illustrate in condensed form the climate of contestation and exchange that enveloped every tactical decision or public gesture.

Finally there is a level of what could be termed "master narration," achieved through the use of a single, flatly intoned voice—the filmmaker's own. The film does not evince a "Voice of God" authority, an unquestioned omniscience for this level of narration in the manner of standard documentary exposés (note, for example, the use of the voice of the ethical guarantor—Edward R. Murrow, Chet Huntley, Charles Kuralt—in the network television documentaries of the 1960s liberal tradition such as *Harvest of Shame* [1960], *Sit-In* [1961], and *Hunger in America* [1968]). Rather, this narrational element achieves its position of mastery by virtue of the greater weight of knowledge and analysis it brings to bear on the issues raised. The classical Newsreel style dictates abrupt, untitled beginnings, often in medias res. In *Summer '68,* the essential terms of the film's problematic are addressed from the outset through the inauguration of a hermeneutic element that traverses the text. It is the master or meta-discursive voice that presses the interrogation in terms that will evolve in conjunction with the events imaged: how to define the "we" of the movement, how to ensure the legitimacy of actions taken in the name of "the people," how to use the lessons of defeat and compromise to make meaningful change in a complex society.

All of this analysis suggests a primacy of the sound track in *Summer '68*. It is therefore important to add that the special attention accorded acoustic elements in no way impedes the development of an image track that, in terms of its diversity of sources and immediacy of impact, is the equal of any of its better-known Newsreel cousins. But it is the layering of commentary and the relationship of sound elements to the structuring principles of the text that make *Summer '68* a richly textured work too long ignored. Norm Fruchter, who recorded sound and codirected, had been a writer of some note before his turn to cinema, both as a novelist and as a member of the editorial boards of arbiters of contemporary Marxist thought such as *New Left Review* and *Studies on the Left*. Although one hesitates to isolate individual contributions within collective endeavors, the sophistication of Fruchter's thought and political insights permeate the text. The final moments of the film offer a dramatic illustration of the potency of effect achieved through the interpenetration of word and image: Robert Kramer addresses a crowd of demonstrators on the streets of Chicago as the end of four days of political engagement draws near. The sudden appearance of troop carriers on Michigan Avenue signals the apogee of confrontational drama. As the camera turns from Kramer to the parade of occupational forces, a kind of visual epiphany or radical defamiliarization occurs. The film becomes, for the moment, a directly transmitted witnessing of history. Refusing the appeal of the unmediated moment, the film returns for the last time to the ceaseless interrogation of historical acts and the meaning they bear for the promulgators of social change.

> Once the troops were called out, we thought we'd won. But won what? All we'd managed was a disruption. But we'd fought for days and so many people had joined us that we felt much more than ourselves. For once, we thought we were the people. [Sound of communal singing, "This Land Is Your Land."] . . . When we left Chicago to go back to our own communities, our sense of triumph quickly became a memory. What we went back to was the tough, day-to-day work of building a revolutionary movement. And what Chicago finally came to, for us, was the feeling of what it might be like after making that revolution, when anyone could say: "We *are* the people!"

[2] The "Real" in Fiction: Brecht, Medium Cool, and the Refusal of Incorporation

"The 'Real' in Fiction," like the Newsreel chapter preceding it, evolved out of my research and teaching on sixties counterculture in the early 1980s, most notably for a class called "The Films of the 1960s" cotaught at the University of California–Santa Barbara with sociology professor Dick Flacks. A version of this chapter was presented at the Society for Cinema Studies conference in 1985, and the essay was revised and expanded for a conference, "Documenting Fictions: Documentary Dimensions of the Fiction Film," held in Luxembourg in 1993. I had long been fascinated with Medium Cool, *a critically acclaimed but commercially disastrous Hollywood film directed by Haskell Wexler in 1969, which seemed to me to stage a rather unique collision of history and fiction. The work of Bertolt Brecht was crucial to my understanding of* Medium Cool, *for it was in part owing to Brecht's influence that traditional notions of drama and subjectivity had been so eclipsed in 1960s political culture. In Wexler's film, set in the streets of Chicago during the turbulent days of the 1968 Democratic National Convention, the fictional characters turn out to be far less important than the history that surrounds them. Subjectivity, considered politically counterproductive in the 1960s, would make a dramatic comeback two decades later.*

The time has arrived for a more decisive theorizing of the tangled relations between fiction and nonfiction. The conference "Documenting Fictions: Documentary Dimensions of the Fiction Film" is but one instance of a salutary trend in recent critical thought aimed at reinvestigating the fiction/nonfiction borderline, a development no doubt accelerated by the growth of hybrid media forms that, while trafficking in the "real," occasionally even miming the tropes of a documentary style, cannot be said to adhere in any meaningful way to the standards of a documentary praxis (as to ethics, rhetoric, or pedagogy) developed over the past seventy years. Here I am primarily thinking of the proliferation of American nonfiction television forms. In a moment of escalating production costs, independents and major networks alike have begun to subscribe to the belief that "truth" is not only stranger but also more profitable than fiction. The result: reality-based programming, capitalizing on the camcorder revolution *(America's Funniest Home Videos, I Witness Video)* or celebrating law enforcement *(Cops, America's Most Wanted)*; tabloid TV's lurid reportage; the talk show wars; and the news magazine with *60 Minutes*—CBS's biggest moneymaker ever—leading the pack.

Considerable theoretical ground has already been cleared on the fiction/nonfiction frontier. Bill Nichols devotes the middle third of his groundbreaking study *Representing Reality* to a sorting out of issues meant to clarify the place of documentary through recourse to a range of discursive filters—semiotics, narratology, and poststructuralism among them. Crucial distinctions, such as that drawn between the respective orientations of fiction and nonfiction, are progressively refined. Fiction he aligns with nonindexical signification and thus with the "likeness," while nonfiction produces "representations" that retain the "stickiness" of the indexical sign. Fiction is oriented toward *a* world, nonfiction toward *the* world; yet in acknowledgment of the thoroughly mediated character of the documentary, Nichols redefines nonfiction some two pages later as *a* view of *the* world ("It is not just any world but neither is it the only view possible of this one historical world").[1]

In my own writing, I have described fiction and nonfiction as representational domains that are enmeshed in each other. While some fiction, and much advertising imagery, does indeed exploit documentary's "lure of authenticity" through a cunning appropriation of particular tactics or stylistic traits (the use of "witnesses"; the low-tech look, shaky camera; grainy, out-of-focus images), nonfiction itself displays a number of "fictive elements"—instances of style, structure, and expositional strategy that draw on preexistent (fictional) constructs or schemata to establish meanings and effects for audiences. Among these are the construction of character as ideal type; the use of poetic language, narration, or musical accompaniment to heighten emotional impact or create suspense; the deployment of embedded narratives or dramatic arcs; and the exaggeration of camera angles, camera distance, or editing rhythms.[2] These elements of documentary practice evoke and express rather than posit sober arguments, but they are no less the province of nonfiction on that account. Indeed, I have argued that documentary shares the status of all discursive forms with regard to its tropic or figurative character, so that the aforementioned elements of nonfiction are *necessarily,* rather than coinciden- tally, fictive. "For, it is not that the documentary *con*sists of the structures of filmic fiction (and is, thus, parasitic of its cinematic 'other') as it is that 'fictive' elements *in*sist in documentary as in all film forms."[3] This claim is consistent with my belief that documentary, construed by Nichols as a "discourse of sobriety," is equally a discourse of *jouissance*—of pleasure, desire, and of appeals to the Imaginary—even of delirium.[4]

Sobriety and delirium should not, however, be understood as mu- tually exclusive terms. To be sure, an impulse toward the revelation of oppressive social conditions and the empowerment of audiences to overthrow those conditions is distinguishable since Vertov, Ivens, and Grierson. Nichols is right to point to the seriousness of such a mandate. Yet, as I have claimed in my work on documentary poetics, the documen- tary theorist cannot afford to privilege nonfiction's undeniable debt to the signified at the expense of the signifier's play.[5] Sober intent has more than once produced delirious results.

In this chapter, I will pursue a rather different line of thought, one that, nonetheless takes up the matter of fiction/nonfiction relations quite explicitly. I will be examining fiction films in which a significant segment of the historical world is contained within the diegesis, intact and recog- nizable, and in which a tension is created between the centripetal force of fiction and the centrifugal power of the "real."[6] The most interesting case, and the one to which I shall devote myself principally, is Haskell Wexler's *Medium Cool* (1969), a film that interweaves the public events of the sum- mer of 1968 (the Chicago Democratic National Convention and the vio- lent clashes between police and demonstrators it provoked) with the pri- vate dramas of several fictional characters. It is no exaggeration to claim that in this film, Wexler—acknowledged auteur of the piece by virtue of his writing, direction, and camera work—has designed a collision of his- tory with fiction, a collision whose outcome is the virtual death of cinema.

Textual analysis, necessary to an understanding of the specific rhe- torical, compositional, and sound design elements through which the encounter between fiction and history is realized, will nonetheless serve a larger purpose. I will be suggesting that the history/fiction contretemps can also be theorized through reference to properly psychoanalytic terms, those of introjection and incorporation as theorized by Nicolas Abraham and Maria Torok.

In a series of texts, Abraham and Torok outlined what Jacques Derrida has termed a *hermetics* rather than a hermeneutics, a science of cryptological interpretation, in which the paradoxical character of incorporation as a function of psychic space is explored. For Abraham and Torok, the crypt is a topos buried within the Self, a place both inside and outside, "sealed, and thus internal to itself, a secret interior within the public square, but, by the same token, outside it, external to the interior."[7] Basing their analysis on the famous case of the Wolf Man, Abraham and Torok submitted the concept of introjection (the transposition of objects and their inherent qualities from the "outside" to the "inside" of the Self)[8] to rigorous reelaboration, arguing for the necessity of an opposing principal—incorporation—to describe the desire for a lost object (frequently a loved one, now deceased), which can be intrapsychically maintained yet simultaneously excluded from assimilation (understood as a kind of gradual dissolution of the other). Simultaneously conserving and suppressing, incorporation came to be theorized by the analysts as "a kind of theft to reappropriate the pleasure object," with the crypt—the place of incorporation—functioning as "the vault of a desire."[9]

It is my intention to use this dizzying topology of inside and outside as a way to theorize a specific instance of the relations between history and fiction within cinematic representation, with *Medium Cool* as a case study. I am thus arguing for the transposition of a term within psychoanalytic discourse to the field of textual and ideological film criticism as a way of providing a framework for analysis that is conceptually precise and mobilizes considerable explanatory power. But before returning to the figure of incorporation near the end of the paper, it is necessary to situate the key film text, *Medium Cool,* within the context of its politico-aesthetic aspirations.

▶ ──────────────────────────────────

History and Its Textual Incorporation

The epic theatre is chiefly interested in the attitudes which people adopt toward one another, wherever they are socio-historically significant . . . In short, the spectator is given the chance to criticize human behavior from a social point of view, and the scene is played as a piece of history.
:: Bertolt Brecht, "On the Use of Music in an Epic Theater"

The new media are not bridges between man and nature: they are nature. Gutenberg made all history SIMULTANEOUS.
:: Marshall McLuhan, *Hot and Cool*

The documentary is a recording of modern history. History is, after all, a recreation of the past by those who have the recording tools.
:: Haskell Wexler, interview by Renee Epstein, *Sight and Sound* (winter 1975–1976)

Wexler's decision to make a film in Chicago during the summer of 1968 that could make use of the confrontational events of the Democratic National Convention as a backdrop for fiction was far more than a creative gamble that paid off; the implications of that choice deserve consideration. Filmmakers have, since the Lumières, recognized the cinema's power to preserve and record the affairs of the world. Less often, however, have they attempted to incorporate historical action into the diegetic domain. Here we are talking not about location shooting or a handheld camera roving city streets but of the inclusion of significant social action—occurring independently of the fiction—and of the historical momentum that real events possess. The vagaries of the historical "real" inevitably threaten to destabilize the mise-en-scène whose control must remain the director's chief concern. Doubtless the economic overlords of any film production shrink from the sheer weight of "discontinuity" that a historical event of any magnitude bears. A brief examination of instances of this strategy of incorporation in two other films will suffice as evidence of the quite remarkable position accorded historical action in *Medium Cool*.

Toward the end of *Breathless* (1959), a restive Michel Poiccard tails a police investigator who in turn is following Poiccard's lover, Patricia Franchini, along a Parisian boulevard. In the midst of this farcical scene, Godard chooses to introduce a wholly contrasting motif, that of history. From an overhead placement, as the camera follows the cat-and-mouse processional along the boulevard, Godard pans to a simultaneous and geographically parallel event. Through the streets another more public processional is making its way at this point in the fiction. A glimpse of a large black limousine flying twin flags—one, the Stars and Stripes; the other, the French tricolor—is all that Godard chooses to include of then-president Eisenhower's state visit and his greeting on the streets of Paris, the liberator returning to admiring throngs. Much of the irony of the sequence is due to the discrepancy between the amount of screen time allotted to the double cordon of motorcycle police leading the entourage and the imaging of the limousine itself. The editing of the scene denies us a view of the celebrated figures themselves, contrasting instead the attention given to pomp and preparation as compared with the meager content of the instantaneous "event." The sound track—recorded "wild" here as elsewhere in the film—is momentarily boosted to include a chaotic blend of crowd noises, police chatter, and the sound of the motorcade. Several placard-waving demonstrators are momentarily visible.

Within the context of the film, heralded from the first as a marvel of ellipsis and energetic economy, this momentary insertion of the "real" is dense with meaning. The Eisenhower/de Gaulle summit conference—a "historic event"—becomes the diplomatic correlative for the Poiccard/ Franchini relationship, in which each lover's desire is invested in the cultural iconography of the other, that of Bogie or of Auguste Renoir. Michel's later remark in the midst of amorous pleasures ("We're helping Franco-American relations") is thus anchored in a material reality.[10] Like the use of the moving camera that repeatedly precedes the couple through bustling city streets, often provoking the glances of curious passersby, this cursory aside to history is also the bravura touch of a fearless young cineast revising the canons. The meaning of this brief historical footnote, while not altogether narrativized, is largely contained within fictional bounds, the potential for a radical dispersal of nondiegetic action and connotation controlled.

In the spring of 1970, Calcutta was gripped by a prolonged season of confrontation between Left and Right forces punctuated by a series of massive demonstrations. Against this background, Satyajit Ray, the highly regarded Bengali filmmaker whose inattention to political issues had long galled his countrymen, began shooting *Pratidwandi* (The Adversary). The film centered on the fortunes of the young, recently graduated Siddhartha, whose immediate future, clouded by a tight job market and family responsibilities in the wake of his father's death, offered an illustration of the moral dilemmas facing the socially conscious youth of Calcutta. Tanu, Siddhartha's younger brother, represented the response of the severely alienated; having lost faith with the established order, he has taken to the streets in league with a militant guerrilla faction. Meanwhile, Siddhartha's path has crossed with that of a shy and beautiful young woman of the sort familiar from so many Satyajit Ray films. In a dramatic scene shot atop a tall building in Calcutta, the woman tells Siddhartha of the family troubles that threaten her happiness. In the background, yet never specifically addressed in dialogue, can be seen the largest mass demonstration ever staged in Calcutta. Here one can distinguish a paradigm of conventional melodrama whose epic dimensions are understated in a manner consistent with the Ray style. Rather than contrast the scale of public and private realms in the manner of, for example, a David O. Selznick (e.g., the lurid craning action that loses Scarlett O'Hara in a sea of wounded men at the Atlanta train depot or the monumental pans in *Since You Went Away* in which Jennifer Jones's parting from Robert Walker is restated by those of dozens more young lovers),[11] Ray chooses to allow the spectator's glance the freedom to inspect what appears to be a human tapestry moving at a distance from the fictional action. One is left to determine the significance of private suffering relative to the tumult of massive social conflict. Ray neither dwarfs his characters in a sea of humanity nor belittles the pain of the sensitive young woman's plight. Rather, the visual strategy is the prototype of Bazinian democracy with the eye and mind left to weigh the valences of both levels of drama—social-historical and interpersonal. Ray's camera placement atop the tall building guarantees the mixture of delicacy and visual potency that has so often prompted critical comparisons with Jean Renoir. The demonstration is rendered visible yet inaudible. The Ray sensibility couples a sincere humanism with a reticence for the rough-and-tumble of upstaged and unrehearsed reality.[12]

> *I would like to make features, go out and see the people, and I would like to find some wedding between features and cinema verité. I have very strong opinions about us and the world, and I don't know how in hell to put them all in one basket.*
> :: Haskell Wexler, interview in *Film Quarterly* (spring 1968)

Medium Cool chooses history's unfolding as the very core of its dramatic concerns. For ten years prior to his departure for Hollywood in 1956, Haskell Wexler had been engaged in making documentary films, many of them in support of various Left organizations in the Chicago area.[13] Wexler had also lent a hand in postproduction work on that most celebrated of blacklist era projects, *Salt of the Earth* (1954). But it was the documentary that had most occupied this young filmmaker, whose first Hollywood assignments as cinematographer, as with *Stakeout on Dope Street* (1958), benefited from Wexler's newsreel eye and his ability to render back alley locations in convincing detail. Says Wexler: "All I knew was reality, the documentary. So my ignorance of the other way sort of helped."[14]

By the time the by now Academy Award–winning cinematographer (for *Who's Afraid of Virginia Woolf?* [1966]) was given the opportunity to direct his first feature in 1968, Wexler had already taken the leap into independent production with a sixty-minute documentary, *The Bus* (1963). With the most skeletal of crews, Wexler had accompanied a busload of freedom marchers on their odyssey from San Francisco to Washington in an effort to capture the sense of commitment and historic purpose shared by the demonstrators. The experience left the filmmaker nearly $60,000 poorer and convinced that independent production without a prearranged distribution deal was an unfeasible course of action. When, in 1968, Paramount Pictures offered Wexler a chance to direct a low-budget, rather saccharine story of a boy and his photographer friend, Wexler had at last begun to realize a dream of many years' standing. In retooling and personalizing the project, Wexler relocated the film's setting (from New York to Chicago), changed the photographic journalist of the tale to a television cameraman, and, most importantly, restructured the entire piece around the upcoming Democratic National Convention. Needless to say, the "scripted" historical events exceeded the limits accorded them; the crucial gesture, however, was Wexler's premeditated inscription of the historical within the fictional.

Given these preliminary remarks on the incorporation of history into a filmic text and Wexler's particular interest in this process, what can be said, in more concrete terms, about the choice of contemporary history as subject matter in *Medium Cool* and about this specific instance of incorporation? The setting or physical environment within which diegetic action transpires is normally considered to be one more or less coequal mise-en-scène element among several (lighting, costume, and figural movement or expression being the others). The most acclaimed of "mise-en-scène directors" are notable either for the meticulous design of their decor (Vincente Minnelli) or for an uncanny ability to enmesh place and action with little sense of contrivance (Nicholas Ray, Anthony Mann). Here, in *Medium Cool*, the dynamics of the relationship between setting and other structural elements are utterly transfigured to the extent that the term "setting" is no longer suitable. In this film, "place" (the summer 1968 Chicago setting) generates dramatic action and, in the end, annihilates it.

The preeminence of the spatiotemporal framework in *Medium Cool* is evidenced by the uneven ontological status of the film's component parts—that is, the disjunction between a constructed, essentially reproducible fictional space and an unframable, nonreproducible "real" space. (There could, of course, be no second takes during the bloody battles outside the Conrad Hilton Hotel.) The history of cinema is replete with tales of the fortuitous "act of God" that creates celestial, one-time-only lighting effects unrivaled in scale and grandeur by the Renaissance masters.[15] In *Medium Cool*, however, the nonreproducible "real" space was a *social space* rather than a natural or elemental environment, a combat zone within which social forces collided with a fury and unpredictability that shocked the international assemblage of journalists and photographers. Wexler's singular attempt to harness that zone of activity within fictional bounds constitutes the basis for substantial critical attention; his awareness that the aesthetic vehicle could not and, in fact, should not contain and subsume that social space merits a great deal more. The analysis of the deepest implications of what might be termed this fiction's disengorgement of history, the text's refusal to sustain its strategy of incorporation, must await further examination of the specificities of the textual system.

The foregoing has attempted to establish the primacy of setting within the ensemble of structuring elements that constitute *Medium Cool* as filmic text. It should now be added that the drama of historical events connected with the convention and its repercussions—the historical profilmic—bore an equally profound relationship to a precise conjuncture of time and geography. To state this fixity less emphatically would be to misconceive the nature of historical phenomena, particularly the summer 1968 debacle in Chicago. Without the atmosphere of strict autocracy of the sort engineered during the Daley years, without a massive police apparatus—high-strung, combat ready, and unflinchingly loyal to the Daley high command—without the demographics of high-density, low-quality housing for blacks and white rural émigrés, and without the stifling wet heat of a Chicago August, the intensity and duration of pitched battle would have been unlikely, if not unthinkable. What occurred, in fact, was a convergence of civil rights and antiwar forces on the turf of a large and supportive Left community on the one hand and a repressive, fundamentally paranoid military encampment on the other. The film's intent was to fix as representation that moment of polarized confrontation in such a way as to implicate the spectator, to force her or him to occupy a position within this politicized landscape. The next step beyond the arousal of consciousness was intended to be social action.

This itinerary is coincidental with Brecht's own, as stated in his essay "Theatre for Pleasure or Theatre for Instruction": "The object of our inquiries was not just to arouse moral objections . . . but to discover means for their elimination."[16] If *Medium Cool* can be said to share this agenda, it is clear that the possibility for its spontaneous fulfillment—political action, the elimination of social ills—was effectively sabotaged by the Gulf and Western Corporation.[17] In a 1975 interview, Wexler maintained that "what actually delayed the release of the film in 1969 was the fear of the attorneys for Gulf and Western Corporation that, after seeing the film, people would go into the streets and perpetrate illegal acts. And if that did happen, the officials of the Corporation could then be subject to court action."[18] Thus the dominant cinema's heavily capitalized mode of production (in comparison with Brecht's, for example) bears with it a conservatism whose economic and political motivations are deeply fused; the corporate response in this case blunted much of the film's immediate political impact.

The focus of my interest here, what remains undiluted in *Medium Cool,* despite the delay of distribution and various editorial tamperings enforced by Paramount, is the gestural and emblematic. The most striking feature of the film's relation to history—its effort to incorporate the "real" within the fictional domain—is not the only one. At least two other formal strategies, significant for their divergence from the filmic norm, deserve mention: a rhetorical strategy, the use of direct address by characters, and a compositional one, the progressive transformation of the relationship between foreground and background, figure and ground. Each contributes to the erosion of fiction's uncontested domination of the discursive system.

Direct address in fictional cinematic discourse is rare indeed, except in instances of comedy. There the fictional character turns raconteur; the Bob Hope or Jerry Seinfeld persona is shed in favor of the comedic presence—the comic himself—in a manner consistent with the stand-up tradition of vaudeville and music hall. Film theorists, most notably Christian Metz in "The Imaginary Signifier," have speculated on the gravity of the returned gaze. If the preservation of a specular unity can be deemed the sine qua non of the fiction film, the sustained direct address of a character from within the diegesis threatens this imaginary plenitude. During a sequence midway through *Medium Cool,* television cameraman/protagonist John Katsellas is confronted by an assemblage of black militants whose hostility is aroused by the presence of this media representative:[19] "When you walked in, you brought La Salle Street with you, City Hall and all the mass communications media. And you are the exploiters. You are the ones who distort and ridicule and emasculate us. And that ain't cool." Theirs is a response to Katsellas's unsolicited appearance in an alien environment (his attempt to follow up a human interest story has brought the newsman to the all-black Southside of Chicago) and his casual disregard for the frustrations of the media lockout they suffer.

The diatribes of the two men are profoundly confrontational; the frontal compositions are insistent and multiform in rhetorical effect. The subjects of this direct address are three in number: the fictional character Katsellas, the filmmaker Wexler, and ourselves, the film's audience.[20] The sudden confluence of these three registers of spectatorship threatens to dislodge *histoire* and its invisible network of suture. The disruptive effect of this mode of address is diminished somewhat by the sense one has of a recurrent play of identity between filmmaker and protagonist. In one case, a group of mock rioters responds to the command "Get the guys with the cameras!" by first rushing toward Katsellas, then engulfing Wexler himself and the "true" recording device that he holds. Here the thrusting forefinger of the militant forces a recognition upon all who share privilege, in life as in fiction; those who tolerate suppression and disenfranchisement (in representation as in commerce or law) are destined to suffer its deadly backlash. By disrupting the binding power of *histoire* that holds every

The direct address of the black militant in Haskell Wexler's *Medium Cool* (1969).

gesture within a web of fictional conceit, by allowing verbal utterance to circumvent the customary relay of character/identification/introjection, Wexler produces a discursive caesura intended to instruct by force of confrontation. A similar tactic has been employed in every patriotic appeal. The unyielding gaze and forward pitch of Uncle Sam's wartime countenance ("Uncle Sam Wants You!") has rousted countless Americans out of peacetime apathy. This figure of rhetorical fusion, the interpellation of audience, filmmaker, and character alike, expresses an urgency of tone reminiscent of Hollywood's most fervent wartime pleas.[21]

There is at least one other key reference for these instances of direct address, that of the Brechtian notion of "social gest." In "Diderot, Brecht, Eisenstein," Roland Barthes proposes a genealogy of the tableau in Western art. Working from Diderot's concept of dramatic unity, which exalts the tableau structure and its succession of cutout settings brimming with signification, Barthes defines Brecht's epic theater as a successor to this tradition. Brecht's writings on epic theater stress the autonomy of each scene and the importance of a staging that challenges its audience through a layering of discrete signifying elements (words, music, decor). This Brecht contrasts with the dramatic theater's muddled flow of sensations, which intoxicate the onlooker. In the course of his argument, Barthes suggests that distanciation, the cornerstone of Brecht's theory of epic theater, is but a particular instance of a more general artistic strategy explored by Diderot, Lessing, and Greuze. The tableau of Brecht, in representing itself for the active criticism of the spectator, discourages the closure of a final meaning (so commonly the intent of the tableau form) in favor of an interactive social meaning constructed in reflection. Furthermore, social attitudes are meant to be derived from the movement and gestural repertoire of the actors. As Brecht specifies in "On the Use of Music in an Epic Theatre," "the actors' social gest becomes particularly important. . . . (Naturally this means socially significant gest, not illustrative or expressive gest.) The gestic principle takes over, as it were, from the principle of imitation."[22]

As Barthes has described this Brechtian neologism, the social gest is "a gesture or set of gestures (but never a gesticulation) in which a whole social situation can be read."[23] If this formulation is applied to these instances of direct address in *Medium Cool*, their gestic function is clearly demonstrated. The unaccustomed centrality of the black militant within the filmic frame, the unswerving eye and advancing forefinger, are joined by an auxiliary array of mise-en-scène elements—a string of love beads, a framed photograph of the Reverend Martin Luther King Jr., a darkened television screen toward which the black-shirted man will soon gesture with disdain. This use of the confrontational filmed interview, framing subject against a flattened backdrop, is also recurrent in the work of Godard. But in *Medium Cool* the portraitist's sensibility, discernible in Godard (only recall Jean Seberg framed against the Renoir painting in *Breathless*), is replaced by a sociological entablature whose peripheral details contribute to historical narration.[24]

In this context of cinematic application of Brechtian theory, it is useful to recall Brecht's descriptions of his own filmic usages in the theater. In "Theatre for Pleasure or Theatre for Instruction," the German dramatist enthused about the potential of projected film segments as contributions toward a process of alienation considered "necessary to all understanding." Like choric chant, placards, or mimed sequences, film was deployed as a breaker of spells, a method of introducing the weight of the "real world" into the airless domain of drama. For Brecht, of course, the illusionism intrinsic to the cinematic image was not at issue; the ontology of the filmic "real" was of no consequence so long as the shock value of the moving image remained intact. "Films showed a montage of events from all over the world. Projections added statistical material. And as the 'background' came to the front of the stage so people's activity was subjected to criticism."[25]

It is this transposition of foreground and background that bears upon the present analysis. What Brecht calls for here, albeit in a largely metaphorical sense, is a radical shifting of figure and ground so that character and dramatic emplotment lose their primacy of place in the refocusing on the broader social horizon. The destiny of the romantic couple or the troubles of the beleaguered protagonist are thus de-emphasized as a vast panorama of historical concerns envelops fictional ones. Several filmic examples of this paradigm have been mentioned, all of which depend on the movement or eccentric positioning of the camera so that foregrounded characters are briefly decentered or optically neutralized. This realignment of foreground/background relations is, in these cases, a temporary one. In *Medium Cool,* however, the hierarchical arrangement of historical milieu and fictionalized, foregrounded action is progressively undermined and at last inverted.

In *Medium Cool,* the romantic interest of protagonist John Katsellas is a woman recently arrived in Chicago from the backwoods of West Virginia; she is the mother of a waif, Harold Horton, whom the camera-man has befriended. It is worth noting that this female character, despite her status (one-half of the romantic couple), is never named. It is only via the film's closing credits that the name "Eileen" becomes attached to her. Since Paramount chose to recut the film before its commercial release, it is possible that this lacuna is simply a product of that evisceration. Nonetheless there is in *Medium Cool* a generalized sense of character as a lure to spectator interest rather than as its final destination. The lack of psychological development of the Eileen Horton character discourages the potential for misplaced psychic investment. It is she who, on the pretext of finding her runaway son, leads us from the provinces of the private and the fictional into the savage underworld of city streets and bloody confrontation. There Eileen encounters the battlements of a furious conflict she has little suspected and an array of combatants whose diversity and number leave her wide-eyed. Eileen is now reduced from character to a site of nominal motivation for the imagery, a figure dispatched to the edges and into the depths of the frame. Traces remain of Horton as picaresque protagonist, a wistful Candide whose canary yellow form, though frequently obscured from our sight, assures us that the fiction endures. Yet there remains no narrational "I" through whom the landscaped is refracted, only an "eye," which is Wexler's own.

The diminution of emphasis on the Eileen Horton character within the visual field is a progressive one. From her foregrounding early in the sequence as she begins her search in the unearthly glow of the elevated train, Eileen is reduced to a status identical with our own—that of history's spectator. Yippies, Young Socialists, bloodied protesters, and smooth-faced National Guardsmen are all systematically drawn into the foreground of a mise-en-scène that Wexler has temporarily borrowed from

Newsmen and fictional characters as history's spectators in the streets of Chicago, August 1968.

brute reality. By the end of the sequence, Horton has become only slightly more distinguishable than a patch of yellow affixed to a passing jeep.

Two formal conditions provide a sense of suture across this dispersal of a scenic space in which narrative development has effectively been frozen. Indeed, this grand spectacle of loosely ordered scenes can be said to supplant fictional syntagma outright. (These sequences were, for good reason, shot silent and handheld and have a decidedly newsreel quality; they occupy something less than twenty minutes of screen time.) The first spur to continuity, then—volition or viewer interest—is a condition of reception and, as such, is subject to the vagaries of time and place. For a knowledgeable audience with a preestablished awareness of the events depicted and an appreciation for the archival value of the footage itself, these sequences are the film's most extraordinary achievement. To the uninitiated, the second formal condition—the sound track—must suffice as a brace to continuity. Composed by Chicago blues and rock musician Mike Bloomfield, the film's score is dominated by the spare melody line of an electric guitar whose bassy tremolo establishes an icy, desperate tone. The hard edge of music offers intermittent accompaniment to Eileen's odyssey through troubled streets. The simplicity of the score, the dependence on the single instrument and reiteration of a now-familiar musical motif, stabilize a restive image track suddenly more documentary and preservational than fictional and narrativizing.

It is ironic that the film of a man with twenty years' experience behind the camera should depend so heavily on its sound track. Without question, *Medium Cool* is as much a film for the ears as for the eyes. It was the sixties media guru Marshall McLuhan who characterized television as "the most recent and spectacular electric extension of our central nervous system."[26] Yet TV was termed "cool" insofar as it was capable of transmitting an image low in resolution and intensity, a mere "mosaic of light and dark spots."[27] Its channels of information remained grossly underdeveloped; the TV was more to be heard than seen. Like the television medium it critiques, *Medium Cool* uses the sound track to much advantage, developing a sound strategy suited to its political-aesthetic aspiration.[28] Indeed, it is the sound track that guarantees the text's annihilation of fiction and its supplantation by history.

Once again it is Brecht who has provided the guideposts for analysis. In his seminal essay "The Modern Theatre Is the Epic Theatre," Brecht emphasized the need for the "radical separation" of formal elements so that neither music nor text nor setting would be degraded in the service of a hypnotic theatrical experience. This "process of fusion extends to the spectator, who gets thrown into the melting pot too and becomes a passive (suffering) part of the total work of art."[29] This "process of fusion," as manifested in the cinema's treatment of auditory elements, means that the sound track is customarily a support of the imagery through synchronous dialogue or "evocative" music used as mood enhancement. In *Medium Cool,* the use of nondiegetic sound, that is, nonsource music and phonic sound whose origins lie outside of the fiction, as well as protracted nonsync passages utilizing sound as counterpoint to image, help to undermine conventional sound-image relations. It can further be claimed that these acoustic elements, functioning as relatively autonomous axes of meaning, contribute to a radical social critique freed from utter dependence on the word.

A great deal of the effectiveness of *Medium Cool*'s attack on the brutal effects of a repressive state apparatus depends on its ability to contextualize violence within American culture and sensibility. The most graphic illustration of this effort occurs early in the film when Katsellas and a woman friend attend the roller derby. In long shot, the camera frames a stream of burly, helmeted women roller-skating around a circular track while attempting to elbow, body-slam, and generally incapacitate one another. This lurid spectacle, which generates much excitement among the "live" audience ("live" because Wexler's telephoto lens focuses largely on the "real" audience rather than on the actors) is wedded not to a sync sound track but to a rendering of Wild Man Fisher's "Merry-Go-Round."

> C'mon let's merry-go, merry-go, merry-go-round.
> Everyone is going merry-go-round.
> Merry-go, merry-go, merry-go-round.

The song's lurching rhythm and ludicrous nursery rhyme lyrics transform high-speed head bashing into comic choreography. The unexpected sound/image mix serves to defamiliarize the staged event, enforcing a tangible distance between spectator and profilmic spectacle. This is a sound strategy that accords with Brecht's dicta regarding the separation of formal elements and the alienation of the audience from an unmediated, predigested experience that contravenes rational thought. The distance between viewer and filmed event is underscored after the fact when sync sound abruptly resumes; a discord of thudding bodies, audible grunts, and a crowd chanting for more now alarms us by its closely miked presence. Our revelation of this ritual performance—part carnival, part public sacrifice—is largely achieved through a syncopation and variegation of sound/image relations. The critique of another public performance, the ensuing "police riot" broadcast around the world, is rehearsed here.[30]

The Wild Man Fisher song was a nondiegetic sound insert, but in a scene toward the end of the film, Wexler juxtaposes source sound from one location with the visual track from another proximate space to great effect. Location one is the interior of the convention hall in which Katsellas witnesses the clamorous demonstration of support for Illinois's favorite son, mayor Richard J. Daley, to the tune of "Happy Days Are

Here Again." The song links this locale with the site of another less celebratory demonstration—the melee at Lincoln Park. Several meaning effects attend this sound/image counterpoint. The spectator is, in the first
place, led to assume a simultaneity of events—the two demonstrations,
both of them "real" and unstaged—which joins them in a historical dialogue. Moreover, the sense of the hollowness of the refrain is dramatically
heightened by the radical contradiction between the lyrics and the scenes
of battle that are their visual counterpart. One is led to recall the genesis
of a tune that has become a fixture of American political campaigns—the
dark days of the depression when Franklin D. Roosevelt's promises of
renewal required melodic support. Through Wexler's strategic counter-
pointing of sound and image, a song built on a wish turns into a taunt,
the more caustic for its moral insensitivity.

But it is the acoustic strategy of the film's conclusion that assures us
of the significance of Wexler's valorization of history over diegesis, the annihilation of the fictional domain previously claimed. Katsellas and Eileen
Horton are shown driving down a deserted highway, presumably in search
of Horton's errant son. The sound track is a continuous barrage of on-
the-scene reportage by an astonished newsman, which issues, one gathers,
from the car radio. (With the exception of several brief intervals, there
has been no sync sound used during the twenty minutes of screen time
devoted to Eileen's street odyssey.) From the camera's position, mounted
on the car's hood, the face of first one then the other of the film's central
characters is obliterated by a wash of reflected light on the windshield.
This prefiguring of dissolution is soon joined by a further disruption of
narrative decorum—a brief aural flash-forward in which Horton's death
and Katsellas's critical injury are announced in the form of a radio news
bulletin. The auditory flash-forward forestalls suspense; a stylized montage sequence, reinforced by grating sound fragments, represents the crash
that follows with an equal disregard for tragic overtones. The camera
zooms out in an inexorable retreat from the burning wreckage. Yet the
stately recessional should not be construed as a sign of mourning for the
fallen protagonists. The camera shrinks from their little story.

These two fictional subjects have been absorbed, bit by bit, into a
bleak landscape of American tragedy whose authenticity mocks fictionalized sorrows. And all the while the live newscaster continues, numbly
describing the carnage outside the convention center in great detail. The
reverse zoom ceases. A pan to the right reveals Wexler himself, posed behind a camera, now panning left to meet the first camera's gaze head-on.
One camera zooms into the black, rectangular matte box of the other.
Even as this act of ritual self-immolation is completed (a warning against

the siren songs of all representational forms?) and the final credits roll, the once radio-drab voice persists, now cracking with emotion and disbelief.

> The policemen are grabbing and beating everyone in sight . . . People are being clubbed, and I mean in technicolor and 3-D . . . Right in front of the nation, right in front of the entire nation, this is happening.

This narration is sustained even after the credits are replaced by black leader; the end of the celluloid strips cuts off the voice at the very moment of a newly forged awareness.

> I've just got out of being smashed against the wall by the skin of my teeth . . . people are being smashed up against the wall and are being hit by the police with clubs, and those are real nightsticks, and people are really being hit.

It is the weight of this final testimony, issuing from an unseen space, that marks as definitive the film's choice of the raw, relatively unprocessed material of history over the manufactured imagery of Hollywood fiction. It is a peroration of mixed function. In formal terms, it offers a final guarantee of the sovereignty of the sound track, freed from mere illustration or reiteration. As an epiphany of consciousness regarding the wanton brutality of a repressive state apparatus, this anonymous narration is proof of the active substitution of the fictional regime by primary, historical source material. For instead of focusing on the final throes of a dawning social awareness in the Katsellas or Horton characters, *Medium Cool* chooses to jettison the fabrication of character and diegesis altogether. By the film's end, the spectator has been prodded toward a recognition of social forces in conflict, much in keeping with the Brechtian prescription. Moreover, the increasingly hortatory character of the work serves to align it with the didacticism of the nonfiction tradition. It is the disembodied plea of the extradiegetic voice that provides the spur to this revelation, not the agencies of character or emplotment. In sum, the success of *Medium Cool* as innovative political art is an effect of its success as an act of deconstruction—of filmic fiction and of itself as fictional film.

▶

The Denial of Incorporation: Annihilating Fiction

Thus far the analysis of one film and its attempts to integrate an uneasy mixture of aesthetic, commercial, and political concerns has provided the focus of critical inquiry. This analysis has attempted to suggest certain points of tangency with other politically motivated aesthetic thinking of this century, principally that of Bertolt Brecht, and to examine the variety of formal tactics in *Medium Cool* whereby directly historical material has been introduced and substantive social critique undertaken. By way of conclusion, a more speculative direction of inquiry deserves further elaboration.

From the outset, it has been the claim of this study that Wexler's film pursues a strategy of incorporation, a "swallowing" of whole chunks of history and an attempted integration of this unstaged reality within the fictional context. Brief analyses of comparable attempts elsewhere—by Godard, Ray, and Selznick—indicate that it is the convulsive or traumatic historical moment that undergoes incorporation (the Civil War, World War II, a pivotal summit conference, a mass demonstration). Like the Chicago riots of August 1968, these are events that exert a domination of sorts over an epoch or historical conjuncture, events that crystallize certain elemental contradictions projected on a grand scale, events about which it becomes difficult to remain silent. The filmmakers surveyed, with the exception of Wexler, have used the historical as controlled counterpoint, situating their own inventions of fictionalized conflict within or against the larger social field used as dramatic foil. But Wexler's inclinations toward cinema verité and his preoccupation with film as political tool altered the balance of diegetic and historical concerns so that the recuperation practiced elsewhere is resisted. The effect of this autonomy accorded the historical "real" is a surrender of certain fundamental narrative aims, particularly that of closure. In the film's final minutes, characters are dispensed with in a laconic, stylized flourish that denies the ties of identification and psychic investment while a continuous flow of live news coverage signals the preferment of "real" social conflict via the sound track.

If we take as our primary object the act of incorporation—of the historical by the fictional—it becomes possible to correlate this condition of aesthetic practice with a phenomenon of psychic production. In a remarkable essay entitled "Introjection—Incorporation: Mourning or Melancholia," Nicolas Abraham and Maria Torok describe in great detail the character and function of incorporation within the metapsychological framework developed by Freud in his efforts to theorize an adequate model of the mind. In contrasting incorporation with introjection, Abraham and Torok are interested in the relationship of each of these phenomena to the maintenance or alteration of the topographical status quo. Fantasy is defined as any representation, belief, or body state that works toward maintaining this topography, while "reality" (in the metapsychological sense) is constituted by "everything that acts on the psychic system so as to bring about a topographical alteration."[31] The function of fantasy, then, is a conservative one insofar as it generates no new ca-thexis or alteration to disturb the psychic equilibrium as does the introjec-tion of external stimuli. The intrusion of the "real" demands some form of accommodation or topographical reordering that is an expenditure in the psychic economy. To quote Abraham and Torok: "Thus our formulation goes back to the view that fantasy is in essence narcissistic: rather than make an attack on the individual, it attempts to transform the world" (4).

Incorporation is a particular kind of fantasy in which a loss of some magnitude (e.g., the death of a loved one) is refused introjection or ac-ceptance within the psychic system ("to admit the true meaning of that loss . . . would make one different" [5]). Thus the fantasy of incorporation is both a refusal of introjection and the denial of a lacuna. Moreover, this inability to mourn or accept loss is figured as a failure of language, the inability of the subject to form words to fill the void. For a fantasy of in-corporation to occur, the loss must be "of such nature as to prohibit com-munication" (7).

Abraham and Torok's description of the conditions that support a fantasy of incorporation suggests an intriguing parallel with the circum-stances under which the incorporation of history within a fictional text takes place. Just as fantasy was deemed an act of preservation intended to withstand the bombardment of the "real" and the concomitant alterations to the *psychic* economy, so too can the fantasy of fiction be termed a con-dition of conservatism in which the historical "real" is refused introjection within *narrative* economy. For the introduction of historical forces and dramas would necessitate a fundamental restructuring of the fabular schema; incorporation is thus a means by which the historical "real" can be swallowed whole without the reordering of generative structures. It should be noted, moreover, that incorporation in its proper sense is to be distinguished from Barthes's "inoculation effect," in which the threat of a contesting value or ideological position is defused by introducing it into the field of representation in meager and manageable proportions. In this way, the integrity of the contesting value is replaced by a decontextualized and insubstantial surrogate.

True incorporation maintains the integrity of the historical event or social phenomenon—renders it intact—while simultaneously circumscrib-ing its access to signification. Of course, such access would unseat the internal logic, the narcissism, of the fiction. Just as psychic incorporation constitutes or makes representable while containing the loss of the loved object, the incorporation of history by fiction produces a representation that at the same time effectively safeguards the diegesis from the contagion of the "real." As Derrida has argued in his own discussion of Abraham and Torok's cryptonomy—their study of incorporation or psychic encrypt-ment: "The crypt hides as it holds. . . . [It] is a place comprehended within another but rigorously separate from it, isolated from general space by partitions, an enclosure, an enclave."[32] History, when encrypted within the fictional diegesis, is allowed to "re-present" lived experience, but it is sealed off, made safe.

This strategy of representation/prohibition can be seen as a means whereby the power of direct address and public appeal (so long the staple of nonfiction) is substantially withheld from history unless costumed in fictional garb or placed discretely to the rear. This is precisely the mode of filmic practice that Wexler rejects with much fervor by the end of *Medium Cool*. The film is a kind of battleground in which continuity and psycholo-gism wage war with the boisterous, unframable streets of Chicago. The corporate tongues of Paramount were dumbstruck by the finished project, over which they had maintained minimal supervision. "They came out looking like somebody hit them on the head," says Wexler. "They literally didn't know what to think. They knew they were in the presence of a kind of film they hadn't seen before. It threatened them. They didn't know how to deal with the film, because most Hollywood films don't have anything practical to do with the real world—certainly not the immediate world."[33]

On the basis of these observations, it is tempting to collapse the conservatism of the fictional text (its refusal of topographical/structural alteration) with the properly political conservatism of the cultural institu-tion. While I do not endorse such a conflation, I do wish to argue for the political and textual cogency of the refusal of incorporation in *Medium Cool* and its resultant confounding both of the textual and of the insti-tutional status quo. That cogency was also perceived as a threat in some quarters. To defy the ground rules of cinematic storytelling, to unleash the representational potency of "real" events undiluted by fictional constraint, is to court the reprisal of a cultural institution whose financial investment is rooted in maintenance and preservation—of form (or formula), of ac-cepted values, and of market position. Wexler's inability to direct a fea-ture for fifteen years following the release of *Medium Cool* is a reminder of the unspoken unanimity through which the Hollywood topography is maintained.

The analysis that these remarks conclude has taken as its object a single film and a set of relations corollary to it. The examination of rela-tions internal to the text (as of sound and image) has been supplemented by an extended inquiry into the relations between textuality itself—the process or structuration of the work—and the social-historical "real" that permeates and finally dismantles that text-in-process. This study is intended as a contribution to the critical thinking about political art and the discourse of history, both considered as acts of representation. The chief claim here has been that the collision of these two regimes, the realm of socially conscious dramatic fiction and the relatively unmediated but diegetically contained realm of historical representation (introjection versus incorporation), becomes, at last, the principal subject matter of the film. In the end, both introjection and incorporation prove inadequate. History-in-representation leaks through, then prevails.

Little wonder that *Medium Cool* explores a path seldom taken in the American cinema. It is a text about textuality, a genre inconceivable to the corporate sensibility. Only recall the final image of the film, which, like Godard's "FIN . . . DU CINEMA" [the end . . . of cinema], the concluding title of *Weekend,* can be taken as a gesture of infanticide—consuming both itself and its future progeny. Wexler images himself as image maker; one camera engulfs its mate. History, which has been freed from its incorporation within the belly of fiction, cannot escape the larger snare of representation. The image, refusing to succumb to its appropriation, swallows itself.

[3] Warring Images: Stereotype and American Representations of the Japanese, 1941–1991

"Warring Images: Stereotype and American Representations of the Japanese, 1941–1991" was a catalog essay for Media Wars: Then and Now, *a publication for a special Pearl Harbor fiftieth anniversary sidebar event at the 1991 Yamagata International Documentary Film Festival. In the context of this book, "Warring Images" is notable for its attention to the ways in which stereotypical discourse, in the service of the state, functions as an aggression against the subject, robbing racialized "others" of their uniqueness and individuality to further wartime aims. This is nowhere more evident than in the propaganda efforts that accompanied the internment of 120,000 Japanese Americans during World War II. The chapter moves through an account of 1940s American propaganda en route to a consideration of the revisionist works of Japanese American artists of the next generation whose films recover and celebrate the em-battled identities of their parents' generation. In reaffirming the historical subjectivity of their forebears, films such as Rea Tajiri's* History and Memory *(1991) and later Ruth Oseki Lounsbury's* Halving the Bones *(1995) and Emiko Omori's* Rabbit in the Moon *(1999) showed that auto-biographical filmmaking could become an act of political resistance.*

> Stereotypes can assume a life of their own, rooted not in re-ality but in the myth-making made necessary by our need to control our world.
> :: Sander L. Gilman, *Difference and Pathology*

> I was drinking about a fifth and a half of whiskey every day. Sometimes homemade, sometimes what I could buy. It was the only way I could kill. I had friends who were Japanese and I kept thinking every time I pulled a trigger on a man or pushed a flamethrower down into a hole: What is this person's family

gonna say when he doesn't come back? He's got a wife, he's got children, somebody.

They would show us movies. Japanese women didn't cry. They would accept the ashes stoically. I knew different. They went home and cried.

:: John Garcia, from Studs Terkel's *The Good War: An Oral History of World War II*

What follows is an attempt to think through several difficult and somewhat disparate questions, all of which bear upon the history of American representations of the Japanese a half century ago. In doing so, I will focus on the notion of "otherness"—defined as a categorical, hierarchical, and, in this instance, racially motivated separation between self and outsider—and the ways in which it can be exploited or countervailed in a contemporary media environment. Toward that end, a number of World War II American tracts—of propaganda and war aims promotion—will be examined, including posters, Hollywood films, and documentaries produced by the War Department. Alongside this material, I propose to consider the more recent work of independent Asian American artists who, in rewriting their own histories, have begun to recover a lost history for all Japanese Americans, domestic victims of America's wartime racism.

Finally, I will discuss one more instance of independent documentary production from the United States, a collaboratively authored series of videotapes entitled the "Gulf Crisis TV Project." Broadcasting the work at the height of anti-Arab hysteria during the recent Gulf War amidst the monolithic cheerleading of CNN and other mainstream "news" entities, the Gulf Crisis TV Project articulated a position critical of the war and its unspoken ideological foundations. A sequence in one of the programs *(Manufacturing the Enemy)* is particularly relevant to this discussion for the parallels it draws between recent expressions of racially based hostility toward Arab Americans and the climate of feeling that resulted in the internment of Japanese Americans a half century earlier.

On the basis of these three historical sites of media production—American World War II propaganda, Asian American independent work since 1970, and the Gulf Crisis TV Project of 1991—I will conclude by arguing for the social necessity of alternative media enterprises capable of countering the streamlined and state-managed images that trade on stereotype, mold prevailing public images to their own ends, and move millions to violence against a perceived other. There was no such venue for public contestation in the 1940s; we have, through the screenings of this festival, ample evidence of the dire result.

I return, then, to a series of questions—and thus to a range of texts and their analysis—that I shall use to frame the discussion. Although fraught with political and ideological complexity, these questions emerge as crucial to heightened historical understanding between Japan and the United States, to the future health of all cross-cultural representations and to the potential role of documentary film and video in the establishment and assessment of public policy goals, including those of war and peace. Among the questions to be explored are the following:

- What is the character and function of stereotyping, particularly in the ideological pressure cooker of wartime?
- What is the "reality effect" of documentary film and video, and what role can these media forms play in the construction or dissolution of stereotypical discourse?
- On what historical grounds can we account for the virulence of the anti-Japanese rhetoric of World War II America, and in what specific ways was it manifest?
- How can the seizure of property and incarceration of 120,000 Japanese Americans during those years be understood in terms of stereotypical discourse, and how have recent Asian American artists sought to recoup their losses through a reinscription of personal memory and public history?
- Is it possible to employ documentary techniques within a mass media context to resist the effects of government-sponsored, racially based stereotyping during wartime? What is the political importance of alternative media making in the current media environment?

▶

Race and Stereotype

> Know Your Enemy—Japan *followed Capra's rule of thumb (Let the enemy speak for himself) in an exceptionally evocative manner. . . . Beneath its dazzling surface imagery . . . the message was simple, conveyed in a stark metaphor and a striking visual image. The audience was told that the Japanese resembled "photographic prints off the same negative." Visually, this was reinforced by repeated scenes of a steel bar being hammered in a forge.*
>
> :: John W. Dower, *War without Mercy: Race and Power in the Pacific War*

Once a Jap, always a Jap . . . you cannot regenerate a Jap, convert him and make him the same as a white man any more than you can reverse the laws of nature.
::   John Rankin, U.S. congressman, Mississippi

Here's a very personal question: Have you killed a Jap soldier today?
::   Opening narration from War Department film, Misc. 1121

It is here within the domain of wartime stereotypes that we encounter the most disturbing and dehumanizing instances of cross-cultural representation, the images and rhetoric that must be confronted if we are to determine their cause and avoid their recurrence. Rather than devote myself to simply reproducing the virulently racist constructions endemic to America's waging of war in the Pacific (John W. Dower's *War without Mercy* offers an exhaustive account of the savagery of the conflict as fought and represented by both sides), it seems to me crucial to dig further in order to theorize an underlying dynamic of the stereotype that can account for all obsessively vilifying characterizations of others. Japanese and American wartime excesses can thus be placed in a broader conceptual framework that engenders understanding in addition to strong emotional response.

Despite this concern for root causes, the concrete features of the wartime encounter between Japan and the United States deserve careful study. Dower is at pains to historicize the race hates and war hates that typified the Pacific conflict and thus offer explanation for the actions on both sides. He argues persuasively that the number of casualties sustained by the principal combatant nations (and by other Asian peoples such as the Chinese, Filipinos, and Indonesians), as well as the sheer intensity of hatred expressed toward the enemy—civilian and soldier alike—are incomprehensible without a grounding in both Japanese and American social history. On the American side—to which I shall confine myself—Dower narrates the historical matrix that prepares the way for wartime excesses: the legacy of nineteenth-century evolutionism and its presumptions of racial superiority; a century of "Yellow Peril" rhetoric in response to Chinese and Japanese immigration; Oriental exclusion laws and enforced segregation by the mid-1920s; limitations on land ownership by alien Japanese; and, at the level of popular culture, an intransigent strain of nativism resulting in a series of books and films warning of Japanese aggression at home and abroad.[1] These are just a few of the significant forces or events that were historically determining (creating a climate of social pressures and limits within which subsequent racist manifestations arose). Any search for the basis of stereotyping must, however, move beyond such a historicizing account.

We might begin this search for the fundamental source and recurrent psychosocial functions of stereotyping with the crawl that introduces the Gulf Crisis TV Project's *Manufacturing the Enemy*. There the producers offer a series of definitions of the stereotype, pieces of a diagnosis that might serve to explain the actions and behaviors that are the subject of what follows.

> A stereotype is a projective device used to make it easy to behave toward people in socially functional ways. . . .
>
> You call a people "barbarians" . . . or you call a group "criminals" if you want to suspend just laws of decency and behave towards them in an otherwise criminal way.
>
> This is a function for coping with threats, for it justifies both dismissing and brutalizing these groups.

Two important points deserve some discussion: first, the notion of "projective device"; second, the assumption of a "social function" for the stereotype. Projection is a psychological term for the attribution of internal states to an externalized object; traits attached to the stereotyped other are said to originate within the psyche of the self. The other is thus a kind of screen or mirror for one's internalized idealizations, both good and bad. This feature of the definition lies firmly within the realm of psychoanalysis and will be discussed further hereafter.

The second point—the social utility of the stereotype—suggests that stereotyping can serve destructive social ends when "managed" by a political party, nation-state, or subculture. The hatred mobilized through recourse to stereotype can fuel violent or discriminatory acts by one group against another on the basis of the latter's (putatively) shared characteristics or physical traits. While this definition leaves unstated the question of intention (is this social function circumstantial or the product of a conspiracy?), it does at least begin to comprehend the critical features of stereotypical discourse within a framework of cause and effect. It is worthwhile to examine the phenomenon of stereotyping in even finer detail.

We might return to Dower's book to pursue our search for a deeper understanding of the stereotype in the context of the Pacific War. There the author expresses some puzzlement about the speed and forcefulness of "the easy transition from antagonistic to congenial images on all sides," the way in which "the demonic Westerners could suddenly become transformed into their tutelary guise" during the postwar occupation.[2]

Conversely, in their own studies on the subject of racial stereotyping, scholars such as Sander L. Gilman and Homi K. Bhabha have emphasized the underlying structures of mind and thought that can account for the deep-seatedness and volatility of stereotypical discourse (what Gilman calls its "protean" character). It seems to me entirely necessary to understand stereotyping as a dynamic rooted in psychical as well as historical processes if we are to succeed in educating ourselves toward its control.[3]

Gilman believes that "stereotyping is a universal means of coping with anxieties engendered by our inability to control the world."[4] He proposes that we require certain "immutable structures" that can assure us of our power to grasp the play of difference that surrounds us at the level of thought, object, or person. Homi Bhabha offers a similar assessment, arguing that "the stereotype is not a simplification because it is a false representation of a given reality. It is a simplification because it is an arrested, fixated form of representation that . . . [denies] the play of difference."[5] In a response to our inability to control an ever-changing environment, we limit the threat that otherness poses through the creation of fixed images. Bhabha goes on to claim that such an arrest of difference facilitates a sense of clear-cut opposition between the self, more or less fluid in its identifications and idealizations, and the stereotyped other, fixed, immutable, and available for appropriation.

The radical split between self and other helps to uphold a racial fantasy discernible in both Japanese and American contexts: "the fantasy that dramatizes the impossible desire for a pure, undifferentiated origin."[6] The racial other as stereotype emerges as both the grounds for anxiety and the source of its relief. As an image, arrested and controlled, it serves as an inverted mirror of identity. In racial terms, the other is the support of a defining hierarchy; mongrelized or fallen from grace, the other defines the purity of one's own lineage.

Gilman traces the origins of stereotyping to childhood development, arguing that the self is itself split into good and bad components. The bad self comes to be identified with the mental representation of the bad object (that which, in the infantile world, causes pain or anxiety); the bad that we perceive within us thus becomes projected or cast out onto external objects. Stereotypes are thus "a crude set of mental representations of the world"; the Manichaean domains that have dominated global history during this century—East and West, Axis Powers and Allies, Communists and the Free World—correspond to this most primitive (but powerful and deeply rooted) dichotomization.[7] We are said to be equally capable of projecting idealized self-images (the good self) onto an other with a dramatic vacillation between the two remaining psychologically viable.[8] Gilman's discussion of the volatility of shifting stereotypical valences offers substantial explanation for the variability of Japanese/American stereotypes that appears to puzzle Dower.

> But the line between "good" and "bad" responds to stresses occurring within the psyche. Thus paradigm shifts in our mental representations of the world can and do occur. We can move from fearing to glorifying the Other. We can move from loving to hating. The most negative stereotype always has an overtly positive counterweight. As any image is shifted, all stereotypes shift. Thus stereotypes are inherently protean rather than rigid.[9]

If we accept this account of the psychic basis of stereotyping, we should not be surprised to discover its ubiquity or even its virulence. Both the Anglo-Saxon and Japanese traditions were notable for deeply rooted racial pride bolstered in the former instance by centuries of colonial occupation around the world and in the latter by a culturally shared conviction as to the racial purity of the Yamato race and its 2,600-year history as an unconquered people. As strongly held as these ideas of racial supremacy might have been in both cases, the culture's potential for projection onto its evil other wielded an equal force. The Japanese were diminutive, childlike in temperament, simian in appearance (scientific proof of their debased evolutionary station), and never to be trusted; the Americans were overgrown and devilish, ill-smelling and licentious.

But the Japanese/American confrontation was not a unique case; indeed, Dower writes of the way in which the Japanese were "saddled with racial stereotypes that Europeans and Americans had applied to nonwhites for centuries: during the conquest of the New World, the slave trade, the Indian wars in the United States, the agitation against Chinese immigrants in America, the colonization of Asia and Africa, the U.S. conquest of the Philippines at the turn of the century."[10] One need only consult Edward Said's classic text *Orientalism* for an extended discussion of the ways in which Europeans have constructed a non-Western other whose chief characteristics remain intact across centuries and major geographic boundaries.

It is crucial that we consider the ways in which a wartime climate can fuel the intensity of racial hatred through a hardening of boundaries along the dichotomous split between "us" and "them." A pressure or ideologically produced and sustained urgency is created culturewide that reinforces consensual behavior through positive rewards (the approbation of top-down propaganda campaigns, peer group support, and traditions of filial piety or team play) as well as negative ones (the death of community members, fearfulness, and a constantly renewed loathing toward those whose actions appear to challenge accepted values). What's more, the intensity aroused through this identification of the enemy as the embodiment of evil and the source of all conflict spirals upward as it confronts its mirror self in the attitudes and behaviors of its other. The underlying dynamic of projection and stereotype that fuels the enemy's hatred is identical to one's own. Certainly, all the governing societal conditions outlined can be applied equally to Japan and to the United States during the Pacific war. Dower notes that many of the stereotypical traits claimed by one combatant nation for the other (e.g., bestiality or barbarism) were mutually attributed.

If, as Gilman states, "stereotypes arise when self-integration is threatened," it becomes possible to see wartime stereotyping as the manifestation of a shared and heavily reinforced perception of a threat to national integrity. A crucial distinction—that between the pathological and nonpathological personality—is equally pertinent to our discussion; the former (person or state) remains "consistently aggressive toward the real people and objects to which the stereotypical representations correspond . . . [while] the latter is able to repress the aggression and deal with people as individuals."[11] A state of war evinces a kind of cultural pathology, a general inability (or unwillingness) to treat people of an other designation as individuals.

The blindness caused by this stereotyping dynamic can be extended to others who may share one's own state citizenship, a fact discovered by the two-thirds of the interned Japanese Americans who were born in the United States. In the words of General John L. DeWitt, head of the West Coast Defense Command: "A Jap's a Jap. . . . It makes no difference whether he is an American citizen or not. . . . I don't want any of them. . . . There is no way to determine their loyalty."[12] What is at stake is the control of one's world, this time understood at the level not of infantile personality formation but of global politics. That which is identified as the source of threat—namely, the enemy—becomes the wellspring of all that is evil, the object of culturally shared projection. It is into this setting of deeply rooted emotion that we must now place the documentary film, without doubt the most effective tool for mass projection ever devised.

▶

Documentary Film: Tool for Mass Projection

The photographic image is the object itself, the object freed from the conditions of time and space that govern it. No matter how fuzzy, distorted, or discolored, no matter how lacking in documentary value the image may be, it shares, by virtue of the very process of its becoming, the being of the model of which it is the reproduction; it is the model.

:: André Bazin, "The Ontology of the Photographic Image"

The photograph . . . becomes meaningful in certain transactions and has real effects, but . . . cannot refer or be referred to a pre-photographic reality as to a truth. . . . we have to see that every photograph is the result of specific and, in every sense, significant distortions which render its relation to any prior reality deeply problematic and raise the question of the determining level of the material apparatus and of the social practices within which photography takes place.

:: John Tagg, *The Burden of Representation*

In his autobiography, *The Name above the Title,* Frank Capra describes his reaction to a first viewing of Leni Riefenstahl's *Triumph of the Will.* In his words, "Satan couldn't have devised a more blood-chilling super-spectacle. . . . I sat alone and pondered. How could I mount a counter-attack against *Triumph of the Will* . . . ?"[13] It should come as no surprise that three terms coalesce in this prelude to Capra's discussion of his own strategies for wartime documentary film production—the demonic, spectacle, and war. It was he, noted American populist and one of Hollywood's premier storytellers, who was tapped by General George C. Marshall to explain to American soldiers, citizens, and allies "Why We Fight" in a series of seven feature-length documentary films. In his effort to make "the best damned documentary films ever made" (his promise to Marshall), Capra seems to have intuited John Tagg's pronouncement "Every photograph is the result of specific and, in every sense, significant distortions."

We might extrapolate on Tagg's dictum to say that every documentary film or videotape is the result of a lengthy series of selections (instances of the maker's interventions that are constitutive)—from the choice of lens, film stock, camera position, and distance to choices surrounding sound recording and mixing techniques, editing strategies, and musical and narrational accompaniment.[14] No documentary image is innocent; it is mistaken for its referent (that which existed before the lens at some other time and place) at our collective peril. Capra knew about the malleability of the image and even more about editing, the power of association. He gave proof of his acumen in *The Battle of China* as he joined newsreel images of Japanese planes firing on an American gunboat to a narrated description of the attack of "the blood-crazed Japs." These images of an air attack—indistinguishable from so many others—instantly evoke, on account of the narration that blankets them, both bestiality and madness (two of the archetypal attributes of America's wartime other).

Time and again, Capra mobilizes words and images to reinforce prevailing stereotypes, both good and bad. The Chinese allies, "spontaneously driven by an epic impulse," embark on "a Homeric journey . . . thirty-million people moving westward . . . westward to freedom" in an effort to evade Japanese coastal encroachment, evoking the westward expansionism of America itself. When the Chinese blow up the dikes that hold back the Yellow River, the Japanese invaders are shown beating a watery retreat, thus calling to Western minds a biblical referent and an act of divine retribution—the drowning of the Egyptian pharaoh and his men as they pursued Moses and the children of Israel across the Red Sea. Images of Chinese labor processes are characteristically collective and patiently painstaking (pulling a barge upstream by hand, children breaking down rocks with tiny hammers), while the archival images chosen to represent the Japanese show them to be vicious and aggressive (shouting their celebrant "banzai," beating or bayoneting the helpless). Even the Disney animation that provides graphic representation of troop movements bears a stereotypical charge; Chinese activity is denoted by white arrows, the Japanese by black. Through these various acts of appropriation, the Asian allies temporarily become white.

The case of the Disney graphics in the Capra films offers apt illustration of the potential for ideological inflection for even the most benign filmic elements. What could be more empirically documentative than a chart of troop movement? And yet opportunities for coloring and connotation abound. In a manner to which the history of the African American experience bears tragic witness, blackness in Western culture has been freighted with notions of evil and moral turpitude. On the basis of a near-subliminal color contrast, Capra is able to cast the Chinese and Japanese as instant hero and villain. Such moments of graphic illustration can be colored in a number of other ways as well, for example, through the use of musical accompaniment, festive or foreboding according to the desired emotional impact. What appears to be a straightforward presentation of factual material can, in fact, be strongly if subtly inflected by authorial choices calculated to sway audiences.

At a time of consensual action, when the enemy is clearly demarcated and the lines drawn, films that rally statistics toward an argument or recontextualize documentary footage retrieved from many sources (including the enemy) can mobilize a persuasive force of staggering proportion. If we, as individuals or nations, believe that the newsreel image is always neutral, that the document cannot lie, or even if we receive no encouragement within our culture to question the status of every image as truth, we become subject to a persuasive force capable of overturning some of our most basic ethical principles.

I have written elsewhere about the several functions that define the documentary film—the preservational, the persuasive, the expressive, and the analytical.[15] At certain moments and in the hands of particular practitioners, one or the other of these functions may be decisively foregrounded. For the historical and ideological reasons discussed earlier, wartime documentary films produced by combatant nations were heavily weighted in the direction of persuasion. The specific character of that persuasiveness—its goals and methods—varied. The Japanese and American documents featured in these festival screenings offer ample evidence of that variability. Certain British war films exemplify an approach to persuasion unlike those of either the Japanese or Americans.

The bulk of British wartime documentary films feature persuasive tactics quite at odds with their American ally's interest in defining the enemy, focusing instead on producing wartime paeans to English stoicism and resilience. Films such as *Listen to Britain* (1942) and *Fires Were Started* (1943)—two remarkable works by Humphrey Jennings—celebrate the common culture and cohesiveness of Britain at war. In *Listen to Britain*, compositional choices (one memorable image—soldiers, silhouetted against the evening sky, guarding the British coastline), picture editing, and the creation of sound bridges all help to orchestrate a vision of a nation, unmarked by class or gender divisions, fighting as one. There are almost no direct references to the German menace, although it is the un-imaged Luftwaffe—for the moment held at bay by the RAF—that prompts repeated glances skyward. Instead the film celebrates Britain's proud past and its sheer indomitability, echoed in the title of another of Jennings's wartime documentaries, *London Can Take It* (1940). Big Ben, the BBC blanketing the globe with its war coverage, the dome of Saint Paul's—these are the audiovisual icons around which Jennings rallies mass support.

No matter the concrete manifestation of the national imperative toward wartime persuasion, however, cinema—and the documentary film form most of all—remains a tool of great potency. This was known to the nations at war in World War II; it was also known some years before to V. I. Lenin, whose maxim "The cinema is for us the most important of all the arts" is a statement about the power of the motion picture to solidify national identity and move great numbers of people toward state goals. All of the filmmaking practices alluded to here—the Soviet efforts of the twenties, the German, British, Japanese, and American propaganda films of the thirties and forties—are inconceivable outside of state authority and guidance. These social visions projected to millions by cinematic means are, in every case, cut to the cloth of government policy. They explain, they celebrate, they predict, they inculpate. And they do so in a manner that maximizes their persuasive force while leaving little space for counter-instances or dissent.

The wartime documentary film can thus be seen as an ideal domain of stereotypical discourse. These are the films that, in their appropriation of apparently evidentiary images (archival footage, newsreels, shots of the recognizable and the everyday), can rally mass support and inspire joint action. Sounds and images projected in the dark can tap popular memory through biblical references or a musical phrase; the most treasured values of American culture, instantly evoked by shots of children at play or the Washington Monument, can be made to seem the direct targets of enemy attack. Responses—elicited on the spot, frequently by recourse to "real" images—can be shaped and intensified by the canny filmmaker, then harnessed to wartime aims. Wartime consensus only fuels the fire that burns against the debased other. It is worthwhile to explore some representations of the Japanese produced in wartime America in greater detail.

▶

"This Is the Enemy"

In the autumn of 1942, the Museum of Modern Art in New York exhibited two hundred war posters from among the thousands submitted to a campaign drive spearheaded by Artists for Victory, a coalition of twenty-six arts organizations dedicated to patriotic service. The images were meant to illustrate one of several war slogans, among them "Deliver Us from Evil," "Buy More War Bonds," "Loose Talk Sinks Ships," "Victory Starts Here," and—the most salient of all for our purposes—"This Is the Enemy." Of the handful of posters featured in *Life* magazine's coverage of the exhibition (December 21, 1942), there is a notable difference between the character of the representations of the European as against the Asian enemy. Four of the six "This Is the Enemy" images depict Nazi violence and sacrilege: a daggered hand smashing through the stained glass of a church window or desecrating an American flag. In the most horrific of them, the superimposed face of Hitler oversees a ravaged landscape. In the background, flames lick over a church spire; the foreground is littered with corpses. Chief among the dead is a woman, pierced through the heart, her body resting against a plaque that reads "God Bless Our Home." Her lifeless hand is held by a hysterically crying child who sits up to his waist in a pool of blood. The evils associated with the Nazi enemy are forcefully invoked: cruelty, antagonism to cherished values of church and family, mass homicide.

The two examples of Japanese "This Is the Enemy" posters provide, however, a considerable contrast to the German; they are both more explicit in their depiction of enemy atrocities and clearly racially driven. While the European nemesis may be figured as a defiler of the sacred, the Japanese are "othered" with far greater vehemence.[16] In one poster, a Japanese soldier, swarthy and simian of posture, stands half erect, with a naked woman slung over his shoulder; the alabaster of her exposed skin contrasts hyperbolically with that of her captor. In yet another instance, a dagger-wielding Japanese soldier, his yellow face drawn wide in a snarl, reaches for a horror-struck white woman fleeing from the lower left edge of the frame. The grotesquerie of the image results from two excessive elements: the teeth and nails (now fangs and claws) of the Asian man are hyperbolized in the direction of the bestial, and a low-key, low-angle lighting effect transforms the painted image into nightmare. While the threat of the other is in all cases figured as the brutalization of the woman, the most fundamental assault within the patriarchal order because it annihilates the medium of exchange and reproduction, the savagery and bestiality of the Asian are crucially foregrounded. Such images are calculated to inspire vengeance for the primordial robbery of the woman and for the violation of the inviolable—white womanhood, anchor of Western morality and aesthetics.

The April 29, 1944, cover of *Liberty* magazine is equally explicit in its projection of animality upon the Japanese. Three uniformed soldiers of the empire—one bedecked in medals, all bucktoothed and bespectacled—are shown perched on a fallen tree trunk as bombs rain down from behind and above. The gestured poses of this figure group—hands placed over ears, eyes, and mouth respectively—enact the "hear no evil, see no evil, speak no evil" adage (with "Japanese-ness" functioning as the visible shorthand for evil). But the cover illustrates far more than a hackneyed moral injunction, for once again these enemy soldiers are imaged as apelike, their dark, fur-covered hands and feet inhumanly outsized and grasping. Such dehumanizing representations as these can, in the end, be said to have a cumulative effect. The atomic resolution to the war could be faced without remorse by a society assured of the enemy's subhumanity.

In wartime Hollywood films such as *The Purple Heart* (1944) and *Guadalcanal Diary* (1943), visual as well as cultural codes were mobilized in the service of stereotype. In the latter film, the enemy was depicted in camouflage, capable of merging with the jungle flora, much as the Vietnamese were in *Platoon* (1986). This is clearly not a Rousseauian

The cover of *Liberty* magazine (29 April 1944) shows the virulence of wartime stereotyping.

reference (the Asian other as idyllically close to nature)—the enemy is "of nature" to be sure, but in a manner suggestive of the simian reference of the *Liberty* cover. He is simply meant to occupy a lower rung on the evolutionary ladder. When, in *Guadalcanal Diary*, a patrol discovers an enemy encampment only recently abandoned, one American soldier cannot conceal his distaste for the alien look and smell of the other's cuisine.

His face a mask of disgust, the GI sniffs gingerly at what look to be the remnants of a rice cake and some raw fish, foods now much in demand by Western sophisticates.

In *The Purple Heart,* Japanese linguistic characters are described as "chicken scratch"; the enemy's most elemental powers of symbolization are devalued at the same moment that the figure of animality recurs. Low-angle placement of camera and light source reinforces the sense of threat and grotesquerie attached to the Japanese characters throughout *The Purple Heart,* a film based on the trial and sentencing of eight pilots (led by Colonel James Doolittle) who had been shot down over China following a Tokyo bombing raid in 1942. By the time of the making of the film, it was widely known that three of the American flyers had been executed (October 1943). Dower's discussion of the case in *War without Mercy* is instructive. The denunciations spurred by the incident were nearly identical on both sides; the acts of the enemy (bombing civilians on the one hand, executing captured combatants on the other) were "barbarous," "uncivilized," "inhuman," and "depraved."[17] In Lewis Milestone's film version, the Japanese soldiers and jurists are leering, bucktoothed aggressors who possess no code of justice. In a detail of casting both fitting and ironic, none of the enemy roles were played by Japanese actors, who, even had they agreed to play the parts, could not have done so. It was they who were the prisoners—in camps not so very far away from the back lots of Twenieth Century Fox. It is unlikely that American audiences knew the difference in any case.

Indeed, the inability to distinguish among Asians—betraying a kind of smug indifference recently parodied in Valerie Soe's tape *All Orientals Look the Same*—came to be a problem when dealing with the Chinese allies during World War II, a problem to which I have alluded earlier in my discussion of Capra's *The Battle of China.* In yet another instance of popular culture's dispatch to war service, cartoonist Milton Caniff contributed his familiar illustrative style to the U.S. Army's *Pocket Guide to China,* a pamphlet for American forces fighting in the Pacific. Using the figure of his fictional character Steve Canyon as the soldier's guide, Caniff provided the pictures that could tell the story.

The task was a challenging one: how to split one stereotype into two. Indeed, Caniff and company were charged with educating the American fighting man to a degree sufficient to distinguish between two racial groups while remaining entirely within the domain of stereotypical speech. And always the connotative meanings of the text had to express praise for the ally while disparaging the enemy. For example, the Chinese are said to be "dull bronze" in color, while the Japanese are "more on the lemon-yellow side"; a precious metal is opposed to a bitter fruit.[18] The pamphlet continues: "Look at their profiles and teeth . . . C usually has evenly set choppers—J has buck teeth . . . the Chinese smiles easily—the Jap usually expects to be shot." The physical characteristics of the two are typically contrasted through some reference to the relative similarity of the Chinese physical type to the Euro-American: "C's eyes are set like any European's or American's—but have a marked squint. . . . J has eyes slanted toward his nose." The Chinese "and other Asiatics" have "fairly normal feet," while the Japanese soldiers will usually have a "wide space between the first and second toes" from wearing his wooden sandals or "geta."

The message is clear: the Chinese are more like us, only we never noticed it before. Their eyes and feet are really like ours; they are a cheerful and attractive people with a ready, even-toothed smile. The Japanese are distinctively othered by comparison. There is a kind of grotesque confusion in the very placement of their facial features; their eyes slant down to where their noses should be. They have bad teeth and misshapen feet and are paranoid—if paranoia is the appropriate term for what is everywhere reinforced as just reward for being a lesser species.

Such racially based disparagement as this would, by necessity, apply equally to Japanese people who happened also to be citizens of the United States. Stereotyping tactics such as these that placed the human integrity of an entire race in jeopardy would have as their historical correlative an unapologetic assault on the rights of many thousands of American citizens and alien residents. It is to the internment camp experience of the 120,000 Japanese Americans of the first and second generations—the Issei and Nisei—that we now turn, with particular regard for the active reinvestigation of that history by artists of the Sansei generation.

▶———————————————————————————

The Return to Manzanar

> FRAMED
> *"It was a bum rap. We were FRAMED."*
> FRAME
> FRAME *of reference*
> ReFRAMED
> :: Bruce and Norman Yonemoto, from *FRAMED*, a video installation

> *I don't know where this came from, but I just had this fragment, this picture that's always been in my mind. My mother,*

*she's standing at a faucet and it's really hot outside. And she's
filling this canteen and the water's really cold and it feels
really good. And outside the sun's just so hot, it's just beating down. And there's this dust that gets in everywhere and
they're always sweeping the floors.*
:: Rea Tajiri, *History and Memory*

According to the *Asian American Media Reference Guide,* second edition (1990), a source book of more than one thousand films and videotapes made by Asian American artists, no fewer than fifteen media
works have been made since the early 1970s that focus on the topic of the
Japanese American relocation camp experience during World War II.[19]
The Yonemoto brothers' *FRAMED,* a video installation twice exhibited
in 1989, is—owing to the site-specific nature of all installation pieces—
unlisted and unavailable for rental. These sixteen works share a common
interest in the radical reexamination of a historical occurrence crucial
to the understanding of American stereotyping of the Japanese during
World War II. For it is only through consideration of the internment
experience—the uprooting and imprisonment of all Japanese Americans
living on the West Coast with inestimable damage done to the health, economic fortunes, and self-esteem of two generations of Americans—that
we can assess the domestic as well as global effects of wartime racism in
the United States.[20]

One element of the incarceration procedure is particularly significant
to this discussion. When the Japanese residents reported to the camps,
federal officials confiscated cameras as "dangerous contraband," an action that effectively robbed the internees of their most powerful tool for
the documentation and potential redefinition of their lives. It was clear
that those who committed the Japanese Americans to these desert camps
would represent them and their history in ways that would serve the
state's best interests rather than any experiential "truth."

According to the government-produced film *Japanese Relocation,*
the internees, in an act of patriotic good faith, are said to have "cooper-
ated wholeheartedly" in their imprisonment. In a scene that echoes the
pioneer (and all-American) spirit alluded to in Capra's description of the
Chinese people's great westward migration in *The Battle of China,* these
thousands of dispossessed Americans are shown being shipped off by
truck and train to lands "full of opportunity." There, anonymously bun-
kered in the desolate locales of ten states, they are to be given the opportunity to make the desert flower. Milton Eisenhower, brother of the great
general, is the spokesman for the enactment of Executive Order 9066,

whose job it is to whitewash wholesale imprisonment on the basis of racial origin. The arrogance and self-serving logic of his explanation is rarely lost on contemporary audiences. The film concludes with the following narration:

> We are setting a standard for the rest of the world in the treatment of people who *may* [italics mine] have loyalties to an enemy nation. We are protecting ourselves without violating the principles of Christian decency [no mention made of Buddhist decency]. And we won't change this fundamental decency no matter what our enemies do. But of course we hope most earnestly that our example will influence the Axis powers in their treatment of Americans who fall into their hands.

It has frequently been repeated that no act of subversion or espionage was ever proved against a Japanese American during the war years. This is significant given the equation that Eisenhower's statement makes between Americans of Japanese descent and the wartime enemy. For of course the harm was entirely one-sided. Generations of Americans were, through the internment experience, inculcated with a sense of guilt and shame that proved indelible for many. But if the majority of the Issei and Nisei found personal expiation a difficult task given their culturally reinforced sense of loyalty to authority—governmental or familial—members of the next generation have remained obsessed with the active reinscription of Japanese American history. The media works that they have produced—from oral histories with internees to meditations on memory—move far beyond apologia. Through the aggressive reinvestigation of the past effected in these pieces, history itself becomes the object of investigation.

It used to be a commonplace that history was the story of great public deeds and, by extension, of great (white) men—as told by other great (white) men. Recent trends in the field have recognized that the distinction between public and private histories is suspect on intellectual as well as ideological grounds. Women, non-Western peoples, and all those who, by virtue of their race, gender, or sexual orientation, have been officially dispossessed of a history have begun to fight back. They have done so by means of the written word as well as by the constructions of sound and image. The seizure of cameras at the relocation camps can now be redefined as a failed attempt on the part of government authorities to rob the interned of any future access to their own past. If the visible evidence is lacking, the intrepid media historiographer can rewrite history through recourse to interview, present-tense footage of past campsites, or the sheer force of creative imagination.

One of the truly trailblazing efforts of this sort is Robert Nakamura's

Manzanar (1971), a short Super-8 film shot by a former internee who, as a UCLA film school student some years later, made a solitary (and aesthetically triumphant) return to his past. It is a viscerally felt meditation on Nakamura's own experience that nonetheless pays homage to two generations of kinsmen. Using a mix of traditional Japanese vocal and instrumental elements as audio accompaniment to the handheld images, Nakamura focuses on the ravaged landscape and the few remaining markers of what took place there. Little is left to testify other than the discards—broken dishes, pieces of a wall—but what remains visible is rendered all the more poignant. An insect crawls slowly across an inscription of a name carved in stone ("Tom Fujisaki 10/7/43"). That deeply etched reminder becomes a hieroglyph bearing witness to a past—and to a person—that can never be erased so long as memory and imagination survive. The film's emotional climax occurs in a flurry of music and handheld images as the filmmaker charges (in a blind rage?) across the desert landscape. It is as though Nakamura's lurching camera is exorcising a past officially buried and mastering it in an act of memorial reconstruction. One feels the unleashing of three decades of anger and frustration through the camera's eye.

In the 1980s, two other Asian American independent filmmakers, Loni Ding and Steven Okazaki, produced significant works on aspects of the wartime Japanese American experience. Ding's *Nisei Soldier: Standard Bearer for an Exiled People* (1984) is a sensitive treatment of the young men who chose to leave the camps to enter military service and in so doing became the most decorated unit in American history. While any film about the storied 442nd Infantry Regiment must tell the tales of struggle and survival endemic to men at war, *Nisei Soldier* is equally intent on asking anew—and for these hero/internees—the question of "Why We Fight." The ironies are bitter and layered. With the unit's casualties running at 300 percent over twenty months, there were many gold stars (denoting a fallen son) hanging on concentration camp doors. Was the bravery of these men a sign of superpatriotism at odds with their treatment? They were, after all, segregated and perhaps too frequently assigned the most dangerous missions. Or was their soldiering the sole legitimate outlet for the fury they felt but could never channel to its proper source? Ding provides no answers but instead offers a gentle tribute; she is the chronicler of men who spoke their history only on the battlefield.

Ding's later film, *The Color of Honor* (1987), returns to the submerged history of the Japanese American GI, in this case focusing on the duties they performed for the U.S. Military Intelligence. The ironies were compounded for these men who fought the invisible war of Special

Services—cracking codes, translating and interrogating the captured Japanese soldiers—while continuing to experience the racial prejudice responsible for their people's mass incarceration at home. But more than that, *Honor* returns to the men themselves. One man's recounting of his return stateside provides a particularly instructive insight into the power of these films to rekindle latent passions. Rudy Tanaka, now partially disabled, tells of the confrontation with his former high school principal, the man responsible for expelling Tanaka and his brother on racial grounds in the days after Pearl Harbor. Finding him before the assembled students, Tanaka demands an apology on the spot, or he will "wipe the stage with him, I don't care which." The principal apologizes.

Ding has said that this moment, of all the film's one hundred minutes, never fails to inspire the most heated debates during postscreening discussions. Some in the Japanese American audience decry Tanaka's threat as a mere reflection of violence absorbed while others applaud it as a gesture of self-determination of a sort all too lacking in the generation as a whole. Ding, a Chinese American aware of the moral compromise of the "good Chinese" role decreed by wartime policy, remains devoted to a kind of historical excavation of the Japanese American experience through the making of her films. They bring a people and their stories to the attention of millions while continuing to inspire controversy and renewed self-awareness within the Japanese American community.

Steven Okazaki's *Unfinished Business: The Japanese American Internment Cases* (1984) is a product of the militancy of the 1980s, the time during which the battle for reparations for internees reached its peak. Okazaki, who consciously uses the term "concentration camp," takes as his focus three men who resisted Executive Order 9066 and challenged government policy. These were the men who chose the public degradation and imprisonment accorded them as conscientious objectors but continued to struggle for their dignity. That struggle became, by the 1980s, a legal battle fought in courtrooms across the land. Okazaki celebrates the resolve of forty years that kept the challenge to the constitutionality of internment alive and the inner strength of those who, in resisting the most popular war of the century, chose prison stripes instead of khaki.

Days of Waiting (1989) is another film about conscious choices. In it, Okazaki mines yet another source of historical irony through the life story of a white woman who chose to share the wartime incarceration of her Japanese American husband and there in the camps discovered for the first time a sense of social identity. As told by the filmmaker, Estelle Ishigo was a kind of artistic waif of fin de siècle San Francisco who found her romantic match in Arthur Ishigo. After more than a decade of marriage,

Ishigo was fired from her art school teaching job on the basis of her interracial marriage. She was soon sharing the indignities and small triumphs of the more than twelve thousand internees confined to a single square mile of land near Heart Mountain, Wyoming.

The strength of the film lies in the way in which the figure of Estelle Ishigo subverts the expected categorizations of insider and outsider that so animated the period. Ishigo's experience proves that race can be a matter of choice as well as birth, that race can be functionally determined through conscious alliances and identifications. If the Caucasian American can begin to see the drama of internment from Ishigo's hybrid position, new sources of empathy may be tapped. And stereotype can thus be deposed.

It is this overturning of the dynamic of the stereotype that binds together these works and establishes their pertinence to this discussion. If we look and listen, the racially grounded generalizations that dictated public policy become untenable, for these films give the lie to the top-down, government-sanctioned pronouncements that were the unchallenged public images of an era. Japanese Americans are accorded the complexity and variability unavailable to them during the 1940s through the appropriation of the means of reproduction by a group of Asian American independent artists. And this means of reproduction amounts to a franchise on history and its active rewriting.

I have saved to the end of my discussion the most recent and perhaps most ambitious of these works. In a manner reminiscent of Robert Nakamura's *Manzanar,* Rea Tajiri's *History and Memory* mixes historical reinscription with autobiography, but with a far more complex weave of image sources and temporalities. Tajiri's address to memory is also a kind of gift; the tape attempts to supply images of her mother's life in the Poston, Arizona, relocation camp. And yet, though the mother's recollection of the camps is uneven, it is the artist herself who most requires the act of visual reconstruction. She narrates her desire very near the tape's opening:

> I don't know where this came from, but I just had this fragment, this picture that's always been in my mind. My mother, she's standing at a faucet and it's really hot outside. And she's filling this canteen and the water's really cold and it feels really good. And outside the sun's just so hot, it's just beating down. And there's this dust that gets in everywhere and they're always sweeping the floors.

Like the child of a Holocaust survivor, Tajiri is obsessed with the pain suffered by family members before her birth, manifest in her case by "the search for an ever-absent image." This is a particularly telling image for its overlay of water, life-giving and beneficent, and the recurring historical motif of resentment at the successes of the Japanese American small farmer. Indeed, these farmers "brought water to the land and made things grow"—according to stereotype but in affirmation of life.

And now, in 1991, Tajiri searches for a memory that is personal, familial, and cultural all at once.

> I remember having this feeling growing up that I was haunted by something, that I was living within a family full of ghosts. There was this place that they knew about. I had never been there, yet I had a memory for it. I could remember a time of great sadness before I was born.

The tone of the tape is confessional in its plumbing of the depths of obsession, testimonial in its expression of the emotional linkage of mother and daughter. Tajiri claims in a crawl that accompanies spoken narration (there are frequently multiple channels of information that compete for our attention) that she was able to intuit the exact location of her mother's barracks when visiting the Poston campsite.

In a strategy of disjunctive layering of image sources, anecdotes, and historical markers that recurs throughout, the theme of obsession with identity is played out in a comic vein through the story of Tajiri's putative sister. She collects pictures of movie stars or cute boys she follows in the park. Most of them are white. The artist's preoccupations, on the other hand, are historically rooted: "There are things that have happened in the world while there were cameras watching, things we have images for." She sets out to transform memory into history and thus depose from

Tajiri retrieves an image of particular intensity from her mother's past. Reprinted with permission from Rea Tajiri.

hegemonic power the false histories of image makers from Hollywood or Washington. Examples of both types of the latter abound, from wartime propaganda tracts such as *Japanese Relocation* or *December 7* to the glossier but still potent fictions—*A Bad Day at Bad Rock* (1954), *From Here to Eternity* (1954), or *Come See the Paradise* (1990).

We know through Nietzsche of "creative forgetfulness," the removal from consciousness of that which denies, rather than affirms, life. And yet, like a time traveler in a Chris Marker film, Tajiri wishes to retrieve an image of particular intensity from her mother's past: her hands filling a canteen with cold water in the middle of the desert. Of course that retrieval is, more than anything, a gift the artist gives to herself and her generation. The tape culminates in a victory that is shared by all the Asian American independent artists through whom the stereotypes—rarefied, abstract, and dehumanized—have been supplanted by the sounds and images of experience, memory, counterhistory. Tajiri concludes: "But now I found I could connect the picture to the story. I could forgive my mother her loss of memory and could make this image for her."

The tape's resolution signals more than personal achievement. It sounds but the most recent note in a rich chorus of contemporary voices engaged in a political act combining creative imagination and the will to document. History has been rewritten.

▶ ───

Media Activism as Counterstereotype

> *Between American TV and the American print media, the war has been presented as if it was a finely engineered piece of art or a high-tech tea party. American troops were uniformly professional, courteous and kind, even toward captured Iraqi weaklings. And anyone who was wounded or died just vanished.*
> :: Carol Squiers, "Screening the War: Filmmakers and Critics on the Images That Made History"

> *The point is to encourage people to take control of their own lives, their own images, to begin representing their own struggles without a high degree of technical expertise, to become speaking subjects, makers of meaning, active participants instead of passive consumers.*
> :: Sherry Millner, "All That Glitters . . ."

Up until the moment that the bombs began to fall on Iraq and the Gulf War began in earnest (mid-January 1991), American mass media coverage of the debates surrounding proposed military intervention in the Middle East presented the image of a nation divided. Within hours of the first air attacks, a veil of self-censorship began to descend upon the land, so that few who tuned into CNN's nonstop war coverage might have guessed that organized acts of resistance to the war continued unabated and in some cases intensified. As Carol Squiers observed, the American news media were transformed into cheerleaders and propagandists: "What happened was a war; what we saw was military promotion. Few in the United States seem to notice a distinction."[21]

There were those who did notice. And some of them, banding together to form the Gulf Crisis TV Project, acted on their political analysis, producing a series of thirty-minute programs that focused on a range of issues related to the war. In the exposé style of another, earlier cultural manifestation—the guerrilla television movement of the early 1970s—these programs provided extensive documentation of antiwar activities as well as political analysis of the motives and methods of government planners. Two decades earlier, collectives such as the Ant Farm, Global Village, Videofreex, and Top Value Television had begun to show Americans electronic versions of themselves never before seen on the CBS Evening News. TVTV's *Four More Years* (1972) provided unique coverage of the 1972 Republican National Convention, spending more time with the antiwar protesters in the streets and the news gatherers on the floor of the convention center—themselves media celebrities such as Walter Cronkite, Dan Rather, and Mike Wallace—than with the party chieftains or their chosen candidates (Nixon/Agnew).

The Gulf Crisis TV Project's immediate predecessors were Paper Tiger TV and the Deep Dish TV Network, both products of the 1980s. Originally formed in New York in 1981 as a cable TV–based platform for media criticism, Paper Tiger has created more than three hundred half-hour programs devoted to countering the prevailing mythologies of American popular culture in a cheaply produced, no-holds-barred format. From attacks on tabloid journalism and TV soap operas *(Joan Does Dynasty)* to diatribes against American TV news *(Brian Winston Reads the TV News),* Paper Tiger has provided scholars, artists, and political activists with the opportunity to share television space with Ted Turner or Arsenio Hall. The Deep Dish TV Network simply expanded on the Paper Tiger insight by renting satellite time and beaming their programs to hundreds of downlinks across America.

With the Gulf Crisis TV Project, media activists took on a concrete challenge: to produce a political counterdiscourse on the same tight schedule as the "big boys." It took thirty years for Japanese American artists to re-create their histories; those dying beneath a hail of missiles could not afford the wait. More than three hundred public-access cable stations across the country took the feed from the Project; thirty PBS stations broadcast the series, often with multiple repeats. It is estimated to have reached 40 percent of the total audience for public broadcasting (itself an admittedly small slice of the TV pie). Canada's Vision TV, Channel Four in the United Kingdom, SBC Australian TV, and national television in Dubai all broadcast the Gulf Crisis programs. It is necessary to say that despite these broadcasts, the war was still fought, and thousands still died. But every program that casts doubt on the wisdom of this and every war, every exposé of ignorance or complacency, affects the fragile balance of support for the deployment of billion-dollar missiles and the endangerment of human lives.

I won't have much to say about the programs themselves, although the episode entitled *Manufacturing the Enemy* made clear that the racism in evidence against Arab Americans in the 1990s had its regrettable antecedents in the Japanese American internment camps fifty years before. It is my contention that the most important thing about the Gulf Crisis TV Project is the fact of its existence. In the media-charged global environment we now share, alternative voices and visions are our best insurance for survival. And the price of that insurance is the creation and support of media groups devoted to the critique and thoroughgoing inquiry of public policy. This means that no national television culture can afford to exist solely for profit or state-guided education. If we accept Louis Althusser's notion that any cultural or educational institution functions within late capitalism as a kind of "ideological state apparatus," we might then say that a minimum of television channel time and space must be systematically devoted to programming that functions with a degree of autonomy—outside of, if not entirely beyond, the sway of state control. Such an initiative can never of course be mandated from above; it requires the collaborative efforts of independent makers. But these artists and cultural workers cannot hope to succeed in the tedious, frequently unrewarding task of networking and downscale production without a degree of public support.

And therein lies the internal contradiction. Alternative visions and social critiques can maintain their integrity only if they are allowed to exist apart, but no capital-intensive operation such as television production can survive without access to the tools or the airwaves. The initiative that will allow alternative media to flourish in market-driven economies from the United States to Europe, Asia, and Africa must begin with public awareness. The establishment and safeguarding of a culture of dissent in any nation is the surest hedge against the violation of human dignity or the wholesale condemnation of a people on the basis of race or class or gender. Fifty years have been required to begin the healing of hatreds that raged across the Pacific, binding American and Japanese alike in a corrosive dynamic of racial stereotype. Atonement for all the deaths and all the liberties lost begins by guarding against any future reenactments. Alternative cultural vehicles might have allowed the thousands of Japanese Americans interned to speak rather than be spoken for; certainly, more cross-cultural traffic in the days before the war would have narrowed the gulf that separated the Issei and Nisei from their neighbors.

What I am calling for is nothing less than the systematic implementation of counterstereotyping, the unfixing of images, the embrace of, rather than recoiling from, difference. Although we indeed stereotype as a means to confirm our control of the world, we need not do so in a pathological manner, unable to differentiate in any meaningful way among the men and women who share our planet. We need not spend another fifty years recovering from the next onslaught of "warring images."

[4] Lost, Lost, Lost: *Mekas as Essayist*

*"Lost, Lost, Lost: Mekas as Essayist," originally written for David E.
James's edited collection* To Free the Cinema: Jonas Mekas and the New
York Underground *in 1992, offers an extended analysis of the essay film
as a mode of autobiographical practice that combines self-examination
with a deeply engaged outward gaze, coupling, in founding essayist
Michel de Montaigne's words, "the measure of sight" with "the measure
of things." Taking Jonas Mekas's monumental* Lost, Lost, Lost *(1949–75)
as case study, the chapter situates this canonical avant-garde film (and,
by extension, the essayistic films of Godard, Marker, and others) in relation to the documentary tradition's historical concern for the expressive
potential of the medium (e.g., the work of Vertov, Vigo, Buñuel, and
the early Ivens). The chapter bridges the gap between filmmaking that
focused on the subjectivity of social actors joined in struggle, dominant
in the 1960s and 1970s, and the first-person forms that developed in the
1980s and 1990s. This chapter bridges another gap as well—the gap between notions of social subjectivity that animate the first part of the book
and the interest in theorizing the subject pursued in Part II.*

> *And so the opinion I give is to declare the measure of my sight,
> not the measure of things.*
> :: Montaigne, *Essays*
>
> *Of course, what I faced was the old problem of all artists: to
> merge Reality and Self, to come up with the third thing.*
> :: Jonas Mekas, "The Diary Film"

In the conclusion of a remarkably perceptive review of Jonas Mekas's
Lost, Lost, Lost appearing soon after the film's 1976 release, Alan
Williams suggests a relationship between the autobiographical project

of this, the first volume of *Diaries, Notes, and Sketches,* and "the spirit of Montaigne and self-examination."[1] In so doing, Williams situates the work within an essayistic tradition whose roots, though traceable to Montaigne's three-volume *Essays* of the late sixteenth century, might be said to include certain writings of Nietzsche, Adorno, and, most recently, Roland Barthes. Indeed, the essay form, notable for its tendency toward complication (digression, fragmentation, repetition, and dispersion) rather than composition, has, in its four-hundred-year history, continued to resist the efforts of literary taxonomists, confounding the laws of genre and classification, challenging the very notion of text and of textual economy. In its heterogeneity and inexhaustibility ("with an 'amoeba-like' versatility often held together by little more than the author's voice"),[2] the essayistic work bears with it a logic that denies the verities of rhetorical composition and of system, indeed of mastery itself.[3] Knowledge produced through the essay is provisional rather than systematic; self and object organize each other, but only in a temporary way—"Nothing can be built on this configuration, no rules or methods deduced from it."[4]

The Montaignean essay derives in part from disparate precursor forms—the confessional or autobiography as well as the chronicle—insofar as its codetermining axes, its concern for self and other ("the measure of sight" as well as the "measure of things"),[5] enact what Gerard Defaux has called the "twofold project" of *Essays.* Descriptive and reflexive modalities are coupled; the representation of the historical real is consciously filtered through the flux of subjectivity. Neither the outward gaze nor the counterreflex of self-interrogation alone can account for the essay. Attention is drawn to the level of the signifier ("let attention be paid not to the matter, but to the shape I give it");[6] a self is produced through a plurality of voices, "mediated through writing, forever inscribed in the very tissue of the text."[7]

This plurality of voices provides a clue to a fundamental if implicit presumption of the essayistic mode, namely, that of indeterminacy. Neither locus of meaning—neither subject nor historical object—anchors discourse so much as it problematizes or interrogates it. This foundation of epistemological uncertainty has been widely theorized, initially by Montaigne himself, as in his essay "On Repentance": "The world is but a perennial movement. All things in it are in constant motion. . . . I cannot keep my subject still. . . . I do not portray being, I portray passing. . . . If my mind could gain a firm footing, I would not make essays, I would make decisions, but it is always in apprenticeship and on trial."[8] That more contemporary essayist Roland Barthes claimed that the fragmentary or discontinuous writing of his latter works enacted a counterideology of form inasmuch as "the fragment breaks up what I would call the smooth finish, the composition, discourse constructed to give a final meaning to what one says, which is the general rule of all past rhetoric. . . . the fragment is a spoilsport, discontinuous, establishing a kind of pulverization of sentences, images, thoughts, none of which 'takes' definitively."[9]

Despite the epistemic distance separating Montaigne and Barthes, their respective writing practices enforce a shared refusal. If neither being-as-essence nor final determinations (neither first nor last causes) arise in the essays of Montaigne or Barthes, this reticence can be attributed in part to the protocols of (essayistic) writing they share. Essayistic practices achieve a degree of commonality not through thematic consistency (as is the case with genre) but through formal and ideological resemblances.

For the young Georg Lukács, the essay was an "intellectual poem" whose first exemplar was not a literary trace but the life of Socrates. Unlike tragedy, whose end informs the whole of the drama, the life of Socrates and the essay form alike render the end an arbitrary and ironic moment. "The essay," declared Lukács, "is a judgment, but the essential, the value-determining thing about it is not the verdict . . . but the process of judging."[10] Socrates as essayistic phenotype comes to stand for a method that is active, fragmentary, and self-absorbing—ever in pursuit of a question "extended so far in depth that it becomes the question of all questions."[11] In Reda Bensmaia's phrase, the essay is an "open-ended, interminable writing machine," for just as the real resists the strictures of representation (how to frame or carve out a historical personage or event without the loss of authenticity), so too are the fixity of the source and the subject of enunciation called into question. The interminability of the essay follows from the process orientation of its activity, the mediation of the real through a cascade of language, memory, and imagination. Montaigne's "book of the self," the essay as autobiography, refuses any notion of simple or self-evident origins in a manner consistent with the Barthesian pronouncement "I am elsewhere than where I am when I write."[12]

In classical poetics, the coherence and the synthetic power of a work are the aesthetic manifestations of a rather different epistemological assumption, that of the unity and stability of the subject. Montaigne's refusal of being-as-stasis is one precursor of the more radical contemporary theoretical position that wishes to suggest otherwise: "In the field of the subject," writes Barthes, "there is no referent."[13] As formulated in the later works of that writer, the essay form is the textual manifestation of indeterminacy par excellence; heterogeneous and resistant to precise boundaries, it is metaphorizable as a Japanese stew, a broken television screen, a layered pastry. Consequently, the essay eschews grand design; Bensmaia characterizes its formal procedure as "tactics without strategy."[14]

Little wonder that films such as *Lost, Lost, Lost* and the remainder of Mekas's *Diaries, Notes, and Sketches*, Raul Ruiz's *Of Great Events and Ordinary People* (1979), Chris Marker's *Sans soleil* (1982), Trinh T. Minh-ha's *Naked Spaces: Living Is Round* (1985), or the pair of television series produced by Jean-Luc Godard and Ann-Marie Mieville, *Six fois deux* (1976) and *France/Tour/Detour/Deux/Enfants* (1978)—all of which could be termed essayistic—have alternately intrigued and puzzled audiences and critics alike with their failure to conform to generic expectation or classical structuration.[15] In all cases, the works would appear to straddle certain of the antinomies that have defined the boundaries of film scholarship: fiction/nonfiction, documentary/avant-garde, even cinema/video. Frequently, the critical appraisal of the taxonomically unstable film or video work returns to the name of the author: the television efforts of the seventies are an extension or revision of earlier Godard obsessions; *Naked Spaces* grapples with issues of Third World feminism and the limits of language as Trinh has done in previous film and literary efforts; *Sans soleil* is the summum of Marker's career as itinerant gatherer of images and sounds. And *Lost, Lost, Lost* is the work of the chief polemicist and celebrant of the New American Cinema. The diary films of Mekas can thus be said to spring from (the) underground; the autobiographical renderings of an artist can only be art.

Yet it is my purpose to speak of Mekas as essayist, to claim for *Lost, Lost, Lost* and the other volumes of *Diaries, Notes, and Sketches* a discursive position shared by the aforementioned as well as by other essayistic works, a position mobile in its resistance to generic encirclement, one that traces a trajectory within and across the historical fields of the documentary as well as of the avant-garde. Far from being a mere quibble over scholarly classification, the discussion of Mekas's work within a documentary context yields several dividends: on the one hand, the relatively moribund critical discourse surrounding nonfiction is enlivened, its aesthetic horizons broadened; on the other, *Lost, Lost, Lost* is more easily delivered of its status as a key work of contemporary film historiography, a work that teaches us about history and about the limits within which the filmic inscription of history is possible. Finally, the placement of *Lost* within a documentary context is essential for the present enterprise in another way. There can be little doubt that Mekas's diary-film project offers one of the most exhaustive instances of self-examination in the history of the cinema. And yet, as has been established, the essayistic is notable for its enmeshing of two registers of interrogation—of subjectivity and of the world. It is my contention that *Lost, Lost, Lost* shares with Montaigne's *Essays* an unyielding attentiveness both to the measure of sight and to the measure of things. My greatest concern in what follows will therefore be for the shape and tactical dynamics of a documenting gaze and a desire—to retrace the visible and the historical—that impels the film.

The placement of *Lost* within the documentary tradition remains consistent with the genesis of Mekas's project. According to the filmmaker, the documentary intent of the earliest diary efforts constitutes *Lost*'s prehistory: "The very first script that we [Jonas and his brother Adolfas] wrote when we arrived in late 1949, and which was called *Lost, Lost, Lost, Lost,* was for a documentary on the life of displaced persons here."[16] Significantly, the kinship between the founding intention and the project's eventual outcome has remained generally unremarked. Indeed, virtually every critic who has written about *Lost, Lost, Lost* has focused on the emergence of an authorial voice that develops over the thirteen-year period covered by the three-hour film (1949–1963), a voice instantiated by a series of visible stylistic shifts.[17] Perhaps inevitably, this pattern is rendered teleological, an ascension toward a full-blown gestural style familiar from the work of Brakhage and others. The steadfastly observational camera of the first two reels devoted to the activities of the Lithuanian exile community becomes the sign of the artist as yet unaware of his true vocation. "When you were first starting to shoot here," asks MacDonald, "did you feel that you were primarily a recorder of displaced persons and their struggle, or were you already thinking about becoming *a filmmaker of another sort?*"[18]

▶

The Documentary Detour

In fact, this assumed pilgrimage toward artistic progress deserves further examination, as does the essayistic character of the film's textual mapping, but not before a brief consideration of the nonfiction realm to which *Lost, Lost, Lost* is here being consigned. What is necessary in this instance is a kind of critical disengagement from the received limits of the nonfiction film in order to comprehend its historical as well as its discursive parameters. Mekas himself talks about his early literary efforts undertaken in Lithuania in the mid-1940s, his pursuit of a kind of "documentary poetry" that employed poetic means—of pace and prosody—to achieve largely descriptive ends. This hybridization of literary modes in itself echoes the essential dialogism of the essayistic enterprise. But, we are told in an interview with Scott MacDonald, this merger of the poetic and the non-fictional did not survive the move into cinema a few years later:

> When I began filming, that interest [documentary poetry] did not leave me, but it was pushed aside as I got caught up in the documentary film traditions. I was reading Grierson and Rotha and looking at the British and American documentary films of the '30's and '40's. I feel now that their influence detoured me from my own inclination. Later, I had to shake this influence in order to return to the approach with which I began.[19]

The notion of a return to origins is intrinsic to Mekas's filmic oeuvre. But the return is always itself a reworking, a movement of recuperation and renewal, in this case to a documentary poetics from which Mekas never entirely retreated. It is worth noting, for example, that the traditional documentary approach to which Mekas unfavorably refers, discernible in the fervent recording of expatriate activities in *Lost*'s early reels, is circumscribed and absorbed by the complex weave of the film's sound/image orchestration. We can only imagine the Griersonian intent of the raw footage, now dialogized by auditory elements (narration and music) and the film's rhythmic self-presentation; for the spectator of *Lost, Lost, Lost*, Mekas's departure is already contained within his return.

The reference to Grierson and Rotha in the *October* interview is significant inasmuch as they were the chief polemicists for a vision of the documentary film as a tool for propaganda and social education during the embattled decades of depression and war. For Grierson, son of a Calvinist schoolmaster, the screen was a pulpit, the film a hammer to be used in shaping the destiny of nations. When Mekas's attachment to the Lithuanian exile community gave way to broader as well as more personal concerns and the engagement with formal questions, when the fixation on national identity subsided, it was historically as well as aesthetically apt that the Griersonian model should cease to hold sway. But a wholesale disavowal of the documentary tradition threatens to obscure the tangency between Mekas's literary and filmic practices of many decades' standing, embroiled as they have been in the materiality of everyday life, and certain currents of work in nonfiction. The diary-film project deserves its place in that filmic domain.

The documentary film has, since its beginning, displayed four fundamental, often overlapping tendencies or aesthetic functions; at some moments and in the work of certain cineasts, one or another of these characteristics has frequently been over- or underfavored. They are stated here in the active voice appropriate to their discursive agency.

1. *To record, reveal, or preserve.* This is perhaps the most elemental

of documentary functions, familiar since the Lumières, traceable to the photographic antecedent. In one of several of Mekas's efforts to parse the filmic firmament (this one circa 1961), the "Realist Cinema"—a category that bridges the fiction/nonfiction divide—is named as one of three general approaches to cinema, the one that most prizes the revelatory potential of the medium:

> The third approach [the others being "Pure Cinema" and "Impure Cinema"] could be called Realist Cinema, and could be summed up as the tradition of Lumiere. The film-maker here is interested primarily in recording life as it is. His personality, instead of creating a new reality, goes mainly into revealing the most essential qualities of the already existing reality, as it is seen at the moment of happening. Flaherty attempted it in *Nanook,* Dziga Vertov ["The Camera-Eye"] devoted his life to it.[20]

This emphasis on the replication of the historical real links anthropology and home movie, since both seek what Barthes in his *Camera Lucida* has termed "that rather terrible thing which is there in every photograph: the return of the dead."[21] The preservational instinct—resisting the erosion of memory, the inevitability of passage—is the motor force behind this, the first of documentary's aesthetic functions.

Mekas remains the visual chronicler throughout *Lost.* The stark black and white of certain images early on evokes the best of thirties documentary photography in its combination of precise compositional values and compelling subject matter: the arrival of displaced persons at the Twenty-third Street Pier, the spare ramshackle of a Williamsburg front stoop or the round faces of the exiled young framed in tenement windows. But the specter of Méliès hovers nearby. Even in the midst of the most faithfully atmospheric renderings of place or person, one recalls the images with which the film commences: the brothers mugging playfully before the camera and Adolfas's magic tricks. Conjury and *actualité* are made to coexist.

Documentary has most often been motivated by the wish to exploit the camera's powers of revelation, an impulse rarely coupled with an acknowledgment of the mediational processes through which the real is transformed.[22] At times, as with Flaherty, the desire to retain the trace of an already absent phenomenon has led the nonfiction artist to supplement behavior or event-in-history with its imagined counterpart. The wish to preserve images of the traditional walrus hunt of the Inuit led Robert Flaherty to suggest the anachronistic substitution of harpoons for rifles in his *Nanook of the North.* In *Lost,* Mekas's voice-over narration speaks his desire for a recovery of the past. This obsessive witnessing of events is frequently accompanied by the spoken refrain "I was there," even while the efficacy of such a return is repeatedly contested by the film's conflictual voices.[23] The spectator is constantly reminded of the distance that separates the profilmic event and the voiced narration written years afterward. Mekas's vocal inflections themselves enforce the separation, the words delivered with a hesitancy, a weary delight in their sonorous possibilities. Thus a discomforting retrospection on an irretrievable past is mixed with a pleasurable if provisional control over its filmic reproduction.

Moreover, the sense of indeterminacy that has been suggested as a crucial ingredient of the essayistic comes to the fore in the choice of sound elements, particularly for several of the early sequences. Rather than reinforcing the pathos of loss and displacement evoked in the scenes that document the activities of the Lithuanian expatriate community, Mekas frequently chooses to play against or at oblique angles to the anticipated emotional response. Early scenes of Jonas walking the streets of New York, alone and dispossessed, gather great force from the plaintive Kol Nidre chant that accompanies them. The reference to the holiest of Hebrew prayers and its call to atonement on Yom Kippur Eve sounds the right liturgical note even while crossing cultural boundaries (and a particularly charged cultural boundary it is, given the troubled history of the Jewish Lithuanian population in this century). The resonances—and frequent dissonances—between sound and image consistently challenge the retrieval of untroubled or available historical meaning from documentary images.

"And I was there, and I was the camera eye, I was the witness, and I recorded it all, and I don't know, am I singing or am I crying?" These words accompany images from the early fifties—of placard-bearing Lithuanians, traditionally clad, marching along Fifth Avenue, protesting the Soviet occupation of their land, or of the impassioned oration of exiled leaders speaking to packed halls. The private and idiosyncratic character of the images enforces Mekas as the first reader of the text; his own uncertainty about the impact or affect engendered by his project demands that we too suspend our own certain judgments. On more than one occasion, *Lost* renders itself as undecidable—at the level of emotional response as well as of historical-interpretive activity.

Mekas's diary images document a variety of historical moments; in fact, *Lost* provides access to a *series* of histories that can be traced across the film. In the first instance, there is the discourse on the displaced person and the Lithuanian community that shares his or her exile in Brooklyn. But if the pictures of life—of work, recreation, family rituals—strain toward faithful evocation, the filmmaker's spoken refrain dissuades us from our apparent comprehension: "Everything is normal, everything is normal," Mekas assures us over the images of everyday life. "The only thing is, you'll never know what they think. You'll never know what a displaced person thinks in the evening and in New York." Occurring in the opening minutes of the film, this is the first lesson to be drawn from *Diaries,* applicable to all forays into historiography through film. Historical meanings are never simply legible or immanent. Understanding arises from the thoughtful interrogation of documents (the real in representation) and the contradictions that are produced through their overlay. Mekas here reminds us of the irreparable breach between experience and its externalized representation, a notion implied by the film's very title. We are all of us lost in the chasm between our desire to recapture the past and the impossibility of a pristine return—no one more so than Mekas himself.

The Lithuanian émigré experience, equivocal though our understanding of it may be, thus emerges as the first strand of *Lost*'s historiographic braid. It is, however, possible to trace a second preservational trajectory through the film's elaboration of a kind of postwar urban geohistory. Mekas's odyssey from Williamsburg to Manhattan crisscrosses virtually every sector of New York—Orchard Street, East Thirteenth Street, Avenue B, Times Square, City Hall, Madison Avenue, Fifth Avenue, Park Avenue South, Washington Square, and the obsessive return to Central Park. There and elsewhere, Mekas finds himself inexorably drawn to the energy and tenacity of the picketers and the poets who agitate for their personal visions. The leaflet women of Forty-second Street (appearing

Lost as postwar urban geohistory: Mekas finds himself inexorably drawn to the energy and tenacity of the picketers and the poets.

near the end of the fourth reel) who face public indifference on the coldest day of the year inspire Mekas's lyric testimonial, evinced at the level of word and image. "I was with you. I had to be. You were, you were . . . the blood of my city, the heartbeat. I wanted to feel its pulse, to feel its excitement. Yes, this was my city."

The cropped and canted composition of the leafleting trio celebrates at a historical—and stylized—remove; it also recalls the Three Graces on the Stony Brook beach near the close of reel 2, the trio of émigrés preserved in a moment of unself-conscious revelry. The leafleteers likewise anticipate the final instance of this figure at film's end—Barbara and Debby wading fully clothed, awash in the same sea as the original celebrant trio, two decades later. Each of the film's three sections thus contains near its close a strikingly composed female figure group. Far from performing a merely decorative function, these imaged women are drawn from milieus particular to each stage of Mekas's life chronicle—from the Lithuanian nationalist period to the years of social activism to the consolidation of artistic identity. These dreamily eroticized avatars—part comrade, part goddess—are apt figures for a sensibility that obsessively couples the historical with the aesthetic. Endowed with a kind of grandeur, even monumentality (evoked through their framing and musical accompaniment), they bestow benediction on memory.

It is worth considering further the figural tableaux that conclude

The Three Graces on the Stony Brook beach: Lithuanian émigrés preserved in a moment of revelry.

each of *Lost*'s three sections. Thick with classical and romantic allusions, their repetition is a marker of the autobiographical in the sense established by Jacques Derrida. In his analysis of Nietzsche's *Ecce Homo,* Derrida approaches the question of signature—and hence the attribution of the autobiographical—for literary and philosophical texts, particularly those that problematize self-presentation. He posits a dynamic borderline between the "work" and the "life," the system and the subject of the system, a "divisible borderline [that] traverses two 'bodies,' the corpus and the body, in accordance with laws that we are only beginning to catch sight of."[24] This borderline—mobile, divisible—is a site of contestation, the place where the proper name or signature is staged. Thus the recurrence of the invested iconographic figure in *Lost, Lost, Lost* can be said to speak the artist's subjectivity even as it reproduces the concreteness of historical detail. As Mekas himself has remarked, "Therefore, if one knows how to 'read' them [the details of the actual], even if one doesn't see me speaking or walking, one can tell everything about me."[25]

In his own writing, Mekas has tended to reduce the dynamism of the work/life borderline through his claim for the primacy of the subjective in *Diaries*. "As far as the city goes, of course, you could say something also about the city, from my *Diaries*—but only indirectly."[26] Indeed, New York is more than a passive wrapping for Mekas's personal odyssey. The fourteen-year period encompassed by the film coincides with a crucial

The play of revision and erasure. "He remembered another day . . . I have seen these waters before."

period of thaw for America's cultural crossroads; New York, fast becoming the lodestone of art movements and accelerating social protest, is shown to experience a maturation in tune with the filmmaker's own.

But the surest focus of Mekas's witnessing throughout much of *Lost, Lost, Lost* is the constellation of creative pressures that produces the New American Cinema. The growth and development of that movement is the subject of a third history charted from the moment of this title card's appearance in the third reel: "*Film Culture* is rolling on Lafayette Street." From the East Thirteenth Street apartment that doubles as *Film Culture*'s headquarters to the New Yorker Theater and its gathering of cinephiles to the Park Avenue South offices of the Film-Makers' Co-op, these are the urban spaces that frame the actions of the New Cinema's protagonists. What they do there is much the subject of the film. But the altered aims and methods of Mekas's creative drive testify to the historical development of the new aesthetic with equal cogency; a heightened spontaneity of camera movement, flickering shot duration, and a series of high-compression vignettes, the Rabbit Shit Haikus, are the chief markers of this shift.

Lost thus documents a succession of events significant in the formation of a cultural moment that holds an equally crucial place in the "discovery" of the artist's vocation. Exemplary instances include the collective efforts around the publication of *Film Culture* from 1955 onward, the shooting of Mekas's first feature, *Guns of the Trees* (1961), and the assault on the self-anointed arbiters of documentary purism at the Flaherty Seminar. The footage from the set of *Guns of the Trees* was, in fact, shot by Charles Levine; the exploration of the artist's subjectivity, increasingly foregrounded in the latter portions of *Lost,* is here suborned to the demands for a physical witnessing, to cinema's preservational function. "It's my nature now to record," says Mekas at the close of reel 4, "to try to keep everything I am passing through . . . to keep at least bits of it. . . . I've lost too much. . . . So now I have these bits that I've passed through."

Mekas's preservational instincts serve to salvage the past for others as well. In this regard, Mekas may, in his later years, have come full circle, from an attention to the needs of the extended family of displaced persons to those of the nuclear family. His sense of the historical or popular memory function of the diary films is expressed with appropriate tenderness in his film notes to *Paradise Not Yet Lost, a/k/a Oona's Third Year* (1979): "It is a letter to Oona [Mekas's daughter], to serve her, some day, as a distant reminder of how the world around her looked during the third year of her life—a period of which there will be only tiny fragments left in her memory—and to provide her with a romantic's guide to the essential values of life—in a world of artificiality, commercialism, and bodily and spiritual poison."[27]

As we shall see, there is no contradiction between the elemental documentary impulse, the will to preservation, and the exploration of subjectivity; indeed, it is their obsessive convergence that marks the essayistic work. It is, however, the irreconcilable difference between retention in representation and experiential loss that lends urgency to the diary project, driving the filmmaker toward an unobtainable, ever-deferred resolution.

2. *To persuade or promote.* This is the dominant trope for many of the films of the Grierson group during the Empire Marketing Board period (*Night Mail* [1936], *Housing Problems* [1935]), and for a majority of state-supported works ranging from Dziga Vertov's *Three Songs for Lenin* (1934) to Santiago Alvarez's *Now!* (1965) or *Hasta la victoria siempre* (1967).[28] While Mekas remained for decades the most visible polemicist for the "new" or personal cinema through *Film Culture* and the "Movie Journal" column in the *Village Voice,* his filmmaking practice exhibits little of the rhetorical intent of a Vertov or an Alvarez. In his "Call for a New Generation of Film-Makers," appearing in *Film Culture* in 1959, Mekas issued a surrealist-inspired manifesto for an American avant-garde: "Our hope for a free American cinema is entirely in the hands of the new generation of film-makers. And there is no other way of breaking the frozen cinematic ground than through a *complete* derangement of the official cinematic senses."[29] This directive is visibly executed in the last third of the film through the gestural style that received Mekas's critical endorsement. But the film exceeds the programmatic; its plurality outstrips polemics. As is the case with essayistic discourse generally, *Lost* is at odds with the kind of epistemological or affective certainty necessary for overt persuasion. Recall herewith the emotional ambivalence ("Am I singing or am I crying?") and the unhinging of interpretive stability ("You'll never know what they think"), both conditions ill suited to the goal orientation of propaganda. The gap of history and feeling that separates the images of 1949 from the voice that reassesses their meaning a quarter of a century later produces resonant or ironic effects rather than discursive streamlining. If there is a promotional impetus to be found in *Lost,* it is for a life defined through a perpetual act of self-creation rather than for a particular political or aesthetic position.

3. *To express.* This is the rhetorical/aesthetic function that has consistently been undervalued within the nonfiction domain; it is nevertheless amply represented in the history of the documentary enterprise. While the Lumières' *actualités* may have set the stage for nonfictional film's

emphasis on the signified, a historically conditioned taste for dynamic if not pictorialist photographic composition accounts for the diagonal verve of the train station at La Ciotat. Most sources agree that Robert Flaherty was the documentary film's first poet as well as itinerant ethnographer. Flaherty's expressivity was verbal as well as imagistic in origin; in addition to the in-depth compositions of trackless snowscapes in *Nanook of the North,* one must consider as well the flair for poetic language ("the brass ball of sun a mockery in the sky"). The cycle of "city symphony" films of the twenties (*Man with a Movie Camera* [1929], *Berlin: Symphony of a Great City* [1926], *A propos de Nice* [1930]) declared their allegiance in varying degrees to the powers of expressivity in the service of historical representation. The artfulness of the work as a function of its purely photographic properties was now allied with the possibilities of editing to create explosive effects—cerebral as well as visceral. The early films of the documentary polemicist Joris Ivens (*The Bridge* [1928], *Rain* [1929]) evidence the attraction felt for the cinema's aesthetic potential, even for artists motivated by strong political beliefs.

In his earliest attempt to categorize film types, Mekas had suggested that the "document film" encompassed both the "interest film" (newsreels, instructionals, films on art) and the "documentary film—realist, impressionist or poetical, the primary purpose of which is non-instructional (though teaching)."[30] Parker Tyler, a frequent contributor to *Film Culture,* suggested his own rather cumbersome category of poetic film, "the naturalistic poetry document," a grouping that included *The River* (1937) and *The Blood of the Beasts* (1949).[31] Difficulties arise in such efforts to distinguish among film forms as ideal types, a problem reduced through attention to discursive function rather than to the erection of discrete categories.

It is important to note in the context of taxonomic confusion that certain works of the avant-garde canon (Brakhage's "Pittsburgh Trilogy" or Peter Kubelka's *Unsere Afrikareise*) share with mainstream nonfiction a commitment to the representation of the historical real. However, the focus of these pieces typically remains the impression of the world on the artist's sensorium and his or her interpretation of that datum (Brakhage's tremulous handheld camera as he witnesses open-heart surgery in *Deus Ex*) or the radical reworking of the documentary material to create sound-image relationships unavailable in nature (Kubelka's "sync event"). Critical differences of emphasis such as these notwithstanding, the realm of filmic nonfiction must be seen as a continuum within which the Mekas diary films constitute a significant contribution. That a work undertaking some manner of historical documentation renders that representation in an innovative manner (in silence or soft focus, for example) should in no way disqualify it as nonfiction, since the question of expressivity is, in all events, a question of degree. All such renderings require a series of authorial choices, none neutral, some of which may appear more "artful" or purely expressive than others. There can be little doubt that such determinations ("artful documentary" or "documentary art") depend on various protocols of reading that are historically conditioned.

One expressive vehicle common to Mekas's diary films deserves special mention: the use of the filmmaker's voice. Rich in performance values, Mekas's voice functions as an instrument of great lyric power—measured, musical in its variation, hesitation, and repetition. The incantatory tone reinforces *Lost*'s bardic quality, inaugurated by the epic invocation that is the filmmaker's first utterance: "O sing, Ulysses, sing your travels." The poetic use of language is strategically counterweighted, however, by the alternation of first and third person in the narration, never more effectively than at the film's conclusion: "He remembered another day. Ten years ago he sat on this beach, ten years ago, with other friends. The memories, the memories, the memories. . . . Again I have memories. . . . I have a memory of this place. I have been here before. I have really been here before. I have seen these waters before, yes, I've walked upon this beach, these pebbles." Spectators are brought to their own recollections from a shared experience of some three hours' viewing; the young Lithuanian women on the beach at Stony Brook, captured in blissful dance, who recur as the leaflet women halfway through the film, are brilliantly recapitulated by the paired female figures at the film's end. We too have been here before. As with the poetic figure anaphora, so frequently invoked in the triplets of the Rabbit Shit Haikus and elsewhere ("the memories, the memories, the memories"), repetition proves to be not simple duplication, but a play of revision and erasure.

4. *To analyze or interrogate.* If the question of expressivity has plagued discussions of documentary, the analytical function has been virtually ignored.[32] The imperative toward analysis (of the enunciated and of the enunciative act) offers an intensification of, and challenge to, the record/reveal/preserve modality insofar as it actively questions nonfictional discourse—its claims to truth, its status as second-order reality. On what basis does the spectator invest belief in the representation? What are the codes that ensure that belief? What material processes are involved in the production of this "spectacle of the real," and to what extent are these processes rendered visible or knowable to the spectator? While many of these questions are familiar from the debates on reflexivity and the Brechtian cinema, applicable to fiction and nonfiction alike (the films of

Vertov, Godard, and Straub and Huillet—essayists all—have most frequently inspired these discussions), their urgency is particularly great for documentary works, which can be said to bear a direct, ontological tie to the real.

As noted in the discussion of expressivity, nonfiction film is the result of determinate mediations or authorial interventions, some of which may be perceived as "style." The analytical documentary is likely to acknowledge that mediational structures are formative rather than mere embellishments. In *Man with a Movie Camera,* the flow of images is repeatedly arrested or reframed as the filmic fact is revealed to be a labor-intensive social process that engages camera operators, editors, projectionists, musicians, and audience members. Motion pictures are represented as photographic images in motion, variable as to their projected speed, duration, or screen direction: galloping horses are capable of being halted midstride, water can run upstream, smiling children can be transformed into bits of celluloid to be inspected at editor Svilova's workbench.

In the sound era, the breach between image and its audio counterpart has rarely been acknowledged; synchronized sound, narration, or music is meant to reinforce or fuse with the image rather than question its status. Such is not the case in Alain Resnais's *Nuit et brouillard* (1955), with its airy pizzicati accompanying the most oppressive imagery of Holocaust atrocities. Chris Marker's *Letter from Siberia* (1958) is another departure from the norm. The connotative power of nonlinguistic auditory elements (music, vocal inflection) is confirmed by the repetition of an otherwise banal sequence; the sequencing of images and the narration remain unchanged while the accompanying music and tonal values of the narrating voice create differing semantic effects. Every viewer is forced to confront the malleability of meaning and the ideological impact of authorial or stylistic choices that typically go unnoticed. In Straub and Huillet's *Introduction to "An Accompaniment for a Cinematographic Scene,"* a musical composition, Schoenberg's opus 34, is "illustrated" by the recitation of Schoenberg's correspondence as well as by his drawings, photographs (of the composer and of the slain Paris Communards), archival footage of American bombing runs over Vietnam, and a newspaper clipping about the release of accused Nazi concentration camp architects. A process of interrogation is thus undertaken through the layering and resonance of heterogeneous elements. Schoenberg's music, the work of a self-professed apolitical artist, becomes the expressive vehicle for an outrage whose moral and intellectual dimensions exceed the parochial bounds of politics proper. Yet the collective coherence of the filmic elements remains to be constructed by a thinking audience. The analytical impulse is not so much enacted by the filmmakers as encouraged in the viewer.

The analytical impulse so rarely activated in mainstream nonfiction is strong in *Lost, Lost, Lost,* primarily due to the distance that separates the images, spanning more than a decade of the filmmaker's life, and the auditory elements, chosen years later, that engage them in dialogue. The relations between sound and image maintain a palpable tension throughout the film's duration, aided by the poignancy of silence. It is largely through the orchestration of acoustic effects (not least among them silence) that the film establishes its tonality. Despite the alterity of word and image, which occupy quite disparate planes of signification, conventional nonsync narrational techniques frequently attempt to sustain the impression of illustration, the visible enacting the spoken. In *Lost,* however, the breach between the seen and the heard remains irreparable; indeed, the sound elements themselves seem rarely to resolve into a "mixed" track—words, music, and effects remain discrete, virtually autonomous. From the clattering of subway trains to the plucking of stringed folk instruments to the subtle voicing of narration, each element retains its sovereign (that is, nonnaturalized) status.

Particularly through his spoken commentary, Mekas seized on the nonfiction film's ability to reassess human action even while revisiting it. Williams concluded his review of the film with a discussion of this aspect of its structure: "*Lost* is a particularly moving film because of the distance between the Jonas Mekas who shot—who wrote—the footage used in the work and the Jonas Mekas who assembled it in the 1970's. In this distance lies the material for powerful interactions between levels of experience."[33]

▶ ───

"When I Am Filming, I Am Also Reflecting"

The reflexive character of the film, its will to analysis of self and events, returns us to the domain of the essayistic. While all documentary films retain an interest in some portion of the world *out there*—recording, and less frequently interrogating, at times with the intent to persuade and with varying degrees of attention to formal issues—the essayist's gaze is drawn inward with equal intensity. That inward gaze accounts for the digressive and fragmentary character of the essayistic, as Andre Tournon's assessment of Montaigne's *Essays* suggests: "Thought can abandon its theme at any time to examine its own workings, question its acquired knowledge or exploit its incidental potentialities."[34]

Long before the appearance of his diary films, Mekas wrote admiringly of Alexandre Astruc's "camera stylo." Indeed, the work of Mekas, like that of Godard, Marker, and other prose writers turned filmmakers, offers important insight into the essayistic as a modality of filmic inscription. In a lecture on *Reminiscences of a Journey to Lithuania,* Mekas addressed the relationship between the diaristic in film and its literary counterpart; his reflections inform our consideration of filmic autobiography and of the defining conditions of historiographic pursuits more generally.

> At first I thought that there was a basic difference between the written diary which one writes in the evening, and which is a reflective process, and the filmed diary. In my film diary, I thought, I was doing something different: I was capturing life, bits of it, as it happens. But I realized very soon that it wasn't that different at all. When I am filming, I am also reflecting. I was thinking that I was only reacting to the actual reality. I do not have much control over reality at all, and everything is determined by my memory, my past. So that this "direct" filming becomes also a mode of reflection. Same way, I came to realize, that writing a diary is not merely reflecting, looking back. Your day, as it comes back to you during the moment of writing, is measured, sorted out, accepted, refused, and reevaluated by what and how one is at the moment when one writes it all down. It's all happening again, and what one writes down is more true to what one is when one writes than to the events and emotions of the day that are past and gone. Therefore, I no longer see such big differences between a written diary and the filmed diary, as far as the processes go.[35]

Mekas's diaristic project is writerly at every turn, both because the process of inscription is foregrounded throughout and because, consistent with Barthes's description of the writerly in *S/Z, Lost* as text approaches the status of the "triumphant plural, unimpoverished by any constraint of representation. . . . We gain access to it by several entrances, none of which can be authoritatively declared to be the main one; the codes it mobilizes extend *as far as the eye can reach.*"[36] It is writing of a certain sort that suffuses the film; the sense of sketch or palimpsest is retained throughout, in contrast with, for example, the florid, unwavering signature of Straub's Bach, whose piety engenders artistic as well as moral certitude in *Chronicle of Anna Magdalena Bach* (1967). The intermittently imaged snatches of written diary in *Lost* conjure for us a process of self-inscription that is painfully, materially etched. "October 3rd, 1950," intones Mekas, from the distance of decades. "I have been trying to write with a pencil. But my fingers do not really grasp the pencil properly, not like they used to grasp it a year, two years ago. From working in the factory my fingers became stiff. They don't bend, they lost their subtlety of movement. There are muscles in them I haven't seen before. They look fatter. Anyway, I can't hold the pencil. So I go to the typewriter and I begin to type, with one finger." Apocryphal or not, this account of graphological vicissitudes is corroborated at every turn of the text. Typographic emendations are foregrounded in Mekas's imaging of the diary pages. Significantly, it is the overstroke rather than the erasure that prevails; the trace of each failed gesture remains legible beneath each correction. As so many theorists of the essay have noted, it is the process of judgment, far more than the verdict, that counts. Mekas is at pains to restore to his filmed diaries the physicality and sheer effort of their provenance.

The diary inserts thus reinforce our sense of the text as a handcrafted and provisional one, always subject to reconsideration. The provisional character of all filmed material in *Lost* is dramatically borne out by its occasional transfiguration in other volumes of *Diaries, Notes, and Sketches*. In addition, then, to the potential reassessment of each image by a narrating agency at great historical remove, these same images can be reinvested and reframed—in a manner consistent with Freud's notion of *nachtraglich-keit,* or deferred action.[37]

The triumphant plurality of which Barthes speaks results from the film text's temporal fluidity, the multiple styles and perspectives it mobilizes (mingling color with black-and-white film stock as well as footage shot by others) and its several historical foci. *Lost* mimes the richness of lived experience through its modulation of a range of filmic elements. It is the sheer extent and heterogeneity of Mekas's *Diaries, Notes, and*

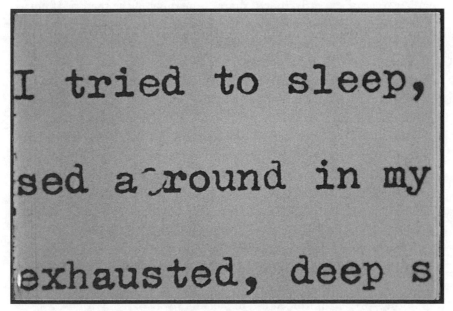

The process of self-inscription—painfully, materially etched.

Sketches that is most responsible for producing the sense of Barthes's inexhaustible text.

But the heterogeneity of Mekas's oeuvre is distinguishable from Godard's unceasing referentiality, Straub's geologic stratification, and Marker's Borgesian labyrinths. While it is likely that, among these film practitioners, Mekas's diary format most approximates Montaigne's flight from final judgments, the writing practices of the two emerge from very different philosophical contexts. Montaigne's refusal of the preexisting limits of thought and literary protocol was vested in an intellectual skepticism that valorized reflection and the ceaseless revisionism it dictated. Mekas, on the other hand, responds to a tradition that embraces spontaneity over thought. The expansiveness of the diaries arises from the conviction that art and life are indissoluble.

> The spontaneity of the new American artist is not a conscious or an intellectual process: it is rather his way of life, his whole being; he comes to it rather intuitively, directly.
>
> The new artist neither chooses this spontaneous route himself nor does he do so consciously: it is imposed upon him by his time, as the only possible route.[38]

That pronouncement, made in 1960, was slightly revised two years later, the emphasis having shifted from the involuntary (and apparently unknowable) source of art making to the art process and its institutional reception. This reassessment, responsive to the politicized environment of the New York art scene of the early 1960s, shares something of the rhetoric if not the material circumstances of the new Latin American cinema emergent at that moment. Mekas, however, spoke his refusal from the very nerve center of dominant culture, rather than from its periphery; he wrote against the art establishment, not against the mass-culture colonizers. "I don't want any part of the Big Art game. The new cinema, like the new man, is nothing definitive, nothing final. It is a living thing. It is imperfect; it errs."[39]

Diaries, Notes, and Sketches owes a great deal to the raw power of the improvisatory art Mekas championed at the time of those writings. Several sequences in *Lost* offer documentation of the people and activities of the Living Theater. In 1959 Mekas awarded the first Independent Film Award to John Cassavetes's *Shadows*; Drew Associates' *Primary,* which was said to reveal "new cinematic techniques of recording life on film," was the recipient of the third award. The 1962 essay "Notes on the New American Cinema" shares the spirit of the Willem de Kooning epigram it quotes in apparent admiration: "Painting—any kind of painting, any style of painting—to be painting at all, in fact—is a way of living today, a style of living, so to speak."[40] Indeed, *Lost, Lost, Lost* shares something of the edgy immediacy of the art that prevailed in the moment of its shooting.

But *Lost* exceeds its roots in improvisation, in the capture of an uncontrolled reality, in a wished-for fusion of art and life. At last, it is through its character as essayistic work that the film yields its surplus. Vast in its purview, elliptical in its self-presentation, complex in its interpolation of historical substrata and textual voices, the film struggles with "the old problem"—"to merge Reality and Self, to come up with the third thing." But *Lost* resists the snares of resolution or completion, even in the dialectical beyond. Moreover, a belief in the revivification or recapture of experience in the crucible of art is actively disavowed, even if, as in Marker's *Sans soleil,* loss itself becomes ritual celebration.

In assessing the film four decades after its inception, the Lukácsian prescription might well apply. *Lost, Lost, Lost* will survive as a triumph of judgment independent of the world or psyche that it reveals. And "the value-determining thing about it is not the verdict . . . but the process of judging."[41]

II The Subject in Theory

5

Charged Vision: The Place of Desire in Documentary Film Theory

"Charged Vision" echoes a position first explored in my introduction to Theorizing Documentary *(1993), which argued that documentary studies had remained largely (and, in my view, regrettably) untouched by the insights of psychoanalytic theory despite its tremendous influence elsewhere in post-1970s film studies. Nonfiction film had come to be regarded as a realm of rationalist inquiry, a filmmaking practice pursuing educational or activist goals; the documentary audience was understood to be under the influence of epistephilia or intellectual curiosity rather than incited by unconscious drives, as had been argued for the audience of the fiction film. Such a view seemed at odds with my experience of many of the early documentary classics (e.g., Joris Ivens's* Rain *[1929] or Jean Vigo's* A propos de Nice *[1930]) and also theoretically insupportable. I argue here that documentary is far from an exclusively "sober" discourse and that documentary reception can be responsive to far less rational principles—erotic desire, horror, whimsy—than those encompassed by rhetoric or epistemology. Subsequent to the writing of this chapter in 1996, several psychoanalytically informed analyses of the documentary project have appeared, chief among them Elizabeth Cowie's "The Spectacle of Actuality," in* Collecting Visible Evidence *(1999), which help historicize and reinforce the claims made here.*

In his seminar "The Line and Light" published in *The Four Fundamental Concepts of Psycho-Analysis,* Jacques Lacan retells the classical tale of Zeuxis and Parrhasios, two painters who engage in a competition to determine who is the more masterful.

> Zeuxis has the advantage of having made grapes that attracted the birds. The stress is placed not on the fact that these grapes were in any way perfect grapes, but on the fact that even the eye of the birds was taken in by them.

This is proved by the fact that his friend Parrhasios triumphs over him for having painted on the wall a veil, a veil so lifelike that Zeuxis, turning towards him, said, *Well, and now show us what you have painted behind it.* By this he showed that what was at issue was certainly deceiving the eye *(trompe l'oeil)*. A triumph of the gaze over the eye.[1]

Consider the inaugurating image of Peter Hutton's *New York Portrait, Part III* (1990), shown here. While only a frame enlargement and therefore robbed of a filmic moment's acoustic, dynamic, durational, and narratological contexts, this still image is less impoverished than most. This is because Hutton's work—shot almost exclusively on black-and-white Tri-X reversal stock—is always silent and organized according to the logic of a mosaic structure consisting of more or less equally weighted vignettes connected by fades to black. Each image remains on the screen for anywhere from ten to thirty seconds, long enough to register perceptually and, in some instances, for some viewers, to begin to resonate, to evoke, to summon forth a response that may elude ready articulation.

It is with this image that I propose to begin my discussion of the place of desire in documentary film theory. What can be said of this image at the level of description? It is veiled in mystery, shot at night from below, looking up toward a window through which we see little more than the silhouette of a banner or flag. At the level of content, in the language of traditional documentary discourse, there is very little here: no person

The lure of the image: the mysterious opening shot from Hutton's *New York Portrait, Part III* (1990).

upon whom to build exposition à la Flaherty, no crisis around which to organize a diegesis à la direct cinema, no retroactive knowledge gained by a return to this window later in the film. But I would argue that this image *signifies* a great deal, and in the manner of Parrhasios, for it evidences in a rather irreducible way the "lure" activated by the documentary image around which this discussion of desire in the nonfiction film will circulate. The image returns us to Lacan's allegory. Here, as in the tale, the gaze triumphs over the eye; our desire to pierce the veil sustains our attention to the image well beyond either perceptual or knowledge-based demands. There is no crisis of referentiality on display as in Paul Strand's *Abstraction—Bowls* (1915) or *White Fence* (1916), photographic works in which Strand produces a kind of retinal tension between the two-dimensional image surface (forcefully stated through the aggressive frontality of the white picket fence) and the three-dimensionality implied by chiaroscuro and deep-focus photography. Neither does Hutton's image offer a visual field particularly rich in data, loaded with diegetic or characterological clues.

"In the matter of the visible, everything is a trap," says Lacan.[2] There is never a question of Hutton allowing the viewer to penetrate this nighttime shadow. What we see and, even more pointedly, what we long to see as we fix our gaze cannot easily be spoken. It is, precisely, the presence of an absence. Hutton's image functions as a figure of metonymy, which Freud argued was the rhetorical correlative of desire. The symptom was metaphor, a vertical domain, a site of condensation, a knot of overdetermination. But desire was irrepressibly horizontal, fugitive, never in its place. In Lacanian terms, desire can only arise in the subject on account of a fundamental separation between the self and its object: "The subject cannot desire without itself dissolving, and without seeing, because of this very fact, the object escaping it, in a series of infinite displacements."[3] Hutton's veiled image, in its play of translucence and opacity, stands for all the desired, infinitely displaced objects that present themselves within the field of vision. It is a metaphor of metonymy. For me, it evokes a foundational component of our reception and understanding of nonfiction images, suggesting something of the mechanism on account of which we return, again and again, to images of the world.

As Hutton's image demonstrates, this lure of "the visible real" is reducible neither to the purely perceptual on the one hand nor to the realm of the signified on the other. That is, it is not simply that the human eye is drawn to two-dimensional depictions of movement in three-dimensional space (though that may be true enough) or that we return to the documentary cinema only for the subjects it treats (though the rich tradition of socially conscious documentary filmmaking might suggest otherwise). Let me be clear that I don't wish to diminish either of these grounds for documentary's appeal, such as it is. It is, rather, my contention that the notion of desire developed in psychoanalytic theory is a crucial and generally neglected component of documentary spectatorship that deserves our careful consideration and one whose neglect has hindered the development of contemporary documentary film theory.

In speaking of desire in documentary, I have in mind not simply the familiar references to an eroticized gaze of the sort found in feminist film theory (e.g., Mulvey's notion of the gendered "pulverizing gaze" of classical narrative cinema)[4] but also notions of a look that Bill Nichols has characterized as epistephilic and Tom Gunning has rooted in "curiositas."[5] Yet while focusing on nonfiction in its specificity, I will nevertheless challenge a position that I consider to be unduly separatist and deeply rationalist in its alignment of documentary wholly with consciousness rather than in traffic with unconscious processes, challenging too that position's preference for knowledge effects over pleasurable or ecstatic looking and for its enthronement of sobriety at the expense of the evocative and delirious. I will instead argue for the documentary gaze as constitutively multiform, embroiled with conscious motives and unconscious desires, driven by curiosity no more than by terror and fascination.

In pursuing my investigation, I will give particular attention to the silent cinema, in which visuality was accorded primacy. This rhetorical choice is not meant to suggest that the introduction of sound alters the terms of the argument. Indeed, in accord with the ways that the invocatory drive has been accounted for by sound theories of the cinema as supplement to a scopically derived explanatory model for psychic engagement, there is much to say about the lure of the audible real.[6] That direction for research is simply beyond the bounds of the present occasion. There are, however, practical reasons to return to the silent cinema for the purposes of illustrating desire's place in documentary spectatorship. In the early works of documentary practitioners such as the Lumières, Shub, Vertov, Ivens, and Vigo, the eye holds sway; visuality is directly addressed and thematized. A return to this work affords us the possibility to ground our investigation into the relations between desire and documentary vision with greatest specificity.

There are other critical and pedagogical reasons to return to the 1920s as a focus for study. It is a historical moment cut off from our present understanding. Documentary history has, to a large extent, been severed of its ties to the 1920s avant-garde, so that current experimental and performative work in film and video appears to be anomalous rather than consistent with documentary's roots.[7] Instead it has been the 1930s and 1960s that have taken center stage. The Griersonian model has functioned as the baseline of documentary persuasion, the sixties as the moment of technical, formal, and ideological reinvention (cinema verité, direct cinema, Newsreel). Indeed, Nichols's model for the modes of documentary exposition really begins with the 1930s (the expository mode) before moving to the 1960s and 1970s (the observational, interactive, and reflexive modes) with only a nod to the 1920s ("poetic exposition"). This inattention to the twenties facilitates the general disregard for the ecstatic and delirious in documentary film theory and criticism. On what grounds do I make such a statement? First because the twenties were the pinnacle moment of modernism, during which the barriers separating the arts were most permeable and in which cinema was widely embraced by cutting-edge artists (Duchamp, Ray, Leger, Richter, Dalí). Their fascination for the medium was due in part to its tangency with the Real, for the camera's ability to create, in Richter's words, "a reservoir of human observation in the simplest possible way,"[8] while remaining capable of effecting a radical derangement of the senses. The twenties were also the apex of the silent era, during which the codes of visual expression had become exquisitely refined, so that "even abstract notions [could be made] concretely visible in the image."[9] The arrival of sound in the 1930s, coupled with the onset of global economic crisis and fascist repression, redirected the documentary emphasis to persuasion and the spoken word. It is crucial, at a time in which documentary is again being revivified by an engagement with avant-garde practices and sensibilities (evidenced through the work of Harun Farocki, Johan van der Keuken, Marlon Riggs, Su Friedrich, Rea Tajiri, and others), that we reinvest our understanding of documentary with its historic encounter with the twenties avant-garde.

These are the historical concerns that inspire this return to early documentary. But what is at stake in this inquiry into desire, visuality, and nonfiction film at the level of epistemology? In *Representing Reality,* Bill Nichols argues that the realm of subjectivity in documentary is of a substantially different order from that which is produced in filmic fiction. He suggests that it is an outwardly oriented, *social* subjectivity that is primarily at issue, as for example with the Griersonian project in which "informed citizenship" was the ostensible goal. Other subjectivities are also possible—from curiosity and fascination to pity and charity, from poetic appreciation to anger or rage, from scientific scrutiny to inflamed hysteria—but all function as modes of engagement with representations of the historical world that can readily be extended beyond the moment of viewing into social praxis itself.

Because affective response can lead to social action, Nichols chooses to define documentary subjectivity in relation to the praxis it may provoke rather than in its own terms. It is on these grounds that Nichols can write that "documentary realism aligns itself with an epistephilia . . . a pleasure in knowing." "In igniting our interest," he continues, "a documentary has a less incendiary effect on our erotic fantasies and sense of sexual identity but a stronger effect on our social imagination and sense of cultural identity. Documentary calls for the elaboration of an epistemology and axiology more than of an erotics."[10] But it is simply not the case that the unconscious component of documentary spectatorship can be subsumed beneath the banner of an eroticism so overtly thematized. As we will see, knowledge and desire are ineluctably entwined.

Nichols's notion of epistephilia situates documentary on the side of conscious rather than unconscious processes, public activity more than psychical reality. Nonfiction is, according to this reading, about *engagement* with representations of the real; what matters is *what you do* with reception rather than how the film is received, how a putative response is evoked. Moreover, for Nichols, nonfiction is differentiated from fiction, which is story based and tied to an imaginary world, by virtue of its being by definition propositional; the nonfiction version of story is "argument," which is understood to be the defining condition of all documentary diegesis.[11] Of course, this view (which I would characterize as deeply rationalist) depends in some measure on the film knowing what it wants to say. I would propose that this is far from the case.

In *The Interpretation of Dreams,* Freud challenged the preeminence of consciousness in Western thought, carrying his radical skepticism to "the very heart of the Cartesian stronghold." Paul Ricoeur has called Freud one of the three "masters of suspicion" who emerged during the nineteenth century (the others being Marx and Nietzsche); their legacy is doubt as to whether or not "consciousness is such as it appears to itself."[12] In his magisterial work on dreams, Freud sought to reverse a rationalist hierarchization alive since the Greeks: "The unconscious must be assumed to be the general basis of psychical life," wrote Freud. "The unconscious is the larger sphere, which includes within it the smaller sphere of the conscious. Everything conscious has an unconscious preliminary stage. . . . the unconscious is the true psychical reality."[13] For Freud, "waking thought" behaved toward perceptual material much in the manner of secondary revision in the dreamwork; percepts were made orderly in conformity with "our expectations of an intelligible whole."[14] Consciousness, for Freud and later Lacan, was in fact erected on "structures of misrecognition" through which the self could assume its status of unicity and self-sufficiency. But as Louis Althusser famously argued in the 1960s in the context of ideological analysis, one could never take the self or its representations at their word. In Althusser's view, psychoanalysis had robbed philosophy of its origins—God, reason, consciousness, history, and culture—erecting in its stead the rigorous study of the discourse of the unconscious. In short, Freud's "revolutionary discovery" challenged the epistemology of presence and of consciousness.[15] Slavoj Zizek's assessment of Althusser's enormous contribution to Marxist analysis returns to the same point: "Habermas and Foucault are the two sides of the same coin—the real break is represented by Althusser, by his insistence on the fact that a certain cleft, a certain fissure, misrecognition, characterizes the human condition as such."[16]

It is important to note that certain strands of philosophical discourse have echoed the psychoanalytic position that identifies desire as the destabilizer of knowledge, understood to be a fully rational domain subject only to the laws of science. Foucault (although insufficiently psychoanalytical for Zizek) devoted his first year of seminars at the Collège de France (1970–1971) to a series of analyses that could gradually form a "morphology of the will to knowledge." Foucault was interested in the contrast between an Aristotelian explanation for the genesis of the desire to know (assumed to be universal and natural) in which knowledge, truth, and pleasure share a harmonious coexistence and a Nietzschean model that posits a primordial conflict among them. With attribution to Nietzsche's *The Gay Science,* Foucault notes that knowledge is an "invention" behind which lies something completely different from itself: the play of instincts, impulses, desires, fear, and the will to appropriate. Knowledge is produced on the stage where these elements struggle against each other.[17]

Of course, Foucault's suspicion toward knowledge depended in large part on his analysis of its institutionalized power.

> When I see you straining to establish the scientificity of Marxism I do not really think that you are demonstrating once and for all that Marxism [substitute here "the documentary project"] has a rational structure and that therefore its propositions are the outcome of verifiable procedures; for me you are doing something altogether different, you are investing Marxist ["nonfiction"] discourses and those who uphold them with the effects of a power which the West since Medieval times has attributed to science and has reserved for those engaged in scientific discourse.[18]

I understand why Nichols might wish to align documentary film with other "discourses of sobriety," nonfictional systems such as science, economics, politics, foreign policy, education, religion, and welfare that "assume they have instrumental power" and "can . . . alter the world itself . . . can effect action and entail consequences."[19] It is a matter of the *critic's* desire—to mobilize through association a greater power of action for documentary. But this wish cannot be confused with conceptual lucidity. I would argue that knowledge as conscious thought cannot so easily be separated from the instinctual domain and that Nichols's attribution of sobriety for documentary obfuscates more than it reveals, for documentary is equally a discourse of delirium. To what, precisely, do I refer when I speak of delirium in this way?

In her essay "Psychoanalysis and the Polis," Julia Kristeva has argued that "the simple knowing subject" is little more than a theoretical fiction. Why?

> The knowing subject is also a *desiring* subject, and the paths of desire ensnarl the paths of knowledge. . . . We normally assume the opposite of delirium to be an objective reality, objectively perceptible and objectively knowable, as if the speaking subject were only a simple knowing subject. Yet we must admit that, given the cleavage of the subject (conscious/unconscious) and given that the subject is also a subject of desire, perceptual and knowing apprehension of the original object is only a theoretical, albeit undoubtedly indispensable, hypothesis.[20]

If we assimilate such a notion of delirium within documentary film theory, it becomes necessary to supplement accounts of nonfiction's sober aspirations with research into the deformations and displacements that desire effects upon the system of perception/knowledge.

To review, then, the assumption of knowledge as unassailable, protected from the vicissitudes of the instinctual domain, has been challenged. So too has the alignment of documentary with the "sober discourses," a claim that suborns the play of the cinematic signifier and its delirious effects to the conscious engagement of maker and spectator to social issues. These challenges were inaugurated through attention to a single image, one that I have argued can be seen as the very emblem of documentary desire, one in which the gaze is entirely separated from its object.

I will now return to some concrete instances drawn from the silent era of documentary practice in the hope of spelling out with greater concreteness the mix of the conscious and unconscious components of documentary spectatorship. There is, as I have suggested, the need to account for a continuum of motives underlying documentary reception ranging from what I would call historiographical curiosity (motivated by our manifest appetite to know the look and feel of a past preserved for our view) to a more freely associative fascination with the image along the lines of Barthes's notion of punctum, the explosive prick of contact with one's own image repertoire evoked by the documentary image.[21] In offering this formulation, then, I am arguing that the documentary image functions in relation to both knowledge and desire, evidence and lure, with neither term exerting exclusive control. Rather, I would echo the Nietzschean position—that knowledge is produced on the stage where instincts, impulses, desires, fears, and the will to appropriate struggle against one another.

Let us take for example Esther Shub's *The Fall of the Romanov Dynasty* (1927), which offers the contemporary viewer representational access to the life and customs of czarist Russia. Given the prevailing antipathies to the old regime, assembling the historical footage was no small task, just a few years after the revolution. Shub writes:

> This and my following two films filled three years with the joy of searching, finding, "opening" historical film-documents—but not in the film-libraries or archives, for there were no such things then. In the damp cellars of Goskino, in "Kino Moskva," in the Museum of the Revolution lay boxes of negatives and random prints, and no one knew how they had got there.[22]

Through her montage choices, Shub brilliantly sets in conflict the aristocracy at their leisure—sipping tea with dog or merrily dancing until the ladies perspired from their exertions—against images of those who indeed *toiled*, whose sweaty brows were hastily mopped only at their own risk. The film responds to and inflames our historiographical curiosity about a world on the brink of cataclysmic change. But even here can be found the occasion of other registers of documentary reception, as illustrated by a sequence in Chris Marker's *The Last Bolshevik* (1994), a videotape composed in the manner of a series of letters sent to the late Alexander Medvedkin.

For Marker, Medvedkin's bittersweet life story is also that of the Soviet Union. Born in 1900, the filmmaker's years span those of the Soviet state; Marker's rendition of the double narrative introduces some unexpected parallels. Amidst his reveries surrounding Medvedkin's early years, Marker notes that Alexander Ivanovitch was only thirteen when the Romanovs celebrated the three hundredth anniversary of their reign. He returns to some of the newsreel footage so masterfully deployed by Shub nearly seventy years previously. In *The Fall of the Romanov Dynasty*, we are shown the ritualistic displays designed to awe the multitudes: the processions of foreign dignitaries joined by the czarist generals and aristocracy parading through the streets. It is just here that Marker offers us his own reading of this processional scene. His narration supplies us with a reading of a single gesture from Shub's film along the lines of the Barthesian punctum, in which a detail, "[occurring] in the field of the photographed thing like a supplement that is at once inevitable and delightful," sparks a powerful response in the viewer.[23] As we watch this stately promenade, step-printed for our obsessional view, the voice-over ironically intones:

> Every documentary on the period shows this parade of dignitaries. But who has looked at it? That gesture of the big chap tapping his own head. What does it mean? That the crowd is crazy? No. He's telling them to take off their caps. You don't keep your hat on before nobility. I imagine what advice a Russian Machiavelli would have given these pompous men. Rule, exploit, kill now and then, but never humiliate.

In Marker's hands, this newsreel becomes the occasion for a speculation that combines whimsy and historical research. There are similar passages in *Letter from Siberia* (1957) and *Sans soleil* (1982). The crucial point here is that the journey to discursive sobriety at the level of documentary reception is set temporarily adrift by fantasy. Marker's text suggests the ways in which documentary images, while denoting history (via the newsreel) and promulgating persuasion (as Shub does), can and do incite a metonymic movement that is the play of desire capable of exploding historical discourse.

I would at the same time argue in the opposite direction: ecstatic viewing can be shot through with sobriety. Take, for example, Joris Ivens's *Rain* (1929), one of the finest examples of the cine-poem, a documentary whose propositional character is far less at issue than its power to evoke sensory experience or create mood. The film is deeply atmospheric—Amsterdam in the rain—yet the depicted space is in part an imaginary one, concocted over a four-month period from ten or more rainstorms.[24] The images, enhanced by the musical accompaniment, are darkly dreamy. Yet despite all appeals to what we might call an Imaginary engagement, *Rain* also responds to spectatorial demands of another sort. Beyond evocation, Ivens allows the viewer to apprehend one crucial feature of the physical world (namely, rain) in a manner available only through the cinematic apparatus. We can—repeatedly and from multiple points of view—watch water flow, drip, streak, puddle, pool, and cascade. We learn something of the optics that produce watery reflections , we see displayed the principle of surface tension as water yields to gravity, we note the power of water to refract light rays in arresting patterns. While we learn something of the look and feel of Amsterdam in the late 1920s, we are equally privy to the unchanging physical laws that determine the behavior of water. In short, *Rain* could play to the scientific curiosity of the student of physics or meteorology as well as to the cinephile. Thus we could say that, lodged within one of the great aesthetic experiences of early documentary film, there is, at least potentially, a scientific viewing lesson of a more sober variety. Again, documentary spectatorship is shown to be the site of multiple, even conflictual, desires that traverse the presumed barriers between conscious and unconscious processes.

It is appropriate that this analysis has drawn the bulk of its examples from films of the 1920s, produced at the peak of the avant-garde's exhiliration for cinematic possibilities. Rationalist aims were far removed from the experimentations of Leger, Buñuel, Vigo, or Vertov. If I have attempted to trace the interplay of epistephilic motives and unspoken desires that fuel documentary reception, no period so amply illustrates this amalgam as the twenties. It was Vertov, in 1922, who could write of a "desire for kinship with the machine," a desire that found its support in the endless perfectibility of the kino-eye.[25] With this utopian phrase and through the dynamism of his imagery, Vertov forever linked the rationalist and scientific potentialities of the medium with the impossible and the fantasmatic. As we attempt to formulate the principles underlying the reception of the documentary film, we would do well to recall the historical lessons before us, to take into account the manner in which cinematic vision has, from the beginning, been charged with a deep yet fugitive desire.

6

The Subject in History: The New Autobiography in Film and Video

First published in Afterimage *in the summer of 1989, "The Subject in History" examines the turn to autobiographical film- and videomaking in the 1980s in relation to post-1960s theoretical interventions that challenged certain fundamental bulwarks of Western thought—the adequacy of history, the centrality of the subject, the coherence of master narratives. In part, the essay is a paean to the film- and videomakers who pursue similar matters in their artistic practice, constructing historical selves that are nonetheless sites of instability rather than coherence. As in chapter 4, there is a return to the model of the (Montaignean) essay and its filmic avatar, Jonas Mekas's* Lost, Lost, Lost, *but the scope of the argument is broader. The emphasis here is on the historical and theoretical underpinnings of the "new historicism" in 1980s autobiographical film- and videomaking.*

> And so the opinion I give . . . is to declare the measure of
> my sight, not the measure of things.
> :: Montaigne, *Essays*

> I am elsewhere than where I am when I write.
> :: Roland Barthes, *Roland Barthes*

The work undertaken here takes as its object "the essayistic in film and video." I borrow the notion of the essay from the literary tradition with caution and am careful to stipulate one trajectory from within a rich and diverse genealogy—that which was initiated by Michel de Montaigne in the late sixteenth century and reprised in recent years in the final works of the late Roland Barthes. Before I examine the specific character of the essayistic for the visual media, however, some clarification of the determining conditions of that version of the essay activated here is required. In *The Barthes Effect: The Essay as Reflective Text,* Reda Bensmaia claims that the essay, as practiced by Barthes and his several precursors from Montaigne to Theodor Adorno, constitutes an "impossible genre . . . combining . . . at the same time theory, critical combat, and pleasure."[1] Epitomized by *Roland Barthes par Roland Barthes* but already in embryo in Montaigne's *Essays* (c. 1580–1588), the essayistic can be said to approach the horizons of the writerly as proposed in Barthes's *S/Z*—the text as a "triumphant plural," reversible, without beginnings, a galaxy of signifiers to which we gain access by several entrances, "none of which can be authoritatively declared to be the main one."[2]

In singling out this version of the essay from all the others (the empiricist, humorous, or confessional modes of Locke, Bacon, Lamb, Augustine, or Rousseau), I privilege a writing practice that couples a documentary impulse—an outward gaze upon the world—with an equally forceful reflex of self-interrogation. This double or reciprocal focus effects an unceasing, even obsessive, exploration of subjectivity that situates itself within a matrix that is irreducibly material and of necessity historical. Crucial to an understanding of such a writing practice is thus its construction of a subjectivity at odds with the dichotomous subject/object model of Descartes.

Much of contemporary theory since Jacques Lacan has presumed the mutually defining (even "circulatory") character of the subject and its other ("we depend on the field of the Other, which was there long before we came into the world, and whose circulating structures determine us as subjects").[3] The Montaignean or Barthesian essay enacts that interpenetration: "in a sense, self and object organize each other, but only in a temporary way."[4] If the subject and the historical field are mutually configuring in essayistic discourse (the measure of sight/the measure of things), so too are author and work, the writing and written selves. "We go hand in hand and at the same pace, my book and I," writes Montaigne. "In other cases one may commend or blame the work apart from the workman: not so here; he who touches the one, touches the other."[5] The essayistic thus shares something of the character of autobiography, which, in the sense suggested by Jacques Derrida, mobilizes meaning along a dynamic borderline between the "work" and the "life," the system and the subject of the system.[6]

As discourse, the essay embroils the subject in history; enunciation and its referential object are equally at issue. The essayistic *stages* subjectivity through a play of successive self-metaphorization in a manner consistent with that "radical heteronomy . . . gaping within man" that Lacan claims as Freud's monumental discovery.[7] The essay (like its kindred autobiographical forms) is that practice of writing responsive to Barthes's pronouncement on metaphor—"you cannot get to the heart of a refrain; you can only substitute another one for it."[8] And for Montaigne's *Book of the Self* as for *Roland Barthes par Roland Barthes*, subjectivity remains the master metaphor.

Of equal significance is the essay's disaffiliation with certainty. The essayistic bears with it a logic that questions the verities of rhetorical composition and of system, indeed, of mastery itself; the status of the subject as transcendental or originary is likewise challenged. Montaigne's self-appraisal in "Of Repentance" ("I do not portray being; I portray passing")[9] is echoed four centuries later in Barthes's quandary over a discourse that, despite its indifference to "truth," remains rhetorically assertive. His remedy—"absurd . . . everyone would surely agree, to add to each sentence some little phrase of uncertainty."[10] The formulation of the Lacanian subject as adrift, fading, ever-eclipsed, posits that indeterminacy as an effect of language, of the "incessant sliding of the signified under the signifier."[11] The essayistic makes practice of that theorization. As announced by the author of *Roland Barthes*, the writing subject's unwillingness to be pigeonholed, even by a discourse of his own making, results in his adoption of an "internal doctrine" pertinent to the essay form in general—"that of *atopia* (of a drifting habitation)."[12]

I have chosen to think of the contemporary work in film and video that shares something of the essayistic agenda as a kind of lifeline between the received categories of the documentary and avant-garde, each of which has been discursively and institutionally cloistered to its disadvantage. The work I will discuss takes up the consideration of what might be called the "new autobiography," with the understanding that the taxonomic limits of terms such as *diary, autobiography,* and *essay* demand to be superseded.[13] Rather than focusing on the distinctiveness or specificity of each, though such a sorting out is essential, I shall speak of the *autobiographical,* which in its adjectival form evokes the activity of self-inscription shared by all. Although I will consider three autobiographical instances—Jonas Mekas's *Lost, Lost, Lost* (1975), Ilene Segalove's *My Puberty* (1987), and Lynn Hershman's *First Person Plural* (1988)—it is the first of these works that will occupy the bulk of my attention, with the latter two functioning primarily to suggest avenues for future elaboration.

One of the most debilitating myths of contemporary North American life is the alleged contrariness of the realms of art and science. We of the humanities are meant to have little in common with those who devote themselves to the "hard sciences"; indeed, it is frequently supposed that the languages that name and govern our respective pursuits are untranslatable. A particularly pernicious effect of this assumed cleavage involves the question of financial support, both public and private. Science grants assume the necessity of the efforts they foster, no matter how arcane they may appear to the layperson; support is bestowed upon the bearers of a special knowledge who labor on our behalf. Since World War II, from which the United States emerged with technological hegemony, the assumption has persisted that the nation's fortunes are tied to surpassing the scientific achievements of first the Soviets, then the Japanese. The rhetoric that accompanied the space race shares with the scramble for the next generation of semiconductors an essentially imperative mode—do or die.

Culture, on the other hand, has in this country been pursued at greater leisure; art or philosophical inquiry is always "in excess" of necessity. The very disciplines whose aims encompass the comprehension and theorization of all forms of human action (philosophy, history—including the history of science—and anthropology) find themselves struggling to attract the institutional support that alone can guarantee their future. It is my assumption that there is a very real linkage between the fortunes of such pursuits and our national destiny. We have always needed technology, from wheel to rocket ship, but we have required with even greater necessity the understanding of the meanings and effects of our handiwork. Our survival has always depended with equal force on a more comprehensive understanding that can situate local knowledges within the largest framework. For what is mere survival without benefit of dignity or intelligence?

If the humanists are undervalued by an instrumentalist perspective that favors the hardware over the less tangible fruits of thought, what more can be said for the artist? What place in society is afforded the one who employs metaphor or abstraction to contemplate the meanings and effects of our collective inventions? And here I dare to distinguish between the fine artist and the one who toils in the vineyards of mass culture. Dwight MacDonald once disparagingly characterized mass art as the work of technicians in the employ of businessmen. Not that I mean to slight those who make their livings on the fragile border of art and entertainment. I live in one of the capitals of the culture industry, and I do not underestimate its virtues. Nevertheless, my concern is with the relatively disenfranchised who work in near isolation, attempting to preserve or refashion our culture, to interpret our lives and emotions for us, to ask questions and suggest answers in terms whose partial opacity is part of the message. This is not "production for use," the realm of practicality or immediate payoff. But it is in this domain of artistic practice—at the margins and interstices—that one can begin to take the measure of a culture, to discover its latencies and phobias as well as dismantle its preconceptions.

This is the work that deserves our attention. And we may very well wish to borrow an idea or two from our scientific colleagues as we consider the art issues at hand. There is great respect in the scientific community for "basic research." Only consider the homage paid to the category of defense appropriations: all hail the repose of laboratory conditions—the place of detached musings and speculation—that gives birth to new strategic defense systems. According to this model, the scientist must be afforded the opportunity to "stumble upon" the next breakthrough that could not have been anticipated within the prevailing paradigms. It is my belief that the independent artist is likewise frequently absorbed in "basic research." Speculative work of this sort can thus be contrasted with the practical application of the entertainment professional who tests the elasticity of preexistent forms, producing, for example, the latest variant of a genre verging on exhaustion.

Lately I have begun to think a lot about a direction of film and video practice that seems to be exploring questions that have occupied the attention of so-called humanists for at least two decades. Since the importation of structuralist (then poststructuralist) thought from the Continent sometime in the 1960s—the work of Claude Lévi-Strauss in anthropology, Michel Foucault in history, and Lacan, Barthes, and Derrida in philosophy and literary theory—certain fundamental questions regarding the ground rules of representation have been activated. How can one *adequately* represent history or ethnological subgroup, through written word or sound/image play, without recourse to emplotment, trope, or narrative convention? If Foucault writes in favor of historical discourse as embracing discontinuity—the attention to rupture, threshold, and transformation rather than to lineage and continuity—domestic scholars such as Hayden White, Clifford Geertz, and James Clifford have added their voices to the questioning of the adequacy of representation for the description of phenomena as well as for the interpretations that follow.

One effect of this mode of thought has been the erosion of the presumed mastery that scientific discourse has claimed to offer since the eighteenth century. Such doubts were perhaps inaugurated by Freud's work on the unconscious, which suggested that analysis of any sort was interminable. All interpretation, in fact all representation, was claimed to depend upon a play of metaphor and metonymy, of condensation and displacement, producing meaning through an endless play of similarity and difference. Barthes's pronouncement that denotation is merely one privileged moment of connotation simply restates that psychoanalytical finding. Anthropologist Geertz's writing evidences the impact that this episte-mological position has made on the social sciences in his acknowledgment of the limits of his own discourse. "I have never gotten anywhere near to the bottom of anything I have ever written about," says Geertz. "Cultural analysis is intrinsically incomplete. And, worse than that, the more deeply it goes the less complete it is."[14]

If poststructuralist philosophy has contributed to the undermining of absolute certainty, its structuralist precursor moved in the direction of systematic knowledge, toward the determination of the rules governing a discourse, the discovery of the paradigms generated within a problematic. The interest in the "authorless text" begun with Lévi-Strauss's studies of myth and kinship structure helped to unseat generations of scholarship that sought to understand art through a critical focus on the artist. The intentionalist fallacy began to nullify the auteurist bias in film studies that had reached its peak with the *Cahiers du Cinéma* writers-turned-cineasts such as François Truffaut, Jean-Luc Godard, and Eric Rohmer. Much theoretically inclined cultural criticism began to abjure the personal in favor of the systematic and its attention to discursive function and effect. Lacanian psychoanalytic criticism, far from hypostasizing a determining or coherent self, shared the semiotic agenda and thus tended to formulate the subject not as a coherent site of knowledge or creativity to be under-stood and interpreted but as an "effect" of the larger play of signification of which it was a part.

But the recent outpouring of work by independent film and video art-ists who evidence an attachment both to the documentary impulse *and* to the complex representation of their own subjectivity leads me to believe that we are witnessing an efflorescence of "basic research" that grapples with—and significantly enriches—questions that theorists have been posing for years. We could say that this recent work, which straddles the received boundaries of documentary and the avant-garde, regards history and subjectivity as mutually defining categories. That the world beyond the self is necessarily filtered through the perceptual apparatus comes as no revelation; it is, however, the process of what Freud calls secondary re-vision that remains at issue here.

Historical discourse has, after all, come to be regarded as the rep-resentation of people, forces, and events from a particular perspective. Feminists, for example, have reminded us that the attention in standard history texts to military milestones rather than to the transmission of societal values merely replicates the patriarchal bias—(his)tory over hers. If we can say that history belongs to those with the power to *re*-present it, little wonder that film and video practitioners have come to share the revisionist historian's suspicion for top-down institutional accounts. Instead, a number of contemporary artists seem to have gravitated toward an approach in which a past, frequently public, event is figured through recourse to the subject, the category of the self, through a variety of modalities I shall discuss presently.

Of equal importance is the recognition that the "return of the subject" is not, in these works, the occasion for a nostalgia for an unproblematic self-absorption. If what I am calling "the new autobiography" has any claim to theoretical precision, it is due to this work's construction of subjectivity as a site of instability—flux, drift, perpetual revision—rather than coherence. Lacan has staked his version of the psyche on the notion that the constitution of the subject depends on a fundamental misrecognition in which the child, aged six to eighteen months, sees in his mirrored image a self well in advance of his true condition, the "motor incapacity and nursling dependence" of the infant. This identification with an "ideal I," in the words of Lacan, "situates the agency of the ego . . . in a fictional direction."[15] The poststructuralist version of subjectivity is thus at odds with the Western tradition since Descartes that posits the "I" of the *cogito* as the anchor and foundation of being, the locus of a certainty that reflects in miniature the sovereignty of god.

The works in question thus undertake a double and mutually defining inscription—of history and the self—that refuses the categorical and the totalizing. An approach such as this—embracing digression, reverie, the revelation of public history through the private and associational—has been argued to be an intrinsic feature of literary autobiography. "Autobiography completes no picture," writes Janet Varner Gunn. "Instead, it rejects wholeness or harmony, ascribed by formalists to the well-made art object, as a false unity which serves as no more than a defense against the self's deeper knowledge of its finitude."[16] The transgressive status that some literary theorists have ascribed to autobiography, "as a formal mutation, a hybrid genre . . . definable neither as fiction nor nonfiction—not even a mixture of the two,"[17] applies with equal force to the film and video variants. The new autobiography, far from offering an unselfconscious transcription of the artist's life, posits a subject never exclusive of its other-in-history. In so doing, it challenges certain of our staunchest aesthetic and epistemological preconceptions.

I have chosen to speak about three very different examples of the new autobiography: one film, Mekas's *Lost, Lost, Lost,* and two videotapes, Segalove's *My Puberty* and Hershman's *First Person Plural.* The choice of such diverse pieces testifies to the range of approaches and tonalities available within the genre. Each combines an explicit and familiar level

of presentation—of the self, the artist in embryo, historically situated—
with another, implicit discursive enterprise, namely, research into the
potentials of self-presentation for moving-image forms. It is through
work such as this that we are brought to reconsider Elizabeth W. Bruss's
pronouncement on filmic autobiography. In her "Eye for I: Making and
Unmaking Autobiography in Film," Bruss makes the claim that literary
autobiographical activity, once central and pervasive, has largely been
displaced by new media forms. "If film and video do come to replace writing as our chief means of recording, informing, and entertaining," writes
Bruss, "and if (as I hope to show) there is no real cinematic equivalent for
autobiography, then the autobiographical act as we have known it for the
past four hundred years could indeed become more and more recondite,
and eventually extinct."[18] My own position would be that autobiography,
far from being an endangered species, shows new signs of life. It is the site
of a vital creative initiative being undertaken by film- and videomakers
around the world that is transforming the ways we think about and represent ourselves *for* ourselves and for others.

▶──

Mekas and the Diary Film

To speak of Mekas's monumental diary project entitled *Diaries, Notes,
and Sketches* (1975) (of which the three-and-one-half-hour *Lost, Lost,
Lost* is but the first volume) is to engage with one of the crucial voices in
the development of U.S. independent cinema. At the time of *Lost*'s release
in the mid-1970s, Mekas had been filming fragments of his life with one
or another spring-wound Bolex for more than a quarter century. Within
two weeks of his arrival from Lithuania in 1949, Mekas and his brother
Adolfas began the obsessive documentation of their lives and activities
with an accelerating focus on the cultural activities that could support
their creative aspirations (Jonas had been recognized in Lithuania as a
young but accomplished poet in the romantic tradition). We know from
Mekas's writings that this process of diaristic image gathering was originally intended as preparation for more conventional efforts. "I thought
what I was actually doing was practicing," he writes. "I was preparing
myself, or trying to keep in touch with my camera, so that when the day
would come when I'll have time, then I would make a 'real' film."[19] But in
the years that followed, Mekas's life became a succession of cultural interventions that reshaped the U.S. cinema. In 1955 he founded the influential
journal *Film Culture,* which combined for the first time examinations
of the Hollywood and European art cinemas with attention to a nascent

independent movement for which Mekas was chief public advocate, most notably in the pages of his "Movie Journal" column in the *Village Voice*. By the late fifties, he had launched the Film-Makers' Cooperative, a collectively organized distribution service aimed at maximizing artists' control at the expense of the institutional middleman, as well as two ongoing exhibition vehicles—Film-Makers' Cinematheque and the Anthology Film Archive. By the early sixties, Mekas had thus been instrumental in creating an alternative media culture that could sustain itself at the levels of production, distribution, and exhibition while furnishing it with a base of critical support. As organizer, polemicist, journalist, and practitioner, Mekas was the linchpin of what he called the New American Cinema.

Recall that my case for the new autobiography is premised on the work as an embroiling of subject in history. Far from positing the autobiographical as solipsistic, this position defines it as a practice of inscription in which the domain of the subject and that of the enveloping world are mutually constitutive: self and other/self through other. As an exemplary instance, *Lost, Lost, Lost,* chronologically the first of many volumes of *Diaries, Notes, and Sketches,* orchestrates public and personal domains while operating at the borders of documentary and avant-garde or privatist practices. Much in the manner of Montaigne's dual focus (on the measure of sight and of things), Mekas redefined the diaristic within the cinematic context, obliging his diary "to register the reality to which I react and also . . . to register my state of feeling (and all the memories) as I react."[20] Authorial style thus becomes the effect of an inevitably mediating subjectivity in its encounter with the world. The full complexity of this encounter is effected only through the interplay of sound and image; Mekas's intermittent narration reassesses the viewed material from as much as a quarter century's remove, installing through this temporal disjunction a prevailing poignancy.

The diary film, like the home movie with which it is aligned, presumes an act of documentation, if only through the preservation of the fragments of everyday life that envelop the self. Of course, the artist may choose to image herself in the isolation of a naked studio, as Lynn Hershman does. In that case, the visual document approaches the rarefied status of the written diary, unburdened with the weight of the visible world. In contrast, Mekas's diary images are subtended by a *series* of histories that can be traced across the film. In the first instance, there is the discourse on the displaced person and the Lithuanian community that shares its exile in Brooklyn. The film, as Scott MacDonald has noted,[21] is organized as three sets of couplets: the first pair focusing on the Lithuanian community in Brooklyn, the second on the formation of a new life in Manhattan and the forging of social and political ties outside the exile community, the last on the development of a cinematic aesthetic of spontaneity and personalism. Mekas remains the visual chronicler throughout. The stark black and white of certain images early on evokes thirties documentary photography in its combination of precise compositional values and compelling subject matter: the arrival of displaced persons at the Twenty-third Street Pier, the spare ramshackle of a Williamsburg front stoop, or the round faces of the exiled young framed in tenement windows. Subsequent portions of the film trace a kind of cross-cultural Oedipal itinerary in which the itinerant poet seeks the moment of spiritual resolution denied him by his exile. Indeed, the film's opening invocation ("O sing, Ulysses, sing your travels") establishes the shape of what follows: a lengthy journey culminating in an arrival that is equally a return. Mekas's personal trajectory is, however, coincident with several others—that of the late fifties peace movement, and more centrally the emergent New American Cinema, within which the filmmaker appears to find his place at last.

But throughout, Mekas's narration testifies to a continuing obsession for the witnessing and documenting of events—an activity whose efficacy is nonetheless repeatedly contested by the film's conflictual voices: "And I was there, and I was the camera eye, I was the witness, and I recorded it all, and I don't know, am I singing or am I crying." These words accompany images from the early fifties—of placard-bearing Lithuanians, traditionally clad, marching along Fifth Avenue protesting the Soviet occupation of their land, or the impassioned oration of exiled leaders speaking to packed halls. In a manner consistent with the poststructuralist conception of the subject, neither fixed nor categorical, the first-person pronominal repetition of this refrain ("And I was there, and I was the camera eye, I was the witness . . .") produces a subjectivity in flux, sliding beneath the verbal signifier. Despite all efforts to remain "true" to personal experience, the autobiographer faces the intrusion of the imaginary into discourse; the self refuses to "sit still" for any singular nomination. "The image-system creeps in stealthily," writes Barthes, "gently skating over a verb tense, a pronoun, a memory, in short, everything that can be gathered together under the very device of the Mirror and its Image: *Me, myself, I.*"[22]

If the pictures of life—of work, recreation, family ritual—strain toward faithful evocation, the filmmaker's spoken refrain dissuades us of our apparent comprehension: "Everything is normal, everything is normal," Mekas assures us over the images of everyday life. "The only thing is, you'll never know what they think. You'll never know what a displaced person thinks in the evening and in New York." Occurring in the opening minutes of the film, this is the first lesson to be drawn from *Diaries,* applicable to all forays into historiography through film. Historical meanings are never simply legible or immanent. Understanding arises from the thoughtful interrogation of documents (the real in representation) and the contradictions they engender. Mekas here reminds us of the irreparable breach between experience and its externalized representation, a notion implied by the film's very title. We are all of us lost in the chasm between our desire to recapture the past and the impossibility of a pristine return, no one more than Mekas himself.

And therein lies the key to the significance of *Lost, Lost, Lost* in the context of the present discussion. For if we can never know what any one of the imaged exiles is thinking despite our rapt attention to the preservational image, what more can we know of Mekas himself? More to the point, what can the Mekas of 1975 know of his 1949 self? If, as this film suggests, memory is, like history, always revision, translation, the gap between experience (the moment of filming) and secondary revision (the moment of editing) produces an ineradicably split diaristic subject. The temporal and epistemological syncopation of selves (the *writing versus written* self) is, I would argue, quite different for the moving form than for the written diary, which instantiates a perpetual present tense ("Right now I am writing my diary").[23]

As exemplified by the Mekas project, the *staging* of subjectivity effected by the film or video diary is consistent with Freud's notion of psychical temporality. As discussed in Jean Laplanche and Jean-Bertrand Pontalis's *The Language of Psycho-Analysis*, Freud's usage of the term *nachtraglichkeit*, or deferred action, is intended to convey the manner by which experiences, impressions, or memory traces are altered after the fact as a function of new experiences and are thus rendered capable of reinvestment, producing new, even unexpected, effects of meaning. As Freud wrote to his confidant Wilhelm Fliess: "I am working on the assumption that our psychical mechanism has come about by a process of stratification: the material present in the shape of memory-traces is from time to time subjected to a *rearrangement* in accordance with fresh circumstances—is, as it were, *transcribed*."[24] The film and video works of self-inscription being considered here, sites of deferral and reinvestment, can thus be said to *enact* what is typically *theorized*, putting certain key assumptions to the test in what could be called (in deference to my opening remarks) "laboratory conditions."

I turn now to two other instances of the new autobiography that treat the issues explored earlier in an altogether different key. Both of the tapes, Segalove's *My Puberty* and Hershman's *First Person Plural,* map private history (the self as microcosm) onto a more comprehensive or macrocosmic plane of social/cultural representation, but with altogether differing effects. Segalove's treatment is gently parodic, situating its retrospection within a popular cultural context of early sixties adolescent Americana. In contrast, Hershman's electronic diary project is deadly serious, assuming the status of "talking cure." It is a working through of the traumas of childhood abuse in a manner that exceeds the personal— in part through its intermittent graphic overlay of archival footage (as of concentration camp survivors), which functions as a gut-wrenching historical corroboration to the scene of auto-analysis.

▶

My Puberty

Segalove has long been engaged in a project of autobiography, dating back to *The Mom Tapes* (1974–1978), a comic mother/daughter dialogue begun in the early seventies, extended over a succession of years. In that piece, Segalove is the interlocutor intent on eliciting a mother's confidences on matters ranging from shopping tips to familial reminiscence. Despite the ironic distance to the material established from the outset, one senses throughout the complicity of the younger Segalove. Indeed, the tape mimes the autobiographical through the figure of the mother, undertaking self-inquiry at a generational remove.

My Puberty is diaristic pastiche. Each segment of the tape begins with the imaging of a literary fragment that evokes the character of the diary—quotidian, unstructured in its seriality, and profoundly anti-Aristotelian. These lead-ins ("Susan came over to visit" or "In seventh grade, I took sewing class") authorize our entry into the representational space of first-person recall, a world of hyperbolic decor—all splashy color and pedal pushers. But *My Puberty* is equally a performance piece, and therein lies its contribution to the diaristic genre. Segalove chooses to cast her present-tense, thirty-seven-year-old self as the preteen Ilene sharing the frame with the preadolescents of memory. The effect is at once comic and uncanny, particularly in the moment at which Segalove freezes on a two-shot of herself in drag with an honest-to-god charming twelve-year-old boy. This *tableau vivant* effects a revisionist translation of past into present tense so as to suggest the failure of its possibility. It is a scene that evokes the hybrid reality of dream. And yet, lurking beneath the mock seriousness of the piece, something of the complex epistemological conditions governing film and video autobiography obtrudes.

Elizabeth W. Bruss's presumption that it is "impossible to characterize and exhibit selfhood through film" is based in part on Frank D. McConnell's narratological insight that "the world seen cinematically" is "the world seen without a self."[25] While this may hold true for the test cases Bruss chooses—among them, Truffaut's *The Four Hundred Blows* (1959) and Federico Fellini's *8½* (1963)—the productive mode of independently produced autobiographical film and video works necessitates neither the delegation of subjectivity to actors nor authorial collaboration with producer, editor, or, for that matter, crew. The defining character of autobiography in Bruss's terms—the conflation of the speaking subject and the subject of the sentence—remains intact and quite literally so; nowhere in the Mekas or Hershman pieces, and rarely in Segalove's tape, can a voice other than the artist's be heard. And in each instance but to varying degree, the speaking subject emerges as the imaged object. In Hershman's electronic diaries, the artist's corporeality is an inescapable fact; her unflinching return of the camera's gaze is a sign of the auto-transference her testimony precipitates.

Segalove's video memoirs, as in *The Mom Tapes* or *I Remember Beverly Hills* (1980), have frequently deployed a subjective camera whose anthropomorphizing pans and tracks evoke the sense of a present-tense exploration of a descriptive narration rooted in the already experienced. In *I Remember Beverly Hills,* Segalove's camera returns to her school playground to stalk the memory of a special friendship; in *The Mom Tapes,* Segalove acts out her belated defiance against maternal prohibitions, tracing a path beneath Wilshire Boulevard along a subway passage once deemed off-limits. The admixture of past and present modes through a first-person reimaging of sites invested with the force of narrated experience blends expressive and descriptive elements, a combination Bruss claims to be essential to the autobiographical act. In *My Puberty,* voiced description (in Segalove's work, retrospection tends to deflate rather than romanticize experience) evokes the past as her nosy camera testifies to the materiality of the present-tense reevaluation. This hybrid temporality is the inverse of Mekas's past image/present narration approach. But in either case, the disjunctive relations between sound and image tend toward a dispersal, rather than a coalescence, of the represented self. Segalove's work, comedic throughout, nevertheless refuses an unproblematic formulation of the remembered life she obsessively reexamines; the memories are held at arm's length, not by the melancholia of Mekas's vocal overlay but by a humor that deflates idealization.

First Person Plural

The title of Hershman's tape plays on the notion of the essential plurality of what we call the first person singular; the graphic display of its nomination as it appears in the tape (the "plural" of the title hounded by a doubling ghost image) states the case succinctly. The reference is less to the grammatically correct "we" than to the plurivocality of the I-in-discourse. Hershman, we learn in this third volume of her electronic diary, was an abused child, whose bones and psyche were battered by her parents. Observant Jews of the professional class, her forebears are alleged by Hershman to have perpetuated in her the violence whose kindred manifestation she takes to be the wholesale slaughter of European Jewry by Adolf Hitler, himself a third-generation abused child. Although *First Person Plural* is far too complex for thoroughgoing analysis here, it is worth roughing out the contours of the subjectivity that Hershman delegates to herself in the work.

The tape stakes its existence on the psychoanalytic presumption of memory retrieval and elaboration as curative treatment for childhood trauma. While occasionally voicing the negation of such a talking cure in whispered tones ("You're not supposed to talk about it"), Hershman proceeds to relentlessly explore the depths of memory and fantasy. "I lost my voice," she says, "and it's taken me nearly forty-five years to get it back." Indeed, the tape is invested with a force attributable to the repression of such a history and to the history of such a repression. While the piece offers a more or less nonstop verbalization—the videomaker's self-narration in language—the image track (which seldom departs from Hershman's tightly composed face) is the site of an insistent discontinuity that underscores multiplicity. The notion of subjectivity as serial, heterogeneous, even conflictual, is established through the use of jump cuts within otherwise continuous takes, the juxtaposition or enforced continuity of separable presentational moments for continuous monologue sequences. The sense of discontinuity is enforced by alterations of angle, hairstyle, or dress, as well as by the vacillation between color and black and white, even the appearance of negative imagery. Self-alienation is further achieved through the framing or inserting of the first-person image, recessing Hershman against a field of black.

But it is the projection of the self onto a broader historical backdrop—the superimposition of the ghastly if familiar images of the victims of other places, other times—that may be the most striking component of *First Person Plural*. Hershman is at pains to break through the barriers that isolate the self who suffers from the world that restates her victimization daily. That escape—and the recontextualization that it demands—is effected through her artifice. But the world-historical suffering figured in the tape is not at all trivialized through such self-referencing. For even while Hershman enacts her therapy on video, that most privatized of public media, she succeeds in framing an audiovisual metaphor for that double gaze inaugurated by Montaigne in the sixteenth century. Indeed, it is through her obsession with the processes of self-healing that she reminds us of the efficacy, as well as the staggering complexity, of self-representation in the moving-image arts of the twentieth century.

The presumption of a necessary or inevitable split between critical and creative practices seems less and less tenable. It seems increasingly clear that artists and critics are replying to the same theoretical debates despite the differences of discursive apparatus. Perhaps this has always been the case. Certainly much of what has come to count as the most significant thought of the past century has required the kind of formal innovation usually attributed to the artist—here I'm thinking of the signifying "play" of Nietzsche, Adorno, Derrida, or Barthes. In part, this is so because the issue for the contemporary artist or theorist remains the same: the ruse of representation. For Nietzsche, all articulation, more so self-inscription, engaged in a kind of necessary charade: "Appearance is for me that which lives and is effective and goes so far in its self-mockery that it makes me feel that this is appearance and will-o'-the-wisp and a dance of spirits and nothing more—that among all these dreamers, I, too, who 'know,' am dancing my dance."[26]

The work addressed here takes as its object the intrinsic plurality of a self that lives, desires, feels pain and pleasure—and re-presents that experience in a dynamic, historicized framework. This is the work that stages a subjectivity that exceeds the difference of a stultifying binarism—or, for that matter, of Freud's tripartite psychic topography. Without question, this attention to differences has underwritten an outpouring of culturally resistant work in the 1980s.

It has been the place of the essayistic—the "new" or historicizing autobiography in film and video—to take up this question of difference at its source, at the level of the subject. It is Barthes whose summary diagnosis *takes* most trenchantly, this despite his abhorrence for the definitive statement ("the fear of not being able to resist the *last word*").[27] "When we speak today of a divided subject," writes Barthes, "it is never to acknowledge his simple contradictions, her double postulations, etc.;

it is a *diffraction* which is intended, a dispersion of energy in which there remains neither a central core nor a structure of meaning: I am not contradictory, I am dispersed."[28] It is in the direction of this diffraction that the essayistic is poised; it is work whose vitality and political efficacy will continue to illumine the media horizon for some time to come.

7

*Filling Up the Hole in the Real:
Death and Mourning in Contemporary
Documentary Film and Video*

*First presented at Visible Evidence III (Harvard, 1995), "Filling Up the
Hole in the Real" proposes that the film or video work can, through its
memorialization of loss, function as a work of mourning that is also and
profoundly an instance of self-inscription. With such work, the self that
is constructed tends to be a conditional one, figured as it is against a
ground of irreparable loss. In various writings of Freud and particularly
Lacan, death is figured as a negativity, a discursive void, which can be
partially and progressively worked through, if not resolved, at the level
of language or imagery, a line of thought that has long been applied to
the study of literature and painting. Inspired by a number of remarkable
films and tapes of the 1980s and 1990s that treat the death of a loved one
or even the self (the key historical point of reference, as in* Blue *[1994],*
Tongues Untied *[1989],* Silverlake Life: The View from Here *[1993], or*
Fast Trip, Long Drop *[1993], is no doubt the AIDS epidemic), I look at
how a work of mourning can be enacted through constructions of sound
and image. It is noteworthy that the central film examined in this context
is* Shoah, *which, more than any other, illustrates the impossibility of anything like a "successful" act of mourning. For in the face of staggering,
epochal loss, art can only hope to signify the limits of its healing powers.*

If you look very carefully at the shots of the actual explosion when the screen is white, in the middle of the screen is
a small . . . boiling black area for, oh, maybe ten or fifteen
frames. That little boiling black area is where the heat from
the first atomic bomb burned a hole through the film in the
camera. It was so hot, and it focused so intensely on the film
in the camera gate, the motion picture camera gate, that it actually burned a hole through the negative. And you can hold
up the negative and actually look at this—this extraordinary

physical imprint of the first atomic bomb on that . . . piece of motion picture film. . . . In many ways, it's the ultimate movie. It's actually a hole in the film. It's not just an image on the emulsion; it's actually a hole in the film.

:: Jon Else, director, on footage used in *The Day after Trinity*

Now, in the days following the fiftieth anniversary of Hiroshima and Nagasaki, it seems appropriate to begin this discussion of the documentary representation of death with this reference to the filming of the first nuclear detonation at Trinity site, July 16, 1945.[1] In the moment of *The Day after Trinity* to which Else refers, the absolute unrepresentability of death is physically, materially realized. The terrifying power unleashed by the blast has caused the film stock itself to combust. This massive release of energy is figurable only as a sheer negativity, commensurable not to the black leader found on every answer print of the documentary but to the void, a hole in the emulsion of the original camera stock, a null set in the domain of indexicality and of signification.

I propose that this eruption of the abyss in discourse be understood in relation to two difficult, and indeed elusive, terms: death and the Lacanian Real. In this chapter, we will arrive at a formulation of the former by way of the latter. Then a range of instances from recent documentary films and videos will be examined in which representations of death figure centrally. It is my sense that such an investigation brings us up hard against the limits of documentary discourse, to the very conditions of its (im)possibility, and, in a movement whose negativity echoes that of our theme, to the potential of documentary inscription as a work of mourning. One final point: this work on film and tape in which the loss of the other elicits signs of grief and memorialization (and here it is worth recalling Lacan: "The one unbearable dimension of possible human experience is not the experience of one's own death, which no one has, but the experience of the death of another"),[2] that work of mourning is also and profoundly an instance of self-inscription. It is in this way that such work can be linked to other variants of autobiographical discourse that I have attempted to analyze, such as domestic ethnography, the video diary, the essay film, the video letter, and the confessional.

It is not simply out of morbidity that I turn to documentary texts on death (although my students at times may think so). For a range of reasons, among them the epidemic of AIDS-related deaths that have vitiated the ranks of the arts community and a general turn to the autobiographical in film and video, a large number of important films and tapes have been made in the past decade that attempt to confront the maker's death or that of a close friend or family member. I am thinking of work such as *Silverlake Life: The View from Here* (Joslin and Friedman, 1992), *Tongues Untied* (Riggs, 1989), *Black Is . . . Black Ain't* (Riggs and Atkinson, 1994), *Thank You and Good Night* (Oxenberg, 1991), *Shadow's Song* (Hershman, 1992), *Everyday Echo Street: A Summer Diary* (Mogul, 1993), *Everything's for You* (Ravett, 1989), *The Last Bolshevik* (Marker, 1993), *Blue* (Jarman, 1994), and, at a slight remove, *History and Memory* (Tajiri, 1991) and *Complaints of a Dutiful Daughter* (Hoffmann, 1994). Of this subset of films and tapes, *Shoah* (Lanzmann, 1985) is at once paradigmatic and eccentric given its vastly larger scale—textual and historical—and the filmmaker's remarkably complex relationship to his topic and subjects. Before turning to a discussion of these texts, however, there is a great deal more that must be said about what is at stake in examining this crucial body of work.

I share something of Roland Barthes's conviction that death is something like the special calling of the camera arts. I also concur with Hans Richter in his assessment of the desire for "factual sustenance" to which early cinema responded in an age in which "reason [had] given rise to a secularization of the divine."[3] If, as Richter claims, "our age demands the documented fact," what better proof than in the image of the dead Paris Communards said to be the first mass-circulation photograph? For it congealed at once the proof of failed resistance against state authority and of the power of the photograph as a reproducible warrant of that authority. In that image, the private horrors of personal loss were suborned to a more public pronouncement; the photograph has come to be received less as a work of mourning for the vanquished than as a sign epiphanous for the state, its discovery of a new and powerful interpellative tool.

In his final work, Barthes indelibly joined the preservational reflex of the documentary project with mortality. "Death must be somewhere in a society," he wrote; "if it is no longer (or less intensely) in religion, it must be elsewhere; perhaps in this image which produces Death while trying to preserve life."[4] Where Barthes confined his analysis to the photographic sign, I take heart in my extrapolation to film and video, for increasingly, the "somewhere" from which the dead are both memorialized and annulled is the moving image form, discernible as a work of mourning.

There is cause, however, to echo Freud's founding question in "Mourning and Melancholia": "Now in what consists the work which mourning performs?"[5] It is necessary to comprehend something of the psychic dynamic underlying every work of mourning if we are to understand the special circumstances that surround the cinematic or videographic variants. Although Freud admits in his 1917 essay that "we do not even know by what economic measures the work of mourning is carried through," he notes that, with "normal" grief, the loss of the loved object is gradually surmounted, libidinal ties are loosened, and the ego emerges triumphant. This positive outcome is characterized as a struggle between the reality principle and its other (perhaps the death drive, perhaps psychosis), occurring only painfully and in stages; its course is not to be interfered with by the analyst. This battle royal that is the work of mourning receives lavish and painstaking description:

> This struggle can be so intense that a turning away from reality ensues, the object being clung to through the medium of a hallucinatory wish-psychosis. The normal outcome is that deference for reality gains the day. Nevertheless its behest cannot be at once obeyed. The task is now carried through bit by bit, under great expense of time and cathectic energy, while all the time the existence of the lost object is continued in the mind. Each single one of the memories and hopes which bound the libido to the object is brought up and hyper-cathected, and the detachment of the libido from it accomplished. Why this process of carrying out the behest of reality bit by bit, which is in the nature of a compromise, should be so extraordinarily painful is not at all easy to explain in terms of mental economics. It is worth noting that this pain seems natural to us. The fact is, however, that when the work of mourning is completed the ego becomes free and uninhibited again.[6]

More than forty years later, Lacan remarks in his interpretation of *Hamlet* that if the mechanism underlying the work of mourning remains poorly understood, it is because "the question hasn't been properly posed."[7] To do so, he says, requires the introduction of certain key terms, among them his notion of the Real.

In the constant renegotiation of Lacan's teachings, the Real remains the most neglected term in the tripartite schema composed of the Imaginary, the Symbolic, and the Real. It is no wonder that this is so if we may judge by its slipperiness as it recurs in various of the seminars. Michael Walsh has made this point in a recent and persuasive essay arguing for the pertinence of the Lacanian Real for film studies.[8] For his part, Slavoj Zizek has written obsessively on the value of Lacan's later formulations, those of the 1960s and 1970s, which, in their attention to various, often puzzling, characteristics of the Real, complicate the "classical" formulations of the Mirror Stage and the linguistic analogy (i.e., the unconscious is structured like a language). Indeed, Zizek has gone so far as to suggest that the immediate coincidence of opposite or even contradictory determinations is what *defines* the Lacanian Real.[9] (According to Zizek, the Real as developed in the 1960s and 1970s approaches more and more what was, in the 1950s, deemed the Imaginary.) For present purposes, however, the Real can be adequately localized in relation to discourse. Lacan variously and over a period of years refers to the Real as "the impossible," "that which always returns to the same place,"[10] as "being without alterity," "undifferentiated,"[11] "that with which all words cease and all categories fail,"[12] as "marked by symbolic nihilation,"[13] and as "what resists symbolization absolutely. . . . [the] literally ineffable."[14] Combining several of these usages, Zizek has deemed the Real "[the] rock . . . the traumatic point which is always missed but none the less always returns, although we try . . . to neutralize it, to integrate it into the symbolic order. . . . That is the Lacanian Real," writes Zizek, "a certain limit which is always missed—we always come too early or too late."[15] It is elsewhere for Zizek, and even more vividly, "the pulsing of the presymbolic substance in its abhorrent vitality."[16] The Real is not to be mistaken for "reality," which is perfectly knowable (think only of the notion of the "reality principle" through which one constantly puts experience to the test), but should instead be understood as a zone outside symbolization from which trauma may erupt as symptom. The traumatic symptom's appearance is thus also a return; the temporality of these effects of the Real is that of the future anterior, a mixture of past and future, that which "will have been."

What, then, is death according to this schema, for I have said that our understanding of death will require the Lacanian Real? Like the Real, death is defined in its negativity. It is, according to Mikkel Borch-Jacobsen, "the absolute Master," "the (impossible, unlivable) absence of all symbols," the "unpresentable *nothing*." But if death is "what negates discourse," it is also what "introduces negation" into discourse. For Lacan, like Kojève before him, "the negativity of discourse" is precisely "its 'manifestation,' in the sense that it 'causes to be what is not.'"[17] As Derrida has written, the sign marks a place of difference; it is the place where "the completely other is announced as such."[18] "Representation is death," says Derrida succinctly in "Freud and the Scene of Writing."[19] "Pronounce the word 'cat,' Blanchot [writes], and 'death speaks.'"[20] Death, like the Lacanian Real, can be understood as a founding negativity.

But how more precisely are these two terms to be understood in relation to each other? Lacan has claimed that "death is never experienced as such . . . it is never real."[21] Freud says something like that in his "Thoughts for the Times on War and Death": "It is indeed impossible to imagine our own death; and whenever we attempt to do so we can perceive that we are in fact still present as spectators."[22] Death and the Real, while conceptually linked, can never coincide. Death, the death of the other, can produce *effects* in the Real. In his work on psychosis, Lacan claimed that the radical foreclosure *(verwerfung)* of traumatic material resulted not in its repression (and eventual return) but in its ejection into the Real: "Everything which is refused in the symbolic by the *Verwerfung* reappears in the Real."[23] Death is formulated as a structurally homologous but inverse formation of foreclosure. "Where is the gap," asks Lacan, "the hole that results from this loss and that calls forth mourning on the part of the subject? It is a hole in the real, by means of which the subject enters into a relationship that is the inverse of what I have set forth in earlier seminars under the name of *Verwerfung* [repudiation, foreclosure]. Just as what is rejected from the symbolic register reappears in the real, in the same way the hole in the real that results from the loss, sets the signifier in motion."[24] Death opens up a hole in the Real that will be filled by a "swarm of images" having perhaps ritual or therapeutic value. Like psychosis, then, mourning can be understood in relation to negativity, to a void. Unlike psychosis, however, mourning is commonly resolved or worked through. That recovery, too little understood by Freud, is, according to Lacan, a function of language. "The work of mourning," writes Lacan, "is accomplished at the level of the *logos:* I say *logos* rather than group or community, although group and community, being organized culturally, are its mainstays. The work of mourning is first of all performed to satisfy the disorder that is produced by the inadequacy of signifying elements to cope with the hole that has been created in existence, for it is the system of signifiers in their totality which is impeached by the least instance of mourning."[25]

We now have a conceptual framework within which to approach the representation of death in relation to the work of mourning: the loss of a loved one produces a gap in the Real, that formless beyond of symbolization, a hole that sets the signifier in motion, filling the void, relieving the pain. We also have a better understanding of the grounds for claiming that the representation of death in some recent films and videotapes may constitute both a public and an autobiographical or intrapsychic activity. But if we are to make sense of Lacan's logocentrism, we must translate it into terms specific to film and video. And there it becomes apparent that "the totality of the signifier" and the particular ways in which it is "set in motion" in cinematic and videographic works must be investigated with rigor and specificity. For far from either *logos* or a "rush of images," the work of mourning in film and video tends to be composed of a combination of words (via first-person voice-over or interview-based testimony) and images (relics of pastness, evocations of memory) whose meaning depends upon their overall arrangement via editing.

Even in the case of the few recent texts mentioned at the outset, there is a tremendous variability as to tactic and effect. Some key distinctions can be made: the extent to which the piece focuses on death, one's own or another's *(Silverlake Life, Blue),* or instead reveals loss as the veiled source of textual desire *(Everyday Echo Street, Tongues Untied);* the choice of direct, relatively unmediated representations of death or dying *(Thank You and Good Night)* versus the oblique or distanced view *(Everything's for You, Blue);* the tonality of the piece—elegiac *(Everything's for You, Shadow's Song)* or laconic *(Thank You and Good Night, Complaints of a Dutiful Daughter).* With this work, every choice is a dangerous one as regards audience response. Deep and painful identifications can arise; a gamut of emotions can be elicited, including anger directed at the filmmaker for her presumed insensitivity, exploitativeness, or narcissism. One person's cathartic experience can be another's exhibitionist display.

Having sketched out some sense of the issues at stake, I will briefly examine a few key moments from a single film to concretize matters. Recall my earlier statement that Claude Lanzmann's *Shoah* is unique. While Lanzmann maintains an inquisitorial distance from his subjects throughout—and these subjects include Holocaust survivors, perpetrators, and fellow travelers—this massive (indeed, obsessive) project can be seen as an effort to shore up a hole in the Real of unparalleled proportion. If the film is a work of mourning from which the subject may emerge more or less intact, one feels it is doomed to failure for Lanzmann, as for many of his witnesses. There will never be words enough to fill the void left by the six million. A more salutary result may be achieved for those who "know" the loss only secondhand or even harbor doubts about the Holocaust's very existence. For those, resistance may be replaced by partial identification; a sense of loss may be absorbed and repaired. But this is not a zero-sum game; the result, where it "takes," is also the replication—indeed, the contagion—of historical memory figurable as the residue of the work of mourning. I will describe one scene among many.

Lanzmann is interviewing Abraham Bomba, a survivor of the Treblinka death camp. Bomba now lives in Israel, where he works as a barber. This choice of vocation can be read as cruelly ironic, as a survival tactic, or as a compulsion to repeat, for it was as a barber that he had proved useful to his captors. Bomba was stationed inside the gas chamber itself, where he was made to cut the hair of women soon to perish; it was cutting rather than shaving, and thus a false and pacifying hope was instilled in the victims. By the time of the filming in the early 1980s, Bomba has survived, physically intact, for nearly four decades. Throughout most of his on-camera testimony, his face remains a mask of implacability.

There is a blankness of affect that one recognizes from psychological accounts of Holocaust survivors. Now, in a moment that has elicited much criticism from audiences, Lanzmann prompts Bomba to speak about a particular past event, a singularly impossible memory. He resists. That resistance is, in psychoanalytic terms, a sign of strong cathection, deep trauma. "Go on, Abe, you must go . . . You have to," Lanzmann prompts his subject from off-camera. "It's too hard," Bomba replies. "Please," says Lanzmann, his voice low but insistent, "we have to do it. You know it . . . You have to do it. I know it's very hard. I know and I apologize." Bomba continues to resist, wiping his face with a handkerchief. "I won't be able to do it. I told you. Today it's gonna be very hard." But in the end, the subject acquiesces. In what follows, Bomba speaks not of cutting the hair of his own friends and family members (an event that remains foreclosed, unsayable) but rather of witnessing a friend and fellow barber as he confronted his own wife and sister about to die.

The kernel of trauma, buried and of the Real, erupts less as language, more as signs of bodily distress—grimacing, tears, the cessation of activity. Lanzmann has chosen to interview Bomba as he works, the repetition of the gesture helping to unleash memory. As for the media specificity of this scene, I would argue that the camera, once called by Jean Rouch a "psychoanalytic stimulant," functions as an incitant to confession. ("Yes, the camera deforms," says Rouch, "but not from the moment that it becomes an accomplice. At that point it has the possibility of doing something I couldn't do if the camera wasn't there: it becomes a kind of psychoanalytic stimulant which lets people do things they wouldn't otherwise do.")[26] Lanzmann's injunction is for speech, but speech *for the camera*, for an apparatus capable of preserving, amplifying, and circulating his testimony. Whether or not we agree with the tactic, we must recognize its force.

But wherein can be found the work of mourning here, and for whom? Not, I would argue, for Abraham Bomba. No "swarm of images," no "setting in motion of the signifier," can repair the damage suffered. As with other Holocaust survivors, "a pathological shade" is cast on grief; the return to a "free and uninhibited" ego position is doubtful. But therapy for the survivors, those like Bomba whose identifications may be irremediably with the dead, is not Lanzmann's object. Nor can a positive resolution achieved through the work of mourning be the chief or even likely result of the project for the filmmaker. His obsessive eleven-year quest (including five years of editing) was to track *shoah*, the European genocide of the Jews (*shoah* is the Hebrew word for annihilation), in the most minute detail and to transform the present-tense testimony of scores of living witnesses into an object of mass culture. If the film functions as a work of mourning (and I think it does), it is primarily for audiences at some remove both from the events chronicled and from the representational act.

And, as suggested earlier, I would argue for *Shoah* as a media-specific work of mourning. As film, it shows as much as it tells. The words of the witnesses reveal only a portion of a complex and subterranean drama. Nonverbal signs abound—the casting down of the glance; the shifting of body weight; the uncanniness of one survivor's masklike facial expression, part smile, part grimace. Freud's case histories and Lacan's seminar anecdotes are rendered exclusively through language at the expense of performance or spectacle. In *Shoah,* we have the opportunity to see and hear former SS officers impugn themselves through the tiniest inflection of tone or usage, to watch as traumatic memory beats its way to the surface. The camera incites, records, and preserves these sustained efforts to speak the most unspeakable of losses.

For the most part, the films and tapes to which I have alluded here respond to private or familial sorrows, though almost always in a manner that implicates others: other black, gay males *(Tongues Untied),* other daughters of Alzheimer's patients *(Complaints of a Dutiful Daughter),* other children of Holocaust survivors *(Everything's for You).* Frequently, however, I have seen these pieces foster identification well beyond that initial audience. I have argued that the film or tape can function as a work of mourning both for the artist and for a community of others who share the experience of loss. In addition, the work may, through the trigger of grief and in spite of cultural or political differences, engender spectator identification with the maker who focalizes loss from a radically alien position.

I will conclude with some brief remarks about Chris Marker's *The Last Bolshevik,* another work whose monumentality outstrips the norm. In a manner familiar from *Letter from Siberia* and *Sans soleil, The Last Bolshevik* is of the epistolary mode. The six letters that make up the tape's structure are addressed postmortem to Alexander Ivanovitch Medvedkin, Marker's dear friend and a Soviet filmmaker who straddles the century, his fortunes and longevity (1900–1989) also paralleling those of the Soviet nation. The event that precipitates this two-hour work is Medvedkin's death. The tape begins with, and returns to, the image of an elderly Medvedkin scolding Marker, his unreliable interlocutor, for his failure to write. "You lazy bastard," Medvedkin berates him on camera, "why don't you ever write. Just a little. Like this." Medvedkin gestures with an outstretched left hand, his thumb and index finger inches apart. The frame freezes. All that follows, two hours of tape time and Marker's commentary on nearly a century of Russian cultural and political history with Medvedkin as dramatic foil, constitute the reply. But it is a reply that arrives too late. Or perhaps not.

If these letters arrive at their destination (in the manner that Lacan described in his famed seminar on "The Purloined Letter"), they do so only as a work of mourning. But far from tracing private grief, *Bolshevik* mourns not only the passing of a benevolent and largely overlooked totemic ancestor (as well as others, purged or fallen—Babel, Meyerhold, Vertov) but also the betrayal of the ideals and principles that underwrote the Russian Revolution and the Left in this century. In consummate essayistic fashion, Marker succeeds in weaving together disparate levels of referentiality and historical narration. As a work of mourning, *The Last Bolshevik* displays a horizon of unrivaled breadth. But more than that, it is the work of a consummate ironist who, as a lifelong activist and cinephile, views the political transformations and cultural wars of the century without nostalgia, aggrieved but not humorless.

In the end, one must recognize that all this filling up and patching over of holes in the Real has its limits. And yet, as regards the work of mourning, cinema and video possess a remarkable potential for creating new therapeutic communities, joined by bereavement, loss, and the need for healing. In *A Very Easy Death,* Simone de Beauvoir wrote about the death of her mother. For Beauvoir, in the solitude of her sorrow and her writing, there was little hope for community. "The misfortune is that although everyone must come to this, each experiences the adventure in solitude. We never left Maman during those last days which she confused with convalescence and yet we were profoundly separated from her."[27] The making and public display of the films and videotapes to which I have referred, all the bathos, the controversies, and resistances they have occasioned, must be understood in relation to the profound separation of which Beauvoir speaks.

In his analysis of *Hamlet,* Lacan made note of the ritual value of mourning, the fulfillment of obligation to what is called the memory of the dead. Ritual value, he wrote, "introduces some mediation of the gap opened up by mourning."[28] Recall Barthes's plaint—"Death must be somewhere in a society"—and his belief that it resided in the photographic image. Perhaps there, in the ritual value we ascribe to the documentary as a work of mourning, we will discover a limited but resilient source of reconciliation for our private losses and public tragedies.

8

Documentary Disavowals and the Digital

"Documentary Disavowals," first presented at Visible Evidence V (Northwestern University, 1997), represents a departure from the approach of the previous three chapters, which examine the construction of subjectivity within documentary film from a largely psychoanalytic perspective. This chapter begins with an overview of Zygmunt Bauman's critique of the modernist project as an adventure in "social engineering," posing it in relation to documentary filmmaking, which, it is argued, has frequently served as a powerful instrument of rationality. Due to its rhetorical potency as a tool for nation building, public education, and advocacy, the documentary form has consistently been harnessed to the manufacture of social consent. This chapter looks at the issues raised by a documentary tradition in which epistemological or rhetorical ends—the acquisition of knowledge or the persuasive delivery of ideas to an audience—override ethical ones. In the ethical context, greater value may be attached to the circumstances surrounding the creative process (the status and conditions of the social interaction, encounter, and exchange) than to the final product, understood in the commercial arena to be the "bottom line." In the instance of some ethically charged works, the openness and mutual receptivity between filmmaker and subject may be said to extend to the relationship between the audience and the film. Open exchange may begin to replace the one-way delivery of ideas. This ethical challenge in the field of documentary practice echoes those in contemporary art and philosophy that question models of mastery or absolute certainty, placing greater emphasis on open-endedness, empathy, and receptivity.

Documentary has, from its inception, been tied up with modernism. If, as Zygmunt Bauman has suggested, the modernist dream was for "a unified,

managed and controlled space" achieved through "projects of global social engineering, [and] the search for universal standards of truth, justice
and beauty," documentary has served as a willing handmaiden.[1] Aspiring
to the post-Enlightenment promise of full legibility, documentary has
displayed "the audacious self-confidence and hubris of modernity,"[2] particularly apparent during the pinnacle moments—the 1920s in the Soviet
Union, the 1930s in Britain. In what follows, I will offer elaboration of
Bauman's critique of the modernist project and suggest its applicability to
documentary film history before counterposing to it a few contemporary
documentary practices that explore digital, frequently interactive, technologies and their ethical potential.

But first it is important to clarify and offer some reservations toward
the polemical, often totalizing, claims of the antimodernist position. Bauman's view of "the modernist project" upon which my own thesis depends
is rhetorically powerful but tends to collapse a tremendously complex set
of terms capable of multiple declension—the modern, modernity, modernism, the modernist, modernization—terms that have been realized quite
differently in varying historical moments and contexts. It is important
to note the variability of the notion of "modernism" (to consider but one
thread of the problematic) in the hands of various cultural critics. One
encounters aesthetic and literary as well as philosophical modernisms,
modernisms inflected by diverse national or regional cultures. In his remarkable essay "The Modernist Event," Hayden White hinges his discussion of the unraveling of certainty in the field of historiography on something like the interminability of analysis as described by Freud a century
ago. White suggests that any claims to an objective account of an event
are undermined by two circumstances: "one is that the number of details
identifiable in any singular event is potentially infinite; and the other is
that the 'context' of any singular event is infinitely extensive or at least is
not objectively determinable."[3] This characterization of "the dismantling
of the concept of the event as an object of a specifically scientific kind of
knowledge" as "modernist" seems entirely at odds with Bauman's view
that regards the modernist agenda as unflinchingly rationalist and even
disciplinary. White attempts to clarify the confusion in a footnote:

> I want to make clear that by the term "modernism" I am not referring to that
> program of dominating nature through reason, science, and technology sup-
> posedly inaugurated by the Enlightenment; I refer, rather, to the literary and
> artistic movements launched in the late nineteenth and early twentieth cen-
> turies against this very program of modernization and its social and cultural
> effects—the movement represented by writers such as Pound, Eliot, Stein,
> Joyce, Proust, Woolf, and so on.[4]

"Modernism" appears to be a cultural term so overdetermined as to contain within itself apparent opposites (e.g., antimodern modernists).

But the confusion proliferates. In his infamous essay on postmodernism, Fredric Jameson singles out more or less the same roster of literary modernists as White, but given Jameson's brief for a theorization of the postmodern, it is no surprise that he prefers to think of them as premature postmodernists. "It may indeed be conceded that all the features of postmodernism I am about to enumerate can be detected, full-blown, in this or that preceding modernism (including such astonishing genealogical precursors as Gertrude Stein, Raymond Roussel, or Marcel Duchamp, who may be considered outright postmodernists, avant la lettre)."[5] I am, however, less concerned with pinpointing the moment of some aesthetic shift, more concerned with the formation of a putative "modernist project" in relation to an epistemological position that evolved in the nineteenth century, dependent on the support of rationalism, technology, and the scientific method. It is this philosophically derived notion of modernity to which I am claiming tangency for the forging of the documentary project in the first decades of the twentieth century.

It is important to note that postmodernism as Bauman has described it in a half dozen of his books is understood not as a matter of chronology, of the replacement of modernism with something new, but rather as an epistemic realignment born of an acknowledgment "that the long and earnest efforts of modernity have been misguided, undertaken under false pretenses . . . [demonstrating] beyond reasonable doubt [modernity's] impossibility, the vanity of its hopes and the wastefulness of its works."[6] For Bauman, the postmodern is an attitude toward knowledge rather than a mere marker of contemporaneity. In much the same vein, Stephen Toulmin has characterized the establishment of modernism's rationalist roots—the turn to rhetoric and logic, the favoring of the abstract over the particular—through Descartes in the seventeenth century as a narrowing of intellectual horizons (and here he has in mind the Montaignean skepticism of the century before). Thus a significant subset of pre- and postmoderns share a distrust of the quest for certainty.[7] From this perspective, postmodernism emerges less as a new idea or fashionable trend than as a moral and intellectual recovery.

I would therefore stress the alignment of the modernist critique with ethical concerns rather than with aesthetic ones and with the concomitant debates surrounding periodization or artistic technique. The rather singular notion of progress that provided the ideological scaffolding for the construction of the modern nation deserves to be strenuously challenged. Social systems charting their courses toward modernity tended to assume the infallibility of rationality and all that it promised—the rewards of science, the ever-greater power of technology to master nature, the heightened efficiency of the bureaucratic order and the social engineering it made possible. But some contemporary critics have claimed that the Holocaust, Hiroshima, and the Gulag are just as surely (perhaps inevitably) the products of that modernist project as penicillin or the fax machine.[8] Bauman has argued for the Holocaust as "a legitimate resident in the house of modernity; indeed, one who would not be at home in any other house."[9] He describes a system in which citizen-workers find themselves immersed in a complex and functionally differentiated bureaucracy, "distantiated from the ultimate outcomes of the operation to which they contribute," so that their primary concern becomes good performance of the job at hand: "morality boils down to the commandment to be a good, efficient and diligent expert and worker."[10] In such a setting, otherwise moral individuals can manufacture napalm or launch cruise missiles at depersonalized targets.

In general, modernity has been charged with remaining wholly incapable of acknowledging its limitations, its aporias that were assumed to be "momentary lapse(s) of reason soon to be rectified."[11] According to the logic of modernism, if technology created new problems ("final solutions," atomic weapons, ozone depletion), it also contained the power to solve them. But that grand certainty, two hundred years in the making, flourishes no longer. In his *Postmodernism and Its Discontents,* Bauman recites the symptoms: "the paucity of sense, porousness of borders, inconsistency of sequences, [the] capriciousness of logic and frailty of authorities."[12] And though Bauman, a sociologist by training, is most attuned to the moral challenges encountered in the current moment, he reinforces his claims for the "uncertainization" of everyday life through recourse to an analysis of social reality: in France in 1994, 70 percent of all new employment was temporary or fixed term; in the United States, 90 percent of vacancies offered in 1993 were part-time, without insurance or benefits.[13] Moreover, within the professional and managerial ranks, there are fewer guarantees; a greater unpredictability of career paths is evident. For the American working person, as for the Continental philosopher, the grand certitude, product of the modern age, has indeed begun to dissipate.[14]

For the present purposes, it is important that this critique of the modernist project be historicized. The principle of universal reason, touchstone of post-Enlightenment thought, was massively facilitated by the growth and refinement of the nation-state during modernity's two-hundred-year reign. It is here that one encounters the confluence of an incipient documentary project, particularly alive in the Soviet Union and Great Britain in the 1920s and 1930s, with the nation-building imperative of that age. The most ambitious documentary efforts have often coupled a zealotry for science and nation. Dziga Vertov is perhaps exemplary:

> Our path leads through the poetry of machines, from the bungling citizen
> to the perfect electric man.
> In revealing the machine's soul, in causing the worker to love his
> workbench, the peasant his tractor, the engineer his engine—
> we introduce creative joy into all mechanical labor,
> we bring people into closer kinship with machines,
> we foster new people. (1922)[15]

Annette Michelson has noted the irony of Vertov's valorization of the forced industrialization and accelerating bureaucratization of the Soviet Union through his published manifestos and films such as *The Man with a Movie Camera* (1929), *Enthusiasm* (1930), and *Three Songs for Lenin* (1934). For despite his devotion to the "chronicling of the production of the new regime," Vertov was himself soon to be crushed beneath the weight of an increasingly restrictive cultural apparatus and would spend the last two decades of his life fruitlessly awaiting a next opportunity.[16]

But no figure has so defined the "project" of documentary as John Grierson, and few have so relentlessly pursued the promotion and advancement of state aims through their creative practices. During his years heading the film unit for the Empire Marketing Board (1928–1934) and then at the General Post Office (1934–1939), Grierson forged a British documentary film movement. Recruiting talented young men fresh out of Cambridge and adding to their number experienced professionals such as Robert Flaherty and Alberto Cavalcanti, Grierson created a sizable and quite prolific film production group enthusiastic in its pursuit of a single mandate: "to bring the Empire alive."

> We were instructed, in effect, to use cinema, or alternatively to learn to use it, to bring alive the industries, the harvests, the researches, the productions, the forward-looking activities of all kinds; in short, to bring the day-to-day activities of the British Commonwealth and Empire at work into the common imagination. . . . If you are to bring alive—this was the E.M.B. phrase—the material of commerce and industry, the new bewildering world of invention and science and the modern complex of human relationship; if you are to make citizenship in our vast new world imaginative and, therefore, possible, cinema is, on the face of it, a powerful weapon.[17]

Aesthetic experimentation was to take a backseat to the expression of filmic statements that were "honest and lucid and deeply felt and which fulfil the best ends of citizenship"; but the unabashed goal of the unit was "to command, and cumulatively command, the mind of a generation."[18]

Such a pronouncement scarcely sounds innocent. It is no wonder that in the midst of a book devoted primarily to the interrogation of the Griersonian realist documentary project, Brian Winston includes a chapter on the work of Leni Riefenstahl.[19] Winston is concerned to trace the effects of "official" or state-sponsored documentary films, which, he argues, always tend to reinforce the existing social order (and are in this sense necessarily conservative) while consistently "running away from social meaning" (by which he means they refuse a more radical or systemic critique of the social ills they survey). It could certainly be argued that the Griersonians, working mostly for Tory governments, helped to put a friendly face on British imperialism in *Song of Ceylon* (1934) or sell a lukewarm reformism in response to pressing slum clearance questions (*Housing Problems*, 1935). In this sense, Grierson is to be faulted for espousing progressive views while delivering social integrationism and upbeat nation-building rhetoric for conservative British regimes between the wars. But my own concern is for tracking the development of documentary film as a potent and highly persuasive vehicle of social engineering, selling rhetorical arguments as truths, visions of the world as objective accounts of history. From this perspective, the problem with Vertov and Grierson (and, by extension, the documentary film tradition they helped to launch) was their aggressive—indeed, pulverizing—self-assurance in the pursuit of Truth, Soviet-style or Tory.

In Dziga Vertov's hands, documentary may indeed have served the rationalist desire for a totalizing, ever-perfectible vision of the social world. But at the close of this century, the optimism of the moderns has given way to a sense of their project's failure. "Reason has given rise to a secularization of the divine," wrote Hans Richter in the late 1930s. "Our age demands the documented fact. . . . The modern reproductive technology of the cinematograph was uniquely responsive to the need for factual sustenance. The (apparent) incorruptibility of optics guaranteed 'absolute truth.'"[20] Can we detect in Richter's words, his phraseology—"the (apparent) incorruptibility of optics"—a tinge of doubt? Richter wrote these lines in Switzerland shortly before his exile to the United States, fleeing from a totalitarianism that some have called the very apotheosis of the modernist project.

Recent scholarship has provided new insights into documentary's historical role as an instrument of rationality; the critiques offered reveal the underside of this century's scientific quest. Lisa Cartwright has brilliantly traced the foundations of the documentary film as a scientific, deeply disciplinary tool used to penetrate and control (often female) bodies,[21] while Fatimah Tobing Rony has shown that the authority of the ethnographic film was, from its beginnings, predicated on its value as "an unimpeachable scientific index of race."[22] In their writings, Cartwright and Rony remind us that modernity, joyous in its constant reinvention of itself, was always also aggressive, ever in need of new frontiers for conquest. The search was for universal standards consistent with the era's "ambitions of homogeneity."[23] *The* article of modernist faith was *certainty*—absolute and unassailable—manifest in a deep belief in the necessity of order making, in progress, in science as a cumbersome but self-correcting mechanism.

Recall that the version of postmodernity developed here refers primarily to an epistemological position, namely, a critical attitude toward absolutist notions of truth through rationality. It is this understanding of postmodernism as the end of a centuries-long refusal, the termination point of an epistemological blindness that guides this consideration of documentary disavowals. While I don't ignore the psychoanalytic connotations of the concept of disavowal, I will not focus on the specifically Freudian conception of the term via the notion of *Verleugnung*, the splitting of belief in defense of the ego.[24] I wish instead to activate the moral charge attached to the figure of disavowal as a complex mode of refusal to acknowledge or to claim responsibility for the meanings and effects of documentary practices devoted to certitude—sober, certain knowledge—in all its epistemological violence and in all its illusions.[25]

I will focus on recent work in video and computer imaging, electronic, and digital forms that call into question many of the Bazinian precepts that underpin documentary practice—indexicality, the ontological, even spiritual, bond between model and image, a deep-seated faith in realism.[26] For while it may have been faith in God rather than science that impelled Bazin's deeply influential writings, the doctrines of film-as-reliable-index, as relic-of-a-retrievable-past, that Bazin so eloquently espoused have functioned as anchoring points for the documentary tradition's self-assurance. To the modernist admixture of reason and history, Bazin simply added an atavistic measure of faith.

But before turning to the case of digital imaging, I want to consider, if briefly, another act of documentary disavowal, that of one recent critic who has inveighed against theoretical writing on documentary film derived "from postmodernist dogma." In a recent essay, Noël Carroll takes as his goal the refutation of what he calls "overly facile skepticism about the possibility of making motion pictures that are genuinely in the service of knowledge."[27] Carroll argues for the efficacy of "established protocols of inquiry" for documentary practitioners that ensure that they, like their kindred spirits the physicists, bring "standards of objectivity to bear."[28] Carroll characterizes the rising tide of skepticism as "philosophically harmless," refusing, for example, the validity of Hayden White's theorization of historical writing as tropological, reading White's position instead as an argument for narrative-as-distortion.

While I was initially puzzled at Carroll's blanket labeling of recent documentary theory as "postmodernist," I have come to understand its sense. Carroll is an apologist for the documentary project in all its modernist ambitions. Despite the fact that myself, Bill Nichols, and Brian Winston (principal objects of attack) have rarely addressed postmodernism in any direct way in our writings on documentary film, Carroll is not so far off the mark. He is correct to note that much current work on documentary acknowledges the tradition's historical alignment with the dreams of universal reason, its predilection for Truth in History. Contingency, hybridity, knowledge as situated and particular, identity as ascribed and performed (ideas now very much alive in documentary studies) seem out of phase with the quest for standards of objectivity, established protocols of inquiry, the belief in disinterested knowledge—the rationalist principles to which Carroll desperately clings. If contemporary cultural theorists tend to regard these latter ideas with indifference, even bemusement, Carroll's tone is that of the reproachful philosopher, scolding the untutored. But it is important to note that the skepticism within documentary theory to which Carroll so disparagingly refers (his essay's title is "Nonfiction Film and Postmodernist Skepticism")— far from being merely trendy and misbegotten—can claim a philosophical pedigree (e.g., Heraclitus, Socrates, Montaigne) at least as ancient and distinguished as his own. My interest in Carroll's critique is a specific one, though, for I propose that in its unwillingness to acknowledge the limits and liabilities of an instrumental rationality in and for the documentary project, it be viewed as an arch instance of "documentary disavowal."

Although I am making a claim here about digital and computer-based media bearing some sort of epistemic relation to the postmodern turn, I want to steer clear of any totalizing claims. Even a brief consideration of the best known of these globalizing analyses of video will show why. Fredric Jameson's "Video: Surrealism without the Unconscious" has been roundly excoriated by those of longer acquaintance with the medium. Jameson deems video "the richest allegorical and hermeneutic vehicle" for the current cultural hegemony and calls experimental video "rigorously coterminous with postmodernism itself as a historical period. . . . the art form par excellence of late capitalism."[29] The grounds for such a statement, indeed, for the entirety of the argument, are shaky. Jameson begins poorly by conflating artists' video and commercial television as the medium's "twin manifestations." He goes on to suggest, in a manner scandalous to those who have been writing on the subject for twenty years, that there is little extant video theory but offers video's alleged "structural exclusion of memory" as a foundational insight. Critics such as Raymond Bellour, Maureen Turim, Marita Sturken, and Erika Suderburg would reply that memory and its vicissitudes provide the ground on which some of video's most profound mediations have been figured.[30] Jameson thematizes video as tied up with the master trope of "psychic fragmentation" (the best term for "what ails us today"). Wholly shorn of referential anchorage, video is claimed to be constitutionally incapable of possessing documentary value. Moreover, at its core, video is alleged to short-circuit traditional interpretive approaches.

> Now reference and reality disappear altogether, and even meaning—the signified—is problematized. We are left with that pure and random play of signifiers that we call postmodernism, which no longer produces monumental works of the modernist type but ceaselessly reshuffles the fragments of preexistent texts, the building blocks of older cultural and social production, in some new and heightened bricolage . . . such is the logic of postmodernism in general, which finds some of its strongest and most original, authentic forms in the new art of experimental video.[31]

While this characterization helps make coherent Jameson's own project—to territorialize postmodern theory—it obscures a great deal more. Jameson's totalizing claims have little to offer us as we interrogate the radical ambivalence of current video practices' confrontation with historical representation. Yes, many of the ontological, epistemological, and textual standards familiar from the cinema—and wholly critical for the documentary project—have been destabilized by the electronic media. But more salient for understanding video in its epistemic moment are the hinge ideas of ambivalence, of vacillation, undecidability, split belief. In the face of certainty, video introduces not absolute uncertainty (i.e., psychic fragmentation writ large) but rather mutability, skepticism, perhaps even a bemused agnosticism.

In a slightly different register, Zygmunt Bauman has nominated video as the postmodern medium of choice for its relation to the problematic of identity. Although I question the value of any and all globalizing characterizations of media forms, Bauman's account has the advantage of referring less to the medium's intrinsic features than to its materiality and functions; his concern is for videotape as a substrate of discursivity in sync with the current moment. What's more, Bauman chooses to set video against its photographic forebear and in so doing has something to say about the convergence of modernist concerns with those of the documentary project.

> If the *modern* "problem of identity" was how to construct an identity and keep it solid and stable, the *postmodern* "problem of identity" is primarily how to avoid fixation and keep the options open. In the case of identity, as in other cases, the catchword of modernity was "creation"; the catchword of postmodernity is "recycling." Or one may say that if the "media which was the message" of modernity was the photographic paper (think of relentlessly swelling family albums, tracing page by yellowing page the slow accretion of irreversible and non-erasable identity-yielding events), the ultimately postmodern medium is the videotape (eminently erasable and reusable, calculated not to hold anything forever, admitting today's events solely on condition of effacing yesterday's ones, oozing the message of universal "until-further-noticeness" of everything deemed worthy of recording). The main identity-bound anxiety of modern times was the worry about durability; it is the concern with commitment-avoidance today. Modernity built in steel and concrete; postmodernity—in bio-degradable plastic.[32]

In accord with modernism, the documentary idea has depended on preservation, durability, capture. In postmodernity, videotape, notable for its ubiquity, endless receptivity, and ephemerality, seems far less suited to documentary's aggressive assertiveness.

While I am intrigued by Bauman's canny pronouncements, I have little interest in parsing out video's inherent properties, a modernist gambit after all. I am more concerned to analyze the ways that some current applications of digital and electronic media have served to undercut the mastery model endemic to the documentary project, a model I have characterized as deeply rationalist. There is in this a kind of historical irony given that these countermodernist applications have evolved within the very crucible of science. Furthermore, in contrast to Jameson, who offers experimental video as the emblem of psychic fragmentation and hence of our current plight, I am interested in new media practices that, in their representation of the real, undercut certainty of any sort (even the certainty of thematization), casting the viewer/participant adrift in an ocean of possibility. I am tracing a movement from the streamlining of vision toward a singular truth (the identifiably modernist documentary project) to the embrace of ambivalence, multiple, even contradictory, belief.

Despite my attention to these specific applications of digital media, I am not, as I have stressed, claiming that there is anything intrinsic to digital media that promotes skepticism. The most commercial uses of this technology work in the opposite direction, for example, through the use of digital compositing techniques to retouch, color correct, even add new details to the mise-en-scène of commercial motion pictures, always with the intention of a seamless result. Illusion rather than critique is the defining aim of digital tools such as the Quantel Domino system, a sophisticated and very costly device that mobilizes science in the service of seamlessness. In Quantel's eighth edition of *The Digital Fact Book,* under "error detection, concealment and correction," the following can be found:

> No means of digital recording is perfect. Both magnetic tape and disks suffer from a few marginal recording areas where recording and replay is difficult or even impossible. However the errors can be detected and some action taken for a remedy by concealment or correction. The former attempts to hide the problem by making it not so noticeable whereas the latter actually corrects the error so that *perfect data* is output.[33]

The presumption is that "perfect data" produce seamless product, providing motion picture producers with alternatives to reshooting scenes, laboriously dressing sets, or hiring large numbers of extras (now that a handful of extras can be digitally duplicated ad infinitum). We are back to the perfectibility of the visual apparatus à la Vertov, but far from "laying bare the device," as the Russian formalists called for, perfection is defined as invisibility, obfuscation. The moment of critique is notably absent.

The goal of such digital sampling systems, then, is transparency, the ability to simulate the look of film in all its photochemical fidelity to the profilmic. Much of the design and refinement of such systems has focused on this goal, as illustrated in a passage from *Film in the Digital Age,* published by Quantel Ltd. for its clientele: "Study of the spatial and dynamic resolution of film has been an essential part of arriving at a suitable digital sampling format. . . . meaning that the digital system, film-to-film is effectively transparent—not only for scene detail but also for the 'filmic' look."[34] The same can be said for the conversion of analog to digital signals for television broadcast. Analog material is converted to digital (with 16 mm, 35 mm or 70 mm film, if necessary, being transferred to high-quality D2 tape stock), and corrections are made or new material introduced in the digital format before the reconversion to analog. In a manner analogous to the sampling application for feature films, the intent here is to "faithfully reconstruct the original analogue signal."[35]

The rhetoric of transparency suffuses the Quantel manuals.

> For the Domino system to be *transparent* it is not necessary to produce an output negative which matches the original in terms of absolute density, but it must match the dynamic range of the region to be printed.[36]

> It is a prime requirement that the use of Domino should be *transparent* to the printed result—with input and output images matching—so input dynamic range must match output dynamic range.[37]

> The Exposure control provides all that is necessary for *transparent* operation from well produced interpositive material.[38]

Seamlessness announces the successful blending of photographic and digitally produced material so that difference is elided, disbelief suspended. The transparency toward which the Domino system strains is the guarantee of illusion, the creation of an invisibility (a signifying absence) endowed with great exchange value. Perhaps, in this "post-legitimation era," this time of dissipating certainty, of fragmentariness and accentuated difference, what these commercial applications of digital media offer is not in fact a guarantee, only its semblance. This spectral guarantee may be understood as a postmodernist gesture of a very limited sort, one whose moral status must be questioned. These industrial usages exist in contradistinction to another mode of current digital media practice that actively cultivates openness and critique.

I would like now to turn to several instances of work in which some tenets central to the modernist project—certainty, the rule of rationality, the pursuit of discursive mastery—are placed in relief: L.A. Link (1995–1998), Daniel Reeves's *Obsessive Becoming* (1995), and the digital interactive art of Jim Campbell (1991–1994).[39] While the examples given do not conform to traditional documentary formats, each of them engages in the representation of "flesh-and-blood" historical events, persons, or experiences rather than fictional ones; each of them intervenes in our perception or understanding of the social world. I wish to draw out the implications of these critical interventions as evidence of what I take to be a significant trend rebutting modernist practices in the field of historical representation.

The first of these examples is the L.A. Link project, in which I have been engaged for the past two years and about which I have written elsewhere in this book.[40] With the project, Hi-8 images are digitally compressed and transmitted over ISDN lines for decompression and display at distant sites. Using computers and videoconferencing technologies, Los Angeles area teens from diverse backgrounds can see and hear one another in something like real time. The project explores the kind of relationships that can be established over the link, the extent to which creative collaborations are possible, the quality of potential encounters between interlocutors who meet "face to face" but only in cyberspace. I would suggest that L.A. Link operates at a great remove from the modernist documentary ethos. It is interested in opening up a space of interpersonal contact, of receptiveness to and "dwelling with" the other, rather than closing down or refining a path of rational inquiry anchored to a territorializing discourse. L.A. Link functions in accord with the concentrated or productive listening that philosopher Gemma Corradi Fiumara has described as the repressed side of a coercive logos. In *The Other Side of Language: A Philosophy of Listening,* she returns to Heidegger's remarks on the etymological linkage of "logos" (in the Greek, *legein*), whose legacy is principally that of "saying," to the German word *legen,* which means to lay down or lay before. Fiumara argues that logos has, within Western culture, devolved into a "saying-without-listening" that subordinates the sheltering and receptive side of language—fundaments of the maieutic method—to the assertiveness of discourse.[41] And no variant of filmic discourse is more assertive than the documentary that Nichols has famously described as constitutively argument based. I therefore pose the L.A. Link project as a sort of tentative antipode to the documentary project as defined in modernist terms. It is an enterprise intended to explore various electronic technologies' listening potential, their ability to provide a shelter for receptivity rather than a scaffolding for argument or a bridge for spatiotemporal conquest.

I want to say only a few things about Daniel Reeves's remarkable videotape *Obsessive Becoming,* although it certainly deserves far more extended treatment than can be accorded it here. I wish to single out for attention the morphing technique utilized in the tape. In the hands of Daniel Reeves, the digital technology that, as with the Quantel Domino system, has proved capable of seamlessly grafting simulated objects onto indexical representations is used instead to undermine verisimilitude. Reeves has called his approach in this tape "ragged magical realism."[42] Through digitizing numerous photographs of various family members and reconfiguring them as discrete computer files, it became possible for Reeves, laboriously and over a five-year period, to control the rate at which a single photographic image liquefies and congeals into another. Lines of gender and generation no longer hold sway; the traumas of Reeves's own childhood are evoked and yet superseded and transmuted under his meditative gaze. Through hypnotic narration (Reeves's own voicings), the overlay of diverse, often haunting musical phrases, and the fluid intermingling of images, Reeves ushers his audience into a "liminal zone," a space of heightened receptivity.

Reeves's is a worldview aligned with Zen Buddhist principles more

In Daniel Reeves's *Obsessive Becoming*, a single family photo liquefies and congeals into another, crossing lines of gender and generation. Reprinted with permission.

than rationalist ones. He suggests that the genetic material that becomes "us" is but one register of our being; we are the source and temporary container of countless other beings to whom we are linked and thus in some measure responsible. To the strains of the Moscow Liturgic Choir and over a liquid array of morphed visages captured from tattered family albums, Reeves intones the following near the end of *Obsessive Becoming*:

If I raise my hand to the light, I can see my dead mother in the palm. I see the way I spring from her in every moment. I see her face. I see her face before she was born and her face before her father was born. They move together in every moment like a garland of water. And like writing on water that cannot be held, they are always becoming, forever moving, forever entwined.

Here we are far from the genealogical models dear to science that trace heredity as linear and irreversible. Modernism, for its part, has given us the eugenics of textbooks and clinics, irrevocably bound to dreams of racial purity. Reeves shows us the cyclical nature of becoming and re-becoming, doing so most dramatically through the plasticity of his digitized portraitures. In *Obsessive Becoming* as in Bauman's characterization of videotape as postmodernist medium, the self is less the repository of sovereign identity than the site of an endless recycling, a surface "calculated not to hold anything forever." If some manner of radical doubt is engendered regarding absolutist notions of truth or knowledge, the deeper challenge is leveled at the ontological status of the image and of the self that is the image's source.

Jim Campbell, trained as an electrical engineer at MIT, is now among the most accomplished makers of digital interactive art. He is something of a *bricoleur*, using an array of materials both strange and familiar, recycled and custom engineered: from weathered family photographs, a cheap Timex pocket watch, and a bucketful of salt to ultrasonic sensors, self-designed computer programs, and custom electronics. But the real substance of Campbell's installations is ideas yielded through a participant's interaction with the work on display. These ideas are often inchoate; they are about the self in relation to time, memory, and desire. But for the present purposes, Campbell's oeuvre is notable for the way in which devices irreducibly scientific in their provenance are used to thwart the rationalist principles so often attributed to modernism, defying the "human demand for factual sustenance" once described by Richter.

The impact of Campbell's work is entirely bound up with its interactive character. If, as has been suggested here, modernism has engendered a search for authoritative discourses and passive recipients, art tailored to that model has proved adept at creating works of great originality and force that nevertheless function as one-way conduits rather than reciprocal conversations. Art is in this sense yet another variant of the logos as assertive discourse with the listening component repressed. In its interactivity, Campbell's work undermines the hierarchical character of traditional art; it requires the participation of the viewer to create its meaning.

In *Digital Watch* (1991), Campbell creates a warp of time and space into which the participant enters. One black-and-white video camera, mounted at right angles to a fifty-inch rear-projection video monitor, captures a small pocket watch ticking inexorably forward. The closed-circuit display of the much-enlarged watch face dominates the screen. As the participant approaches the screen, a second video camera mounted atop the monitor introduces one's own image into the scene in real time at the edges of the projected image, but with a five-second delay for the portion of the frame overlapping the watch face (thanks to Campbell's algorithmic concoctions). The participant's delayed self-image has the appearance of cinematic step printing; Campbell's custom electronics stutter human movement at the precise rate of the sweep of the watch's second hand. Entering the space of the installation, the interactive participant is propelled into the breach, forced to confront a body marching to the beat of institutionalized time yet radically out of sync with itself. This syncopation of subjective time and space does not result in yet another effect of Jamesonian psychic fragmentation but rather, I would argue, encourages a more open, playful, but still radical doubt born of contradiction. It is technology, after all, that delivers the goods here, throwing the self massively out of joint, but only at the participant's behest.

In another of Campbell's installations, *Shadow (for Heisenberg)* (1993–1994), a figurine of the Buddha in a teaching pose is placed within a glass cube at the far end of a small room. The Buddha is placed atop a sheet of text indecipherable at that distance. As the viewer approaches for a better look, a motion detector triggers the release of LCD (liquid crystal display) material, fogging the glass and obscuring one's view. The closer the approach, the more opaque the recently translucent casing. The reference in the piece's title is to physicist Werner Heisenberg's uncertainty principle, the proposition that the very act of observing and measuring a phenomenon alters it, a theorem that implanted a seed of doubt at the heart of empirical proof. *Shadow (for Heisenberg)* forces desire to consciousness, drawing our attention to an epistephilic demand, only to stymie it. It performs sadistically on the gaze producing, if Laura Mulvey is right, a perfectly reflexive gesture. The piece, savagely comic, may produce discomfort in some just as Maurice Blanchot might have predicted: "So an art which has no answers but only questions, which even questions the existence of art, cannot fail to be seen as disturbing, hostile and coldly violent."[43]

Campbell, who has spoken of his desire to create interactive works that are "responsive" rather than "controllable,"[44] is interested in promoting dialogue between the artwork and the user rather than reproducing models of mastery and submission as has been the case for so many computer-based applications. With the dialogue model, the participant engages in an encounter with the art device in which the progress and

In Jim Campbell's *Shadow (for Heisenberg)*, an epistephilic demand is stymied. Images reprinted with permission.

outcome of the interaction depend upon, and are sensitively calibrated to, the choices made by the participant. The machine "listens" to its other and responds rather than delivering one out of a menu of preprogrammed mechanical replies.

> I find it useful to put interactive work on a dynamic spectrum with controllable systems on one end and responsive systems on the other. In controllable systems the actions of the viewer correlate in a one-to-one way with the reaction of the system. Interactive CD-ROM's are on this end of the spectrum and generally speaking so are games. In responsive systems the actions of the viewer are interpreted by the program to create the response of the system. . . . If a work is responding in a predictable way, and the viewer becomes aware of the correlation between their action and the work's response to their action then they will feel that they are in control and the possibility of dialogue is lost. The first time I walked through an automatic door at the supermarket I thought the door was smart and was responding to me. Now I step on the mat to open the door on purpose. The point is that often the first time an interface is experienced it's perceived as being responsive but if the interface is experienced again it becomes controllable. The second time it's not a question but a command.[45]

Campbell's explanation helps us to see that it is not the newness of the technology that should govern the critic's determination of the "postness" of the work, the status of the digital or computer-driven application as postmodern aesthetic practice; it is rather the relation to knowledge and the power dynamics it entails. Which is to say that postmodern art, like postmodernity itself, cannot be periodized through recourse to chronology alone (i.e., art made after the end of modernism). Campbell's work, like L.A. Link and Reeves's *Obsessive Becoming,* fashions itself as dialogue rather than as aggressive, pulverizing discourse. His installations require an active but receptive engagement with their participant other. The actions of the other are interpreted by the system along a continuum of response, sensitively calibrated and reversible at every moment. This openness of the text, its incorporation of response capable of altering the path of the work, reconfirms its distance from the single-minded self-assuredness of the documentary tradition. Grierson saw the cinema as a pulpit from which to espouse values, the camera as a hammer through which to shape public opinion. Documentary practitioners have frequently assumed their right to didacticism based on assumptions of truth (through rigorous methods of research or fidelity to political doctrine) or at least standards of objectivity. The recent work to which I have been referring offers dramatic reappraisal of that tradition.

In the current moment, there is, to be sure, far less consensus around standards, far more doubt as to the reliability of systems of thought or social organization. As Zygmunt Bauman has argued in the case of postmodern ethics, this unraveling of consensus presents an opportunity as much as a challenge in that it returns moral responsibility to the individual rather than to the ethical system—which is where that responsibility rightly belongs. In a comparable manner, these current instances of electronically and digitally based representations of the historical real have begun to shed the epistemological and ethical burden of single-minded truth telling, the mainstay of one hundred years of documentary practice deeply linked to the modernist project. Instead they have opened up a field of uncertain but open-ended exploration that sets aside rational proof in favor of receptivity, understanding that, as moral philosopher Emmanuel Levinas has described, "problems of knowledge and truth must . . . be put in relation to the event of meeting and dialogue."[46]

According to this view, then, documentative work that invites radical doubt, ambivalence, and the embrace of contingency rather than certain knowledge should not be viewed as simply fashionable or facile in its skepticism. Its value exists both as challenge and affirmation: provocative in its refusal of individualist truth, profoundly moral in its call for, and reliance on, individual moral responsibility.

[**9**] <u>Technology and Ethnographic Dialogue</u>

Originally presented at Visible Evidence IV (Cardiff, 1996), "Technology and Ethnographic Dialogue" pursues the ethical dimension of documentary discourse, as in the previous chapter. My thinking here is deeply indebted to the writings of the late ethical philosopher Emmanuel Levinas, who, in daring to challenge rational inquiry as an absolute good, points to the violence inherent in the acquisitive, totalizing quest for knowledge ("an appropriation of what is, an exploitation of reality"). But what is proposed in its stead? What is "the mode of thought better than knowledge" to which Levinas alludes, and how can it be approached through an aesthetic practice such as documentary filmmaking in which (documentary) "subjects" are transformed into "objects" (of knowledge)? In his books, Levinas chooses infinity, that which "escapes all human calculation," over totality, charging the subject with an ethical obligation, an "unlimited responsibility" for the Other. It is the stuff of weighty philosophical inquiry. But what lessons can be learned for the construction of the subject in documentary discourse? What follows is less an attempt to offer answers than to lay the groundwork for a deeper consideration of the ethical conditions that surround the documentary project. My tentative insights are offered in relation to the L.A. Link project, in which teens from diverse backgrounds communicated with each other over a several-month period through a real-time videoconferencing hookup. With L.A. Link, Levinas's belief in the power of the face-to-face "encounter" and its possibilities for human exchange was tested in a novel, technology-driven setting.

An order higher than knowing. An order that, resounding like a call, touches the human in his individuality. . . . From unique

*to unique, from one to the other . . . the wonder of a mode of
thought better than knowledge.*
:: Emmanuel Levinas, *Outside the Subject*

For the past several decades there has been considerable debate around
the status, even legitimacy, of the "human" in the humanities. In the late
1960s, Louis Althusser went so far as to argue that the crucial theoretical
task of the Communist movement, in its struggle against the bourgeois
and petit bourgeois world outlook, was to combat the effects of econo-
mism on the one hand and humanism on the other.[1] While there is no
doubt that Althusserian scientism long ago relinquished its hold on film
theory, the move in film studies both toward cognitivism and empirically
based ethnographic research testifies to the lure that the "harder" sciences
have for media studies. Moreover, the explosion of computer-mediated
communication and its study have placed technology—the digital, the virtual, the hypertextual—at the center of emerging media discourses, with
humanist or community issues frequently rendered peripheral.[2] And yet,
in the face of this empirical turn, many questions have been raised about
the status and effects of the knowledge that can be produced within the
human sciences.

The problem has been posed in various ways: To what extent is
epistemological certainty itself credible in postmodernity, and on what
grounds? To what extent can we speak of a *violence* associated with the
production of cultural knowledge?[3] Might not there be other valued registers of experience not derived from rationalist inquiry? While these doubts
have gathered momentum in philosophy, anthropology, and across cultural studies, a resilient tendency in film studies, best typified by Bordwell
and Carroll's recent *Post-Theory*, has argued against such skepticism. But
the knowledge debate is severely impoverished when limited to the terms
provided by scientific method and verifiable evidence. What if, as Levinas
argues, there is a mode of thought outside the domain of rationality, one
that is "better than knowledge," to which we in the world of media studies might profitably attend?

A return to the passage from Levinas with which we began allows
us to consider the aims of our research within the human sciences—
research, you will recall, in which technology plays an increasingly central role—from a relatively unaccustomed vantage point, that offered by
moral philosophy. "It is not a question of putting knowledge in doubt,"
writes Levinas. "The human being clearly allows himself to be treated as
an object, and delivers himself to knowledge in the *truth* of perception
and the light of the human sciences. But, treated exclusively as an object,

man is also mistreated and misconstrued. . . . We are human before being learned, and remain so after having forgotten much."[4]

In a series of texts written over several decades, Levinas has suggested that a crucial element of our humanness eludes the very project of rational inquiry, the knowledge-producing enterprise that Stephen Toulmin, in a rather different context, has traced back to the twin pillars of modern thought: modern science as inaugurated by Isaac Newton and modern philosophy and the method of reflection initiated by René Descartes.[5] Levinas has proposed a *phenomenology of the other* through which the fundamental condition of alterity can be grasped, creating a metaphysics that affirms the philosophical primacy of the idea of infinity over that of totality, human or divine. His is a system of thought that, while accounting for the temptation to reduce difference to sameness (the "imperialism of the same"), offers the hope of a coexistence in which otherness can remain intact. As Levinas attempts to demonstrate in *Totality and Infinity,* all knowing, indeed the ontological status of the subject, "already presupposes the idea of infinity." This turns out to be an argument in favor of ethics over epistemology in which the terms "totality" and "infinity" bear the weight of centuries of philosophical debate. Totality is understood to be the province of systematic knowledge, that is, reason. It is moreover aligned with freedom, but a freedom that levels all in its path: "That reason in the last analysis would be the manifestation of a freedom, neutralizing the other and encompassing him, can come as no surprise once it was laid down that sovereign reason knows only itself, that nothing other limits it."[6]

The infinite, for its part, is a more elusive term. It is "non-thematizable, [it] gloriously exceeds every capacity";[7] "Whether great or small, the Infinite escapes all human calculation";[8] "the infinite is the absolutely other."[9] Above all else, infinity is predicated on the inescapable encounter with the absolutely Other. The awareness of alterity provokes a responsibility for the Other ("The unlimited responsibility in which I find myself comes from the hither side of my freedom, from a 'prior to every memory'"),[10] an ethical obligation, and it is for this reason that infinity is aligned with justice. In an extended formulation, Levinas argues that the relation with the absolutely other leads to a metaphysical transcendence that dissolves the traditional opposition between theory and practice: "The aspiration to radical exteriority . . . the respect for this metaphysical exteriority which, above all, we must 'let be,' constitutes truth."[11] Levinas, like Lacan, thus argues for the Other as the precondition for the self ("Being in general cannot *dominate* the relationship with the Other. The latter relationship commands the first")[12] but on ethical rather than psychoanalytic grounds.[13]

In a move of astounding import, metaphysics displaces ontology; freedom—the imperative to maintain oneself against the other—gives way to justice. Why? "'I think' comes down to 'I can,'" writes Levinas, "to an appropriation of what is, to an exploitation of reality. Ontology as first philosophy is a philosophy of power. . . . Possession is preeminently the form in which the other becomes the same, by becoming mine."[14] Justice, on the other hand, depends on the willingness to *receive* from the Other beyond the capacity of the I. This relation is an ethical one and is epiphanous: "reason, without abdicating, is found to be in a position to *receive*."[15]

Language emerges as the constitutive medium in the *relation* between self and Other. Influenced by, but recasting the thought of, Martin Buber, Levinas argues that "persons who speak to one another confirm one another, unique and irreplaceable. . . . Never coincidence, always proximity. . . . The problems of knowledge and truth must thus be put in relation to the event of meeting and dialogue."[16] It is in this attribution of primacy to the relation, the meeting, the encounter, that Levinas comes to place great emphasis on the notion of "face-to-face," which he defines not as a modality of coexistence or even of the knowledge one can have of another but as "the primordial production of being on which all the possible collocations of the terms are founded."[17] The face becomes the very figure of the infinite: "the way in which the other presents himself, exceeding *the idea of the other in me*."[18] The meeting—"face-to-face"—is an encounter of unique beings that respects both separation and proximity; it is a breach of totality in which "thought finds itself *faced* with an other refractory to categories."[19]

But how do these concerns for a Levinasian metaphysics relate to the "trouble with ethnography," those myriad challenges to ethnography raised since the mid-1980s? In what follows, I will first suggest the relevance of Levinasian principles to the project of the ethnographic film, then explore a particular case study, L.A. Link, in which the intersubjective relations familiar from the ethnographic tradition—subject/object, knower/known—give way to a dynamic of the dialogue, the face-to-face encounter. I will close by returning to the question of new communications technology, originally posed as a diversion from humanistic concerns, in order to suggest some possibilities for a fruitful engagement of technology and ethics.

In his "Beyond Observational Cinema," written more than twenty-five

years ago, David MacDougall assailed the standard method of the ethnographic filmmaker, which, he argued, "reaffirms the colonial origins
of anthropology."[20] MacDougall took note of the "distinctively Western
parochialism" of the observational film in which the maker, pretending
invisibility, translates and reshapes cultural otherness. In doing so, he
mimes the omniscience of conquerer or expert. It is Levinas's "imperialism of the same" as filmmaking practice.

MacDougall echoes the terms that Buber and Levinas have so forcefully introduced into ethical philosophy: meeting, encounter, dialogue.

> The traditions of science and narrative art combine in this instance to
> dehumanize the study of man. It is a form in which the observer and the
> observed exist in separate worlds, and it produces films that are mono-
> logues. . . . No ethnographic film is merely a record of another society: it is
> always a record of the meeting between a filmmaker and that society. If eth-
> nographic films are to break through the limitations inherent in their present
> idealism, they must propose to deal with that encounter. Until now they have
> rarely acknowledged that an encounter has taken place.[21]

Seen from the current vantage point, MacDougall's essay offers a political
and theoretical rationale for the historical movement from the observational mode of documentary exposition to the interactive and reflexive. But
can we say that the quality of "encounter" as a breach of totality can be
imputed to the succeeding modes of documentary exposition, even to the
performative that Bill Nichols has most recently deemed the fifth mode?[22]

While the acknowledgment of self in relation to other that we associate with the later modes may have signaled a significant movement beyond
the effacement of enunciative agency, we must distinguish between the
foregrounding of the appropriative gesture and its elimination. In the interactive, reflexive, and performative modes, the viewer is far more likely
to understand the formal and ideological conditions within which the
process of production occurs but the film remains, for all that, the con-
ceptualization of the maker. Can we imagine that, following these methods, thought finds itself faced with an other refractory to categories? We
know how easily the subject of documentary discourse is transformed into
witness or symptom for purposes of persuasion; in other instances, the
expressivity of gesture, setting, or the very surface of the image becomes
an aesthetic end in itself. In such cases, the quality of listening, of receptiveness, called for in the encounter is unlikely to occur. In Levinasian
terms, these later modes, like the expository mode before them, produce
works that can surely be deemed acts of possession of the other, appropriations of what is, exploitations of reality. But are these not the ethical
limits within which all ethnographic practice must reside? Is this not the

price of any textual authorship? Can any documentary act hope to escape unscathed?

But our queries are prematurely posed. To refine our understanding of the prospects for ethnographic dialogue, let us return to our sources and briefly consider what Martin Buber meant by "meeting" or "encounter." Writing in the 1930s, Buber called for a philosophical anthropology that, in seeking to answer Kant's question "What is man?", moved beyond the two prevailing methods or worldviews: individualism and collectivism. Modern individualism was said to be a glorification of the despair of man's solitary state, while collectivism, though embracing the masses, failed as "a joining of man to man." In its pledge to provide total security, collectivism "progressively deadened or desensitized" that "tender surface of personal life which longs for contact with other life."[23] Instead Buber valorized neither the individual nor the aggregate but rather what he called "the sphere of 'between'": "It is rooted in one being turning to another as another . . . in order to communicate with it in a sphere which is common to them but which reaches out beyond the special sphere of each." Only in such a circumstance is "real conversation" possible, and here we might want to pose this construct alongside the standards of the ethnographic film. "Real conversation" is one whose individual parts have not been "preconcerted, but one which is completely spontaneous, in which each speaks directly to his partner and calls forth his unpredictable reply. . . . it takes place between them in the most precise sense, as it were in a dimension which is accessible only to them both."[24]

Given such a description, it is difficult to imagine what a "real conversation" or dialogue might be on film or tape. Even if the exchange were to escape the preconceptions or dictates of one or another of the interlocutors, and even were the final product to be jointly edited, its spontaneity and unpredictability could only occur in real time. Indeed, the examples Buber gives of such meetings tend to be the "tiniest and most transient events which scarcely enter the consciousness," as in the chance encounter of two strangers who "suddenly meet for a second in astonishing and unrelated mutuality" in an air-raid shelter or concert hall.[25] It is likely that the meeting Buber has in mind could never coexist with the conditions of reproducibility (not to mention commodification) that the documentary form bears with it. Moreover, the sphere of "between," the stepping into a living relation with another human being as Buber describes it, cannot exist for others; it must occur in "a dimension which is accessible *only to them both.*"

It might, however, be possible to consider the Buberian encounter as a kind of ethical limit case or asymptote against which a particular documentative practice can be measured, in this case, L.A. Link. L.A. Link is a project that connects teens from diverse backgrounds through computer and videoconferencing technologies whose on-line phase occurred from February to May 1996. It is a collaboration among video artist Wendy Clarke, media theorist Marita Sturken, and myself, supported by a grant from the Annenberg Center for Communication with some additional funding from the AT&T Foundation. Two very diverse sites with five participants each, aged fourteen to eighteen, were chosen. Crossroads School is a progressive private school (K–12) located in Santa Monica with an especially strong arts program including six film studies courses. KAOS Network is a media arts center in the Crenshaw District of South Central L.A., founded by UCLA film school–trained Ben Caldwell well over a decade ago. KAOS has recently attracted considerable local media attention for its "Project Blowed," featuring weekly open-mike sessions for rap and spoken-word artists. The two sites are separated less by geography than by socially constructed barriers of race and class of the sort that have historically fueled civil unrest in L.A.

The basis of the apparatus is a codec system capable of compressing the electronic signal, allowing it to pass through multiple ISDN (Integrated Services Digital Network) Basic Rate Interface (BRI) lines at a rate of 384 kilobytes per second before decompressing it for display at the other end. Users are thus able to talk with and see one another in something very close to real time. The frame rate of the display depends entirely on the data rate: the more information passing over the lines, the closer the frame rate to the thirty-frames-per-second standard of broadcast television. (For lots of reasons, L.A. Link's frame rate is closer to fifteen frames per second.) The apparatus supporting L.A. Link was designed by Richard Williams, a Santa Monica computer engineer and entrepreneur whose codec system is PC based, unlike those of his larger corporate rivals, Panasonic and PictureTel. Thus our system is first and foremost a computer with software programs that allow us to input external sound and image sources. Hi-8 cameras are used at both sites to produce the signal transmitted over the ISDN lines, document every aspect of the process, and allow all participants to keep diaries to share with others or keep for themselves. An essential element of all teleconferencing systems is their ability to produce simultaneous images of self and other, often through a PIP (picture-in-picture) feature, the typical format being a small rectangle from one's own site contained within the larger rectangular image source received from the other end. With the L.A. Link computer-based system, the formatted contours and relative size of the images from both sites can be controlled as windows on the respective computer screens.

There were many kinds of exchanges over the link given the primary goal of exploring the effects of on-line as opposed to face-to-face encounters among the teens. Another large aim of the project was to engender creative collaborations across the gaps of space and cultural difference. To these ends, a great deal of time was spent in the first months with one-on-ones, that is, relatively open-ended private conversations between individuals from either site with no others present. Participants had the opportunity to engage in periodic exchanges of this sort with everyone at the other site. The teens were indeed face-to-face, or perhaps more correctly, face-by-face. What do I mean by this?

One of the real breakthroughs of a link project of this sort is the transformation of the screen itself into a simultaneous amalgam of window and mirror. It is a window into another space, onto another subjectivity; it is also a mirror in which one sees the self projected, in minute and unflinching detail. The doubling of the window and mirror functions produces an effect that I believe is altogether unprecedented. During the on-line one-on-one sessions during which participants come to know one another, self and other are structured through the representational apparatus as equivalent, coequal (though fluid as to relative image size). Each exists for the self *exactly* as she does for the other; each sees herself *exactly* as she is seen, knowing that the same holds true for both parties. There is no parallax effect, no reverse angles possible. Two people share equal footing in a virtual terrain. The temporality of the exchange is markedly present tense. It is who you are for the other at that moment that counts, not your future aspirations or your past accomplishments. What matters the most is the degree to which you are open to the encounter, willing to expose parts of yourself and to hear the same from others. For it is through the sharing of intimacies that a "therapeutic spiral" is effected in which the openness of the one induces ever greater openness in the other.[26] Upon closer inspection, the temporality of the encounter, markedly present tense for the interlocutors, slips away from a simple designation ("immemorial, unrepresentable . . . the past that bypasses the present, the pluperfect past"); it is of the order of infinity.[27] As we shall see, however, pastness (and totality) intervene when the encounter is made to respond to the demand for reproducibility.

Without question, there is something new and transformative about the possibilities of computer-mediated "face-to-face" encounters. Might these exchanges be said to offer the possibility for the sort of non-preconceived and spontaneous encounters that Buber describes as the basis of the meeting or dialogue? Did these meetings exist in a sphere of "between," accessible only to the interlocutors themselves? Was there here the potential for proximity without the violence of appropriation? For the most part, the answers are probably no, and for several reasons. In the first place, there was no avoiding the sense of a laboratory setting for these dialogues. Given the group dynamic—two after-school meetings a week, always the same participants—there could be no chance encounters, no evanescent moments in which glances could meet and souls commune. There were, doubtless, occasional sparks of fellow feeling or special communion experienced. And the air of spontaneity was ever present, though the affective ambience often seemed more a mix of chaos and ennui than soulful improvisation. Furthermore, the encounters were, by definition, accessible to anyone who viewed the tapes. The only private materials were the video diaries each participant kept. The one-on-ones were never monitored, nor have they been publicly screened thus far, but some sort of exhibition was always intended. This was a case of balancing the privacy of the exchanges with their heuristic value. We had set out to address a series of questions, after all: Can computer-mediated face-to-face encounters provide a useful or meaningful avenue for human interaction? What are the character and limitations of such relationships? Can people create collaboratively in such circumstances?

The answers to all such questions would need to be demonstrable in some way, and there we, the investigators, were faced with an encounter of our own—with totality. Just as Levinas had described the process, human beings were being delivered to knowledge in the name of the human sciences. The Other, far from remaining refractory to all categories, was instead the "living proof" of the efficacy of computer-mediated communication technology. For while otherness may have been respected for its simultaneous proximity and radical exteriority by the participants in the initial encounter, the overall design of the project demanded that every moment of dialogue be made to submit to a totalizing impulse of a second order, along the lines of Barthes's sign-to-myth model from *Mythologies*.[28] If the investigators were to share the results of our experiment in interpersonal communication, we simply couldn't "let be" the fragile alterity of our subjects. How could we show the world, our funders, our scholarly peers—indeed, *you*—the evidence of our experiment in metaphysics if we eschewed reproducibility?

Recall, however, that I posed Buber's and Levinas's notion of the encounter or dialogue as a kind of ethical asymptote, which, as Webster's tells us, is a straight line always approaching but never meeting a curve, a tangent at infinity. And it is precisely infinity that is at stake in this formulation, for that is the term Levinas chooses to oppose to the totalizing grasp of certitude. Infinity, the very condition of transcendence, is posed in terms of a desire that no satisfaction can arrest (again, the Lacanian parallels are striking). Given the conditions of capture and reproducibility that govern nonfiction media, we can assume that no documentative practice can meet the ethical standards of the encounter, simulating a mode of thought better than knowledge. Yet if we wish to explore the ethical dimension of documentary practices in this way, it may be useful to measure particular instances against the metaphysical limit I have described. The work of certain communication theorists suggests that there are indeed significant ethical distinctions to be made among media forms.

James W. Carey has distinguished between two alternative conceptions of communication alive in American culture since the nineteenth century.[29] On the one hand, there is the transmission view of communication, in which power or control is always at stake. According to this paradigm, communication is important because, through the use of "space-binding media" such as the telegraph, telephone, radio, television, or computer, territorial claims can be expanded, the scale of social organization enlarged. This is the majority view in the United States and is consistent with the pursuit of what Carey calls a "high communications policy" aimed solely at spreading messages further in space while reducing the cost (and time) of transmission. The second, minoritarian conception, the ritual view of communication, is linked to terms such as "sharing," "participation," and "the possession of a common faith"; it plays upon the etymological proximity of "communication" with "community." According to this model, the spatial imperative is less important than the temporal dimension; the maintenance of society and its values in time takes precedence over the "calculus of commercialism and expansionism."[30] It is not the imparting of information that counts so much as the representation of shared beliefs; the archetypal case under the ritual view is "the sacred ceremony that draws persons together in fellowship and commonality."[31]

L.A. Link conforms to the ritual view.[32] This experiment in computer-mediated communication technology, though it displays the capacity to bind space, to expand the physical limits of the face-to-face encounter, serves neither commercialism nor expansionism. L.A. Link explored a new species of dialogic encounter, creating a vehicle of communication both for the eye and the ear. But despite the unyielding fascination with the yoked image of self and other that the apparatus makes possible, it is the ear that dominates. L.A. Link, at its best, was a tool for reception, for listening. Such a circumstance is consistent with the Levinasian critique of vision as totalizing. Levinas wrote that ethics is an optics, but "it is a 'vision' without image, bereft of the synoptic and totalizing objectifying virtues of vision."[33] Audition, in its intransitivity, is a laying open of the self, a voluptuousness of listening.[34]

Inspired by the early writings of John Dewey, Carey has argued that problems of communication are linked to problems of community. All models of communication have different ethical implications because they produce different forms of social relations. In the case of L.A. Link, the social relations produced are dialogic, rooted in the face-to-face experience, yet novel in their hybridization of human and electronic connection. At least potentially, distance and intimacy are fused. The distance is the result of the bar to physical contact, nearness the result of an intensity of discourse, a zeroing in on the other's affective domain.[35] While neither L.A. Link nor any documentative format can ever achieve the transcendent moral status of the Buberian or Levinasian encounter, arriving at that order of experience higher than knowing, L.A. Link's ethical aspirations and complex potentialities are perhaps its chief contribution to the field of media studies. Moreover, it is absolutely crucial that ethical discourse never be allowed to drop out in our rush toward the technologized future and in our research related to these emergent practices. It is perhaps in this way that we can hope to retain something of the human for the human sciences.

[10] The Address to the Other: Ethical Discourse in Everything's for You

Like the previous two chapters, "The Address to the Other" explores ethical questions pertinent to the making and study of the documentary film. The focus here is on Abraham Ravett's Everything's for You *(1989), a film that seeks to create a dialogue between the filmmaker and his deceased father, a man who survived Auschwitz but lost his first wife and two children. Shot over a fifteen-year period, completed years after the elder Ravett's death,* Everything's for You *is a meditation on a father/son relationship, on an unspeakable and inaccessible history, and on the potential for film to reanimate the past. The film reminds us that autobiography, as the encounter between self and other, can be ethically charged in profound ways. For in addition to being an act of historical recovery, self-expression, and memorialization, the autobiographical film can also be a debt fulfilled. Here,* Everything's for You *serves as a locus for the teachings and insights of Emmanuel Levinas, who asserts that "nonindifference to the other" is the very precondition for the construction of subjectivity.*

> The other is in me and in the midst of my very identification.
> :: Emmanuel Levinas, *Otherwise Than Being, or Beyond Essence*

The work of Emmanuel Levinas attracts our attention today because of his elevation of the ethical domain over the generally privileged philosophical categories of "being" and "knowing." This prioritizing of the ethical could have important consequences for documentary theory, whose most notable debates have focused on the ontological status of nonfiction discourse and on its claims to truth and knowledge—in short, on "being" and "knowing." In what follows, I will pursue ethical concerns, beginning with a schematic description of the Levinasian view before turning to a single film, *Everything's for You* (1989), by Abraham Ravett, in which the ethical dimension emerges as the film's chief concern. In this way, I hope to contribute to the larger project of placing ethics squarely at center stage of documentary studies.

In his *Totality and Infinity* and *Otherwise Than Being, or Beyond Essence,* as elsewhere, Levinas argues boldly for the primacy of justice over freedom, for responsibility, being-for-the-other, as predating consciousness. According to Levinas, the encounter with the other, the ethical encounter, antedates and is the very precondition of the construction of subjectivity, for being-in-itself. This encounter, effected through proximity, uncovers a receptivity, a primordial vulnerability to the other, and in the process the self discovers its substitutability for its neighbor. In this formative moment of the one-for-the-other, signification with its play of endless substitutions is born. Thus, before being, before language, before subjectivity, before knowledge, there is this encounter with radical exteriority, with obligation and with the Good. This encounter defies logic.

> It is not because the neighbor would be recognized as belonging to the same genus as me that he concerns me. He is precisely other. The community with him begins in my obligation to him. . . . The neighbor assigns me before I designate him. This is a modality not of a knowing, but of an obsession, a shuddering of the human quite different from cognition. Knowing is always convertible into creation and annihilation.[1]

This "nonindifference to the other" is the founding moment of self-hood. "Responsibility," "obligation," "sacrifice," "indebtedness"—these are the terms of the ethical encounter, while knowledge comes to be construed as appropriative, aggressive, territorializing, even violent. It is worth noting that *Otherwise Than Being, or Beyond Essence,* the book from which the foregoing quotation is excerpted, bears the following dedication: "To the memory of those who were closest among the six million assassinated by the National Socialists, and of the millions on millions of all confessions and all nations, victims of the same hatred of the other man, the same anti-semitism" (v). "Knowing is always convertible into creation and annihilation," writes Levinas, the former Nazi labor camp prisoner. One hears the echoes here of many scholars of the Holocaust, among them Raoul Hilberg, Jean-François Lyotard, and Zygmunt Bauman, who have termed the Final Solution—genocide as a finely tuned machine, authorized and ennobled by the state—the very apotheosis of the modernist project. In this sense, the philosophical writings of Levinas are indissociable from their historical moment. Yet Levinasian ethics do not indict knowledge in toto so much as they register concern for the primacy accorded to rationalist pursuits. For Levinas, knowledge is aggressive and self-aggrandizing, in the service of the ego. Yet the subject also holds the potential for an emptying of its being, a turning itself inside out, pursuing in its subjection to responsibility the underside of being, the "otherwise than being."

This pitting of ethics against epistemology is highly pertinent for documentary studies. When we talk about the prospects for documentary representation, we are most likely asking about knowledge: what can we know of history from this film, what can we learn about this person or that event, how persuaded can we be by this filmmaker's rhetorical ploys? The ethical view refuses this appropriative stance, choosing instead receptivity and responsibility, justice over freedom. "The more I return to myself, the more I divest myself, under the traumatic effect of persecution, of my freedom as a constituted, willful, imperialist subject, the more I discover myself to be responsible; the more just I am, the more guilty I am. I am 'in myself' through the others" (112).

Recall, in this regard, that it is the Holocaust that has been viewed by Hayden White as the event that has "jammed the system" of historiographical knowledge in the current epoch, unmooring "fact" and "event" from their certain anchorage in historical discourse.[2] Too many details to chronicle, too many frames of reference to choose the definitive one, too much trauma blocking memory, too few surviving witnesses to narrate. Dori Laub, a psychoanalyst and cofounder of the Video Archive for Holocaust Testimonies at Yale University, has characterized the Holocaust as an absolutely unassimilable event because it was "an event without a witness," and here he refers both to those who perished and to those for whom painful memories are foreclosed.[3] If, as George Steiner has proposed, "the world of Auschwitz lies outside speech as it lies outside reason,"[4] the Holocaust offers itself as aporia for aesthetic representation just as it does for historiography. In the words of Lyotard, Holocaust art "does not say the unsayable, but says that it cannot say it."[5]

It is here at the junction of ethics and the unrepresentable that we return to Abraham Ravett's *Everything's for You,* a work that reflects upon the filmmaker's relationship with his deceased father, Chaim Ravett, a man who survived both the Lodz Ghetto and Auschwitz but lost his "first family," a wife and two young children. Shot and edited over a fifteen-year period, the film depends upon Ravett's retrospection, his need to revisit footage shot years before and to reexamine his highly charged relationship with his father. *Everything's for You* was prompted in part by the discovery, years after the elder Ravett's death, of several old family photographs of Chaim and his first family. It is these relics of an unknowable past, a time of which Chaim could not speak even while alive, that prompt the filmmaker's reveries. The film is more a vehicle for meditation than a source of knowledge for either the film's maker or its audience. As with other instances of Holocaust art, there can be no question of "knowing" the elder Ravett's experience, of ever penetrating the "gaping, vertiginous black hole" that is the trauma of the ghetto and the camp.[6] Dori Laub has described the relationship that the children of concentration camp survivors bear toward the unspeakable past of their forebears: "It is thus that the place of the greatest density of silence—the place of concentration where death took place—paradoxically becomes, for those children of survivors, the only place which can provide an access to the life that existed before their birth."[7] Laub describes the need to listen through this silence, through the black hole of knowledge and of words. This prescription aptly describes the Levinasian idea of proximity, the call for a communication with the other effected through an openness and a passivity, a state in which the self is an unconditional hostage, responsible for the other "to the point of substitution."[8]

In such a situation, knowledge little avails. Abraham Ravett speaks intermittently on the sound track over black-and-white images of old Jewish men sitting in the park—in Yiddish, his father's first tongue. His address is equivocal, repetitive, inconclusive. How could it be otherwise?

> Now I see. Now I see everything. I understand now a little more. Now I see. It was so hard for you to tell me that you loved me. It was hard for me to let you know I loved you. I don't understand it now. I don't understand it. What were you afraid of? What can I know? I can't know anything. You were always quiet. You sat so quietly. I knew that you were. . . . I knew that something was brewing inside you. You always sat so quietly. You never said anything. You always sat so quietly. You never said anything. Now I remember. Now I remember.

Within a matter of moments, Ravett can see, can see everything, can understand a little more, can't understand, can know nothing, and can at last remember. But remember what? That his father could not speak. We are returned to the aporetic character of Holocaust art, to art "which does not say the unsayable, but says that it cannot say it."

Judged by standards derived from epistemology, this would have to be termed unreliable narration, no basis for knowledge. But we would do better to consider this narration in relation to Holocaust testimony, as second-generation testimony made possible through a kind of substitution of the self for the other that Levinas describes as the sine qua non of responsibility. The son's equivocal speech attempts to speak through the silence, offering itself as a testimony that, in Laub's terms, finds its truth

From Abraham Ravett's *Everything's for You* (1989). The film is more a vehicle for meditation than a source of knowledge for either the filmmaker or the audience.

through a commitment to "a passage through, an exploration of, differences, rather than an exploration of identity."[9] These spoken words indeed offer passage, oscillating rather than zeroing in, narrating inconclusiveness rather than deducing identity. The words are directed toward a father, now beyond the reach of words, for whom words offered little solace or understanding even in life. This narration is also self-directed, an act of mourning, but it is also for us.

I would like now to close with a meditation of my own, on the title of Ravett's film, which is, it seems to me, the most Levinasian of titles. This tack will display, I confess, an obsession for interpretation on what might be considered a fine point, the film's three-word title, but it is in keeping with my subject. "You don't have to be Jewish to be a compulsive interpreter," writes Harold Bloom, "but, of course, it helps."[10] "Everything's for you" says *being* in its abjection before the other. Taken by surprise, the subject is at once obliged without that obligation having begun in her, "as though," writes Levinas, "an order slipped into my consciousness like a thief, smuggled itself in . . . [from] 'who knows where.'"[11] The self, seized through an involuntary election, is charged with a responsibility that alters being irrevocably and from which compassion, solidarity, and social justice emerge. "Everything's for you" might be the shorthand for this ethical scenario. But how precisely are we to understand this injunction here? Who speaks, and to whom, and what are the implications that this unqualified gift entails?

Levinas describes the communicative act, the saying before the other, as a laying bare, "a denuding beyond the skin, to the wounds one dies from, denuding to death."[12] Such a description is certainly an apt one for Abraham Ravett's renewed listening, his return to his father's silence a decade after his death. This exposure to the other is not without its risks. Most studies of second-generation Holocaust survivors have described a transmission of pathologies resulting from an overidentification with the parent (often reinforced by the child's naming after a murdered relative). As evidenced by the study of clinical psychologist Aaron Hass, the second generation tends to describe itself as depressed, angry, fearful, mistrustful, and cynical.[13] Recognizable in the context of such research as yet another instance of overidentification, Ravett's obsessive return to his father through the reworking of footage shot a decade previously can be seen in another light, as enacting what Levinas would call his election "to bear the wretchedness and bankruptcy of the other."[14] This reading would mark the title as the announcement of a son's filial obligation, the return on an irredeemable debt.

But there are other readings possible. In an earlier Ravett film, *Thirty Years Later* (1974–1978), completed while the elder Ravett was still alive, Abraham constructs a dual portrait. It is, on the one hand, an autobiographical investigation of the filmmaker's state of misery caused by the departure of his lover (and beneath that by feelings of self-loathing) and, on the other, a gentle portrait of his survivor parents. Ravett's on-camera rants and self-pitying offer sharp contrast to his father's dark silences or his mother's stoic efforts to share her unspeakable past (she too has lost a first family, husband and child). There is a remarkable sequence toward the end of the film in which Ravett confronts his mother from behind the camera just as he has his old girlfriend Nina previously. Ravett attacks Nina for loving him no longer; here he challenges his mother for having loved him too much, for not preparing him for the harshness and betrayals of the world outside.

"Everything I said was right," Ravett accuses his mother, "the world doesn't treat me like that." His mother chides him, lovingly, of course: "You cannot compare strangers to your parents who love you! Why are you comparing people who have no family ties to you with parents? . . . You have to be realistic . . . You have to adjust yourself, to behave according to the outside world. You cannot be all the time Abeleh, the only child." Abeleh, the beloved only child, the only survivor among his parent's four children. His early life is revealed to have been lived as though "everything was for him." Not a recipe for success. And this too is a trope familiar from the survivor literature, parents overinvesting in their children, sacrificing themselves to the next generation, whatever the cost. By the time of the 1989 film, "everything's for you" can be understood as a gesture of reciprocity. Although Levinas stresses that the responsibility for the other in no way entails a like response (we are responsible even for the other's responsibility), we now have a context for seeing the film's title as a simple inversion: once, everything was for me; now, it's all for you.

Here we must pause to consider a salient point. The other of this discussion is, in fact, a unique other, not just a neighbor, a stranger, or wayfarer but the father, the patriarch. "Everything's for You." The film's title is an enactment, in extremis, of the Fifth Commandment, "Honor thy father and thy mother." Only instead of honor, Ravett offers his father the whole package; he offers everything. Or does he?

In the course of the film, in the portion shot in the late 1980s, we are shown Abraham caring for his own son, whose name is Chaim. It is the custom among Ashkenazi Jews to name children after deceased family members only, so we know that the boy's grandfather is dead. Abraham treats the child with the greatest tenderness, lavishing time and attention on him, sharing physical intimacy with him as one suspects his own father could not. We see Abraham diapering the boy, putting him to bed, asking him about his dreams, showering with him. This is the namesake; he too is Chaim Ravett. As such, he is another plausible object of the title's address.

But there are other registers of interpretation as well. The "you" of the title is, as always, undecidable as to number: it could be a singular or plural "you." Perhaps the film's title simply echoes the motive of every entertainment: "Ladies and gentlemen, everything's for you." This reading has little to recommend it, though, because it corresponds very poorly with the film's tone or substance.

But the assumption of a plural "you" for the title's address does suggest another possibility, one that plays off the film's Jewishness. Since the destruction of the Second Temple in the first century, Jewish life has been conducted in exile. The great rabbinic tradition, from the Talmudic period ending in the fifth century right through the Middle Ages, stressed through its biblical commentaries and teachings the absolute necessity for a kind of historical memory, enacted through ritual and recital, so as to ensure the continuity and survival of the Jewish people.[15] As described by Jewish historian Yosef Hayim Yerushalmi, the command to remember is absolute: "the verb zakhar (remember) appears in its various declensions in the Bible no less than one hundred and sixty nine times, usually with either Israel or God as the subject, for memory is incumbent upon both" (10, 5). There is no memory charge more sacred, no agreement more binding in perpetuity, than the covenant between God and Israel outlined in Deuteronomy 29:13–14: "I make this covenant, with its sanctions, not with you alone, but both with those who are standing here with us this day before the Lord our God, and also with those who are not with us here this day" (10). Remarkably, the contract between God and people is made, in absentia, in the name of all the generations to come. The death of the six million placed that covenant at risk, issuing a near-fatal blow to a culture of European Jewry that had flourished for one thousand years, even in the face of the forced movement eastward after the expulsions from western Europe (from England in 1290, France in 1306, and, most crushingly, Spain in 1492) (59). Particularly in the wake of genocidal assault, a few short decades after the launching of the State of Israel as a Jewish homeland, "Everything's for You" resonates with that first and most irreducible principle of Jewish thought, the survival of the Jewish people.

Finally, Ravett's title can be understood as a dedication of another sort. In Martin Buber's *I and Thou* (1923), a work to which Levinas is both responsive and oppositional, a great deal of attention is given to the "you" of the "I-you" dyad. For it is the "you" that ushers the "I" into the world of relation, offering the possibility for a human encounter unavailable through the machinelike "I-it" relation that Buber saw dominating modern life. Although Buber articulates three spheres in which the world of relation arises—the natural, the human, and the spiritual—spirituality suffuses the entirety of the brief text: "In every sphere, through everything that becomes present to us, we gaze toward the train of the eternal You; in each we perceive a breath of it; in every You we address the eternal You, in every sphere according to its manner."[16] "In every You we address the eternal You," writes Buber, a pronouncement applicable in the present case. If we take the "you" of the title to be divine and eternal, the film becomes a prayer or supplication, dedicated to the memory of the father, pledged to the future of the son and of the Jewish people, set forth in the presence of God.

Given the principle of overdetermination at work in cultural criticism for a century now—a product, Bloom would say, of the quintessential Jewish compulsive interpreter, Sigmund Freud—we don't have to choose meanings. We can instead acknowledge them all, aware of the complex manner in which apparently contrary meanings (the "yous" of father, self, son, people, God) are in fact woven into one another. But all these "yous" share an investment in otherness, in the necessity of responsibility and of the ethical encounter, directing our consideration to moral concerns rather than to the more familiar terrain of ontology and epistemology. "The for itself signifies self-consciousness," writes Levinas, "the for all, responsibility for the others, support of the universe."[17] Documentary has gloried in its access to the everyday, digging beneath the grimy exterior of things, showing us the forgotten gesture or the unacknowledged glance. But that documentary gaze can also be an inward one, steeped in memory, capable of plumbing the depths of the soul, in search of the ineffable: support of the universe.

III Modes of Subjectivity

New Subjectivities: Documentary and Self-Representation in the Post-verité Age

This chapter, first written in 1995 for the Japanese magazine Documentary Box, *offers a historical overview of a broad shift in documentary filmmaking style over a twenty-five-year period (1970–1995). If many of the founding ambitions of nonfiction filmmaking were congruent with those of the natural or social sciences as argued in chapter 8—the gathering of "facts," the careful preservation of imperiled folkways, the construction of arguments through demonstrative proofs—the work of later practitioners bears the marks of a radical shift of values associated with the emergence of second-wave feminism by the early 1970s. A new foregrounding of the politics of everyday life encouraged the interrogation of identity and subjectivity and of a vividly corporeal rather than intellectualized self. Struggles for equity in the public sphere were now joined by interrogations of (inter)personal conflict, of private histories and interiorized struggles. The dramatic growth of personal documentary filmmaking in the post-1960s era thus comes to be understood in relation to an emergent cultural moment in which politics were not so much abandoned as transformed. This essay provides a sense of historical context for the chapters of the third part of the book, "Modes of Subjectivity," in which various modalities of autobiographical practice are explored.*

▶

Cinema and the Secularization of the Divine

The documentary film has long been tied up with the question of science. Since the protocinematic experiments in human and animal locomotion by Eadweard Muybridge and others, the cinema has demonstrated a potential for the observation and investigation of people and of social/historical phenomena. In the 1930s, noted avant-garde filmmaker Hans Richter described this potential with particular urgency:

> Technology, overcoming time and space, has brought all life on earth so close together that the most remote "facts," as much as those closest to hand, have become significant for each individual's life. Reason has given rise to a secularisation of the divine. Everything that happens on earth has become more interesting and more significant than it ever was before. Our age demands the documented fact. . . . The modern reproductive technology of the cinematograph was uniquely responsive to the need for factual sustenance. . . . The camera created a reservoir of human observation in the simplest possible way.[1]

As an instrument of "reproductive technology," the cinema was endowed with the power to preserve and represent the world in real time. "The (apparent) incorruptibility of optics," wrote Richter, "guaranteed 'absolute truth.'"[2]

But as Richter's parenthetical qualification of cinema's veridical status indicates ("the [*apparent*] incorruptibility of optics"), few have ever trusted the cinema without reservation. If ever they did, it was the documentary that most inspired that trust. For the young Joris Ivens, the small, spring-driven Kinamo camera was a tool for investigating the natural world. Having learned "all its advantages and also its weaknesses from Professor Goldberg, the inventor of this practical little instrument," Ivens set out in 1928 to make a film about a railroad bridge over the Maas River in Rotterdam:

> For me the bridge was a laboratory of movements, tones, shapes, contrasts, rhythms and the relations between all these. I knew thousands of variations were possible and here was my chance to work out basic elements in these variations. . . . What I wanted was to find some general rules, laws of continuity of movement. Music had its rules and its grammar of tones, melody, harmony and counterpoint. Painters knew what they could do with certain colors, values, contrasts. If anyone knew about the relation of motion on the screen he was keeping it to himself and I would have to find out about it for myself.[3]

Ivens was researching the unique characteristics of a *cinematic* rendering of the world, already aware that the laws of optics and of chemistry alone could guarantee nothing. If, as he was to discover in his making of *The Bridge,* there were real possibilities for a felicitous translation onto film of this engineering marvel, there remained much to be discovered about how this medium could best evoke the dynamism of the bridge's mechanical action without, for example, sacrificing a sense of the monumentality of its scale. The making of the film was a kind of laboratory experience.

Of course, Ivens's enthusiasm for a systematic understanding of cinema's representational potential was partially historical, a by-product of modernism. Note in this context the writings of Dziga Vertov, who in his "We: Variant of a Manifesto" (1922) produced blissful accounts of man's "desire for kinship with the machine" and of "our path [which] leads through the poetry of machines, from the bungling citizen to the perfect electric man."[4] Vertov, trained in medicine, described his cinematic labors as a "complex experiment" and film itself as "the sum of the facts recorded on film, or, if you like, not merely the sum, but the product, a 'higher mathematics' of facts."[5]

All of these desires evinced by the early practitioners of the cinema—factual sustenance, the discovery of the laws of cinematic motion, and the perfectibility of perception—are deeply implicated with the scientific project. It is the domain of nonfiction that has most explicitly articulated this scientistic yearning; it is here also that the debates around evidence, objectivity, and knowledge have been centered. I would argue, then, that nonfiction film and the scientific project are historically linked. The work of a number of scholars offers further corroboration of this point.[6] I would also argue that the perceived relations between the two (perceived, that is, by the community of practitioners, critics, and scholars) have shifted in important ways over the years. In the post–World War II period, the status of the documentary/science dyad has most frequently centered on the particularly vexed question of objectivity.

While the difficulties surrounding the distinctions between subjective and objective knowledge in the European intellectual tradition are ancient, Raymond Williams points to the developments in German classical philosophy from the late eighteenth century on as crucial to current understanding. Especially in the aesthetic realm, an explicit dualism was forming by the mid–nineteenth century. But important changes were under way. Whereas in previous centuries, the prevailing scholastic view of *subjective* was "as things are in themselves (from the sense of subject as substance)," and *objective* was "as things are presented to consciousness ('thrown before' the mind)," the emergence of positivism in the late nineteenth century effected a radical reorientation of meaning. Now *objective* was to be construed as "factual, fair-minded (neutral) and hence reliable, as distinct from the sense of *subjective* as based on impressions rather than facts, and hence as influenced by personal feelings and relatively unreliable."[7] Attentive as ever to the "historical layering" of meaning in intellectual concepts, Williams suggests that the coexistence of an increasingly dominant positivist ideology with the residual idealist tradition has created considerable misunderstanding:

In judgments and reports we are positively required to be *objective:* looking only at the facts, setting aside personal preference or interest. In this context a sense of something shameful, or at least weak, attaches to *subjective,* although everyone will admit that there are *subjective factors,* which have usually to be put in their place. . . . What must be seen, in the end, as deeply controversial uses of what are nevertheless, at least in *subject* and *object,* inevitable words, are commonly presented with a certainty and at times a glibness that simply spread confusion.[8]

Given nonfiction's historical linkages to the scientific project, to observational methods and the protocols of journalistic reportage, it is not at all surprising that, within the community of documentary practitioners and critics, subjectivity has frequently been constructed as a kind of contamination, to be expected but minimized. Only recently has the subjective/objective hierarchy (with the latter as the favored term) begun to be displaced, even reversed.

▶

The Observational Moment

In his elucidation of four documentary modes of exposition, Bill Nichols has described the observational mode as that approach to documentary filmmaking often called direct cinema, characterized by the prevalence of indirect address, the use of long takes and synchronous sound, tending toward spatiotemporal continuity rather than montage, evoking a feeling of the "present tense."[9] Throughout the 1960s and well into the 1970s, this mode was in its ascendancy in the United States and Canada, with a related but philosophically antagonistic approach (deemed by Nichols the interactive mode) developing in France at about the same time under the aegis of Jean Rouch. Brian Winston has argued that the American practitioners tended, like Richard Leacock (trained as a physicist) and Albert Maysles, to be under the influence of the natural sciences in their early pronouncements of an ethic of nonintervention, even artistic selflessness: for example, one critic's description, "It is life observed by the camera rather than, as is the case with most documentaries, life recreated for it," or Robert Drew's statement "The film maker's personality is in no way directly involved in directing the action."[10] Winston suggests that Rouch, an anthropologist, and his occasional partner Edgar Morin, a sociologist, had "the advantage of a more sophisticated conception of the problems raised by participant observation" than their American counterparts.[11]

But even in the heyday of direct cinema, the specter of subjectivity could not be wholly expunged. According to Stephen Mamber's account, a disagreement arose between producer Robert Drew and D. A. Pennebaker during the shooting of *Jane* (1962) about whether or not the sound of the camera should be filtered out during an extended sequence with Jane Fonda, sitting alone before her dressing-room mirror: "Pennebaker felt that the noise should remain, making it clear that the audience was not seeing Jane alone in her dressing room, but Jane alone in her dressing room with a camera observing her."[12] By the time of the making of *An American Family* (a twelve-part documentary series about the William C. Loud family of Santa Barbara, California, shot in 1971, broadcast on the Public Broadcasting System in 1973), there could be little doubt that the filmmaker's personality was rather intimately involved in the creation of the final product.

In several scenes with Lance or Grant, the two most active "performers" among the five Loud siblings, a conspiratorial glance is exchanged with the camera as a kind of confirmation of its role as witness. In episode 4, Pat Loud journeys to Eugene, Oregon, to help celebrate her mother's birthday. As Pat and her mother settle down with cocktail glasses in hand, the daughter offers a toast to her aging parent: "To lots of birthdays!" Apparently misunderstanding the intent of the wish (she reads it as a toast to all those celebrating their birthdays rather than as a wish for many more years of her own good health), Mrs. Russell replies, "Who else has a birthday?" From off-camera, Pat rather flatly intones, "Susan has a birthday." Mrs. Russell's gaze shifts from her daughter to some point off-screen and to her right: "Oh yeah, sure, I knew it was something else. I'm not the only one having a birthday." This rather puzzling exchange is clarified only with the realization that mother and daughter are sharing this scene with filmmakers Alan and Susan Raymond, the latter of whom is the Susan in question. Indeed, the Raymonds shared a life with the Loud family for seven months, this despite the fact that their off-camera presence and the effects of their personalities on the seven principal subjects are only rarely acknowledged. By the time of the Raymonds' *American Family Revisited* (broadcast in 1983, updated in 1990), only remnants of the invisible fourth wall remain. Each of the Louds in turn speaks to the occasionally imaged filmmakers about the impact of the series on their lives as well as the effects of the presence of the camera on their behavior. (Remarkably, the ever rational Bill Loud calibrates his response to Pat's on-camera announcement that she is filing for a divorce in episode 9 in the following way: 80 percent or 90 percent spontaneous, only 10 percent for the camera.) The Raymonds choose to end the follow-up piece on the fate of this American family, which had unraveled years earlier for all the world to see, with a reference to themselves, announcing that indeed *they* were still married and that in 1988 Susan had given birth to a son, James. Covering nearly two decades, the updated *American Family* saga offers dramatic evidence of the shift away from a self-consciously observational approach to a more interactive, even reflexive, modality. Again, as with the modernist yearnings of Vertov, Ivens, and Richter, this transformation is historically contingent.

▶

Performing the Self

By 1990, any chronicler of documentary history would note the growing prominence of work by women and men of diverse cultural backgrounds in which the representation of the historical world is inextricably bound up with self-inscription. In these films and tapes (increasingly the latter), subjectivity is no longer construed as "something shameful"; it is the filter through which the real enters discourse, as well as a kind of experiential compass guiding the work toward its goal as embodied knowledge. In part, this new tendency is a response to the persistent critique of ethnography in which the quest to preserve endangered authenticities "out there," in remote places, is called into doubt. In his introduction to *Local Knowledge: Further Essays in Interpretive Anthropology,* published in 1983, Clifford Geertz suggested that the predilection for general theories in the social sciences had given way to a "scattering into frameworks." This meant a movement away from "universalist moods" toward what he called "a keen sense of the dependence of what is seen upon where it is seen from and what it is seen with."[13] It is not difficult to imagine observational cinema of the 1960s as a cinematic variant of the social scientific approach to which Geertz disparagingly refers, an approach in which generalizable truths about institutions or human behavior can be extrapolated from small but closely monitored case studies (e.g., *Primary* [1960], *High School* [1969], *An American Family*).

In the domain of documentary film and video, the scattered frameworks through which the social field came to be organized were increasingly determined by the disparate cultural identities of the makers. The documentative stance that had previously been valorized as informed but objective was now being replaced by a more personalist perspective in which the maker's stake and commitment to the subject matter were foregrounded. What had intervened in the years between 1970 and 1990 that might have contributed to this effusion of documentary subjectivity?

The cultural climate of this period, at least in the West, has been characterized by the displacement of the politics of social movements (e.g., antiwar, civil rights, the student movement) by the politics of identity. According to this scenario, the clarion call to unified and collective action came to be drowned out by the murmur of human differences. Instrumental to this sea change was the feminist movement, whose revaluation of the prior alternative political structures suggested that social inequities persisted, internal to the movement. Young men challenged the authority of their fathers to establish state policy but left intact gendered hierarchies. Women and the issues that mattered to them—forthright interpersonal communication; equal stress on the integrity of process as well as product; open and universally accessible structures for decision making; shared responsibility for the domestic and familial—received scant attention. The women's movement changed all that and helped to usher in an era in which a range of "personal" issues—race, sexuality, and ethnicity—became consciously politicized (evidenced by the post-Stonewall gay rights movement as well as the intensification of racially or ethnically based political initiatives). In all cases, subjectivity, a grounding in the personal and the experiential, fueled the engine of political action. While some have seen the emergence of identity politics as an erosion of coalition, a retreat from meaningful social intervention, other cultural critics have argued loudly and persuasively for its efficacy. Stanley Aronowitz has suggested that the current emphasis on multiple and fluid identities (and the critique of "essential" identity as the underpinning for social collectivities) is entirely consistent with post-Newtonian physics:

> The sociological theory, according to which individuals are crucially formed by a fixed cultural system containing universal values that become internalized through the multiplicity of interactions between the "person" and her external environment, now comes under radical revision. We may now regard the individual as a process constituted by its multiple and *specific* relations, not only to the institutions of socialization such as family, school, and law, but also to significant others, all of whom are in motion, that is, are constantly changing. The ways in which individuals and the groups to which they affiliate were constituted as late as a generation earlier, may now be archaic. New identities arise, old ones pass away (at least temporarily).[14]

If indeed we now live in an age of intensified and shifting psychosocial identities, it should surprise no one that the documentation of this cultural scene should be deeply suffused with the performance of subjectivities.

While never considered a part of the mainstream documentary tradition, video artist Wendy Clarke has produced work that foreshadows current developments as well as echoes important discoveries of the past. Beginning in 1977, Clarke began experimenting with the video diary format, attempting to use the camera as a tool to plumb the depths of her own psyche. This concept evolved into the *Love Tapes* project, in which individuals of all ages and backgrounds are given three minutes of tape time in which to speak about what love means to them. Each love tape, while identical in length and subject matter, announces difference at the level of sound and image; Clarke renders each subject the *metteur-en-scène* of her own discourse through a choice of visual backdrop and musical accompaniment. Each individual is seated in a booth with only a self-activated camera, monitor, and the concept of love as a spur to performance. In all instances, those who might, in the interactive mode, have been the interview subject become the source and subject of enunciation; differences of experience, affiliation, and identity join with the unpredictability and variation of desire to make each of these monologues unique. Thousands of love tapes later, the project offers testimony to the absolute heterogeneity of the historical subject.

Some years previously, Jean Rouch, a prime shaper of the interactive mode in which the filmmaker-subject encounter takes precedence over externalized observation, had begun to explore the power of the camera to induce the display of subjectivity. Far from avoiding or disavowing the potential influence of the camera on its subjects, Rouch had from the late 1950s on employed the cinematic apparatus as a kind of accelerator, an incitation for "a very strange kind of confession."[15] Replying to an interviewer's question regarding camera influence in 1969, Rouch replied: "Yes, the camera deforms, but not from the moment that it becomes an accomplice. At that point it has the possibility of doing something I couldn't do if the camera wasn't there: it becomes a kind of psychoanalytic stimulant which lets people do things they wouldn't otherwise do."[16] The famous sequences with Marilou and Marceline in *Chronicle of a Summer* (1961) in which the subjects choose to probe memory and emotion *for,* rather than *in spite of,* the camera offer an apt illustration of Rouch's concept.

But *The Love Tapes* and the films of Rouch are only precursors for the new subjectivity on display in documentary film and video of the 1980s and 1990s. The work to which I refer may rework memory or make manifesto-like pronouncements; almost inevitably, a self, typically a deeply social self, is being constructed in the process. But what makes this new subjectivity new? Perhaps the answer lies in part in the extent to which current documentary self-inscription enacts identities—fluid, multiple, even contradictory—while remaining fully embroiled with public discourses. In this way, the work escapes charges of solipsism or self-absorption. In her recent book titled *Family Secrets: Acts of Memory and Imagination,* Annette Kuhn offers an eloquent rationale for the use of some of her family photographs as case studies for a work of personal and popular memory. In terms that echo the feminist precept that the personal is the political, Kuhn argues that memory work, when properly conceived, folds public and private spheres into each other:

> The images are both "private" (family photographs) and "public" (films, news photographs, a painting): though, as far as memory at least is concerned, private and public turn out in practice less readily separable than conventional wisdom would have us believe. . . . if the memories are one individual's, their associations extend far beyond the personal. They spread into an extended network of meanings that bring together the personal with the familial, the cultural, the economic, the social, and the historical. Memory work makes it possible to explore connections between "public" historical events, structures of feeling, family dramas, relations of class, national identity and gender, and "personal" memory. In these case histories outer and inner, social and personal, historical and psychical, coalesce; and the web of interconnections that binds them together is made visible.[17]

Kuhn's description of the coalescence of outer and inner histories offers an overarching characterization for the recent documentary works to which I refer.

In a number of instances, the maker's subjectivity is explicitly aligned with social affiliations. As in Kuhn's description, a network of familial, cultural, economic, and psychical forces converge and find expression in an act of historical self-inscription; but in these instances, autobiographical discourse is conditional, contingent on its location within an explicit social matrix. A particularly rich example of this phenomenon occurs with works that explore exilic identity, films such as Jonas Mekas's *Lost, Lost, Lost* (1975), Chantal Akerman's *News from Home* (1975), Raul Ruiz's *Of Great Events and Ordinary People* (1979), Marilu Mallet's *Unfinished Diary* (1983), Meena Nanji's *Voices of the Morning* (1991), Rea Tajiri's *History and Memory* (1991), and Dick Hebdige's *Rambling Man* (1994). The exploration of displacement and cultural disorientation bridges the divide between the self and an Other who is specifiably kindred. In the first two of *Lost, Lost, Lost*'s six reels, Mekas focuses on the Brooklyn-based community of Lithuanians, the Displaced Persons, who in escaping Soviet persecution in the immediate post–World War II years experience profound dispossession—of land, climate, custom, language, and cultural context. The poets and statesmen of Lithuania find themselves without familiar mooring in a land whose size and world stature doubles that of the Soviet Union, reinforcing their sense of oppression at the hands of the "big nations." Although Mekas's magisterial film has most frequently been categorized as an autobiographical work of the American avant-garde, in fact it charts at least three histories over a fourteen-year period

(1949–1963)—that of the Lithuanian exiles, the ban-the-bomb social protest movement of the late 1950s and early 1960s, and the emergent underground film scene of the same period. This filmic documentation takes as its pivot Mekas's own history and experience but envelops it in layers of historical documentation. Mekas's subjectivity is eloquently performed across decades of real time, three hours of film time, but his is an identity constituted, as Aronowitz has argued, by multiple and specific relations to institutions and significant others, all of whom are in motion.[18]

During the post-vérité period between 1970 and 1995, documentary explorations of gay and lesbian identities have exhibited a particular dynamism and vitality. In this category I would include works such as *Territories* (Sankofa Film and Video Collective, 1984), *Tongues Untied* (Marlon Riggs, 1989), Gurinder Chadha's *I'm British But . . .* (1989), Su Friedrich's *Sink or Swim* (1990), Sadie Benning's prolific output from 1988 through 1992—including *If Every Girl Had a Diary* (1990), *Jollies* (1990), and *It Wasn't Love* (1992)—*Thank You and Good Night* (Jan Oxenberg, 1991), Sandi DuBowski's *Tomboychik* (1993), and Deborah Hoffmann's *Complaints of a Dutiful Daughter* (1994). There is no template to which these works conform; only a few of them feature a coming-out scenario, and those that do (*Tongues Untied,* for example) often discover ways to reinvent the form. Riggs's controversial piece may be the most outspokenly politicized of the group from its opening incantation ("Brother to brother, brother to brother . . . brother to brother, brother to brother") to its iconoclastic summary claim, "black men loving black men is *the* revolutionary act." From the outset, Riggs puts himself and his body on the line. In an opening sequence, Riggs, undulating and unclothed, moves rhythmically against a black, featureless background, riveting us with his fiery gaze and dramatic narration. But the temptation to read the tape as an exclusively first-person discourse is undermined by the recurring presence of a black men's group, which functions as a rapping and snapping Greek chorus. It is this collectivity of black gay men (of whom Marlon is but one) that occupies the film's political and ethical balance point. Successfully fusing the personal with the social, *Tongues Untied* is both a germinal political manifesto of its epoch and a paradigmatic instance of the new documentary subjectivity.

Other gay- and lesbian-identified pieces take up the maker's sexuality less explicitly. Frequently these works attempt to situate the artist-subject in the familial order, to witness or account for the difficulties of accommodation within rigid family structures to queer sensibilities and life choices. In these cases, identity comes to be constructed less in relation to the family as a relatively abstract institution than to particular, well-loved family members with whom the maker must nevertheless settle accounts. Often, this relative (the mother in Hoffmann's tape, a grandmother in DuBowski's and Oxenberg's pieces) is ill, dead, or dying. Sexuality and its sources or etiology are only occasionally the overt subject matter of such work. Instead these films and tapes affirm the degree to which the (queer) identities of the makers are bound up with those of certain special (but straight) family members. These mothers and grandmothers, heterosexual but unerringly eccentric, have helped create the people the artists have become. Works such as these mourn and memorialize loss, yet they testify with equal force to continuity, to the intransigence of subjectivity, a process charged and revivified by contact with significant others in life and in memory. These works are perhaps the next generation of the new queer subjectivity on film and tape. Janus-faced, looking behind as well as ahead, personal yet embedded in the commonality of family life, these are works that bridge many gaps of human difference—those of generation, gender, and sexuality.

How can we account for the dramatic, even explosive, appearance of new subjectivities on film and tape as the century comes to a close? Julia Watson has written about the historical conditions in which women have voiced their "unspeakable differences" through autobiographical discourses: "For the immigrant or multicultural daughter, naming the unspeakable is at once a transgressive act that knowingly seeks to expose and speak the boundaries on which the organization of cultural knowledge depends and a discursive strategy that, while unverifiable, allows a vital 'making sense' of her own multiple differences."[19] Such a statement well summarizes the circumstances in which this latest phase of documentary exposition has arisen. During the direct cinema period, self-reference was shunned. But far from a sign of self-effacement, this was the symptomatic silence of the empowered, who sought no forum for self-justification or display. And why would they need one? These white male professionals had assumed the mantle of filmic representation with the ease and self-assurance of a birthright. Not so the current generation of performative documentarists. In more ways than one, their self-enactments are transgressive. Through their explorations of the (social) self, they are speaking the lives and desires of the many who have lived outside "the boundaries of cultural knowledge."

[12] *The Electronic Essay*

"The Electronic Essay," first presented at the Society for Cinema Studies conference in 1995, is the first of four chapters that investigate specific modalities of subjectivity in documentary film- or videomaking. The reference to video is vital here, as I argue that the electronic medium offers possibilities for self-presentation unknown to film. First-generation videomakers adopted the tools of the new medium to pursue their prior interests as conceptual or body artists; the camera and monitor became extensions of the artists' sensorium. They also began to work with video's unique and quite complex temporality—its ability to combine and oppose taped and real-time material. In this chapter, I offer a tentative "critical encounter" between the electronic medium and the essay form as theorized in philosophy and literary theory. I look at Jean-Luc Godard's remarkable Scenario du film Passion, *in which the artist uses the video apparatus to compose an imagined script for a feature film* (Passion) *that he has already made. This convoluted temporality and the labyrinthine textuality it helps make possible echo the conditions of essayistic discourse already surveyed in chapters 4 and 6.*

> *The essay's innermost formal law is heresy.*
> :: Theodor W. Adorno, "The Essay as Form"

Much has been written on the status of the essay and from innumerable perspectives: philosophers have principally sought to position the essay in relation to knowledge, while literary theorists have struggled with definitions, typologies, and exegeses of this ever elusive writerly mode. It is perhaps appropriate to begin my own account of the video essay in the manner of evocation, with Adorno's sense of the heretical establishing the prevailing tone. The essayistic—I prefer the adjectival usage despite

Barthes's protestations ("a relationship which adjectivizes is on the side of the image, on the side of domination, of death")[1]—is the undoer of dualist hierarchies; it is the stuff of paradox. For Spanish philosopher Eduardo Nicol, the essay is *almost* literature and *almost* philosophy,"[2] while Walter Pater and Adorno have deemed its approach "methodically unmethodical."[3] For Georg Lukács, citing the elder Schlegel, the essay was an "intellectual poem,"[4] while for Reda Bensmaia, the essay is atopic, eccentric, in short, an "impossible" genre.[5] The essayistic emerges as a kind of limit text, akin to Barthes's invocation of the writerly. It is also a projective screen for many of its commentators, supplying a discursive arena well-suited to their vision. For Jean-François Lyotard, the essay is postmodern; for Adorno, "the essay is what it was from the beginning, the critical form par excellence . . . it is critique of ideology."[6] But more than that, Adorno can claim, a few pages later, that "the essay approaches the logic of music, that stringent and yet aconceptual art of transition, in order to appropriate for verbal language something it forfeited under the domination of discursive logic."[7] For R. Lane Kauffmann, the essay— given its "antinomian" character ("poised between literature and philosophy, art and science, holding the antinomies of imagination and reason, spontaneity and discipline, in productive tension")—is "the most adequate form for interdisciplinary research and writing."[8] In an epoch in which ideas such as hybridity, nonidentity, contingency, indeterminacy, the reflective, the interdisciplinary, the transient, and the heterotopic (pedigreed essayistic characteristics all) resonate both with prevailing theoretical paradigms and with vast sectors of social life, the essay deserves the renewed critical attention it has begun to receive.

In true essayistic fashion, then (for indeed, the essay must "reflect on itself at every moment"),[9] let me place my own intentions tactlessly on trial and in so doing challenge my own appropriative gesture.[10] To what end do I propose a critical convergence of video and the essayistic? It would not go well simply to aver that video has yet to sustain for itself an adequate theorization (which it hasn't) or to suggest a kind of ontological inevitability to the rendezvous between video and essay, given Adorno's aphoristic reminder that "the essay abandons the royal road to the origins, which leads only to what is most derivative—Being, the ideology that duplicates what already exists."[11] Instead it is my intention to suggest the fruitfulness of initiating a critical encounter between the electronic medium and the essay form. I will further argue for the appropriateness of the encounter based on grounds that are historical, theoretical, and tropological, with particular attention given to the temporality of self-inscription in Godard's *Scenario du film Passion* (1982).

Everything attests to the fact that video is more deeply rooted
in writing than is cinema.
:: Raymond Bellour, "Video Writing"

While the convergence of video and essay has received little direct attention, there are a number of writings that posit a discursivity for video congruent with the essayistic. In his analysis of esteemed video artists such as Gary Hill and Bill Viola and the Japanese poets Shito Terayama and Shuntaro Tanikawa (authors of *Video Letter,* a brilliant exchange of electronic missives), Bellour deploys a notion of writing to which any commentator of the essay might aspire: "Writing is conceived here as a particular type of image, fragmented, intermittent, a network of raw significations that allows the image to become unstuck from itself without, for all that, causing it to lose its seductive force."[12] In a lengthy interview/dialogue between Bellour and Viola, the specificity of video is much at issue. Video is contrasted with film in that the latter is composed of "frozen, discrete moments," whereas video is, according to Viola, "a living, dynamic system, an energy field. . . . It's sort of like a light is on when you come into the room. It's all there already. . . . You see the effects of your actions on the image while you are carrying them out."[13] Viola has spoken of his work in certain of his video pieces as "sculpting with time" (with partial fields of past- and future-tense images keyed over present-tense material); indeed, video's real-time potentialities proved immensely attractive to 1960s kinetic sculptors and performance artists who saw in the emergent electronic medium an opportunity to expand their vernacular.

In his interview with Viola and elsewhere, Bellour has insisted on a certain corporeality that characterizes video in contrast to film. The *paluche* minicamera developed in France is the quintessence of this alleged connectedness of artist's body and creative praxis; abandoning the viewfinder, the videomaker "thinks with the hands." In his discussion of a Gary Hill installation, *Crux* (1983–1987), Bellour describes the use of five monitors reproducing "the partial images from five cameras attached to the author-actor's body: two on his feet, two on his hands and one at his waist, aimed toward his face."[14] Perhaps the corporeality of video is a residue of its performative, installation-based infancy. Over the years, video art making has increasingly been forced to depend on the reproducible artifact made possible by institutional support (Hill and Viola are among the few video artists still able to produce large-scale installations). And yet even in single-channel tapes such as Viola's *I Do Not Know What It Is I Am Like* (1986), the video apparatus remains capable of evoking the shock of sensation even if the condition of nonreproducibility (for

Peggy Phelan and other theorists of performance, the sine qua non of the phenomenon) no longer obtains. Interestingly, Phelan has pointed to essayistic writing such as Barthes's *Camera Lucida* and *Roland Barthes by Roland Barthes* as precisely the kind of literary endeavor that seeks to do the impossible—preserve the unreproducible. This she calls "the act of writing toward disappearance," in contrast to the act of writing toward preservation, noting that "the after-effect of disappearance is the experience of subjectivity itself."[15] If the videographic essay can be said to induce a similar kind of aphanisis of the subject (a fading or sense of self-dissolution consistent with the experience of subjectivity), perhaps it is due in part to its genealogical ties to performance.

But my intention is not to make claims for video's defining properties, an activity that Marita Sturken has characterized as video's "ticket of admission to modernist art theory."[16] Rather, I wish to suggest that video has, from its mythic inception via the early 1960s antiart installations of Nam June Paik and Wolf Vostell, retained an attachment to the performative and the corporeal that is historical and is distinct from the cinema. All commentators of video's history acknowledge the impact of its first-generation practitioners—the painters, sculptors, and conceptual, body, and performance artists who lent institutionalized credibility to a nascent medium (e.g., Paik, Bruce Nauman, Vito Acconci, Richard Serra, Lynda Bengalis, and Peter Campus). The work of these artists inspired Rosalind Krauss in an early and infamous essay to suggest that "most of the work produced over the very short span of video art's existence has used the human body as its central instrument" and that narcissism could be generalized as *the* condition of the whole of artists' video.[17]

Beginning with Montaigne, the corporeal self has been the linchpin of essayistic discourse: "I study myself more than any other subject. That is my metaphysics, that is my physics."[18] When Montaigne writes that "no man ever penetrated more deeply into his material or plucked its limbs and consequences cleaner," or begins "Of Vanity" with mention of an acquaintance who was so self-obsessed that he placed on display at his home "a row of [his] chamber pots, seven or eight days' worth," since "all other talk stank in his nostrils," the bodily emerges as an intransigent, inescapable source of self-knowledge.[19] For Roland Barthes, the body is nothing less than the mana-word, the "word whose ardent, complex, ineffable, and somehow sacred signification gives the illusion that by this word one might answer for everything."[20]

Marshall McLuhan hyperbolized that television was an extension of the central nervous system, but it has been independent videomakers who have demonstrated the medium's capabilities to write *through* the body, to write *as* the body. Durable, lightweight, mobile, producing instantaneous results, the video apparatus supplies a dual capability well suited to the essayistic project: it is both screen and mirror, providing the technological grounds for the surveillance of the palpable world, as well as a reflective surface on which to register the self. It is an instrument through which the twin axes of essayistic practice (the looking out and the looking in, the Montaignean "measure of sight" and "measure of things") find apt expression. Eduardo Nicol's description of the literary essay ("a theatre of ideas in which the rehearsal and the final performance are combined")[21] discovers grounds for its amplification in video's real-time capabilities. In this regard, I will focus on one videographic figure in particular.

The inclusion within the video image of a monitor, even if obliquely or inconsequentially framed, in which the artist's self-semblance is re-inscribed affords both viewer and producer access to a perpetual inter-weaving that is the essay's textuality ("lost in this tissue—this texture—the subject unmakes himself, like a spider dissolving in the constructive secretions of its web").[22] The *mise en abyme* effect of the inset self-image-in-process is an enunciative trait available to the electronic, but not the cinematic, essay; through it we are reminded that the body of the artist is literally at stake through these constructive secretions and that the un-folding has real-time implications. It is as Viola has stated: "You see the effects of your actions on the image while you are carrying them out."[23] Such a potentiality is entirely consistent with the essayistic as described by Max Bense:

> This, then, is how the essay is distinguished from a treatise. The person who writes essayistically is the one who composes as he experiments, who turns his object around, questions it, feels it, tests it, reflects on it, who attacks it from different sides and assembles what he sees in his mind's eye and puts into words what the object allows one to see under the conditions created in the course of writing.[24]

In *Scenario du film Passion* (1982), Jean-Luc Godard engages in just such a critical operation with his object, his film *Passion,* completed only months before. *Scenario* functions as a kind of prolegomenon for the film, akin to a book's introduction, which, though placed in the beginning, can only be written last. Godard does, as Bense suggested, turn his object around, test it, reflect on it, attack it from all sides. His desire is to create *Passion*'s pre-text, a scenario to be seen as it is written, one that can attest to his intentions as well as their enactment. To this end, Godard employs video, a medium whose density of sound and image tracks can be scrupu-lously re-layed as he sits before the editing console and as we watch. The primary space of the tape's realization is a small editing room in which a large blank screen ("le plage blanche" after Mallarmé) faces Godard at the controls. The most favored camera placement is at the videomaker's back so that we share his view of the dazzling white screen. But because *Scenario* repeatedly replaces this scene or overlaps it with a second image source—frequently from the film about which Godard speaks—we see both what lies before the maker (tabula rasa as incitation) and the future anterior that he describes. This bizarre temporality has been described by Lyotard:

> The artist and the writer, then, are working without rules in order to formulate the rules of what *will have been done*. Hence the fact that work and text have the characters of an *event*; hence also, they always come too late for their author, or, what amounts to the same thing, their being put into work, their realization *(mise en oeuvre)* always begins too soon. *Post modern* would have to be understood according to the paradox of the future *(post)* anterior *(modo)*.
>
> It seems to me that the essay (Montaigne) is postmodern, while the fragment *(The Athaeneum)* is modern.[25]

But such a scheme—the stark, present-tense studio occasionally inhabited by the lush specter of the future anterior—could install a kind of illusionist hierarchy in which the materially constituted scene (a performative Godard hypothesizing, narrating, and gesticulating before the screen) would be superseded by the "magical" composite image that he calls forth. This is not the case owing to the inclusion in the studio location of three monitors offering miniaturized, angled, and partially obscured versions of the larger composite image that we are ourselves watching. As Godard's hand moves to the fader switch, we see both the in-studio gesture (an act of labor) and its result (the displacement by, or superimposition of, another, seemingly Imaginary, cinematic scene). The monitors, even as they produce a vertiginy of images, paradoxically provide a kind of double anchorage—in the present tense of the productive process and in a space traversed both by a socially constructed Symbolic and by a register of sounds and images redolent of the Godardian Imaginary.

I would argue that these multiple, involuted textual articulations produce an essayistic effect resembling that which critic Andre Tournon has adduced to Montaigne's *Essays:* "The reader, however, is confronted with an uneven textual surface, broken in places and wound around itself like a Moebius strip—'Nous voyla embourbez' . . . ['There we are stuck in the mud'].''[26] I would also argue that the density of *Scenario*'s discursive presentation results from the canny but rather minimalist use of video's capabilities in a manner consistent with Maureen Turim's early and influential analysis:

> What is special about video is its ability to move between different image registrations, to perform these shifts in coding. By splitting the image or superimposing images, video can present different views or temporal instances simultaneously. Each of these views may already be a "processed" image, that is, an image transformed by a process of shifting graphic values and codes or representation . . . The results are images that challenge and train human perception.[27]

The essayistic, a mode to which Godard has long been habituated, reveals itself as ideally suited to the videographic apparatus. Video's potential for textual "thickness," its facility in shuttling between or keying in diverse image sources, can ably serve the essay's discursive goals. Numerous critics have noted that the essay's value is derived from the dynamism of its process rather than its final judgments ("The essay is a judgment, but the essential, the value-determining thing about it is not the verdict . . . but the process of judging")[28] and from the richness of its textuality ("Thought does not progress in a single direction; instead, the moments are interwoven as in a carpet. The fruitfulness of the thoughts depends on the density of the texture").[29] Video's process orientation and its tendency toward discursive density are deeply consonant with the essayistic project.

But if we return to Tournon's evocation of the Möbius strip as analogue to essayistic textuality and to its realization in the *mise en abyme* structure of the monitored self-image, we discover the extent to which descriptions of the essay as the heretical, the impossible, discourse mirror contemporary theorizations of subjectivity itself. In a brilliant essay on the tensions within psychoanalysis between scientific explanation and hermeneutics, Slavoj Zizek writes of Lacan's obsession with topological models of "curved" space in the 1960s and 1970s (the Möbius strip, the Klein bottle, the inner eight, etc.).

> Such a "curved" surface-structure is the structure of the subject: what we call "subject" can only emerge within the structure of overdetermination, that is, in this vicious circle where the cause itself is (presup)posed by its effect. . . . In order to grasp the constitutive paradox of the subject, we must therefore move beyond the standard opposition between "subjective" and "objective," between the order of "appearances" (of what is "for the subject") and the "in-itself."[30]

The "bizarre temporality" of *Scenario du film Passion,* in which the videographic pretext produces the already written, Lyotard's future anterior, evokes the conditions of traumatic memory as described by Zizek:

"This paradox of trauma *qua* cause, which does not pre-exist its effects but is itself retroactively 'posited' by them, involves a kind of temporal loop: *it is through its 'repetition,' through its echoes within the signifying structure, that cause retroactively becomes what it always already was.*"[31] This is so because the trauma is, in Lacanian terms, of the order of the Real and can gain entrance to the signifying chain only through its eruption in language; this "primordially repressed" traumatic kernel, this remainder, this object "which remains stuck in the gullet of the signifier," can never effectuate its causal power in a direct way. "In short," writes Zizek, "the real is the absent cause which perturbs the causality of symbolic law. On that account, the structure of overdetermination is irreducible: cause exercises its influence only as redoubled, through a certain discrepancy of time-lag, that is, if the 'original' trauma of the real is to become effective, it must hook onto, find an echo in, some present deadlock."[32] The Real thus returns to the place in which it never ceased to be. But it is a return with a difference, because now, rather than haunting the subject as an unsymbolizable shard of experience, it is rendered articulate. The temporal logic of this articulation, however, challenges the regime of the discursive order into which it enters.

To review: Godard's video can be characterized as enacting a paradoxical temporality in which anticipated effects (the film that the tape as scenario or pre-text serves to image forth) are at the same moment past causes (a residue or remainder from Godard's experience of the film). Through its instantiation of the future anterior, *Scenario du film Passion* displays an uneven temporal surface; like the Möbius strip, it is neither one nor two, a model incapable of being seen "at a glance," a structure altogether consistent with the essayistic. In terms derived from Lacanian psychoanalytic theory, the images from *Passion* that, owing to their specular, even dreamlike, quality, we have previously aligned with the Imaginary register (with the visibly produced, present-tense footage staunchly Symbolic) now become the traumatic, "Real" kernel of experience reentering the discourse whose source it has always already been. This uncanny object that is Godard's *Scenario* echoes the constitutive disposition of the subject itself. More than that, it is the site at which a model of subjectivity, the potentialities of essayistic discourse, and those of videographic inscription momentarily converge.

While there is a great deal more to be said on behalf of the appropriateness of the encounter between the essayistic and video (particularly with regard to video's current and global utilizations at the technological low end), I have chosen to focus on certain aspects of Godard's *Scenario du film Passion* to examine in detail some tactical as well as epistemological issues that arise. This excursus into a single text offers illustration of the correspondences between certain textual features of the essayistic and some recent theorizations of the subject (Lyotard, Lacan, Zizek), correspondences that find particularly acute expression in the video essay. In the spirit of these proceedings, I close with the acknowledgment of my uncertainty toward the present analysis. After nearly a decade of study, I am more daunted by my object than convinced by my formulations of it. I find some solace in the ministerings of Adorno as set forth in his *Minima Moralia:*

> When philosophers, who are well known to have difficulty in keeping silent, engage in conversation, they should try always to lose the argument, but in such a way as to convict their opponent of untruth. The point should not be to have absolutely correct, irrefutable, water-tight cognitions—for they inevitably boil down to tautologies—but insights which cause the question of their justness to judge itself.[33]

13

Video Confessions

Like the previous chapter, "Video Confessions" examines a mode of autobiographical discourse that is medium specific. In fact, the chapter was first published in a collection of essays entirely devoted to the diverse uses and effects of video, Resolutions: Contemporary Video Practices *(Minnesota, 1996). I begin with an overview of the rich history of confessional culture in the West, a history that encompasses the theological, juridical, and psychoanalytic contexts. I then move to an examination of the ways in which film- and videomakers have used the camera as a tool to probe the psyches of their subjects en route to eliciting confessional testimony. Video, I argue, has had a special confessional vocation owing to its potential for intimacy and near-instantaneous feedback. In the final sections of the chapter, I focus on the work of video artist Wendy Clarke, my collaborator in the L.A. Link project discussed in chapter 9, who has created a series of projects (*The Love Tapes *since the late 1970s and* One on One *in the early 1990s) that have allowed subject-participants to engage in remarkable acts of self-disclosure and to explore emotion and experience in depth.*

> *Every fidelis of either sex shall after the attainment of years of discretion separately confess his sins with all fidelity to his priest at least once in the year. . . . Let the priest be discreet and cautious, and let him after the manner of skilled physicians pour wine and oil upon the wounds of the injured man, diligently inquiring the circumstances alike of the sinner and of the sin, by which he may judiciously understand what counsel he ought to give him, and what sort of remedy to apply, making use of various means for the healing of the sick man.*
>
> :: Canon 21, Fourth Lateran Council of 1215

Confession increasingly takes the place of penance. This development can best be recognized by considering the fact that, in its early period, the Church ordered the sinner to make a public confession as an exercise of penance. Modern Protestantism actually puts coming to terms with one's own conscience in the place of the external confession, thus unconsciously preparing for the future development that will go beyond confession and perhaps replace religion by other social institutions.

:: Theodor Reik, *The Compulsion to Confess* (1925)

Dear Lord, I'm sorry I fight with my mother, but my underwear is my own business and the business of my audience. It ain't that yellow.

:: George Kuchar, *Cult of the Cubicles* (1987)

▶

The Confessional Subject

In an interview shortly after the publication of his groundbreaking first volume of *The History of Sexuality,* Michel Foucault suggested a trajectory of continuity that linked his latest work with earlier projects such as *Madness and Civilization.* In both cases, the problem was to find out how certain questions—of madness or sexuality—"could have been made to operate in terms of discourses of truth, that is to say, discourses having the status and function of true discourses."[1] For in his work on sexuality, Foucault had discovered "this formidable mechanism . . . the machinery of the confession," by which he meant "all those procedures by which the subject is incited to produce a discourse of truth about his sexuality which is capable of having effects on the subject himself."[2] Like autobiography, with which it can be aligned,[3] confession was, for Foucault, a discourse "in which the speaking subject is also the subject of the statement," but unlike other autobiographical forms (e.g., the diary, journal, or Montaignean essay), confession was, by definition, "a ritual that unfolds within a power relationship, for one does not confess without the presence (or virtual presence) of a partner who is not simply the interlocutor but the authority who requires the confession, prescribes and appreciates it, and intervenes in order to judge, punish, forgive, console, and reconcile." And, finally, confession was a ritual "in which the expression alone, independently of its external consequences, produces intrinsic modifications in the person who articulates it: it exonerates, redeems, and purifies him; it unburdens him of his wrongs, liberates him, and promises him salvation."[4]

According to Foucault's formulation, psychoanalysis figured as simply the most recent and most scientifically explicit development of a confessional apparatus that could be traced back to Tertullian and to Augustine. In all cases, confession was understood to be a restorative vehicle, of mind or spirit, yet one in which power was necessarily implicated. In the manner of the Augustinian model (Augustine's *Confessions*, a thirteen-volume work of the late fourth century, is universally cited as originary), confession could provide "a way to escape madness, to reveal secret, hidden places, and to face the world with a new and 'easeful' liberty."[5] But according to confessional logic, the cure could be bestowed only through the guarantee of God or psychoanalyst; confession required submission to authority, divine or secular. Significantly, in neither case was the confessor the bona fide recipient of the confessant's unburdening. The priest was only a go-between in the dialogue between God and supplicant, while the analyst was the site of a transference, the object of "certain intense feelings of affection which the patient has transferred on to the physician, not accounted for by the latter's behaviour nor by the relationship involved by the treatment."[6] The implications of this dependency—confession as a play of authority, a regulation of desire—were the provocation for Foucault's critique of confessional "truth telling."

A very great deal is at stake in this critique, far more than simply a revisionist view of religious ritual or psychoanalytic practice. As so many critics have noted, Western epistemology presumes a subject who must submit to the Truth, one whose substance and identity are constructed in relation to an authoritative Other (the truth as divine, God as the "transcendental signified," the final guarantor of meaning).[7] One could then say that the Western subject finds his sweetest repose in confessional discourse. Moreover, it was not just the individual-as-subject who had been conditioned by confession, as sacrament or compulsion; social effects followed. In *The History of Sexuality*, Foucault traced the influence of the confessional mode at the level of the organization of social life in the West:

> We have . . . become a singularly confessing society. The confession has spread its effects far and wide. It plays a part in justice, medicine, education, family relationships, and love relations, in the most ordinary affairs of everyday life, and in the most solemn rites; one confesses one's crimes, one's sins, one's thoughts and desires, one's illnesses and troubles; one goes about telling, with the greatest precision, whatever is most difficult to tell. . . . Western man has become a confessing animal.[8]

Risking a fall into absolutism, such a notion of confession is nonetheless compelling for the way in which it organizes an extraordinarily dense discursive domain (theological, juridical, psychoanalytic) articulated around the confessional act into an epistemological praxis, thoroughly imbued with relations of power.

▶

The Therapy of Self-Examination

But few commentators, Foucault chief among them, construct confession solely in terms of submission to an authorizing and exteriorized source of power; confession has customarily been assigned a complex therapeutic value.[9] Peter Brown, author of the definitive English-language biography of Augustine, judged the Augustinian model of confession to be a precursor for the modern obsession for self-scrutiny: "It is this therapy of self-examination which has, perhaps, brought Augustine closest to some of the best traditions of our own age. Like a planet in opposition, he has come as near to us, in Book Ten of the *Confessions,* as the vast gulf that separates a modern man from the culture and religion of the Later Empire can allow."[10]

In the mid-1920s, psychoanalyst Theodor Reik pronounced Augustine "one of the greatest psychologists of Christianity."[11] For Reik, confession was a fundamental trope of psychic life, one response to repression: "The general urge of unconscious material to express itself sometimes assumes the character of a tendency to confess."[12] Functioning at the join of public and private domains, confession as public discourse (confessional literature or performative display) can be understood either as a kind of self-interrogation that produces spiritual reconciliation while implicitly challenging others to ethical action (a theological reading)[13] or as an acting-out of repressed material that, when subjected to analysis, can facilitate the transfer of unconscious psychic material to the preconscious (a psychoanalytic reading)—therapeutic ends, both of them. And, of course, therapy has emerged as one of the growth industries of our age. Given an understanding of the multiform historical role that confession has played in the development of Western thought, how can we now begin to talk about the transformations of confessional culture in the late twentieth century? And what place should we give to video in this account? Foucault's theorization remains pertinent.

Despite the historical sweep of Foucault's formulations, which take as their point of departure the advent of the "age of repression" in the seventeenth century, *The History of Sexuality* draws our attention to the dynamic and protean character of confessional utterance, particularly in this century. Far from censoring speech, repression has produced "a regulated and polymorphous incitement to discourse,"[14] which, as Reik notes in the opening epigraph, can find expression outside religion or the therapist's couch. Many commentators have remarked on the decline of confession in its most parochial or doctrinal sense: William James, writing at the turn of the century, refers to "the complete decay of the practice of confession in Anglo-Saxon communities";[15] Norberto Valentini and Clara di Meglio, citing a dramatic statistical decline in the level and frequency of confessional participation in the Italian Church in the 1970s, deem confession to be "in crisis."[16]

And yet in the 1990s, confessional discourse proliferates. In what follows, I will look beyond both church and couch to the aesthetic or cultural domain and indeed to a very particular corner of that domain—toward independently produced low-end video, which I will position against capital-intensive, industrially organized, mass-market cultural commodities, on film or tape. In doing so, I take as my focus selected work by independent videomakers working consciously (sometimes parodically) within the context of confessional and therapeutic discourses. What I will say about video confessions is not, therefore, ontologically grounded. I don't wish to make claims for something like a confessional potentiality intrinsic to the electronic medium; what I say will be limited and contingent. And yet I will argue for a uniquely charged linkage between "video" and "confession" in the current cultural environment for reasons that I will return to later in the essay.

Regarding the aesthetic domain, it should be said that there are substantial grounds for a turn of the confessional impulse toward specifically artistic ends (never, of course, to the exclusion of coexistent theological, psychoanalytic, or criminological contexts). At least since the Greeks, art has been judged capable of yielding "cathartic" effects for artist and audience alike through the public disclosure of concealed impulses and secret wishes, secondarily revised. Indeed, a large number of books have been written on the topic of confessional literature (among the chief objects of inquiry, Augustine, Chaucer, Shakespeare, Rousseau, De Quincey, Dostoyevsky). But in the latter half of the twentieth century, the vehicles of cultural hegemony have been transformed dramatically, along the lines of what Raymond Williams has identified as a kind of ongoing but interstitial struggle of dominant, emergent, and residual cultural forces.[17] For while it can be said that there has been an explosion of confessional and therapeutic discourses within the public sphere of American culture, that efflorescence has been less "literary" than popular cultural—in the form of tabloid journalism, talk radio, and commercial television.

Mimi White's insightful book on American television's place within this emerging landscape of public confession, *Tele-advising: Therapeutic Discourse in American Television*, examines a range of TV formats (daytime soaps, religious broadcasting, game shows, prime-time series, advice shows, shop-at-home television), all of which decisively if unpredictably generate narrative and narrational positions for their audience.[18] White ingeniously shows how television programs not only borrow from the world of psychological theory and clinical practice but also "construct new therapeutic relations."[19] Following closely on Foucault's premise that the production of confessional knowledge is equally an exercise of power and regulation, *Tele-advising* nonetheless points to the multiplicity of subject effects created by these TV therapies, outlining as well the possibilities of resistant positions.

But I want to distinguish between White's field of inquiry and my own, between the worlds of broadcast television and independent video, and thus to begin to account for the very different confessional manifestations produced in each domain. Throughout White's discussion, it is clear that confession is not only narrativized but commodified. (One could say, as Nick Browne has argued, that the master narrative of television, in line with its "supertextal" function, *is* commodification.)[20] Given the profit orientation of broadcast television, all confessional transactions—from Dr. Ruth to *The Love Connection*—are also commercial ones. If successful, the show's presentation of embarrassing disclosures of newlywed couples entices a generous share of the viewing audience and thus higher advertising rates from sponsors. The lifeblood of such commercial ventures must be mass appeal, a requirement to which confession responds, if we may judge by the number and variation of talk therapy vehicles. These therapeutic discourses offer illustration of Reik's characterization of confession as a kind of repetition compulsion[21] ("everyone confesses over and over again to everybody else," says White of TV talk formats),[22] only these secrets are made available to home audiences rather than professional auditor/confessors. As participatory as televisual therapy may appear to be ("telling one's story on television is part of the process of recovery"),[23] there can never be a thoroughgoing disengagement from the consumer culture of which the confessional scene is a support. As we shall see, there is a rather different dynamic to be discerned in the realm of video confession.

▶

Camera: Instrument of Confession

> *We have learned from Freud that verbal presentations are necessary to make consciousness possible. It is only the con-*

*fession that enables us to recognize preconsciously what the
repressed feelings and ideas once meant and what they still
mean for us, thanks to the indestructibility and timelessness
peculiar to the unconscious processes. By the confession we
become acquainted with ourselves. It offers the best possibility
for self-understanding and self-acceptance.*
:: Theodor Reik, *The Compulsion to Confess*

*Yes, the camera deforms, but not from the moment that it be-
comes an accomplice. At that point it has the possibility of
doing something I couldn't do if the camera wasn't there: it
becomes a kind of psychoanalytic stimulant which lets people
do things they wouldn't otherwise do.*
:: Jean Rouch

Chronique d'un été (1961), Jean Rouch and Edgar Morin's monumental
experiment in direct cinema, can also be seen as a milestone in the development of "camera confessions" in the documentary mode, an embryonic
instance of what I have elsewhere called "techno-analysis."[24] There are
two key confessional scenes enacted in the film: Marilou's face-to-face
encounters with Morin, in which corruscating self-inquisition brings her
to the edge of emotional collapse, and Holocaust survivor Marceline's soliloquy of wrenching wartime memory delivered to a Nagra she carries in
her handbag as she strolls through Les Halles. These are two of the most-
criticized moments of the film during *Chronique*'s famous penultimate
sequence, in which the subjects themselves argue over the sincerity of the
personal testimony and the film's overall merits. The filmmakers, though
far from sanguine about the prospects of success for their experiment, are
convinced that they are on to something. In Rouch's words:

> Very quickly I discovered the camera was something else; it was not a brake
> but let's say, to use an automobile term, an accelerator. You push these people
> to confess themselves and it seemed to us without any limit. Some of the
> public who saw the film *[Chronique]* said the film was a film of exhibition-
> ists. I don't think so. It's not exactly exhibitionism: it's a very strange kind
> of confession in front of the camera, where the camera is, let's say, a mirror,
> and also a window open to the outside.[25]

The camera is for Rouch a kind of two-way glass that retains a double
function: it is a window that delivers the profilmic to an absent gaze and,
at the same moment, a reflective surface that reintroduces us to ourselves.
Rouch's insight brilliantly anticipates what the video apparatus (with the
playback monitor mounted alongside the camera) realizes.

As founding a moment as Rouch's experiments may be in the history of filmic confession, a crucial break occurs when the camera as confessional instrument is taken up by the confessant herself. In this configuration, the camera becomes the "camera-stylo" first described by Alexandre Astruc, a moving-image equivalent to the pen that has so assiduously transcribed two millennia of confessional discourses. There are indeed exemplary instances in which filmmakers have committed to film the ebb and flow of conscience and moral evaluation: Jonas Mekas, for one, whose ongoing project *Diaries, Notes, and Sketches*, reinscribes and puts to the test the artist's life since his emigration to the United States in 1949. In a film such as *Lost, Lost, Lost* (1975), Mekas lays his narration, steeped in the memory of the people and places we are shown, over footage excerpted from fourteen years of filming (1949–1963). The "present-tense" voice interrogates "past" images through a temporally disjunctive diaristic method that produces the confession of his own cinematic practice as a compulsion to remember: "It's my nature now to record, to try to keep everything I am passing through. . . . to keep at least bits of it. . . . I've lost too much. . . . So now I have these bits that I've passed through."[26]

But the first-person, artisanal style that has been refined through five decades of the New American Cinema (Deren, Mekas, Brakhage, Baillie, et al.) has always strained against an industrial bias as economically grounded as it is ideological.[27] The legendary spring-wound Bolex—so light, so durable—even Brakhage's handwrought signatures, etched into the emulsion itself, could not free the cineast from a dependence on large-scale manufacturers who could discontinue stocks (even whole formats) if profit margins sagged. Then too there were the vagaries of the local labs to contend with.

The development of the Sony Portapak in the mid-1960s provided visual artists with a greater possibility of relative autonomy. Not that the portapak, designed and manufactured as it was by a major Japanese conglomerate, and its descendants can be deemed a more artisanal format than 16 mm film. Indeed, the potential for the handcrafting so beloved by 16 mm and 8 mm enthusiasts has been lost in the transition to electronic pixels.[28] In exchange, the independent videomaker or home consumer has been relieved of certain mediating contingencies—material, temporal—that separate shooting from viewing, production from exhibition. It is the systematic solipsism and "immediacy" of video (the latter, in particular, a notion to be approached with much caution for its implicit metaphysical implications) that suit it so well to the confessional impulse. No technician need see or hear the secrets confided to tape. None but the invited enter the loop of the video confession.

The Electronic Confessional

In its nearly thirty years of existence, the mass-marketed video apparatus has succeeded in colonizing the business of the preservation of family ritual (home video, wedding video), of information exchange (dating services, instructional media—from closed-circuit patient education in hospitals and clinics to aerobics tapes), and, in a less systematic fashion, of do-it-yourself or "techno-therapy."[29] All of these are nonfiction applications consistent with that most elemental of documentary functions, the preservational.[30] Certain of the aforementioned instances combine preservation with persuasion or instruction (e.g., health education or exercise tapes), while others (such as the home video) provide a moving-image catalog of domestic life to be stored and perused at will. But as compared to generic "home video," video confessions are deictic. (Most of the confessional video with which I am familiar is also artfully crafted. The distinctions I am delimiting here are based primarily on discursive function rather than aesthetic value.) Confessions of the sort that I am examining can also be functionally opposed to other preservational formats, such as the wedding video, in that they are autobiographical and counterindustrial.[31]

It is necessary to resolve the precise object of the present inquiry with an even finer grain. There have, for example, been some important confessional works in video made outside the autobiographical ambit, such as Maxie Cohen's *Intimate Interviews: Sex in Less than Two Minutes* (1984) and *Anger* (1986). In these pieces, Cohen expertly (and from off-camera) elicits the disclosure of intense emotion from a series of interview subjects. In *Anger,* for example, a man calling himself "Master James," a black hood masking his features, confesses to the pleasures he experiences through the whipping of compliant females; he traces his sexual preference to a mother who, though they shared a single room, punished him as a boy for looking at her unclothed body. Another man admits on-camera to four murders. While he displays no remorse for the crimes, only one of which he claims to have committed in anger, he does evidence an ironic self-knowledge. He describes the irreparable atrophy of his liver tissue caused by years of alcoholism and notes that Eastern medicine aligns that organ with one emotion—anger. In each of *Anger*'s seven sequences, people (as individuals, couples, or gangs) speak about an emotion that is very near the surface; anger is the lever whose expression frees discourse from repression. The confessing subjects have been raped, slashed with knives, betrayed, abused, and abandoned and have responded with tears, embitterment, or violence. The unresolved emotion they have lived with has in some cases driven them to unspeakable acts, which they nonetheless offer freely to the camera with only the occasional encouragement from Cohen off-screen. Clearly, as Reik predicted, confession has taken the place of penance. The subjects seek not forgiveness but expressive release in the form of dialogues—between imaged subject and a present but unimaged interlocutor —from which only monologues survive. I am suggesting that first-person video confessions, addressed to an absent confessor/Other, mediated through an ever-present apparatus, constitute a discursive formation significantly different from the truncated dialogue, one that offers particular insight into the specificities and potentialities of the medium itself.[32]

First-person video confessions satisfy Foucault's formulation of confession as "a discourse in which the speaking subject is also the subject of the statement," with the "speaking subject" understood as necessarily and simultaneously the "enunciating subject." (Here enunciation entails the repertoire of tasks required to conceive, shoot, and edit a confessional tape.) The subjects of Cohen's works are thus "speaking," but not "enunciating," subjects. Indeed, it might be argued that *Anger*'s subjects, like those of other documentaries of the interactive mode in which the interview format prevails,[33] are more spoken than speaking. The distinction is pertinent to my earlier claim that confessional discourse is particularly well suited to the solipsistic potentiality of video.

With regard to the therapeutic value of diaristic video confessions, I do not wish to suggest that these practices provide actual substitutes for professional therapies. For its part, traditional psychoanalytic theory is fairly categorical with regard to the distinction between analysis and catharsis or "acting-out," which Reik, for one, never accepts as a therapeutic end in itself:

> Acting-out, if elevated to be the dominating element of psychoanalysis, ruptures the frame of the treatment and transforms the provisional device of analytical experience into a final phase which is nowhere essentially different from the experiences "outside." That technique gives the suppressed impulses and wishes, as well as the need for punishment, full gratification, while we wish to avoid just that in psychoanalysis, which should, according to Freud, be accomplished in abstinence. We said earlier that acting-out is not an emotional end in itself. . . . the analyst reopens to him [the confessant] the way from acting-out to remembering which we expect. In this sense, acting-out, too, is an unconscious confession in the form of representation or display; its interpretation is an essential part of analysis.[34]

Of course, the reference to "abstinence" here is indicative of the distance that separates a monastic Freudianism from the free-for-all that is artistic expression. It is worth noting that autobiographical forms, particularly in the public realm in which film and video reception gets defined, are frequently labeled "self-indulgent." The asceticism that effectuates analysis (and the narrative economy of popular cinema is, in its own way, ascetic) is anathema to the self-immersion of first-person video confessions that obsessively track personal truths. It could hardly be otherwise. According to the Freudian orthodoxy, then, "acting-out" (first-person confession) demands its analytical Other (the analyst-confessor). Could it be, however, that, in the stages of secondary revision we call editing, the videomaker/confessant has the potential, in working through the material, to produce, if only implicitly, something like an analysis, to move from acting-out to remembering, from the unconscious to the preconscious or even to consciousness?

▶

First-Person Video Confessions

A particularly telling instance of the transition from Rouch's incitational camera to first-person video confession occurs in Arthur Ginsberg's notorious documentary soap opera *The Continuing Story of Carel and Ferd* (1970–1971), in which the San Francisco–based videographer set out to chronicle the vicissitudes of a former porn queen turned independent filmmaker and a one-eyed, bisexual junkie, who choose to marry and live their lives before the camera in a videofreex version of *An American Family*.[35] When, months down the line, celebrity and the connubial luster begin to wane, Carel and Ferd wrest the camera from "Awful Arthur," the better to probe the depths of their unhappiness through a one-on-one confrontation. (It seems that the couple had been "seeing a shrink"— Ferd's description—in the period just previous.)

Toward the end of an hour-long précis of the *Continuing Story* produced by WNET's Television Laboratory (1975) in which a reunited Carel and Ferd provide in-studio commentary for the edited compilation, the latter-day Carel describes this appropriation of the apparatus: "It was important for us to use the camera therapeutically. . . . So we took the cameras alone and used them." "And Arthur had nothing to do with it?" asks their on-camera interviewer. "He couldn't use this stuff," replies Carel. "It was too real."

But the footage is used in the hour-long version (now distributed by Electronic Arts Intermix). Ferd and Carel in turn focus in unflinching close-up on the fine gestures and bodily details of the other (Carel's fingers nervously flicking ashes from her cigarette, Ferd's unsmiling lips as he smokes, eats, and talks). The one interrogates the other, posing difficult questions from behind the lens, the camera straining to catch out truths betrayed or, better yet, get under the skin. It is a kino-eye usage, an attempt to extend the perfectibility of the human eye to intrapsychic ends. While the ploy inevitably fails (at least their union—as well as the melodrama—dissolves), *The Continuing Story of Carel and Ferd* establishes the paradigm of interpersonal video therapy with an intensity appropriate to the genre.

In the twenty years since the completion of *Carel and Ferd*, there have been a great number of first-person video confessions produced by independent artists. And while I think it important to draw attention to the range and particularities of this work, I will only be able to discuss a few tapes in any detail. The criterion for selection is primarily a heuristic one (which pieces most vividly illustrate a particular discursive strategy or conceptual affiliation). Artists who have produced video confessions of the sort I have described include Ilene Segalove (*The Mom Tapes* [1974–1978], *The Riot Tapes* [1983]), Skip Sweeney (*My Father Sold Studebakers* [1983]), George Kuchar (the *Weather Diary* series, *Cult of the Cubicles* [1987]), Lynn Hershman (*Confessions of a Chameleon* [1986], *Binge* [1987]), Vanalyne Green (*Trick or Drink* [1984], *A Spy in the House That Ruth Built* [1989]), Sadie Benning (virtually all of her work to date, including *If Every Girl Had a Diary* [1989], *Me and Rubyfruit* [1989], *Jollies* [1990], *It Wasn't Love* [1992]), Susan Mogul (*Everyday Echo Street: A Summer Diary* [1993]), and Wendy Clarke (*The Love Tapes* project [1978–1994], the *One on One* series [1990–1991]).

> Right now I'm sitting here with no cameraman in the room. I'm totally alone. I would never, ever talk this way if somebody were here. It's almost as if, if somebody were in the room, it would insure lying . . . just like eating alone. I think that we've become kind of a society of screens, of different layers that keep us from knowing the truth, as if the truth is almost unbearable and too much for us to deal with, just like our feelings. So we deal with things through replications, and through copies, through screens, through simulations, through facsimiles, and through fiction . . . and through faction.
> :: Lynn Hershman, *Binge*

Lynn Hershman's on-camera monologues in the various entries of her *Electronic Diary* (1985–1989) tend toward the overtly confessional.

Her pronouncements in *Binge* certainly lay out some of the issues to be confronted in the analysis of first-person video confessions. It is a central premise of my argument that taped self-interrogation can achieve a depth and a nakedness of expression that is difficult to duplicate with a crew or even camera operator present. At first glance, the physical isolation of the confessant appears to be at odds with the dynamic of religious and psychoanalytic confession, each of which requires a confessor. To return to Foucault's characterization, "one does not confess without the presence (or virtual presence) of a partner who is not simply the interlocutor but the authority who requires the confession, prescribes and appreciates it, and intervenes in order to judge, punish, forgive, console, and reconcile."[36]

This model would seem, however, to apply to work, like Maxie Cohen's, that depends on the artist's solicitation and preselection, varying degrees of intimacy or distance toward the subjects during production, the introduction of gestural or verbal cues to induce expansiveness, closure, and the like. But this method entails, precisely, "direction" of the more traditional sort; confession is coaxed and elicited rather than simply given the opportunity to issue forth as occurs in the first-person mode. In contrast, the work of the priest or analyst is typically undirected; it is the ear of the other as an organ of passive listening, mirroring rather than choosing, that facilitates confession. With the interactive or directed variant, confession is tendered (not always consciously) to the videomaker herself; confessional discourse of the diaristic sort addresses itself to an absent, imaginary other. Consider, for example, Cohen's *Intimate Interviews: Sex in Less than Two Minutes,* in which four men and women speak directly to the camera about the personal idiosyncracies of their sexual lives. It is a compressed, parodic play of souped-up self-disclosure, confession reduced to the edge of legibility (TV-fashion), much in contrast to the extended, purgative narration—glorying in every pause, every parapraxis—in which Hershman engages in *Binge.* The latter approach, through its willingness to give center stage to unexpurgated self-disclosure as the enunciative act, tells us more about the specific character and potentiality of video as a medium suited to confession. From this point of view, video can be seen as a format historically joined to the private and the domestic, a medium capable of supplying inexpensive sync sound images, a vehicle of autobiography in which the reflex gaze of the electronic eye can engender an extended, even obsessive, discourse of the self.

From a crudely developmental perspective, one could say that first-person video confession has simply built on an evolutionary dynamic in which the public confession initially ordained by medieval church doctrine gave way to a private, one-on-one ritual. Then, in the sixteenth century, Protestantism eliminated the externalization of confession as a face-to-face ritual of reconciliation, fostering a kind of spiritual entrepreneurship. Video preserves and deepens that dynamic of privatization and entrepreneurship. Now, with the help of their cameras, videomakers can exhume their deepest fears and indiscretions all on their own—then put their neuroses on display. In a sense, first-person video confession is uniquely suited to its moment. Born of late-stage capitalism, it endows therapeutic practice with exchange value.

There are other ways to understand the advantage of the first-person format. As Rouch demonstrated with Marceline's soliloquy in *Chronique d'un été,* the presence of the camera or recorder is sufficient to spur self-revelation. In the case of video confessions, the virtual presence of a partner—the imagined other effectuated by the technology—turns out to be a more powerful facilitator of emotion than flesh-and-blood interlocutors. Camera operators, sound booms, cables, and clapper boards are hardly a boon to soul confession. Hershman's statement, in the epigraph at the beginning of this section, the claim that she would "never, ever talk this way" if there were another person in the room, returns us to the heart of the matter.[37]

Given that Hershman's telling describes the travails of an eating disorder in which she ravishes a host of "caloric strangers," frequently in the privacy of her boudoir, we can assume that the artist knows something about the solitary character of compulsive behavior. But is the tape simply another repetition of binge behavior, or does it enact a level of analysis sufficient to move it beyond the realm of catharsis or "acting-out" against which Reik warns us? I would argue that the control Hershman exerts over the structure and design of her tape, signs of secondary revision, suggests that once-repressed unconscious material has been, at least temporarily, rendered conscious and malleable. There is also a way in which Hershman refuses to let herself off the hook in what she shows us of herself. She warns that we are a society that functions most comfortably by means of simulation rather than authentic action or emotion. As she intones her critique of the growing inauthenticity of everyday life ("so we deal with things through replications, and through copies"), her imaged self begins to reduplicate itself in an infinite regress of video boxes. Hershman's self-indictment might also be seen as a further indication of the analytical insight foreign to brute cathartic displays. Her sense of the limits of her "cure"—her confession as itself a kind of artful, socially acceptable repetition of her condition—speaks to the internally contradictory character of confessional discourse that contains the symptom within the cure.[38]

Although there are many more video confessions deserving of discussion, I would like to turn to the work of Wendy Clarke, whose twin vocations—as performance artist/videomaker and psychotherapist—make her the ideal subject for this inquiry. Specifically, I want to focus on two of her projects, each of which explores video's confessional and therapeutic potentialities in new and surprising ways. The place to start is with Clarke's *Love Tapes* project, which since 1978 has afforded thousands of individuals a chance to voice deep emotion through a process of mediated self-interrogation. The minimalism of the concept is compelling: individuals of every age and background are given three minutes of tape time in which to speak about what love means to them. Clarke facilitates rather than directs the process; she supplies her subjects with the opportunity to make tapes and the requisite tools to accomplish the task. A small, booth-like structure is erected, usually at a public site (a mall, a bus station, a prison), containing a chair, a video camera mounted for a frontal, medium close-up, and a monitor.[39] Each participant chooses a backdrop and musical accompaniment as mood dictates before activating the camera. The subject is necessarily the first audience of the piece, for it is only upon the granting of permission that the tape becomes a part of the installation—instantly available for public viewing—and of the larger project.

Clarke's only other role is as the bestower of a single animating word: *love.* As "anger" was the incitation for Cohen, so is "love" the emotional levering point that explains the power of *The Love Tapes.* It

Love Tapes setup. Drawing by Loring Eutemey.

is the mana-word that spurs confession.[40] The performance produced is undirected, but not, I think, unprompted. I would argue that it is the video apparatus as "pure potentiality"—its capabilities for preservation, instantaneous replay, repeated consumption, mass duplication, and public broadcast (all of which have been realized by *The Love Tapes* project)—that effectuates response. Admittedly, the myriad soliloquies collected by Clarke are not so pointedly therapeutic as those contained in *Chronique d'un été* or *Carel and Ferd*. They may not, in fact, conform so closely to what Lacan has termed "full speech"—the talking cure that works through past trauma as an effect of language. The tapes do, however, tap remarkable, and unpredictable, affective wellsprings in troubled youths, guilt-stricken fathers, adoring dog owners, those who have lost or never known love, others whose capacity for love has been revived. The monologues, which frequently pivot on the confessant's (in)ability to experience physical or emotional intimacy, repeatedly speak the unspoken. Why, we might ask, do these individuals, many of whom claim to be incapable of expressing their innermost feelings to those closest to them, choose to eviscerate themselves so profoundly for the camera?

It is as if, in an age in which the information superhighway breeds a kind of "knowledge dependency" via antenna, cable, and optical fibers, *The Love Tapes* effect a temporary inversion of techno-polarities. Instead of spewing a one-way stream of words and images (which, at another level, only soften up the consumer for the kill), Clarke's installed monitor shows the subject only herself as she (re)produces herself. The screen/ mirror also becomes a blank surface on which an active projection of the self, rather than a strictly receptive introjection, reigns triumphant. At last, in a reversal of broadcast fortunes close to Brecht's dream, the television stops talking and just listens.[41] Video becomes the eye that sees and the ear that listens, powerfully but without judgment or reprisal. As for the potential critique of the tapes—that they simply commodify emotion or gratify narcissism—the truth is that only a tiny fraction of these pieces have ever been publicly viewed, and fewer still have been broadcast. The charge of media celebrity is unconvincing for work whose cumulative impact begins to feel more and more species specific, less and less individuated.

I remain convinced that it is video-as-potentiality that fuels the emotional impact of *The Love Tapes*. What makes the experience of the tapes so powerful for subjects and audiences alike can never be duplicated on the couch. Clarke's success taps into the staggeringly hegemonic media current and temporarily redirects the flow. The very force that, while informing and entertaining us, delivers us to the advertisers now becomes a vehicle for performing ourselves for ourselves. The professional analyst can elicit, mirror, and interpret the subject's desire but lacks the levering capacity that the media apparatus inchoately mobilizes.

One on One

> The main object that I really want is to see how open I can get to be, and I think this is a unique opportunity for myself because I don't know you, you don't know me. We don't have to ever know each other besides these tapes.
> :: Ken from *Ken and Louise*

> It's possible I could say things to you that I couldn't say to anybody else . . . Maybe, we'll see.
> :: Louise from *Ken and Louise*

> I find that it's that vulnerable place that I have to address. And you have let me touch yours in a short time. Sometimes people can be married even for years and years and never have allowed their partner to touch that place. And for that I'm very grateful. I'm very grateful. It was a type of a freedom because I knew I was like you. . . . When you said it, I felt what you were saying.
> :: Ken

While *The Love Tapes* may be the most streamlined and populist of first-person video confessions, Wendy Clarke's *One on One* series may be the most complex, bearing as it does the traces of confessional discourse's triple legacy—the theological, the psychoanalytic, and the criminological. For four years, Clarke was an artist-in-residence at the California Institution for Men, a minimum-security prison in Chino, during which time she led workshops in poetry writing, painting, photography, and videomaking. Late in 1990, Clarke proposed a new project to her video workshop: a series of video letters to be exchanged between the class members and people on the outside. Like *The Love Tapes*, these video letters would be intimate and self-regulated but, unlike them, would be addressed, directly and exclusively, to an individual who would respond in kind.[42]

Clarke's concept included another key proviso: the relationship between subjects was to remain a video exchange only. "I wanted them to have a very pure video experience," Clarke has said. "And I felt that the relationships would be changed if they met in any other way outside of this video space."[43] To that end, Clarke functioned as a go-between, minimally facilitating the tapings (usually made in solitude, *Love Tapes* fashion), allowing participants to play back the entry and reshoot if they so chose, then shuttling the tapes to their proper recipients. And, indeed, the connections made between these individuals are remarkable, crossing as they do barriers of race, class, gender, age, and sexual orientation. Those incarcerated are mostly young men of color (black, brown, and red), while the "outsiders" are typically older, both black and white, and frequently female. (Members of the latter group were drawn either from the membership of a progressive church in Santa Monica or from a community of successful African American businesspeople in the Crenshaw district of Los Angeles.) Beyond this sketchy description, few generalizations can be made that apply equally to all fifteen of the tapes in the series except to note that the linkages among participants are in every instance effected entirely through a media apparatus. In this regard, the *One on One* series is a remarkable case study, one in which, in the words of one critic, "the camera, instead of blocking communication, seems to be a two-way umbilical cord that nourishes the candor of both parties."[44]

In an age in which face-to-face encounters have tended to be displaced by mediated ones (e.g., American political campaigns) and in which that development is inevitably figured as a loss, *One on One* demonstrates that the contrary can also be true. "I can express all of my emotions and everything to you," says Raul, a twenty-three-year-old Latino, father of two, who struggles with alcoholism and is estranged from his wife. As the exchange progresses, Raul digs deeper: "To tell the truth, I'm happy without drinking, real happy without having the bottle and getting drunk, all of that. Because all of that time, I might have been with a smile but I was crying inside." How is it that Raul is capable of revealing himself in this way to the video camera? Is the answer to be found in the particular wisdom of his interlocutor, Jeanene, a Caucasian woman in her late thirties who teaches high school in a Latino section of Los Angeles? Or can it be that the *One on One* concept engendered a therapeutic experience for its participants and that, in certain cases, we witness something akin to a positive transference, as described by Freud, in which the removal of repression is aided by the formation of an attachment to the analyst, an attachment properly belonging to earlier (often parental) relationships?

If the latter is so (transference mingling with incipient bonds of kinship or affection), the wonder of the *One on One* tapes is that the transference tends to be both mutual and reciprocal. In almost every instance, vulnerabilities are shared, positions of confessor/confessant exchanged. In fact, the psychodynamic is such that the openness of the one induces greater openness in the other in a kind of therapeutic spiral. In *Ken and Louise*, a black man—married, restrained but confident, a talented songwriter and vocalist—exchanges tapes with an upbeat but somewhat distant white woman of similar age and interests. He suggests that she is putting on an "air." She replies that she is "afraid I'm going to say something wrong to you"; her distance is the result of an excessive sensitivity to racial politics ingrained from childhood. (Her father, once a member of the Communist Party, had been jailed for his political affiliations in the early 1950s.) With each tape exchanged, the emotional intimacy gathers a greater force. Ken writes and sings a song to Louise about the colors not of the skin but of the heart. He is a startlingly gifted singer whose lyrics reveal a delicacy and depth of feeling. In reply, Louise shares with him a small stuffed animal, a monkey named Lucky, whom she cuddles and kisses, giggling with nervous excitement. "Every day I hug her and squeeze her, and you're just about the only person who knows about this." His gift to her has inspired an even riskier display of her secret self. ("It's possible I could say things to you that I couldn't say to anybody else . . . Maybe, we'll see.") And it is through the incitation of the video medium that so powerfully fuses distance and intimacy that this cathartic pas de deux is effected.

As the exchange progresses and Ken nears his date of release, many of the viewer's expectations are overturned. Ken is increasingly buoyant of spirit, self-assured, offering more than receiving emotional support. Louise strips herself bare, revealing layer after layer of emotion testifying to the loneliness of her life, her inability to find a man to love. Her mood darkens. Given the audio/visibility of the process, we are able to judge these interior changes through outward signs—gesture, facial expression, posture, choice of attire, as well as vocal tonalities. Our initial assumptions about these tapes are likely to include an implicit belief in the position of the "outsider" as the more powerful and empowering one (with the attention paid to the inmates restoring their damaged self-esteem). And while the assumption may hold initially and even throughout many of the fifteen *One on One* dialogues, it proves to be far from universal. By her fifth tape, Louise is slumped deep into her chair. Her unmade-up face a mask of despair, she announces that she is in a "state of grief." In Ken's reply, he assures her that her "dark, overclouded look upon things" will pass. He speaks of wanting to reach out to her "in a real way," adding, "I don't necessarily mean the man-lady type of thing."

Both Ken and Louise struggle to define the growing connection between them. There is the flicker of sexual attraction, particularly in Louise's flirtatious beginnings. That edge never entirely disappears, evidenced by

Ken from Wendy Clarke's *Ken and Louise* (1991).

Louise's embarrassment well into the tape when she realizes that she has casually addressed Ken as "hon." And, indeed, what names do we have for such a hybridized relationship—intimate yet remote, equal parts human and electronic? The distance is the result of the bar to bodily contact, nearness the result of an intensity of discourse, a zeroing in on the other's affective domain. After Louise shares her Lucky with Ken, he shows her the guitar that he has played in previous tapes. He has christened it "Louise" in her honor, adding, "It's like a lady—curves and stuff like that. It happens to be brown, but that's no reflection on you." Exchanged confidences are gifts bestowed, producing and eliciting confession. As per the psychoanalytic literature, unconscious material is transferred into verbal presentations and perceptions, repressed material unleashed, preparing the way for "the possibility for a better kind of adjustment to reality."[45]

But there are more directly political considerations to be encountered alongside the therapeutic ones. In the context of Brecht's critique of radio (see note 41), video exchanges such as those of the *One on One* series constitute a kind of resistance to the commercial broadcast model, which offers a "mere sharing out" of entertainment. Brecht imagined the potential of radio as "the finest possible communication apparatus in public life," as "a vast network of pipes" if only it "knew how to receive as well as to

Louise from Wendy Clarke's *Ken and Louise* (1991).

transmit, how to let the listener speak as well as hear, how to bring him into a relationship instead of isolating him."[46] If it can be said of the series that transferential relations between insiders and outsiders are mutual and reciprocal, it can also be said that the clear-cut distinction between producer and consumer is obviated. While a claim of media empowerment can be made for other public art projects such as *The Love Tapes* in which thousands of individuals from all walks of life have made tapes by themselves about themselves, here the gains are even greater. Here, in a precise miming of the Brechtian prescription, "the listener speak[s] as well as hear[s]," indeed, speaks only after listening, perhaps speaks even while hearing. This delicacy of listening is in fact enhanced by the mediated circumstances; there are no auxiliary sources of information for these interlocutors. The subjects of the video letter exchanges learn to listen with a special intensity, frequently replaying the tape just received several times before beginning their own reply. Theirs is a special kind of speech, one that teaches listening.

These exchanges are also profoundly communitarian in their power to overcome the isolation of those incarcerated. How rarely do contemporary media forms work to build bridges across human differences rather than simply make spectacles of those differences? In this instance, the bridges built transcend their apparent limits in demonstrable ways. People who have never and will never meet enter into relations in which trust grows incrementally, in which vulnerabilities are increasingly shared, in which emotions attached to long-buried experiences are allowed to surface. In *Rickey and Cecilia,* Rickey, a young Latino man serving a sixteen-month jail sentence on drug charges, develops a video relationship with Cecilia, a fifty-one-year-old white woman. In his first tape, Rickey speaks about the mix of feelings he has for his younger brother, who is also serving time. Rickey is sorry to have failed as a role model, regretful that their relationship has soured. In her reply, Cecilia replies in kind:

> I was very close to my younger sister, and we were very good friends when I was in my twenties and she was in her teens. Then she became mentally ill, and later, when she was in her twenties—and it was related to the mental illness—she died. I lost her completely except in my memories and feelings. So maybe you have a fear that you'll lose your brother. But maybe you won't, maybe there's still hope for you two, and you'll be able to connect up when you're both out of prison.

The young man is clearly moved by this disclosure; he returns to the topic of his estranged brother several times more during the remainder of their exchanges. Cecilia has struck a nerve. In *One on One,* relationships of trust are built upon a foundation of reciprocal confession, freely given and exchanged. Confidences, painful memories, the willingness to allow the other to touch one's own place of vulnerability and vice versa become the basis for a connection between people who will never meet except on videotape.

The *One on One* dialogues are remarkable from another perspective as well. If, as I have claimed, the confessions exchanged are freely given, they can be contrasted to another kind of self-disclosure well known to the incarcerated subjects. Confession plays an important role in criminology and the practice of law, as evidenced in prime-time cop shows such as *NYPD Blue.* Detective John Kelly's most outstanding police skill is his ability to induce confessions through recourse to an emotional repertoire ranging from the quiescence of feigned sympathy to the near edge of violence. If Kelly can move from tough guy to father confessor so adroitly, it is because, in ushering the accused into those airless rooms, he shares with them a zone of liminality. In criminological terms, confession is a threshold moment, marking the possibility of the criminal's first step on his way back to society. "By confessing, he finds the first possibility of a return to the community after he had put himself, through his deed, outside its limits."[47] In that liminal zone, no emotion, no promise, no sign of remorse remains unthinkable. Kelly's weekly performances are staged both for the perpetrators and for an audience of millions. But there is a particular legacy—visual representation as an apparatus of social control—that haunts this spectacle.

Photographically based representation has played a substantial historical role in the recent history of state power. As John Tagg writes in *The Burden of Representation*, photography began to function as a regulatory and disciplinary apparatus in the aftermath of the failed rebellions of the late 1840s, just at the moment of the consolidation of power of the modern state.[48] Tagg traces a rendezvous between a "novel form of the state and a new and a developing technology of knowledge," in which photography could contribute to the control of a large and dangerously diversified workforce newly arrived in the urban centers.

> Like the state, the camera is never neutral. The representations it produces are highly coded, and the power it wields is never its own. As a means of record, it arrives on the scene vested with a particular authority to arrest, picture and transform daily life, a power to see and record. . . . If, in the last decades of the nineteenth century, the squalid slum displaces the country seat and the "abnormal" physiognomies of patient and prisoner displace the pedigreed features of the aristocracy, then their presence in representation is no longer a mark of celebration but a burden of subjection. A vast and repetitive archive of images is accumulated in which the smallest deviations may be noted, classified and filed. The format varies hardly at all. There are bodies and spaces. The bodies—workers, vagrants, criminals, patients, the insane, the poor, the colonized races—are taken one by one: isolated in a shallow, contained space; turned full face and subjected to an unreturnable gaze; illuminated, focused, measured, numbered and named; forced to yield to the minutest scrutiny of gestures and features. Each device is the trace of a wordless power, replicated in countless images, whenever the photographer prepares an exposure, in police cell, prison, mission house, hospital, asylum, or school.[49]

Like the confession, the mug shot plays a recurrent role in *NYPD Blue*. Eyewitnesses whose testimony will be needed to convict are frequently given pages of images—head shots that have been illuminated, focused, measured, numbered, and named—from which they are asked to choose and thus provide the crucial ID. In *One on One*, the incarcerated, while also "isolated in a shallow, contained space; turned full face," are not subjected to an unreturnable gaze. These prisoners, after all, have already been "subjected" in countless ways: removed from social contact and from their families; given clothing, living space, and food meant to reinforce a regimen of mind-numbing uniformity. Indeed, the experience of incarceration is calculated to strip the inmate of all the trappings of individuation through which subjecthood is achieved. But in seizing the opportunity to return the media gaze, to speak as well as listen, these men are endowed with a measure of subjectivity denied the most privileged TV viewer tuned to the broadcast signal.

The *One on One* project attests to a power latent in the video medium, a power that has seldom been explored. It is a power that is political, psychological, and spiritual: a power to facilitate the reversal of repression at the level of (confessional) speech and of experience and in so doing forge bonds that are wholly media specific. Contrary to expectation, these media-specific relationships appear to engender effects (the visible signs of bolstered spirits as well as audible testimony) that are bidirectional, experienced by both video partners. It is my contention that this new kind of relationship is a fundamentally therapeutic one rooted in confession, freely and mutually exchanged. In *One on One,* the inmates' confessions—the uncoerced expressions of unspoken pain or pleasure—elude authority rather than wholly submit to it as Foucault would have it. These unsanctioned utterances serve no institutional master.[50] While indeed judgment, consolation, even reconciliation, may be sought from the interlocutor "outside," the dynamic of dominance and submission is everywhere reversible. If the ear of the other indeed contributes to the (re)construction of the speaking self, it is only on condition that the positions of self and other, confessor and confessant, remain fluid and reciprocal.

▶

Conclusion

As I stated near the beginning of this chapter, I have little interest in the ontological purity of my claims for video confessions. I have, following Foucault, been interested in tracing a skeletal history of confession and of the forces of repression that have produced in the Western subject a "regulated and polymorphous incitement to discourse." I have claimed that a new and particular variant of ritualized self-examination has arisen over the past two decades in the form of the first-person video confession, with video understood as a format uniquely suited to that purpose owing to its potential for privatized production and consumption. While pointing to a considerable body of recent work made by video artists that I have characterized as confessional, I have given special attention to two projects undertaken by Wendy Clarke, *The Love Tapes* and *One on One.* In the tapes of these series, people of disparate background and life experience are given the opportunity to reveal hidden parts of themselves through direct address to a camera that they control. Video, as apparatus and potentiality, becomes in these works a facilitator to self-examination.

But this is confessional discourse produced neither for profit nor for temporary celebrity in the manner of commercial talk formats on radio or TV. Rather, I have argued, most pointedly in reference to the *One on One* tapes, that video confessions produced and exchanged in nonhegemonic contexts can be powerful tools for self-understanding as well as for two-way communication, for the forging of human bonds and for emotional recovery. In contrast to the legacy of photographic representation as a regulatory and disciplinary apparatus, first-person video confessions of this sort afford a glimpse of a more utopian trajectory in which cultural production and consumption mingle and interact, and in which the media facilitate understanding across the gaps of human difference rather than simply capitalizing on those differences in a rush to spectacle.

14

Domestic Ethnography and
the Construction of the "Other" Self

First presented at Visible Evidence II (Los Angeles, 1994) and pub-
lished in Collecting Visible Evidence *(Minnesota, 1999), "Domestic*
Ethnography and the Construction of the 'Other' Self" stakes out a mode
of autobiographical practice that couples self-interrogation with eth-
nography's concern for the documentation of the lives of others. But the
Other in this instance is a family member who serves less as a source of
disinterested social scientific research than as a mirror or foil for the self.
Due to kinship ties, subject and object are embroiled in each other. The
result is self-portraiture refracted through a familial Other. But the notion
of domestic ethnography has become an increasingly useful classificatory
term for a documentary film type that has proliferated. In an era of great
genealogical curiosity such as our own, shared DNA becomes a power-
ful incitation to documentary practice. Festivals and student screenings
abound with films about aging or eccentric family members whose lives
provide, if only implicitly, insight into the maker's own psyche or cor-
poreal self. Moreover, the reciprocity of subject and object positions is
echoed by a recurrent trope in these works, that of the exchanged camera
as the object of the gaze is temporarily allowed to become its subject.
Nothing less than "textual authority" is at stake in this trope, the extent
to which the semiotic power of authorship is rendered reversible.

> If the West has produced anthropologists, it is because it was
> tormented by remorse.
> ::   Claude Lévi-Strauss, *Tristes Tropiques*

The ethnographic project has long been haunted by the legacy of its colonialist past. Over the past fifteen years, critiques have been launched
from many quarters against the premises of participant observation,

which James Clifford has described as "shorthand for a continuous tacking between the 'inside' and 'outside' of events," but Johannes Fabian has understood more radically as a *disjunction* between experience and science, research and writing, and thus "a festering epistemological sore" in the discipline.[1] Peter Mason has traced the philosophical problem of alterity (and the necessary setting of boundaries between self and other) to the work of Emmanuel Levinas, for whom the construction of the alterity, the absolute exteriority of the other, is a function of desire.[2] Mason notes Levinas's concern for understanding the other without recourse to the "violence of comprehension" whereby the other is reduced to self, deprived of the very alterity by which the other *is* other.[3]

Trinh T. Minh-ha has, rather more stringently, declared that anthropology's romance with the Other is "an outgrowth of a dualistic system of thought peculiar to the Occident (the 'onto-theology' which characterizes Western metaphysics)" in which difference becomes a tool of self-defense and conquest. Anthropological discourse, according to Trinh, produces "nothing other than the reconstruction and redistribution of a pretended order of things, the interpretation or even transformation of [information] given and frozen into monuments."[4] Most recently, Michael Taussig, returning brilliantly to the work of Walter Benjamin, has written of the mimetic faculty as the compulsion to become the Other through the magic of the signifier. "I call it the mimetic faculty, the nature that culture uses to create second nature, the faculty to copy, imitate, make models, explore difference, yield into and become Other."[5]

All of these critical perspectives converge around the problems entailed in representing the other. For some, it is representation itself that is the problem. Stephen A. Tyler has called for the practice of what he terms "post-modern ethnography," whereby the inherited mode of scientific rhetoric is jettisoned; "evocation" displaces representation. In Tyler's view, the ethnographic text, long treated as an "object," is more appropriately understood as a "meditative vehicle."[6] George E. Marcus has pointed to the essay form as practiced by Adorno—fragmentary, reflective, final judgment suspended—as a way out of the trap of realist convention. Formal experimentation, attention to the dialogical context of fieldwork, the incorporation of multiple authorial voices, a retreat from an illusory holism—all can contribute to "a particularly appropriate self-conscious posture," one "well suited to a time such as the present, when paradigms are in disarray, problems intractable, and phenomena only partly understood."[7]

So many replies to this crisis of ethnographic authority: calls for coevalness, evocation, fragmentation, magic, "understanding" shorn of the violence of comprehension, the unlearning of privilege, even silence.[8]

My interest here is in work currently being made by independent film and videomakers that suggests itself—at least to me—as yet another response to the ethnographic impasse. If indeed participant observation founders in its tacking between "inside" and "outside," a passage that restages the subject/object dichotomization installed in the post-Enlightenment West, the films and tapes that I term *domestic ethnography* play at the boundaries of inside and outside in a unique way. This work engages in the documentation of family members or, less literally, of people with whom the maker has maintained long-standing everyday relations and has thus achieved a level of casual intimacy. Because the lives of artist and subject are interlaced through communal or blood ties, the documentation of the one tends to implicate the other in complicated ways; indeed, consanguinity and co(i)mplication are domestic ethnography's defining features. By *co(i)mplication* I mean both complexity and the interpenetration of subject/object identities. To pursue the point yet further, one could say that domestic ethnography is a kind of supplementary autobiographical practice; it functions as a vehicle of self-examination, a means through which to construct self-knowledge through recourse to the familial other.

But domestic ethnography is more than simply another variant of autobiographical discourse, given its explicitly outward gaze; nominally, at least, this mode of documentation takes as its object the father, mother, grandparent, child, or sibling who is genetically linked to the authorial subject. Care must be taken in defining the particular relations that obtain between the domestic ethnographer and her subject. There is a peculiar sort of reciprocity (which might equally be termed self-interest) built into the construction of Other subjectivities in this para-ethnographic mode. There can be no pretense of objectivity for an investigation of a now-dead mother whose alcoholism has helped give rise to the eating disorder of the videomaker in Vanalyne Green's *Trick or Drink* (1984), just as there is little doubt that Kidlat Tahimik's eldest son (also named Kidlat), with whom the filmmaker travels and to whom he frequently addresses his insights and admonitions throughout *The Rainbow Diary* (1994), functions both as heir apparent and as autobiographical foil. Familial investigation in these recent films and tapes is, on one level, a kind of identity sleuthing in which family-bound figures—progenitors and progeny—are mined for clues to the artist's vocation, sensibility, or pathology. Domestic ethnographies tend to be highly charged investigations brimming with a curious brand of epistephilia, a brew of affection, resentment, even self-loathing. The point to stress is that for this mode of ethnography, the desire for the other is, at every moment, embroiled with the question of self-knowledge; it is the all too familiar rather than the exotic that holds sway.

I do not wish to suggest, however, that domestic ethnography of the sort I am outlining is exclusively an exercise in self-inscription. Put another way, these works could be said to enact a kind of participant observation that illumines the familial other while simultaneously refracting a self-image; indeed, the domestic ethnographic subject exists only on condition of its constitutive relations with the maker. Here there is little sense of a tacking back and forth between insider and outsider positions, the ethnographic norm. For the domestic ethnographer, there is no fully outside position available. Blood ties effect linkages of shared memory, physical resemblance, temperament, and, of course, family-forged behavioral or attitudinal dysfunction toward which the artist—through her work—can fashion accommodation but no escape.

In a limited way, domestic ethnography occasions a kind of inter-subjective reciprocity in which the representations of self and other are simultaneously if unequally at stake. This kind of work is all but indemnified against the charges often made against the pseudopositivism of the anthropologist who treats the human subject as scientific datum or statistical proof. The domestic ethnographer qua social scientist can never wholly elude her analytic scene. It has, of course, been argued that this is ever so and from several perspectives: Clifford Geertz has addressed the "signature issue," the ways in which the authorial voice necessarily enters into ethnographic discourse, echoing Hayden White's notion of the "tropic" dimension of scholarly discourse (the play of language) as "inexpungeable" from the human sciences.[9] For its part, psychoanalytic criticism assumes that authorial desire is figured in all texts, never more so than when the Other is the subject of representation. With domestic ethnography, authorial subjectivity is explicitly in question or on display. There exists a reciprocity between subject and object, a play of mutual determination, a condition of consubstantiality. The desire (figurable as dread or longing) of the domestic ethnographer is for the Other self.

▶

Fathers and Daughters

Desire is always destabilizing and delirium inducing, and instability is particularly inscribed in discourses of domestic ethnography. Su Friedrich's remarkable *Sink or Swim* (1990) evokes the artist's family history through a succession of twenty-six titled segments, each beginning with a one-word chapter heading framed against black leader, one for each letter of the alphabet displayed in reverse order, beginning with "z" for "zygote" and the artist's conception. The sound track is composed of what seem to be memory fragments, voiced by a younger Friedrich surrogate, in relation to which the accompanying images (all of them black-and-white and asynchronous, some of them drawn from Friedrich family home movie footage) seem at times illustrative, at times responsive to the previous narration, at times linked only through an associational logic. Despite the elliptical (though chronological) character of the narrated segments, the viewer is lured toward a thematically coherent reading of the text through the chapter titles, which function as a semic reservoir for the family romance: "virginity," "temptation," "seduction," "pedagogy," "kinship," "bigamy."

The film's textual coherence is uneven despite the fact that *Sink or Swim*'s narrative continuity remains more or less intact: the "zygote" section properly launches the film's autobiographical trajectory, and each fragment supports the "life story" trajectory. The sense of linearity is undermined by the thematic discontinuities among the lexia, as well as by the frequently oblique character of the sound/image relations, but these tactics are altogether consistent with the dream logic of recovered memory. As the meaning of the piece gathers force, the film's focus increasingly becomes the identity-defining relations between the father

This dreamlike image of the female bodybuilders from *Sink or Swim* accompanies a story about temptation. Photograph courtesy of Su Friedrich/Downstream Productions.

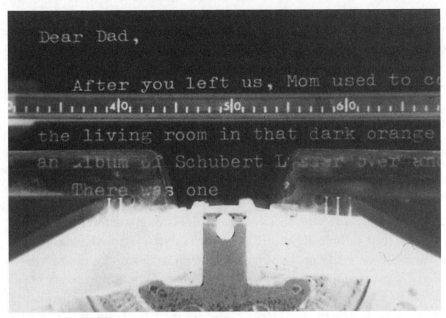

In *Sink or Swim,* filmmaker Su Friedrich types the letter she'll never send to the father who abandoned her. Photograph courtesy of Su Friedrich/Downstream Productions.

(accomplished, demanding yet remote) and the artist/daughter. "Sink or swim" is the dictum that defines the father's philosophy of parenting; his is a world of maleness and action, aloof from the reactive feminine, which tends toward lamentation and numbing resentment. After the father's departure from home and family, Friedrich's mother spends her evenings weeping to obsessively played Schubert lieder while the filmmaker resorts to consulting her anthropologist father's academic tomes, vainly searching—long after the fact—for the emotions he refused to share with the family he was abandoning at the time of their writing.

By the film's close, Friedrich has assembled a cumulative portrait of a father whose once-unassailable authority has begun to unravel. Always the source of judgment, the father is now himself exposed to the collective appraisal of the film's audience, who, in one notable example, are led to intuit the father's sense of sexual rivalry toward his adolescent daughter's admirers during a trip to Mexico. The film is, in part, her delayed revenge for his having unceremoniously sent her home for her transgressions against his incestuous authority. Hers cannot be an outright victory, however. Recall that the defining characteristics of domestic ethnography are *consanguinity* and *co(i)mplication*. Even as *Sink or Swim* moves toward its conclusion and a sense of the artist's vindication through a willful act of historiographical revisionism, the final roundelay of acoustic elements and the double printing of the home movie footage in the film's coda return us to the instability of the domestic ethnographic locus. Over home movie images of the artist as "the girl," clad in swimsuit, ready to sink or swim, Friedrich sings the "ABC Song" in a round of overlapping voices that rhyme with the ghostly doubling of the image. The final and fateful words of her song are, of course, "tell me what you think of me." Only on that concluding, deeply other-directed phrase do the discrepant voices and images coalesce.

But even as we gaze at the now-unified semblance of an achingly fragile young girl, we are filled with the knowledge that Friedrich can never entirely elude her father's grasp. Their histories are forever intertwined, their pathologies enmeshed in each other's. Filmmaking as therapeutic discourse, like analysis, remains interminable, always unfinished. Equally germane to this discussion, the particularity of this instance of domestic ethnography—*Sink or Swim* as Su Friedrich's family history—is countervailed by the familiarity of the dynamic displayed. It is on this account that identification (more with dynamic than with character or situation) is engendered.

It is the depth and indelibility of familial attachment that make the domestic subject such a special ethnographic case. And I would argue that *Sink or Swim* functions as a kind of ethnography—instructive and generalizable—for the way in which it exceeds the bounds of family portraiture. The film is structured by a series of generic elements that reinforce the universality of the subject matter: the use of the alphabet as structuring device, the elemental chapter headings, the constant use of the third person ("the girl," later "the woman") rather than first person, the generic home movie images, the concluding childhood anthem. The specificity of the narration is sustained in tension with the universality of these elements, and through that tension domestic ethnography is forged.[10]

▶

Sharing Textual Authority

The growing attention being accorded indigenous media making at film festivals and conferences and in professional journals speaks to the desire to share textual authority in matters of cultural representation. The frontispiece of Edward Said's *Orientalism* contains a quotation from Marx's *The Eighteenth Brumaire of Louis Bonaparte*: "They cannot represent themselves; they must be represented."[11] The book goes on to perform an extended critique of the epistemological arrogance of such pronouncements.

More than thirty years ago, Paul Ricoeur could write about the dawning of a "universal world civilization" and the disorientation it would bring to the waning colonial enterprise: "When we discover that there are several cultures instead of just one and consequently at the time when we acknowledge the end of a sort of cultural monopoly, be it illusory or real, we are threatened with the destruction of our own discovery. Suddenly it becomes possible that there are just *others,* that we ourselves are an 'other' among others."[12] To that sense of aborted cultural monopolies must be added the tremendous growth of access to the representational tools. What once might have occasioned the bewilderment or disdain of social scientists—this vision of ethnography as a free-for-all—is now routinely reinforced by the camcorder documentation of police abuse in Compton or crumbling Giotto frescoes at Assisi. Given the explosive growth and curious coalescence of travel and surveillance technologies, representational authority no longer resides solely with the professional classes of scholars, journalists, and state functionaries.

In this context, I propose to consider a particular textual gesture, what amounts to a moment of authorial crisis occurring in certain of the domestic ethnographies. I am referring to moments at which the maker hands over the camera to his subject, at the subject's request, moments at which filial obligation outpaces directorial control. This sharing of textual authority is born not of egalitarianism or of a penchant for the hyper-reflexive; instead, it is an outgrowth of the domestic ethnographer's intimate relations with her subject. When, in *Tomboychik* (1993), Sandi DuBowski's grandmother takes his video camera, then rolling, she intends only to "snap a picture" of her "adorable grandson." The camera is a mysterious toy to the erstwhile subject of the piece. We, on the other hand, know the game and strain to see a face already described in detail by the grandmother. *Tomboychik* is a search for the roots of DuBowski's sexual identity by way of the memories of his forebear—reminiscences of the grandmother's gender-blending childhood and of the mannish strength of her mother before her, who routinely lifted 100 -pound sacks of sugar unaided while making chocolate. The presumption may be that DuBowski's gayness can be explained genetically; the tape may also function as an unspoken reply to Nana's occasional references to a wished-for wedding and great-grandchildren.

DuBowski elicits memories of the young Nana's gendered identity. She had once been thought transgressive, a "boy/girl": she wore pants rather than dresses, fought like a boy, ran as fast and jumped as high as any of them. But Nana playfully turns the discussion—as well as the camera—to DuBowski himself. She can do this because she is Nana and because this is her dear grandson toward whom there can be no barriers. Such an exchange would not be possible with an "outsider," but this is "insider" discourse. If *Tomboychik* is ethnography, it is all but absent of the sort of description or explanation we associate with that mode of discourse. But the piece is about shopping for sexual identity in grandma's closet and about the performance of an intergenerational family masquerade (complete with wigs). The point I wish to stress is that the trope of the "shared camera," which effects an erosion of textual authority or directorial control, is endemic to domestic ethnography, one measure of the intersubjective reciprocity I have previously described.

The sharing of the apparatus with the subject packs a particular wallop in Mindy Faber's *Delirium* (1993), an essayistic investigation of her mother's madness and, more broadly, of the history of women and madness and of the link between depression and domesticity. Faber made the tape at the moment of her own motherhood, presumably to break the cycle of family horrors. Through a series of intensely framed interview sequences, we learn about the mother's symptoms, the threat she had posed to her children, as well as the mother's own memory of childhood abuse at the hands of her mother. Faber's voice—pressing for details, unsatisfied by partial explanations—is never long absent from the sound track. We learn of the husband/father's paternalism, the mother's repeated institutionalizations and escapes, her suicide fantasies, her inability or unwillingness to recall her children's fright. These on-camera recitations, prompted and in dialogue with the videomaker, are interspersed with other registers of material: archival footage of madwomen, vignettes from Faber's imagined sitcom about her mother's middle-class doldrums, printed excerpts from the clinical diagnoses of hysteria as female malady, a discursus on the career of Jean Martin Charcot and his famous clinic at Salpêtrière, a music-video-like performance sequence of a nude woman as a puppet controlled by and for the pleasure of men.

Near the end of the piece, as Faber—with intentionality but little aggressivity—presses her mother to remember the details of her abusive behavior toward the young Mindy, the mother says, "Here, give me the camera." Unprepared for the turnabout, the now-imaged videomaker struggles to hold her ground against her mother's version of their past. The authorial subject now objectified speaks to the camera at point-blank range about the terrors of returning from school to a Mom who threw pots and pans at her head. But equally terrifying is the sense of Faber's loss of control in the present-tense interaction. As with Su Friedrich's treatise on her father, but with greater empathy, Faber's task is, at least

Mother and daughter share textual authority in Mindy Faber's *Delirium*.
Photographs courtesy of Video Data Bank.

in part, a therapeutic one—a setting to rights of a painful family history in which the daughter has the last word. It is precisely this power to shape discourse that is temporarily ceded along with the camera. Of course, the footage need not have been included in the final tape. It is to Faber's credit that she recognized the sequence as consistent with her theme: the delirium-inducing potency of family-forged relations across lines of gender and generation. When the videomaker recovers the camera, it is because she has her own idea for an ending for the tape: a staged scene in which the mother's revenge (a slow-motion stabbing of the father with a banana) is enacted from the point of view of the daughter, a primal scene of retribution.

Delirium offers a striking illustration of domestic ethnography's potential to mine cultural memory with a level of intensity unavailable to outsiders. Afforded a depth of access to its subjects, domestic ethnography discloses secrets, performs masquerades of identity, and, temporarily at least, rearranges familial hierarchies. Its sleight of hand is the rendering public of private-sphere material, but not, I would argue, as spectacle.

▶ ───────────────────────────────────────

Families We Choose

Despite the attention given here to the biological family as the nexus within which identity is constructed, in which self-inscription and the representation of the familial other are reciprocally determined, it is important to note that our understanding of "the domestic" has undergone significant change in recent decades. In contrast to the family as ascribed or inherited, Kath Weston has drawn attention to an ascendent paradigm, namely, "families we choose." Weston's specific reference is to the emergence of gay and lesbian families and the reconfiguration of the inherited model they have enacted. "Chosen families do not directly oppose genealogical modes of reckoning kinship. Instead, they undercut procreation's status as a master term imagined to provide the template for all possible kinship relations."[13] Far from aligning themselves with the conservative rhetoric of "family endangerment," many commentators see the "chosen family" paradigm as pluralizing (rather than destroying) the received model of kinship structure: "The more recent forms of alternative life styles have now become part of the official fiber of society, because they are now being tolerated much more than in the past. In short, what we are witnessing is not a fragmentation of traditional family patterns, but, rather, the emergence of a pluralism in family ways."[14]

This pluralization of the familial is dramatically rendered in Thomas

Allen Harris's recent tape *Vintage: Families of Value* (1995), in which the artist explores issues of influence and identity among three sets of African American gay siblings. Harris announces his interest in a tactics of pluralized family identities with the utmost directness; his voice-over, accompanied by black leader, precedes the first image:

> In 1990, I wanted to celebrate the intensity of my relationship with my brother Lyle. I was twenty-eight years old and just beginning to explore feelings of ambivalence, fear, and hope regarding my family. I recruited two other groups of siblings, members of my community who are also queer, to join me in taking a critical look at their own families. This film is a family album created over the course of five years.

It is a family album constructed through recourse both to heredity and to choice, affirmed at every turn by the active participation of all three sets of siblings: Harris and his brother Lyle Ashton Harris; sisters Adrian Jones, Anita Jones, and Anni Cammett; and a brother-sister pair, Paul and Vanessa Eaddy. If domestic ethnography's defining features are consanguinity and co(i)mplication, *Vintage* pushes the latter term to new ends.

Harris rarely backs off from the heat of the relationships he shows us, least of all his own complex interaction with his brother, fellow artist Lyle Ashton Harris. But in a manner consistent with the pluralization of the family model, *Vintage* chooses to focus on *queer siblings*, three groups of individuals each of which is linked internally by blood ties and, across the biological family groupings, by affinity. Although this is not the precise "families we choose" template discussed in the recent sociological literature (i.e., gay or lesbian couple plus adoptive child[ren]), the horizontalizing emphasis on multiple sets of queer siblings positions community alongside biological family grouping and introduces the element of choice. Harris's editing scheme establishes the mutuality of horizontal *and* vertical family investigation throughout the tape's seventy-two minutes. We are never allowed to settle in on any of the three family narratives; just as we become thoroughly engrossed in the hermeneutic tensions of one sibling set, we find ourselves elsewhere. Harris consistently reminds us of the resonances and overlappings of sexual fantasies, family secrets, and shifting alliances narrated and performed—within and across families. We thus see for ourselves the complex, multilayered character of sexual identities, for while the siblings define themselves with, against, and through one another at the level of the biological family, they are also defined, at the level of the text, by a shared identification of queerness that links each to all.[15]

Moreover, all of the tape's participants share another sort of community affiliation: all are African American. Yet each challenges stereotypical gender roles recognizable within the black community: Thomas and Lyle celebrate their masculinity—baring sinewy bodies for the camera—yet identify with their mother; Vanessa Eaddy, not her brother Paul, talks of having idolized her father, tagging along after him and his pals; Anni Cammett shares a passionate commitment to basketball and her young daughter. Yet it is to *Vintage*'s credit that neither "blackness" nor "queerness" is accorded primacy of influence in the work of identity formation. They are all queer, all black, but their queerness and blackness never cease to mutate despite the "family resemblances." Difference and repetition, self and community, race and sexuality, are experienced as interpenetrating categories, mutually determining (indeed, undecidable) rather than contradictory or self-canceling.[16]

What we see and hear are three sets of siblings—mobile in their affinities, desires, and familial identifications—narrating their life stories, interrogating the discrepancies of family histories, questioning the hierarchies and psychosexual dependencies that formed each of them. This interrogation of the past, at times singular and introspective (here the expository mode is decidedly interactive, with Harris focusing his camera and attention on one or another sibling),[17] can also be undertaken sibling to sibling. In the latter instances, brothers or sisters exchange versions of their shared histories, at times firing questions at one another from behind the camera. At such times, the trope of shared textual authority discussed earlier comes into play, reminding us that the operation of the camera is also always a wielding of power. "Were you ashamed of the way I acted?" Vanessa Eaddy asks her brother Paul. Vanessa, though younger, had been out as a dyke while Paul was still closeting his sexuality. Pressing a momentary advantage, a camera-wielding Vanessa suggests that "Mommy is gonna want to talk to you!" The brother hesitates to reply, shifting uneasily beneath his sister's and the camera's gaze. He rises first to grab a cigarette, then returns to his perch, only to pop up again, demanding, in an attempt to regain control of the situation, that Vanessa "Move the camera! Where's Thomas?" The younger, female sibling is now asking the questions of the elder brother, unsettling his inherited authority, overturning the hierarchies. In other sequences between them, it is also clear that Paul and Vanessa (two among eight siblings) are in fact quite close. Their relationship, like that of the other sibling sets, is intense, shifting, co(i)mplicated.

In all instances of domestic ethnography, the familial other helps to flesh out the very contours of the enunciating self, offering itself as a precursor, alter ego, double, instigator, spiritual guide, or perpetrator of trauma. Domestic ethnography entails but exceeds autobiography. In

Thomas Allen Harris's tape, it is not just Harris who matters—it is also his brother Lyle, as well as the other members of an aggressively extended family who perform a shared identity, that of black queer sibling. In so doing, they redefine the family as the crucible of identity and the locus of domestic ethnography.

▶

Conclusion

What brings out the "ethnographic" in the domestic ethnography is the way in which the work calls attention to the dynamics of family life as the most fundamental (which is not to say universal) crucible of psychosexual identity. Universality is at odds with the historical, cultural, and psychosocial differences encountered in any examination of family structures, as exemplified by the variations apparent in four recent pieces. Domestic ethnography offers up the maker and her subject locked in a family embrace; indeed, as we have seen, subject/object positions are at times reversed. I have argued for domestic ethnography as an extension of autobiography, a pas de deux of self and other. It is discursively unstable. If it tells us about cultures and societies (as Fabian claims that all ethnography must), it does so only in miniature. But by abandoning any pretense to authoritative or generalizable knowledge of the one for the other, domestic ethnography eludes the colonialist remorse to which Lévi-Strauss once referred.[18] Self and other encounter each other at home rather than in the village square, but the dynamics of social and sexual identity formation that encounter rehearses leave few of us unscathed.

15

The End of Autobiography or New Beginnings? (or, Everything You Never Knew You Would Know about Someone You Will Probably Never Meet)

This final chapter, originally presented at Visible Evidence VII (1999), examines a relatively new autobiographical phenomenon, the personal Web page. Written near the height of dot-com market mania, the chapter analyzes the unique material and discursive conditions of the autobiographical Web site. "The End of Autobiography" is inspired by Walter Benjamin's prescient insights regarding the constantly evolving organization of human sense perception and of the complex relationship between the perceptual world and the media practices that both shape and reflect it. To his everlasting credit, Benjamin understood the emergence of new communication technologies to be both destructive and cathartic, exhilarating and annihilating. In contrast, then, to those who have, for decades, bemoaned the end of traditional literary autobiography, the chapter sets out to interrogate some new Internet-based forms of self-presentation that have transformed and enlivened contemporary autobiographical culture. Central to my approach is a consistent attentiveness to the twin manifestations of commercial cultural production on the one hand and alternative or artisanal media making on the other. I close with an extended discussion of the work of Amy Miller Gray, whose personal Web site illustrates some ways in which old (diaristic) forms can be wedded to new (technological) practices without the sacrifice of their noncommodity status. In hindsight, the chapter is a bit breathless in its acceptance of the hype surrounding all things Internet in the late 1990s, but it does sound an appropriately forward-looking note for a book devoted to the emergence and constant reinvention of the autobiographical impulse in the late twentieth century.

Nearly twenty years ago, Elizabeth W. Bruss wrote about the disappearance of autobiography, a literary genre that has enlivened Western thought for more than 1,500 years. In describing autobiography's demise, Bruss argued that a shift had taken place, that an activity "once central and pervasive" had loosened its hold over both its practitioners and audience. A displacement had been effected through a change in the dominant systems of communication. Film and video had begun to replace writing as the chief means of recording, informing, and entertaining, a fact of signal importance, given Bruss's claim that there was "no real cinematic equivalent for autobiography." While I strenuously disagree with that assessment (I'll say why shortly), I find her description of the disappearance of the genre quite insightful.

> How does a genre like autobiography, a genre characterized by its durability and flexibility, disappear? Not, I would propose, all at once, in a flaming apocalypse. Not with a melodramatic bang, not even (necessarily) with a whimper, not with clear symptoms of internal decay, disaffection, or cynicism. The disappearance of a genre is both subtler and more gradual; it is not a change in one genre alone but a change of the total environment, especially in the relative strength of alternative modes of expression.[1]

The question of the transformation and displacement of autobiographical modes is my topic here. Having spent more than a decade teaching and writing about autobiographical film and video, I want to examine an important emergent trajectory of autobiographical practice, that of the personal Web page produced for, and accessible through, the Internet. But before doing so, it is worth returning to Bruss's argument for what it can tell us about the social and ideological meanings of dramatic shifts within the cultural sphere.

Published in the context of a major collection, indeed a now-classic text—James Olney's edited volume *Autobiography: Essays Theoretical and Critical*—Bruss's pronouncement on the displacement of literary autobiography by newer cultural forms sounded a warning to the literary-critical community that echoed those of other twentieth-century critics. As Walter Benjamin had noted in "The Work of Art in the Age of Mechanical Reproduction" some decades before, human sense perception and the schemata we use to organize perceptual data are profoundly historical, subject to change, always affected by the introduction of new technologies. "During long periods of history, the mode of human sense perception changes with humanity's entire mode of existence. The manner in which human sense perception is organized, the medium in which it is accomplished, is determined not only by nature but by historical circumstances as well."[2] Unlike many modernist commentators whose pronouncements skew toward utopian or dystopian poles, Benjamin was keenly aware of the mixed blessings of the new. He wrote of the "tremendous shattering of tradition" effected through the cinema: "Its social significance, particularly in its most positive form, is inconceivable without its destructive, cathartic aspect, that is, the liquidation of the traditional value of the cultural heritage."[3]

In her essay, Bruss is responding to what seems to her the liquidation of the cultural heritage of the literary autobiography, but unlike Benjamin, she fails to see the positive side. To her dismay, film and video have begun to displace literature as the preferred system of representation, as the communicative mode best attuned to miming contemporary sensibilities. This is no impartial diagnosis but rather a doomsday message. Since there is no cinematic equivalent to literary autobiography, "the autobiographical act as we have known it for the past four hundred years could indeed become more and more recondite, and eventually extinct."[4]

While I don't disagree with Bruss's overall assessment of the representational shift, I am not inclined to despair; in fact, autobiographical practices of all sorts have thrived since the time of Bruss's writing. I also think she vastly overstates her case when she argues for the outright impossibility of filmic autobiography. Bruss's reasons boil down to this: cinema is simply incapable of producing autobiography's discursive conditions of existence, in which the speaking subject doubles as the subject of discourse. For Bruss, such a doubling would amount to the unity of the observer and the observed, to being in two places at once—both in front of and behind the camera. This makes sense given the exemplars of filmic autobiography she invokes—Truffaut, Fellini, and Woody Allen—whose films restage personal experience. But the work of cinematic and videographic autobiographers such as Jonas Mekas, George Kuchar, Ross McElwee, Lynn Hershman, and Susan Mogul shows that the filming subject can also be the filmed subject, thanks in no small measure to those handy props, the mirror and the tripod.

But the deeper question addressed by Bruss's essay, and the reason to return to it now, regards how the culture comes to grips with profound and deep-seated shifts of communicative modes or representational systems. At one level, the author is simply asking, "Can autobiography survive? Can literary critics stay in business?" At another, she is alerting us to the ways in which filmic and videographic modes of autobiographical practice are themselves subject to dramatic transformation. That is indeed the subject of my own concerns. It is my view that the existence of the Internet and the emergence of the personal Web page have radically altered the culture of autobiography in the late twentieth century.[5] In what follows, I will focus first on the commodity status of this new object within media culture, then briefly on its discursivity—the functions and effects of its self-presentation—with some attention given to a few examples.

The commodity status of the personal Web page is complex and equivocal. Web pages can be advertising vehicles, wholly given to commercial pursuits; or as personal pages, they can be low-cost and quirky bastions of refuge from the marketplace. Web pages find their existence on and through the Internet, a mode of delivery and consumption demanding some level of analysis in itself. This will not always be so. It is as if one were writing in the decades following the invention of the printing press and felt the need to discuss the economics of movable type before every act of literary criticism.

As is well known, the Internet, child of the U.S. Department of Defense in collaboration with the American research university, is now widely and wildly accessible. Capital has colonized the Net with breathtaking speed. Indeed, an explosion of Internet company mergers has made it difficult to know who owns a given company from one day to the next; the volatility of this market sector has been unprecedented. The recent merger mania, now cooled, was fueled by the skyrocketing stock values of many publicly held Internet companies. Dow Jones launched a special Internet Index in February 1999; that index rose by more than 50 percent in its first six months, almost four times faster than the Standard & Poor's 500 index, the standard measure of blue-chip stocks.[6] The major players were in a rush to position themselves within what was believed to be a huge growth industry in which the Net would be the nexus for most purchasing decisions as well as entertainment delivery and information exchange. Said one online advertising executive who likened this merger/buyout frenzy to a second California gold rush: "The first phase is staking out the gold mines, the second phase is building the mines, and the third phase is selling the gold."[7] This at a time when most developed nations have moved off the gold standard. The new gold was virtual, instantaneously traded and colossally expansive. Its chief domain was the Internet.

One such claim staker is Yahoo!, currently the largest portal or gateway to the Internet, which acquired five Net companies with a value of $10.5 billion in the first half of 1999 alone.[8] Yahoo! is the home of more than 48,000 personal pages (http://dir.yahoo.com/Society_and_Culture/People/Personal_Home_ Pages/). As a clearinghouse for the makers and browsers of these pages, Yahoo! may appear to the casual Web surfer to be a neutral vehicle, but it is, on the contrary, a massive capital enterprise valued at more than $40 billion (its first-quarter 1999 profits surged to $25 million from just over $3 million in a single year).[9] Because it reaches so many people, second only to America Online, Yahoo! can charge advertisers more than its competitors such as GeoCities (which it is threatening to gobble up), functioning much in the manner of a television network. The TV tie-in is even more explicit now that Yahoo! has begun to advertise on Fox and other youth-targeted broadcast venues. But the crossover is only beginning. Fearing duplication of "the cable mistake" when the big three U.S. TV networks held pat while ESPN, CNN, and Nickelodeon ate into their market share, many of the largest media conglomerates are now moving aggressively into the Internet. Walt Disney Co., which owns 42 percent of the Web company Infoseek, has announced its intention to absorb that established portal into a new publicly held, separately traded company, go.com, that will consolidate all its Internet interests, including travel-oriented sites, Disney's mail-order catalog business, and its various international ventures such as Britain's popular Soccer.com site.[10] NBC has made its own efforts to join the ranks of the superportals by spinning off its various Internet holdings into a separately traded company. NBC Internet will absorb both Snap.com and Xoom.com, which command the eleventh- and twelfth-largest audiences in the United States. The idea, of course, is that, as with the Disney move, the new portal will cross-promote NBC's broadcast wares and help build a younger, hipper market niche.[11]

This digression into the vagaries and volatility of the Internet's political economy is meant to underscore the unique status of autobiographical expression on the Internet. I will be focusing on the phenomenon of the personal page, tens of thousands of which have been designed and built by individuals around the world. Disparate as to levels of technological expertise or design sophistication displayed, devoted to political passions or personal peccadilloes, these pages, though often deeply personal, are necessarily imbricated within an infrastructure of staggering proportion and immense economic significance. This infrastructure imposes on every purveyor of the medium and every signifying instance a profound social and political valence. It is my belief that, as with Marx's earliest formulations of the commodity in the nineteenth century, the forces and relations of production leave their mark on every item produced. These personal Web sites—evanescent, whimsical, radical though they may at times be—depend for their existence on the high-combustion engine of capital formation that is the Internet in the late 1990s. What follows will, I hope, demonstrate the richly complicated character of personal expression and entrepreneurialism that these personal pages entail.

I have suggested that autobiographical Web sites exist in a very mixed economy. Take, for example, the existence of hybrids such as People Chase (http://www.rainfrog.com/pc/), a Web ring that doubles as a Web site award for personal home pages and other noncommercial sites deemed outstanding in content and design. People Chase, home to and sponsor of numerous autobiographical sites, was founded and continues to be administered by a single individual with the support of volunteers. But sites and rings and portals interweave with one another; a People Chase or GeoCities site can be accessed through Yahoo!

Jacques Lacan described all signification through recourse to a complex topological metaphor, borrowed no doubt from the natural sciences, that of a multileveled signifying chain in which a necklace composed of many rings was itself, at another level, but one ring of a larger necklace.[12] The Internet has immeasurably complicated this notion of the signifying chain with its already interlocking, multidimensional grids of meaning. To the play of the linguistic signifier, already mind-bogglingly complex, must now be added the snowballing effects of technology and market forces that drive this new language system. The Internet is a necklace of a higher order of complexity than natural language, a topos of rings, nets, and webs.

The Internet is also, as we have seen, a media environment in which megacorporations coexist with Mom and Pop and a handful of volunteers, a domain in which some players are creating massive wealth while others are carving out small, alternative spaces. David E. James has written incisively of the small victories of alternative cultural forms, those modes of nearly autonomous cultural production that exist just beyond the reach of capitalist culture in the realms of literature, film, and music. Whether garage bands, amateur pornography, or zines, these cultural forms, peripheral though they may be, can achieve a measure of autonomy and relatively free circulation, mobilizing values other than those current in mainstream culture.[13] In the nineteenth century, Marx described the ways in which residual or emergent forms of material production could coexist with dominant modes; cultural hegemony is porous. But in the case of the Internet, at least to date, noncommodity forms don't just coexist with, but are deeply enmeshed within, the most high-powered sector of venture capital. It is as if the theater premiering the latest episode of the *Star Wars* saga were also to show my home movies.

But it is not simply a matter of artisanal sites squatting within the precincts of high-powered corporate culture. Small-scale entrepreneurialism has also invaded the domain of Web-based autobiographical discourse in the form of numerous sites devoted to selling consumers "how-to" autobiography kits. The "Memories & Reflections" Autobiography Kit (http://www.personalprofiles.org/mem.htm) is a product offered by Personal Profiles, a company billing itself as an "expert in preserving the memories of a lifetime." For $49.95, the buyer receives a kit designed to inspire the "do-it-yourselfer" to preserve her family history, memories, and experience for future generations. Milli Brown, the founder of Personal Profiles and, according to the site, a "renowned family biographer," explains that the business was created to make family history-taking fun, easy, and affordable. The Cyberscribes site (http://www.ellipys.com/cyber/cb5_0.html) offers one-stop shopping for prospective Web writers—journalists, interactive storytellers, and autobiographers. Two volumes of helpful tips are available from Ellipsys International Publications, Inc., of San Diego at $24.95 each. The book's ethos can be intuited from an excerpt from chapter 5 of *Cyberscribes 1: The New Journalists devoted to "Writing the Story of Your Life"*: "Define and design yourself as if you are a product to be sold." MY BIO (http://www.erols.com/mybio/), a $14.95 offer, provides a blueprint for writing one's life story, complete with clues for triggering memories to "enhance the episodes you are capturing on paper." For $89.95, the company, based in Richmond, Virginia, will ship you a MY BIO gift box set in a protective weatherproof covering. MY STORY (http://mystorywriter.com/home.htm) promises a complete autobiography writer system for $19.95. Unlike the print-based Personal Profiles, Cyberscribes, and MY BIO products, MY STORY is an "easy to use" but innovative software system that will help you "describe who you really are in your own words." Reluctant customers are reminded that "no one like you has ever been, you and your life are unique." The profusion of such commercial "how-to" autobiography sites suggests that the culture of autobiography, far from being extinguished, has in fact proliferated, percolating down to the level of popular commercial culture. This is but one manifestation of that "tremendous shattering of tradition" of which Benjamin wrote.

Alternative cultural producers, those relatively autonomous autobiographers of the Web, exist alongside the autobiography pitchmen. The variability of the scale, technical expertise, and content on display in these autobiographical personal pages is astounding; their tonalities range from the homespun to the whimsical, from the lyrical to the mordant. Grandma Sue's Place (http://www.northwinds.net/susanna/default.htm) is the Web home of Susan Anderson: Proud Grandma, Quilter, Engineer, Breast Cancer Survivor. That list of attributes pretty well sums up the diversity to be found within and across these sites. The breast cancer survivor thread of the discourse describes Anderson's experience of breast cancer: early detection via mammogram, mastectomy, chemotherapy treatments, activism in a local breast cancer support group in her Minnesota community. This narrative of disease and healing recurs in many autobiographical sites, the pages offering testimony to survival and the strength afforded by community during the process of recovery.

Of course, the Internet has itself helped to redefine the meaning of therapeutic communities. Steve's Crohn's Page—My Story (http://home.swbell.net/force/mystory.htm) tells of the challenges experienced by Stephen Beauchamps of Dallas, Texas, a forty-seven-year old man living with Crohn's disease, a debilitating illness that has necessitated long periods of hospitalization, multiple surgeries, and recurrent post-op setbacks. Constantly updated, filled with details of the latest flare-ups, struggles with medications, and a deep appreciation for his physicians, Steve's Crohn's Page links to myriad other pages on Crohn's disease, including medical information sites, a contact center for e-mail networking, and other personal pages authored by fellow Crohn's patients.

I have saved my personal favorite for last, a site authored by Amy Miller Gray (http://home.fuse.net/bailiwick/), a thirty-something former journalist and single mother who is, to my mind, among the most compelling of Net autobiographers. I have taken the legend sprawled across her home page as the ideal alternative title for my own discussion: "everything you never knew you'd know about someone you'll probably never meet." Now this description seems appropriate to the work of most autobiographers, literary and cinematic, whose audiences exceed their circle of family and friends. But it is this sense of the "everything" that really sets the auto-Webographer apart from her precursors in print and celluloid. Here it is necessary to say a few words about the quite different discursivity found on the Web. If the commodity status of Internet autobiography is a mixed one, the same can be said for its discursivity, in which the literary is not so much banished as reduced to one of many available tools.

Strange to say, given literary autobiography's death notice à la Bruss, but the personal Web page phenomenon has forcefully reintroduced the writerly into the sphere of self-representation. This should come as no shock; it is never the case that one media form merely cancels out another. As Carolyn Marvin has noted: "New practices do not so much flow directly from technologies that inspire them as they are improvised out of old practices that no longer work in new settings."[14] It turns out that writing, as well as photography, film, video, and the digital arts, provides some of the building blocks for personal Web pages, which are decidedly composite products. Indeed, it might be more accurate to say that the Internet has absorbed rather than displaced prior representational forms in a media setting that emphasizes speed of transmission and breadth of accessibility. And here the examination of discursive conditions becomes equally a matter of ideological analysis.

Without question, the autobiographical Web page responds to the demands for speed and accessibility as no antecedent form has. But speed and accessibility are not, in and of themselves, to be misrecognized as absolute goods, though they may be greeted as such in the marketplace. These would be the space-binding properties crucial to media imperialism about which James W. Carey has written so eloquently. At least since the advent of the clipper ship, telegraphy, and now the Internet, speed of transmission has provided a crucial underpinning for power, for the expansion of empire, and for the accumulation of personal wealth. This is what economic historian Harold A. Innis meant when he argued that the spatial bias of modern communication had been aggressively exploited at the expense of the temporal dimension through which forms of communication can provide a container for enduring human interaction and the affirmation of values.[15] I would propose two perhaps countervailing properties of the Internet as determined by its (im)material character and mode of consumption, that is, its ephemerality and the unpredictability of its reception.

First, regarding the matter of its ephemerality, I would argue that the personal Web page is a species of autobiographical discourse that has sacrificed its object status. Instead of a book or tape to be collected (or fetishized), the Web page tends to be retained only as a bookmark without guarantee; clicking on it may return one to the site as it once existed. It bears a certain resemblance to performance art. Of course, one could download any number of screens from the site, that is, create an object, but only at the expense of the interactive, present-tense character that defines it. As regards reception, it is possible to count hits on sites as a way to quantify spectatorship, but it is far more difficult to measure the depth of the encounter. Many Web authors, Amy Miller Gray among them, maintain guest books that allow users to share their responses, which can be quite wide-ranging. It is worth noting, however, that the common metaphors for Internet use emphasize the casual and the temporary—"surfing" and "cruising." For this media form, speed of transmission and breadth of accessibility seem to be purchased at the price of permanence and depth. The spatial bias described by Innis seems to dominate.

But the example of Amy Miller Gray's Web site reminds us that depth can be measured in a different way, as discursive density, the extent to which the site becomes a table of discrete, sometimes overlapping, sometimes contradictory, signifying chains. Philippe Lejeune has written of the "autobiographical pact," which is the unspoken compact that binds readers and writers of autobiographical discourse. Autobiography is a form of personal writing that is referential (that is, imbued with history), mainly retrospective (though the temporality of the telling may be quite complex), and in which the author, the narrator, and the protagonist are identical.[16] Gray stretches the terms of the autobiographical pact to its limits, promising us not just knowledge of the author but a surprising, totalizing knowledge ("everything you never knew you would know about someone you will probably never meet"). It is the links to diverse pages provided on Gray's home page that attempt to deliver the "everything." We can, for example, gaze upon but not read many of Amy's journals, begun when she was eleven years old (http://home.fuse.net/bailiwick/journal.htm). She scans in a page or two to give us the look and texture of the writing; an early entry is about first menstrual periods and assorted heartthrobs.

Instead of offering to our view the journal pages themselves (we're told Gray has, over the years, filled up several thick volumes), we're given instead something like a history of Amy's diaristic practice, a meta-discourse on the virtues of personal writing and, a familiar autobiographical trope, the revelation of her diary as the source and proving ground of her writerly vocation. There is both modesty ("No, I won't put my personal journal online. Seriously, I think you'd be bored by it") and self-affirmation: "I received an e-mail in response to this web site telling me

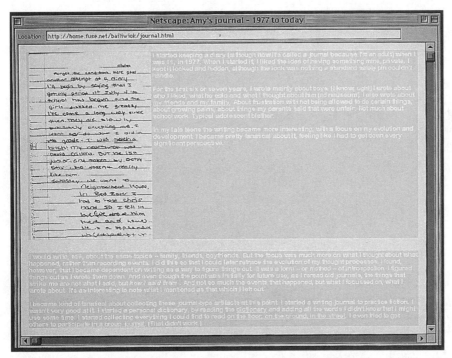

Amy Miller Gray's personal Web site traces her autobiographical habit to childhood diaries. Reprinted with permission of Amy Miller Gray.

(no, ORDERING ME!) to "WRITE A BOOK DAMMIT!" and I e-mailed back
that I kind of have. This web site was a lot of work and it's a work in
progress. It will never be done. I prefer hypermedia to restrictive pages."
By this statement, the author refines her promise of the everything. The
site, although it may not deliver all the goods all at once, will extend to
infinity, mirroring the open-endedness of experience.

One linked page, entitled "Things I Find on the Ground," may be
the most indicative of this site's discursive tactics and of the ways in which
many autobiographical Web sites create textual density. Gray has again
scanned in an array of items, this time found objects, scraps of paper on
which poems, notes, essays, and assorted scribblings can be seen. These
objets trouvés are displayed on the page against a background that simu-
lates the look of once-crumpled stationery. The page is a place of rever-
ence and resurrection for signs gone astray. Gray begins the page with an
admonition:

> Read everything you can find.
> That's what Keith Haring told his little sister and I think it's great advice.
> Okay, you can't read everything, but try.

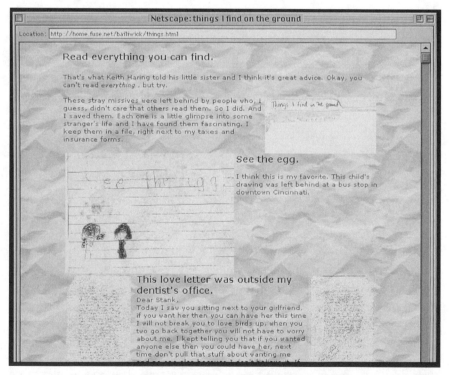

One page of Gray's Web site, "Things I Found on the Ground," maps the author's
inner landscape of fascination. Reprinted with permission of Amy Miller Gray.

These stray missives were left behind by people who, I guess, didn't care that others read them. So I did. And I saved them. Each one is a little glimpse into some stranger's life and I have found them fascinating. I keep them in a file, right next to my taxes and insurance forms.

Various artifacts are displayed on the page, along with a faithful transcription of the written contents, some amount of authorial commentary, and a reference to the scrap's precise location at the moment of its discovery. Included are a child's drawing left behind at a bus stop in downtown Cincinnati, a trodden-upon sheet of paper found two blocks west of the entrance to the University of Arizona, and a love letter plucked from the street outside Amy's dentist's office. These items are charged with the power of the chance encounter once ably exploited by modernists such as Stéphane Mallarmé, Kurt Schwitters, and John Cage. But they are also signposts of another sort, mapping as they do the author's own inner landscape of fascination. Each of these random objects becomes a relay point for a shared identification, a moment of communion with Gray, the curator of this strange show. In the author's hands, these fragments become profound instruments of autobiography. The page effects the extension of the horizon of autobiographical discourse to infinity, since it is no longer just what the author does or thinks that matters. What counts is also the measure of her desire, which is, after all, of the order of the drive, not the object. With her "Things I Find on the Ground" page, Gray shows us why autobiography has no end, only material limits that the Internet proves capable of reworking and extending ad infinitum. Finally, the site may not tell us everything about Amy, but it does tell us a great deal about autobiography.

But I now want to explore another dimension of Gray's autobiographical practice in relation to an accomplished piece of video art. Gray's "Things I Find on the Ground" page bears a striking resemblance to Jem Cohen's brilliant work *Lost Book Found* (1996), in which a lost notebook filled with a selection of apparent ephemera—addresses, times of day, lists of things—is regarded as a now-irretrievable interpretive compass for the urban narrator. I want to suggest some of the resonances between the two works as a way to explore how contemporary autobiographical discourses of diverse sorts can share common structural and epistemological ground.

From the outset, I should say that Cohen's film/video composite may be autobiography only indirectly. The narrating voice is not Cohen's, it turns out, but this is in itself trivial. Does not the use of another's voice and narrational presence only make *Sans soleil* a more acutely autobiographical work, Markerian through and through? We are told that the "I" of *Lost Book*'s telling had, upon arriving in New York ten years earlier, been employed for a time as a pushcart vendor and had briefly possessed a notebook whose seemingly random contents may have been a code, a key to the understanding of an invisible order through which the welter of "things" might at last make sense. The book is almost certainly the artist's conceit (and here I would return once more to Marker's epistolary conceits in *Letter from Siberia* or *Sans soleil* by way of reference). The book is not an autobiographical fact but a tool, an opportunity that Cohen seizes on to offer up his vision.

It is, in fact, a vision about vision and its vicissitudes, about how that which lies beneath the visible world, beyond the reach of order manmade and imposed, may in fact provide the foundations for meaning. Of course, such a statement can be read either as a profound critique of rationality or as a recipe for psychosis. The tape remains equivocal on this point, as art is prone to do. On the one hand, Cohen's narrator says he knows that "not everything can be important," yet he is haunted by the book, which "stays in his head like a song I didn't know I knew and parts of the book come back in flashes, bits and pieces." What is crucial is that the book has inspired the narrator to inspect the world with newfound care and openness. His experience as a pushcart vendor had begun the process, for he found that just as he had begun to become invisible to others, he began to see things that had once been invisible to him. As viewers and auditors of this netherworld, we are invited to share that transformative spectator position.

The book is perhaps a relic of internalized faith. It offers a reply to a nihilism that seems endorsed by Cohen's immersive technique: we are thrown into a world of discount stores and arcades, whirling detritus and peeling signage. Alternating silence and direct sound, Cohen makes his way through the urban object-world in close-up, his postproduction effects producing a stuttering glissando effect. Immersed in a ragged postmodernity in which, as the narrator says, there is no longer any weather and in which "the seasons are marked by different kinds of sales," it would be easy for us too to lose our way. And yet the book returns as a fragmentary and atavistic hope for epistemological redemption.

Little wonder that *Lost Book Found* is dedicated to Walter Benjamin whose own profound ambivalence for the future provided this chapter's point of departure—Benjamin, a man whose greatest ambition was to produce a work consisting entirely of quotations, a man for whom the size of an object was in inverse ratio to its significance, and for whom metaphor poetically brought about the oneness of the world.[17] By turns agnostic and messianic, *Lost Book Found* effects a vision that embraces the fragmentary, the miniaturized, and the metaphorical, one that might well have pleased Benjamin. But it is also a work that, like Amy Miller Gray's "Things I Find on the Ground" page, is cut to the measure of the artist's desire, a desire that entails both epistemology and ethics. Despite some important differences (in the melancholic *Lost Book Found*, the book's hermeneutic power may arrive too late, whereas Amy Miller Gray seems to suggest it's never too late to wrench the meaning from things, even or especially random things), there is strong structural congruence between the two pieces. The fragment is valorized, its horizon and possibilities uncontainable. The two artists (one well esteemed, the other unknown) share a moral compass. How are we to determine what matters in the world? Both ask us to look down on the ground, to regard what is hidden or discarded with newfound care. Is it difficult to imagine that the same openness of vision accorded to things may lead to new possibilities for human encounter? And through this revelation of ethical vision, the artists' self-understanding is also illumined.

I have only begun to suggest what is at stake in the appearance of autobiographical Web sites, the personal pages that litter the Internet. I have argued that this new site of (im)material production has begun to transform the culture of autobiography, situated as it is at the intersection of artisanal practice and explosive capital formation. I have also made some claims for the unique discursivity of the autobiographical Web site, arguing for the depth and breadth of the self-presentational potential it offers. Finally, I have suggested some important resonances between one exemplary personal Web site and a celebrated work of videographic autobiography. In the age of the Internet, I don't believe that autobiography is on the brink of extinction. Unrecognizable to some, disdained by many, practiced by thousands, it has been reborn.

Notes

Surveying the Subject

1. Philippe Lejeune, "The Autobiographical Pact," in *On Autobiography,* trans. Katherine Leary (Minneapolis: University of Minnesota Press, 1989), 3–30.
2. See chapter 6 of this book, "The Subject in History: The New Autobiography in Film and Video."
3. Sidonie Smith and Julia Watson, *De/Colonizing the Subject: The Politics of Gender in Women's Autobiography* (Minneapolis: University of Minnesota Press, 1992), xviii. In this regard, it is worth noting that one of the media darlings of the 1990s was Sadie Benning, a Milwaukee teenager whose diary tapes, made in her bedroom using a Fisher-Price Pixelvision camera, earned her the status of outlaw princess.
4. Elizabeth W. Bruss, "Eye for I: Making and Unmaking Autobiography in Film," in *Autobiography: Essays Theoretical and Critical,* ed. James Olney (Princeton: Princeton University Press, 1980), 296–97. For a more extended discussion of Bruss's position, see chapter 15, "The End of Autobiography or New Beginnings? (or, Everything You Never Knew You Would Know about Someone You Will Probably Never Meet").
5. Jerome Bruner, "The Autobiographical Process," in *The Culture of Autobiography: Constructions of Self-Representation,* ed. Robert Folkenflik (Stanford: Stanford University Press, 1993), 55.
6. Neal Gabler, "Focusing on Oneself in the 'Epoch of Ego,'" *Los Angeles Times,* 2 January 2000, M1-2.
7. The following is but a short list of the books that I have found most useful in charting the ebb and flow of debate around the subject in the context of the autobiographical project: *Autobiography: Essays Theoretical and Critical,* ed. James Olney (Princeton: Princeton University Press, 1980); Paul Smith, *Discerning the Subject* (Minneapolis: University of Minnesota Press, 1988); Philippe Lejeune, *On Autobiography* (Minneapolis: University of Minnesota Press, 1989); *De/Colonizing the Subject: The Politics of Gender in Women's Autobiography,* ed. Sidonie Smith and Julia Watson (Minneapolis: University of Minnesota Press, 1992); *The Culture of Autobiography: Constructions of Self-Representation,* ed. Robert Folkenflik (Stanford: Stanford University Press, 1993); *The Politics of the Essay: Feminist Perspectives,* ed. Ruth-Ellen Boetcher Joeres and Elizabeth Mittman (Bloomington: Indiana University Press, 1993); *Supposing the Subject,* ed. Joan Copjec (London: Verso, 1994); Elizabeth Grosz, *Volatile Bodies: Toward a Corporeal Feminism* (Bloomington: Indiana University Press, 1994); *Getting a Life: Everyday Uses of Autobiography,* ed. Sidonie Smith and Julia Watson (Minneapolis: University of Minnesota Press, 1996). I cannot fail to add that the writings of Michel de Montaigne, Roland Barthes, Charles Taylor, Zygmunt Bauman, and Emmanuel Levinas have been extremely influential in the formation of my own sense of the autobiographical subject.
8. Georges Gusdorf, "Conditions and Limits of Autobiography," in *Autobiography: Essays Theoretical and Critical,* ed. James Olney (Princeton: Princeton University Press, 1980), 29.
9. Arlie Russell Hochschild, "Coming of Age, Seeking an Identity," *New York Times,* 8 March 2000, D1, 10.
10. For further discussion on this point, see Diane Waldman and Janet Walker, eds., *Feminism and Documentary* (Minneapolis: University of Minnesota Press, 1999), particularly Waldman and Walker's important introductory essay, 1–35.

11. Michel Foucault, "The Subject and Power," in *Art after Modernism: Rethinking Representation,* ed. Brian Wallis (New York: New Museum of Contemporary Art, 1984), 420.

12. Doris Sommer, "'Not Just a Personal Story': Women's *Testimonios* and the Plural Self," in *Life/Lines: Theorizing Women's Autobiography,* ed. Bella Brodzki and Celeste Schenck (Ithaca, N.Y.: Cornell University Press, 1988), 111.

13. Bill Nichols, *Representing Reality* (Bloomington: Indiana University Press, 1991), 179. In his subsequent book, *Blurred Boundaries* (Bloomington: Indiana University Press, 1994), Nichols offers an altered and expanded account of the role of subjectivity in documentary filmmaking. Indeed, he suggests that a fifth mode of documentary exposition—the performative—must now be added to the four-part typology described in *Representing Reality.* ("Things change. The four modes of documentary production that presented themselves as an exhaustive survey of the field no longer suffice" [93].) For unlike the classical styles of documentary filmmaking developed over seventy years—the expository, observational, interactive, and reflexive modes—the performative mode stresses "subjective aspects of a classically objective discourse" (95). Nichols's account historicizes this turn to subjectivity in the documentary practices of the 1980s and 1990s, suggesting this mode of performance and self-interrogation as the latest and most notable documentary trend.

14. While *Man with a Movie Camera* was a product of the silent era and should by rights be limited to the visual rather than auditory register, Vertov does manage to mime audition in his 1929 film through the imaging of listening poses. Since one of Vertov's earliest creative efforts was a Laboratory of Hearing, this attentiveness to sound can come as no surprise.

15. Joris Ivens, *The Camera and I* (New York: International Publishers, 1969), 32.

16. Ibid., 50.

17. Ibid., 88.

18. Although Ivens's move toward a politicized practice is an important historical footnote and helps to explain documentary filmmaking's stylistic shifts from the 1920s to the 1930s, it is equally important to recall Pudovkin's allusion to "tension and emotion." His comments suggest that the creation of arguments on film and the documentation of world-historical events, vital roles for nonfiction to play, suffer without the personal and passionate engagement of the maker.

19. Hochschild, "Coming of Age," D1.

20. This period of documentary filmmaking in America is examined with much clarity by William Alexander in his *Film on the Left: American Documentary Film from 1931 to 1942* (Princeton: Princeton University Press, 1981).

21. For the definitive account of guerrilla television's genesis and reinvention, see Deirdre Boyle, *Subject to Change: Guerrilla Television Revisited* (New York: Oxford University Press, 1997).

22. Newsreel has in fact survived in much-altered form. Its twin incarnations are California Newsreel, a San Francisco–based collective devoted primarily to the distribution of films on diverse social topics, and Third World Newsreel in New York, a leading source of personal films by people of color.

23. Stephen Mamber, *Cinema Verite in America: Studies in Uncontrolled Documentary* (Cambridge: MIT Press, 1974), 2.

24. Cited in Charles Taylor, "Focus on Al Maysles," in *The Documentary Tradition: From Nanook to Woodstock,* ed. Lewis Jacobs (New York: Hopkinson and Blake, 1971), 401.

25. Brian Winston, "The Documentary Film as Scientific Inscription," in *Theorizing Documentary,* ed. Michael Renov (New York: Routledge, 1993), 37–57.

26. The most sustained English-language treatment of Rouch as filmmaker is Mick Eaton's *Anthropology/Cinema/Reality: The Films of Jean Rouch* (London: BFI, 1979). See also Paul Stoller, *The Cinematic Griot: The Ethnography of Jean Rouch* (Chicago: University of Chicago Press, 1992).

27. See, in particular, Bill Nichols, "Embodied Knowledge and the Politics of Location: An Evocation," in *Blurred Boundaries,* 1–16.

28. The narrating voices in Chris Marker's films are typically performed by surrogates and, despite their frequently diaristic/confessional character, are equivocal expressions of Markerian subjectivity. Sometimes the vocal presence is even female, as is the case with Alexandra Stewart's narration in the English-language version of *Sans soleil* (1982). Of course, "Chris Marker" is itself a nom de plume; no filmmaker has veiled his interiority with greater panache.

29. No discussion of documentary voice-over can fail to mention Luis Buñuel's *Las Hurdes* (1932), whose narrational voice-over has perplexed, enraged, and entertained audiences since the film's initial release. Some critics have lauded Buñuel's purportedly surrealist agenda, while others, including the Franco government, have simply banned the film; it is either a grossly insensitive treatment of the impoverished Hurdaños of central Spain or a veiled but savage attack on the indifference of church and state to the disenfranchised. No matter how it is read, the film's

voice-over (most versions feature a coolly detached male voice describing the horrors of the villagers' daily life) is a brilliant, if somewhat opaque, vehicle of Buñuelian subjectivity.

30. Elizabeth Cowie, "The Spectacle of Actuality," in *Collecting Visible Evidence*, ed. Jane M. Gaines and Michael Renov (Minneapolis: University of Minnesota Press, 1999), 19–45.

31. Ibid., 25.

32. Noël Carroll, "Nonfiction Film and Postmodernist Skepticism," in *Post-theory: Reconstructing Film Studies*, ed. David Bordwell and Noël Carroll (Madison: University of Wisconsin Press, 1996), 293.

33. Dziga Vertov, *Kino-Eye: The Writings of Dziga Vertov*, ed. Annette Michelson, trans. Kevin O'Brien (Berkeley: University of California Press, 1984), 17–18.

34. Nichols, *Representing Reality*, 156.

1. Early Newsreel

1. Michel Foucault, *Power/Knowledge: Selected Interviews and Other Writings, 1972–1977* (New York: Pantheon Books, 1980), 96–97.

2. Michel Foucault, *The Archaeology of Knowledge* (New York: Harper and Row, 1972), 12.

3. Raymond Williams, *Marxism and Literature* (Oxford: Oxford University Press, 1977), 114.

4. Ibid., 112.

5. *The Sixties without Apology*, ed. Sohnya Sayers, Anders Stephanson, Stanley Aronowitz, and Fredric Jameson (Minneapolis: University of Minnesota Press, 1984).

6. With its twentieth anniversary fast approaching (December 1987), Newsreel, despite its many transformations of political strategy and personnel, has remained a fixture of the left-wing film community since its beginnings. The precise itinerary and various incarnations of Newsreel remain the subject for further inquiry; at present, two functioning entities carry on the political activism of the founding moment. California Newsreel produces and distributes films about work and the changing character of the workplace (including its own *Controlling Interest* [1978] and *The Business of America* [1984]), in addition to administering the Southern Africa Media Center, featuring the world's largest collection of films on apartheid. Despite its history of privileging distribution over production, Cal Newsreel has begun developing an ambitious new project—an extended critique of media within U.S. society—intended for public broadcast. Third World Newsreel is a collective that has focused on producing films that "give voice to the voiceless." Since the early 1970s, the leadership of Third World Newsreel has been provided by filmmakers of color (mostly women) whose work has offered representations of the struggles of the exploited and the marginalized (battered women, Chinese garment-district workers, Vietnamese refugees, to name only a few). More recent Third World Newsreel projects have included a series of traveling film exhibitions featuring the work of African, black American, and Asian American cineasts, as well as the organization of the Minority Media Development Program, intended as a comprehensive study of the crisis in media production among minority practitioners in New York State.

7. At the height of its oppositional powers in the late 1960s, Newsreel could boast offices in New York, Boston, San Francisco, Los Angeles, Detroit, Chicago, and Atlanta; there was a degree of communication and strong familial ties with groups in London, Paris, and Tokyo. Newsreel's film vaults contain at least one film sent from Japan during the peak period of confrontation, which has never yet been translated or titled.

8. The Imaginary, in its Lacanian usage, is one of the three essential orders of the psychoanalytic field: the Real, the Symbolic, the Imaginary. The latter term refers to a type of apprehension in which the subject constructs a false and, in Lacan's system, founding unity between self and other, based on some factor of resemblance or homeomorphism. According to Laplanche and Pontalis, the Imaginary implies "a sort of coalescence of the signifier with the signified," a collapsing of difference in favor of a deceptive identification. See J. Laplanche and J.-B. Pontalis, *The Language of Psycho-Analysis* (W. W. Norton, 1973), 210.

9. Herbert Marcuse, *An Essay on Liberation* (Boston: Beacon Press, 1969), 53.

10. It should be added that all wholesale labels—the movement, the counterculture, the New Left—are concatenations of disparate elements and tendencies that threaten to self-destruct at every moment. These terms are necessary but inadequate ones; each requires a considerable degree of qualification impossible to offer here. For a valuable discussion and clarification of this problem, see Todd Gitlin, *The Whole World's Watching: Mass Media in the Making and Unmaking of the New Left* (Berkeley: University of California Press, 1980), 293–96.

11. *Rat* 1, no. 20 (15–28 November 1968): 3.

12. *Rat* 1, no. 21 (3 December 1968–2 January 1969): 15.

13. Susan Sontag, "One Culture and the New Sensibility," in *Against Interpretation* (New York: Dell, 1966), 302.

14. *Rat* 1, no. 2 (22 March–4 April 1968): 8.
15. Jonas Mekas, *Movie Journal: The Rise of the New American Cinema, 1959–1971* (New York: Collier Books, 1972), 306.
16. Bill Nichols, *Newsreel: Film and Revolution* (master's thesis, University of California–Los Angeles, 1972), 73.
17. Norm Fruchter, telephone interview with author, 3 November 1984. According to Fruchter, a founding member of Newsreel, prints were routinely rented to political groups until they failed to return the third film. California Newsreel's present collection contains a major gap owing to the hasty departure of an Iranian student group after the 1978 revolution, with Newsreel films in tow.
18. David Armstrong, *A Trumpet to Arms: Alternative Media in America* (Los Angeles: J. P. Tarcher, 1981), 375.
19. *Film Quarterly* 21, no. 2 (winter 1968–1969): 46.
20. Mekas, *Movie Journal,* 306.
21. *Rat* (29 October–12 November 1969): 8.
22. Jonas Mekas, "Movie Journal," *Village Voice,* 29 February 1968, 40.
23. Norm Fruchter, telephone interview with author, 3 November 1984.
24. Ibid.

2. The "Real" in Fiction

1. Bill Nichols, *Representing Reality: Issues and Concepts in Documentary* (Bloomington: Indiana University Press, 1991), 113–15.
2. See my "Introduction: The Truth about Non-Fiction," in *Theorizing Documentary,* ed. Michael Renov (New York: Routledge, 1993), 2–3, 198.
3. Ibid., 3, 10.
4. Delirium has been theorized by Julia Kristeva in "Psychoanalysis and the Polis," in *The Kristeva Reader,* ed. Toril Moi (New York: Columbia University Press, 1986), as a name for the process through which discourse strays from "a presumed reality." According to Kristeva, access to knowledge or human experience is more problematic than usually supposed. Why? "Because the knowing subject is also a *desiring* subject, and the paths of desire ensnarl the paths of knowledge. . . . we normally assume the opposite of delirium to be an objective reality, objectively perceptible and objectively knowable, as if the speaking subject were only a simple knowing subject. Yet we must admit that, given the cleavage of the subject (conscious/unconscious) and given that the subject is also a subject of desire, perceptual and knowing apprehension of the original object is only a theoretical, albeit undoubtedly indispensable, hypothesis" (307). This formulation—particularly applicable to the problem of the interview format, but fundamental to nonfiction discourse generally—raises a serious challenge to Nichols's notion of discursive sobriety.
5. See my "Toward a Poetics of Documentary," in *Theorizing Documentary,* ed. Michael Renov (New York: Routledge, 1993), 13.
6. The notion of the historical "real" is a problematic one tied to debates around nominalist versus realist epistemological positions. See, for example, Barry Hindess and Paul Hirst's now-legendary critique of the notion of the "real" in their *Pre-capitalist Modes of Production* (London: Routledge and Kegan Paul, 1975): "History is not a real object, an object prior to and independent of thought, it is an object constituted within definite ideologies and discourses" (318). Furthermore, historical events as represented, even with a minimum of directorial control or conscious mediation as in cinema verité, are constructions embedded within a complex of ideological determinations ranging from decisions at the editing bench to the perspectival relations ground into the lens system. *Medium Cool* places the notion of the "real" in particular crisis. One example will suffice as illustration. In the midst of a confrontation between police and demonstrators (the film contains a great deal of such documentary footage that is incorporated into the fiction), a tear gas canister is thrown. As the camera shakes and wobbles with the operator's (Wexler's) hasty retreat, the soundman's warning is clearly audible: "Look out, Haskell, it's real!" The term "historical real" will be retained (although under erasure) to signify profilmic elements existing outside of or beyond the filmmaker's control. The quotation marks surrounding the word "real" will thus indicate the status of the term as necessary but inadequate.
7. Jacques Derrida, "Fors—the Anglish Words of Nicolas Abraham and Maria Torok," trans. Barbara Johnson, foreword to *The Wolf Man's Magic Word,* by Nicolas Abraham and Maria Torok, trans. Nicholas Rand (Minneapolis: University of Minnesota Press, 1986), xiv.
8. J. Laplanche and J.-B. Pontalis, *The Language of Psycho-Analysis* (New York: W. W. Norton, 1973), 229.

9. Derrida, "Fors," xvii.

10. The American presence in France is treated with progressively darker irony in Godard's later films. By 1965 in *Masculine–Feminine*, the official vehicle of the American consulate becomes a moving billboard for the Jean-Pierre Leaud character's spray-painted "Peace in Vietnam." Increasingly, as in *Two or Three Things I Know about Her* in 1966, references to U.S. political influence give way to a critique of Americanized commodification. Still later, in the Dziga Vertov Group period, the United States and all its emblems become the face of the principal enemy.

11. Despite the monumentality of scale of Selznick's historical interpolations, there is no significant incorporation of the historical "real" distinguishable among these turgid backdrops. While elaborate dramatic conflict and character development are hallmarks of the Selznick style, the history so dutifully attended to is reduced to stasis or clichéd tableau.

12. One might do well to add that Ray is one of the most meticulous of preproduction planners in all of cinema history, with a penchant for sketching out each setup in miniature. Such an approach is ill suited to the incorporation of large-scale historical events.

13. For a fuller account of Wexler's formative years as political documentarist, see David Talbot and Barbara Zheutlin, *Creative Differences: Profiles of Hollywood Dissidents* (Boston: South End Press, 1978).

14. Ernest Callenbach and Albert Johnson, "The Danger Is Seduction: An Interview with Haskell Wexler," *Film Quarterly* (spring 1968): 4–5.

15. The point can be illustrated by a scene from John Ford's *She Wore a Yellow Ribbon* (1949), in which the cavalry accompanies a wagon train across the plain in extreme long shot. The deeply brooding sky enhances the menace of Indian attack with great economy.

16. Bertolt Brecht, "Theatre for Pleasure or Theatre for Instruction," in *Brecht on Theatre* (New York: Hill and Wang, 1964), 75.

17. Paramount Pictures, a subsidiary of Gulf and Western at the time that it distributed *Medium Cool*, is but the tip of the corporate iceberg, accounting as it does for less than 10 percent of the total revenues of a vast multinational conglomerate. In 1977 Gulf and Western ranked fifty-ninth among *Fortune* magazine's listing of the five hundred largest industrial firms. Thomas Guback, "Theatrical Film," in *Who Owns the Media? Concentration of Ownership in the Mass Communications Industry*, ed. Benjamin M. Compaine (New York: Harmony Books, 1979), 202.

18. Haskell Wexler, interview by Renee Epstein, *Sight and Sound* 45, no. 1 (winter 1975–1976): 47.

19. The correct spelling of the protagonist's name is the subject of an enigma worthy of mention. Is it "Katsellas," as my ear suggests, or "Cassellis," as Talbot and Zheutlin—mistakenly, I think—render it in their chapter on Wexler? Researching the answer proves to be a formidable task. Because *Medium Cool* was buried by its Paramount distributors, never opening for an official New York run, the film was never reviewed by the *New York Times*. The standard reference for credits does not exist; a kind of "exnomination" or official silence enshrouds the film.

20. One is tempted to disengage the spectator of 1968 or 1969 from the subsequent audience, at least insofar as the shock of recognition is concerned. The young contemporary audience, unacquainted with the powder keg politics of ghetto uprising and police reprisal, tends to view this sequence as an unmotivated breach of film etiquette.

21. The concept of interpellation—the hailing of the subject through a rhetorical figure—was developed by Louis Althusser in his oft-cited essay "Ideology and Ideological State Apparatuses," in *Lenin and Philosophy* (New York: Monthly Review Press, 1971), 127–86. For an application of the term to the World War II context and filmic representation, see Michael Renov, "The State, Ideology, and *Priorities on Parade*," *Film Reader* 5 (1982): 216–26.

22. Brecht, "On the Use of Music in an Epic Theatre," 86.

23. Roland Barthes, "Diderot, Brecht, Eisenstein," in *Image/Music/Text* (New York: Hill and Wang, 1977), 73–74.

24. The flattened portraiture motif remains insistent in Godard's use of direct-address interviews even after the aesthetic imperative yields to a staunchly rhetorical one (see *Tout Va Bien* [1972], in which extended monologues by fractious labor militants are flatly shot against bold color panels).

25. Brecht, "Theatre for Pleasure or Theatre for Instruction," 72.

26. Marshall McLuhan, "Television: The Timid Giant," in *Understanding Media: The Extensions of Man* (New York: McGraw-Hill, 1964), 317. With regard to this naturalizing of technology as body part endemic to the expansionist sixties, *Medium Cool* actively tempers McLuhan's New Age optimism with suggestions of the dehumanizing effects of the electric environment. The Marxian notion of commodity fetishism is certainly evoked by an offhand remark made by Gus, Katsellas's sound recordist sidekick, when he describes himself as "just an elongation of a tape recorder."

27. Ibid., 313.

28. One of the most pervasive ironies in *Medium Cool*, a film deeply embedded within the ironic mode, is the title's McLuhanesque reference. It was McLuhan who celebrated television (the protagonist's métier) as a vehicle for high audience involvement and participation. "If the medium is of high definition, participation is low. If the medium is of low intensity, the participation is high" ("Television: The Timid Giant," 319). In fact, *Medium Cool* mobilizes an unstinting attack against the television medium as practiced in America on the grounds that it functions as an agent of social control, glorifies rather than explains violence, and induces a deeply rooted passivity in its audience.

29. Bertolt Brecht, "The Modern Theatre Is the Epic Theatre," in *Brecht on Theatre* (New York: Hill and Wang, 1964), 38.

30. The Kerner Commission, a committee appointed by President Nixon to investigate the causes and effects of civil unrest in the sixties, termed the series of violent clashes at the Chicago Democratic National Convention a "police riot."

31. Nicolas Abraham and Maria Torok, "Introjection—Incorporation: Mourning or Melancholia," in *Psychoanalysis in France,* ed. Serge Legovici and Daniel Widlocher (New York: International Universities Press, 1980), 3.

32. Derrida, "Fors," xiv.

33. David Talbot and Barbara Zheutlin, "Haskell Wexler," in *Creative Differences: Profiles of Hollywood Dissidents* (Boston: South End Press, 1978), 113.

3. Warring Images

My thanks to Loni Ding, Linda Mabalot, Steven Okazaki, Rea Tajiri, and Bruce Yonemoto for access to, and discussion of, their work.

1. I am grateful to Gregory Waller for his useful study of American film treatments of the Japanese in the period between 1909 and 1915. While there has been extensive scholarship on works of popular fiction such as Homer Lea's *The Valor of Ignorance* (1909)—which predicted the successful invasion of the U.S. West Coast by the Japanese and was reprinted in 1942 as a prophetic work—far less is known about the more than one hundred films from forty different companies that conditioned American response to Japan and the Japanese during this period. Gregory A. Waller, "Historicizing, a Test Case: Japan on American Screens, 1909–1915," paper delivered at the Society for Cinema Studies conference, Los Angeles, May 1991.

2. John W. Dower, *War without Mercy: Race and Power in the Pacific War* (New York: Pantheon Books, 1986), 308. In fairness, it should be noted that Dower amply historicizes the shifting stereotypes of Japanese and American during and after the war, noting "the malleable and double-faceted nature of the dominant wartime stereotypes" (308). The antecedents and points of reference to which Dower turns for explanation of the radically shifting stereotype—for example, the demonic outsider of Japanese folk culture—are surely useful historical markers. There is no effort made, however, to locate the dynamic of stereotyping at the level of psychic operations, another crucial dimension for historical understanding.

3. Gilman describes the long-term social utility of his analytic endeavor in this way: "The need for stereotypes runs so deep that I do not think it will ever be thwarted; nor do I think that it will ever be converted to purely harmless expression. But I believe that education and study can expose the ideologies with which we structure our world, and perhaps help put us in the habit of self-reflection." Sander L. Gilman, *Difference and Pathology: Stereotypes of Sexuality, Race, and Madness* (Ithaca: Cornell University Press, 1985), 12.

4. Ibid.

5. Homi K. Bhabha, "The Other Question—the Stereotype and Colonial Discourse," *Screen* 24, no. 6 (November–December 1983): 27.

6. Ibid., 33.

7. For a clear but extended account of the psychic origins of the stereotype, see Gilman's introductory essay in *Difference and Pathology:* "Introduction: What Are Stereotypes and Why Use Texts to Study Them?" 15–35.

8. I have pursued the logic of the idealized other in my "Imaging the Other: Representations of Vietnam in Sixties Political Documentary," in *From Hanoi to Hollywood,* ed. Linda Dittmar and Gene Michaud (New Brunswick, N.J.: Rutgers University Press, 1990), 255–68.

9. Gilman, *Difference and Pathology,* 18.

10. Dower, *War without Mercy,* 10.

11. Gilman, *Difference and Pathology,* 18.

12. John Morton Blum, *V Was for Victory: Politics and American Culture during World War II* (New York: Harcourt Brace Jovanovich, 1976), 159.

13. Frank Capra, *The Name above the Title* (New York: Macmillan, 1971), 328–29.

14. For more discussion on the range and effects of the filmmaker's creative choices, see my "Re-thinking Documentary: Toward a Taxonomy of Mediation," in *Wide Angle* 8, nos. 3–4 (1986): 71–77.

15. See my "Toward a Poetics of Documentary," in *Theorizing Documentary*, ed. Michael Renov (New York: Routledge, 1993), 12–36.

16. I undertake a similar analysis of the racist depiction of the Japanese enemy during World War II, this time as the historical context for representations of the Vietnamese two decades later, in "Imaging the Other: Representations of Vietnam in Sixties Political Documentary."

17. Dower, *War without Mercy*, 49.

18. This description is taken from a *Life* magazine story on Caniff's wartime contribution, "Speaking of Pictures," *Life*, 1 March 1943, 12.

19. Copies of this media reference guide can be obtained from Asian CineVision, Inc. For further information see http://asiancinevision.org.

20. It was not until 1988 that the U.S. Congress conceded to the award of financial compensation and the offering of an official apology to those who lost their liberty behind barbed wire.

21. Carol Squiers, "Screening the War: Filmmakers and Critics on the Images that Made History," *International Documentary: The Journal of Non-fiction Film and Video*, no. 8 (spring 1991): 21.

4. *Lost, Lost, Lost*

1. Alan Williams, "*Diaries, Notes, and Sketches*—Volume I *(Lost, Lost, Lost)*," *Film Quarterly* 30, no. 1 (1976): 62. Although Williams reviewed *Lost, Lost, Lost* soon after its release, he was already familiar with the third volume of the autobiographical project *Walden* (1968), filmed between 1964 and 1968.

2. Reda Bensmaia, *The Barthes Effect: The Essay as Reflective Text*, trans. Pat Fedkiew (Minneapolis: University of Minnesota Press, 1987), ix.

3. In an appendix to *The Barthes Effect: The Essay as Reflective Text*, Reda Bensmaia offers the historical and theoretical grounds for his claims for the essay as an "impossible" genre: "Among all the terms that relate to literary genres, the word Essay is certainly the one that has given rise to the most confusion in the history of literature. . . . A unique case in the annals of literature, the Essay is the only literary genre to have resisted integration, until quite recently, in the taxonomy of genres. No other genre ever raised so many theoretical problems concerning the origin and the definition of its Form: an atopic genre or, more precisely, an eccentric one insofar as it seems to flirt with all the genres without ever letting itself be pinned down, the literary essay such as Montaigne bequeathed it to posterity has always had a special status. . . . the Essay appears historically as one of the rare literary texts whose apparent principal task was to provoke a 'generalized collapse' of the economies of the rhetorically coded text" (95, 96, 99). In my writing on the essayistic in film and video, I have chosen to resist the lure of genre, preferring instead to consider the essayistic as a modality of filmic inscription. The invocation of mode rather than genre sidesteps the difficulties raised by the latter's far greater historical stake in taxonomic certainty, as well as the presumption of thematic consistency attached to it. Conversely, the determining principle of resemblance for the mode is a formal or functional one. As Jacques Derrida notes, quoting a distinction framed by Gerard Genette: "Genres are, properly speaking, literary or aesthetic categories; modes are categories that pertain to linguistics or, more precisely, to an anthropology of verbal expression." Jacques Derrida, "The Law of Genre," *Glyph* 7 (1980): 210. In the instance of the essayistic for film and video, formal, functional, and ideological commonalities converge as defining characteristics.

4. Graham Good, *The Observing Self: Rediscovering the Essay* (London: Routledge, 1988), 4.

5. Michel de Montaigne, *The Complete Works of Montaigne*, trans. Donald M. Frame (Stanford: Stanford University Press, 1948), 298.

6. Ibid., 296.

7. Gerard Defaux, "Readings of Montaigne," *Montaigne: Essays in Reading, Yale French Studies* 64, trans. John A. Gallucci (1983): 77.

8. Montaigne, *Complete Works*, 610–11.

9. Roland Barthes, *The Grain of the Voice: Interview, 1962–1980*, trans. Linda Coverdale (New York: Hill and Wang, 1985), 209–10.

10. Georg Lukács, "On the Nature and Form of the Essay," in *Soul and Form*, trans. Anna Bostock (Cambridge: MIT Press, 1974), 18.

11. Ibid., 14.

12. Roland Barthes, *Roland Barthes*, trans. Richard Howard (New York: Hill and Wang, 1977), 169.

13. Ibid., 56.

14. Bensmaia, *The Barthes Effect*, 51.

15. There is considerable elasticity inherent in my formulation of the essayistic, with the result that

no enumeration of exemplary texts will suffice to name its borders. Of course, laws of membership and exclusion always pose a problem for aesthetic taxonomies, which must remain open and therefore "impure" sets. Certain principles of composition do, however, remain useful indicators of the essayistic enterprise for film and video, as they have for literature. The "twofold project," descriptive and reflexive, enfolding self and other, the outward (documentary) glance coupled with the interrogation of subjectivity—these are the signs of a discursive practice termed "essayistic." For further discussion of the essayistic for film and video, see my "History and/as Autobiography: The Essayistic in Film and Video," in *Frame/Work* 2, no. 3 (1989): 5–13.

16. Jonas Mekas, interview by Scott MacDonald, *October* 29 (summer 1984): 84.

17. See in particular Scott MacDonald, "Lost Lost Lost over *Lost Lost Lost*," *Cinema Journal* 25, no. 2 (winter 1986): 20–34, as well as his *October* interview with Mekas. A more conceptually ambitious account of Mekas's career and achievements, contained in David James's *Allegories of Cinema: American Film in the Sixties* (Princeton: Princeton University Press, 1989), 100, continues to treat the development of an increasingly personal style throughout the *Diaries* as a kind of spiritual elevation, producing a filmic mode that "entirely fulfills [underground film's] aesthetic and ethical program." This tendency to describe a progressive stylistic shift as a heightening or purification of form is a romantic notion traceable in the first instance to the filmmaker's own writings over several decades. To be sure, some notion of historical development is inescapable in the discussion of *Lost*, inasmuch as the film's image track appears to be structured chronologically. That irreversibility is, however, consistently undone by the voice-over, which ranges across time and memory, speaking from a place of knowledge: "Paulius, Paulius—I see you. Remember, that day, that evening, that evening we all danced around a young birch tree outside of the barracks. We thought it will all be so temporary, we'll be all home soon." MacDonald ("Lost Lost Lost") suggests that the six reels of the film can be grouped as three couplets: the first pair focusing on the Lithuanian community in Brooklyn, the second on the formation of a new life in Manhattan and the beginnings of a new community around *Film Culture*, the last on the development of a cinematic aesthetic of spontaneity and personalism. Any critical engagement with the film must, in the first instance, comprehend this play of the progressive and the reversible.

18. MacDonald, in Mekas, interview, 84; italics mine.

19. Mekas, interview, 93–94.

20. Jonas Mekas, introduction to "The Frontiers of Realist Cinema: The Work of Ricky Leacock (from an Interview Conducted by Gideon Bachmann)," *Film Culture* 22–23 (1961): 12.

21. Roland Barthes, *Camera Lucida*, trans. Richard Howard (New York: Hill and Wang, 1981), 9.

22. For a further discussion of the necessity and variability of mediation for the documentary film, see Michael Renov, "Re-thinking Documentary: Toward a Taxonomy of Mediation," *Wide Angle* 8, nos. 3–4 (1986): 71–77.

23. The notion of a preservational obsession held in tension with its opposite, the need to release the past or deny its efficacy in the present through representation, provides a crucial underpinning for *Lost, Lost, Lost*. Another film to be situated within the realm of the essayistic, Chris Marker's *Sans soleil*, explores similar terrain through an equally variegated textual mapping of temporality and experience. Even while fragments from the filmmaker's past return obsessively—from his own films such as *La jetée* (1962) or *Le mystère Koumiko* (1964) or from Hitchcock's *Vertigo* (1958)—Marker celebrates their annihilation through a ritual destruction that in turn memorializes their loss; representation becomes the system through which retention and dissolution can be fused. "Memories must make do with their delirium, with their drift," says Marker in *Sans soleil*. "A moment stopped would burn like a frame of film blocked before the furnace of the projector." *Lost* and *Sans soleil* share a fascination for cinema's special admixture of presence and absence, a chemistry examined by generations of film theorists.

24. Jacques Derrida, "Otobiographies," in *In the Ear of the Other*, trans. Avital Ronell (New York: Schocken Books, 1985), 5–6.

25. Jonas Mekas, "The Diary Film (A Lecture on Reminiscences of a Journey to Lithuania)," in *Avant-Garde Film: A Reader, Theory and Criticism*, ed. P. Adams Sitney (New York: New York University Press, 1978), 193.

26. Ibid.

27. Jonas Mekas, "Film Notes," in *Jonas Mekas*, ed. Judith E. Briggs (Minneapolis: Film in the Cities/Walker Art Center, 1980).

28. In Guido Convents's "Documentaries and Propaganda before 1914: A View on Early Cinema and Colonial History," *Framework* 35 (1988): 104–13, it is argued that the documentary film was recruited for the purposes of propagandizing colonialist efforts in Africa as early as 1897.

29. Jonas Mekas, "A Call for a New Generation of Film-Makers," *Film Culture* 19 (1959): 3.

30. Jonas Mekas, "The Experimental Film in America," *Film Culture* 3 (1955): 15–16. Besides the

"document film," Mekas's categorization of cinematic forms includes the film drama, the film poem, and the cinema of abstraction or "cineplastics."

31. Parker Tyler, "Poetry and the Film: A Symposium, with Maya Deren, Arthur Miller, Dylan Thomas, Parker Tyler," in *Film Culture Reader*, ed. P. Adams Sitney (New York: Praeger, 1970), 173.

32. The many studies of reflexivity in cinema have focused on fictional works almost exclusively (e.g., the *Screen* debates on Brecht from the 1970s or Martin Walsh, *The Brechtian Aspect of Radical Cinema* [London: BFI, 1981]). Among the writings that do address this problem in the documentary context, the best may be Jeanne Allen, "Reflexivity in Documentary," *Cine-tracts* 1, no. 2 (summer 1977): 37–43; Annette Kuhn, "The Camera I—Observations on Documentary," *Screen* 1, no. 2 (summer 1978): 71–83; and Jay Ruby, "The Image Mirrored: Reflexivity and the Documentary Film," in *New Challenges for Documentary*, ed. Alan Rosenthal (Berkeley and Los Angeles: University of California Press, 1988), 64–77.

33. Williams, "*Diaries, Notes, and Sketches*," 62.

34. Andre Tournon, "Self-Interpretation in Montaigne's *Essays*," *Montaigne: Essays in Reading*, *Yale French Studies* 64 (1983): 61.

35. Mekas, "The Diary Film," 191–92.

36. Roland Barthes, *S/Z*, trans. Richard Miller (New York: Hill and Wang, 1974), 5–6.

37. As discussed in Jean Laplanche and Jean-Bertrand Pontalis, *The Language of Psychoanalysis*, trans. Donald Nicholson-Smith (New York: W. W. Norton, 1973), 182–83, Freud's use of the term *nachtraglichkeit* is intended to convey the manner by which experiences, impressions, or memory traces are altered after the fact as a function of new experiences and are thus rendered capable of reinvestment, producing new, even unexpected, effects of meaning. As Freud wrote to his confidant Wilhelm Fliess: "I am working on the assumption that our psychical mechanism has come about by a process of stratification: the material present in the shape of memory-traces is from time to time subjected to a rearrangement in accordance with fresh circumstances—is, as it were, transcribed."

38. Jonas Mekas, "Cinema of the New Generation," *Film Culture* 21 (1960): 19.

39. Jonas Mekas, "Notes on the New American Cinema," in *Film Culture Reader*, ed. P. Adams Sitney (New York: Praeger, 1970), 88.

40. Ibid.

41. Lukács, "On the Nature and Form of the Essay," 18.

5. Charged Vision

1. Jacques Lacan, *The Four Fundamental Concepts of Psycho-Analysis*, trans. Alan Sheridan (New York: W. W. Norton, 1977), 103.

2. Ibid., 93.

3. Jacques Lacan, *The Seminar of Jacques Lacan—Book II*, trans. Sylvana Tomaselli (New York: W. W. Norton, 1988), 177.

4. Laura Mulvey, "Visual Pleasure and Narrative Cinema," *Screen* 16, no. 3 (autumn 1975): 6–18.

5. See Bill Nichols, *Representing Reality* (Bloomington: Indiana University Press, 1991), 178–80; and Tom Gunning, "Embarrassing Evidence: The Detective Camera, the Revelation of Daily Life, and the Documentary Impulse," in *Visible Evidence*, ed. Jane Gaines and Michael Renov (Minneapolis: University of Minnesota Press, 1999), 46–64.

6. See in this regard Michel Chion, *La voix au cinema* (Paris: Cahiers du Cinema/ Editions de l'Etoile, 1982); Mary Ann Doane, "The Voice in the Cinema: The Articulation of Body and Space," *Yale French Studies* 60 (1980): 33–50; and Kaja Silverman, *The Acoustic Mirror: The Female Voice in Psychoanalysis and Cinema* (Bloomington: Indiana University Press, 1988).

7. I don't mean to suggest that the twenties have always been slighted in the writing of documentary history. Erik Barnouw's *Documentary: A History of Non-fiction Film*, still the most significant account of nonfiction's development more than twenty years after its publication, treats this period with depth and subtlety. Most recent historically oriented writing on documentary, however, has tended to take as its focus the thirties in Europe and North America (the Grierson group, Workers' Film and Photo League, Nykino, Frontier Films, etc.) or the emergence of the direct cinema/cinema verité phenomenon in Canada, France, and the United States during the 1960s.

8. Hans Richter, *The Struggle for the Film*, trans. Ben Brewster (New York: St. Martin's Press, 1986), 44.

9. Ibid., 78.

10. Nichols, *Representing Reality*, 178. I don't mean in this discussion to single out for attack Bill Nichols, without doubt the most significant critical voice in contemporary nonfiction studies. His formulations are, I think, symptomatic of the more general view that documentary film is

grounded in consciousness and thus simply not subject to the claims made by psychoanalytically oriented film theorists of the 1970s.

11. Ibid., 107–33.
12. Paul Ricoeur, *Freud and Philosophy: An Essay on Interpretation,* trans. Denis Savage (New Haven: Yale University Press, 1970), 33.
13. Sigmund Freud, *The Interpretation of Dreams,* trans. James Strachey (New York: Avon Books, 1965), 651.
14. Ibid., 537.
15. Here I am drawing on two remarkable essays: Louis Althusser, "Freud and Lacan," in *Lenin and Philosophy,* trans. Ben Brewster (New York: Monthly Review Press, 1971), 189–219; and Shoshana Felman, "Jacques Lacan: Madness and the Risks of Theory (The Uses of Misprision)," in *Writing and Madness (Literature/Philosophy/Psychoanalysis)* (Ithaca, N.Y.: Cornell University Press, 1985), 119–40.
16. Slavoj Zizek, introduction to *The Sublime Object of Ideology* (London: Verso, 1989), 2.
17. Michel Foucault, "History of Systems of Thought," in *Language, Counter-memory, Practice: Selected Essays and Interviews* (Ithaca, N.Y.: Cornell University Press, 1977), 201. Years before Freud, it was Nietzsche who could write: "For the longest time, conscious thought was considered thought itself. Only now does the truth dawn on us that by far the greatest part of our spirit's activity remains unconscious and unfelt. . . . *Conscious* thinking, especially that of the philosophers, is the least vigorous and therefore also the relatively mildest and calmest form of thinking; and thus precisely philosophers are most apt to be led astray about the nature of knowledge." Friedrich Nietzsche, *The Gay Science,* trans. Walter Kaufman (New York: Random House, 1974), 262.
18. Michel Foucault, "Two Lectures," in *Power/Knowledge: Selected Interviews and Other Writings, 1972–1977,* ed. and trans. Colin Gordon (New York: Pantheon Books, 1980), 85.
19. Nichols, *Representing Reality,* 3.
20. Julia Kristeva, "Psychoanalysis and the Polis," in *The Kristeva Reader,* ed. Toril Moi (New York: Columbia University Press, 1986), 307.
21. Roland Barthes, *Camera Lucida: Reflections on Photography,* trans. Richard Howard (New York: Hill and Wang, 1981).
22. Cited in Jay Leyda, *Kino: A History of the Russian and Soviet Film* (New York: Collier Books, 1960), 224.
23. Barthes, *Camera Lucida,* 47.
24. Joris Ivens, *The Camera and I* (New York: International Publishers, 1969), 37.
25. Dziga Vertov, *Kino-Eye: The Writings of Dziga Vertov,* ed. Annette Michelson, trans. Kevin O'Brien (Berkeley: University of California Press, 1984), 7.

6. The Subject in History

1. Reda Bensmaia, *The Barthes Effect: The Essay as Reflective Text,* trans. Pat Fedkiew (Minneapolis: University of Minnesota Press, 1987), 98–99.
2. Roland Barthes, *S/Z,* trans. Richard Miller (New York: Hill and Wang, 1974), 5.
3. Jacques Lacan, *The Four Fundamental Concepts of Psycho-Analysis,* trans. Alan Sheridan (New York: W. W. Norton, 1977), 246.
4. Graham Good, *The Observing Self: Rediscovering the Essay* (London: Routledge, 1988), 4.
5. Michel de Montaigne, *The Complete Works of Montaigne,* trans. Donald M. Frame (Stanford: Stanford University Press, 1948), 611–12.
6. Jacques Derrida, "Otobiographies," in *The Ear of the Other: Otobiography, Transference, Translation,* trans. Peggy Kamuf (New York: Schocken Books, 1985), 5.
7. Jacques Lacan, *Écrits: A Selection,* trans. Alan Sheridan (New York: W. W. Norton, 1977), 172.
8. Roland Barthes, *Roland Barthes,* trans. Richard Howard (New York: Hill and Wang, 1977), 127.
9. Montaigne, *Complete Works,* 611.
10. Barthes, *Roland Barthes,* 48.
11. Lacan, *Écrits,* 154. Or to declare the impermanence of meaning another way: "We can say that it is in the chain of the signifier that the meaning 'insists' but that none of its elements 'consists' in the signification of which it is at the moment capable" (153).
12. Barthes, *Roland Barthes,* 49.
13. There is some irony in my claim for the "new autobiography," since a similar pronouncement was made more than a decade ago in P. Adams Sitney's "Autobiography in Avant-Garde Film," in *The Avant-Garde Film: A Reader of Theory and Criticism,* ed. P. Adams Sitney (New York: New York University Press, 1978), 199–246. What struck Sitney as "one of the most vital developments in the cinema of the late Sixties and early Seventies" (202)—the autobiographical films of Mekas, Hollis Frampton, Jerome Hill, Stan Brakhage, and James Broughton—was its

tendency to engage with certain fundamental questions about the "nature of cinema, and often on its ambiguous association with language" (ibid.). The film and video works that inspire my critical efforts are engaged in questions that have motivated artists and theorists primarily in the eighties, in response to positions advanced beneath the rubrics of poststructuralism and feminism—issues of plurivocality and (gendered) identity, the efficacy of historical representation, the meanings engendered by the friction between public and private spheres. While I admire Sitney's groundbreaking work on filmic autobiography—and share his enthusiasm for certain key texts—the disparity of our respective political and historical coordinates suggests that the "new autobiography" discussed here is, if not novel, at least renewed.

14. Clifford Geertz, "Thick Description: Toward an Interpretive Theory of Culture," in *The Interpretation of Cultures* (New York: Basic Books, 1973), 29.
15. Jacques Lacan, "The Mirror Stage," in *Écrits*, 2.
16. Janet Varner Gunn, *Autobiography: Towards a Poetics of Experience* (Philadelphia: University of Pennsylvania Press, 1982), 25.
17. Louis A. Renza, "A Theory of Autobiography," in *Autobiography: Essays Critical and Theoretical*, ed. James Olney (Princeton: Princeton University Press, 1980), 273.
18. Elizabeth W. Bruss, "Eye for I: Making and Unmaking Autobiography in Film," in Olney, *Autobiography*, 296–97.
19. Jonas Mekas, "The Diary Film," in Sitney, *The Avant-Garde Film*, 191.
20. Jonas Mekas, "Notes on *Walden*," in *Film-Makers' Cooperative Catalogue* (New York: Film-Makers' Cooperative, 1975), 178.
21. Scott MacDonald, "Lost Lost Lost over *Lost Lost Lost*," *Cinema Journal* 25, no. 2 (winter 1986): 20–34.
22. Barthes, *Roland Barthes*, 105.
23. For an incisive discussion of the formal and epistemological conditions of the written versus filmed diary formats as they pertain to the work of Mekas, see David James, "Diary/Film/Diary Film: Jonas Mekas' *Walden*," *Frame/work* 2, no. 3 (December 1988).
24. Quoted in Jean Laplanche and Jean-Bertrand Pontalis, "Deferred Action," *French Freud/Yale French Studies*, no. 48 (1972): 182–83.
25. Bruss, "Eye for Eye," 298.
26. Friedrich Nietzsche, *The Gay Science*, trans. Walter Kaufman (New York: Vintage Books, 1974), 116.
27. Barthes, *Roland Barthes*, 94.
28. Ibid., 143.

7. Filling Up the Hole in the Real

1. Else's statement in the epigraph occurs in an audio commentary contained on the recently released laser disc and CD-ROM versions of the 1981 Academy Award–nominated documentary (Voyager Company, 1995).
2. Jacques Lacan, "Desire and the Interpretation of Desire in *Hamlet*," *Yale French Studies* 55–56 (1977): 37.
3. Hans Richter, *The Struggle for the Film*, trans. Ben Brewster (New York: St. Martin's Press, 1986), 43, 42.
4. Roland Barthes, *Camera Lucida: Reflections on Photography*, trans. Richard Howard (New York: Hill and Wang, 1981), 92.
5. Sigmund Freud, "Mourning and Melancholia," in *General Psychological Theory: Papers on Metapsychology*, ed. Philip Rief (New York: Collier Books, 1963), 165.
6. Ibid., 166.
7. Lacan, "Desire and the Interpretation of Desire in *Hamlet*," 37.
8. Michael Walsh, "Returns in the Real: Lacan and the Future of Psychoanalysis in Film Studies," *Post Script* 14, nos. 1–2 (fall 1994–spring 1995): 22–32.
9. Slavoj Zizek, *The Sublime Object of Ideology* (London: Verso, 1989), 162, 171.
10. Alan Sheridan, "Translator's Note," in *Écrits: A Selection*, by Jacques Lacan (New York: W. W. Norton, 1977), x.
11. Mikkel Borch-Jacobsen, *Lacan: The Absolute Master*, trans. Douglas Brick (Stanford: Stanford University Press, 1991), 192.
12. Jacques Lacan, *The Seminar of Jacques Lacan: Book II*, trans. Sylvana Tomaselli (New York: W. W. Norton, 1988), 164.
13. Jacques Lacan, *The Seminar of Jacques Lacan: Book III*, trans. Russell Grieg (New York: W. W. Norton, 1993), 148.
14. Jacques Lacan, *The Seminar of Jacques Lacan: Book I*, trans. John Forrester (New York: W. W. Norton, 1988), 66, 86.

15. Zizek, *The Sublime Object of Ideology*, 69, 173.
16. Slavoj Zizek, *Looking Awry: An Introduction to Jacques Lacan through Popular Culture* (Cambridge: MIT Press, 1991), 14–15.
17. Borch-Jacobsen, *Lacan: The Absolute Master*, 166, 125, 103.
18. Jacques Derrida, *Of Grammatology*, trans. Gayatri Chakravorty Spivak (Baltimore: Johns Hopkins University Press, 1974), xvi.
19. Jacques Derrida, "Freud and the Scene of Writing," trans. Jeffrey Mehlman, *Yale French Studies* 48 (1972): 114.
20. Borch-Jacobsen, *Lacan: The Absolute Master*, 193.
21. Lacan, *The Seminar of Jacques Lacan: Book I*, 223.
22. Sigmund Freud, "Thoughts for the Times on War and Death," cited in Borch-Jacobsen, *Lacan: the Absolute Master*, 95.
23. Lacan, *The Seminar of Jacques Lacan: Book III*, cited in Walsh, "Returns in the Real," 26.
24. Lacan, "Desire and the Interpretation of Desire in *Hamlet*," 37–38.
25. Ibid., 38.
26. Jean Rouch, cited in G. Roy Levin, *Documentary Explorations: Fifteen Interviews with Film-Makers* (Garden City, N.Y.: Doubleday, 1971), 137.
27. Simone de Beauvoir, cited in Nancy K. Miller, "Autobiographical Deaths," *Massachusetts Review* (spring 1992): 46–47.
28. Lacan, "Desire and the Interpretation of Desire in *Hamlet*," 40.

8. Documentary Disavowals and the Digital

I wish to acknowledge the generosity and assistance of Daniel Reeves and Jim Campbell, without whose cooperation this essay could not have been written.

1. Zygmunt Bauman, *Life in Fragments: Essays in Postmodern Morality* (Oxford: Blackwell, 1995), 186, 239.
2. Ibid., 200.
3. Hayden White, "The Modernist Event," in *The Persistence of History: Cinema, Television, and the Modern Event*, ed. Vivian Sobchack (New York: Routledge, 1996), 22.
4. Ibid., 38.
5. Fredric Jameson, "The Cultural Logic of Late Capitalism," in *Postmodernism, or The Cultural Logic of Late Capitalism* (Durham, N.C.: Duke University Press, 1991), 4.
6. Zygmunt Bauman, *Postmodern Ethics* (Oxford: Blackwell, 1993), 10.
7. Stephen Toulmin, *Cosmopolis: The Hidden Agenda of Modernity* (Chicago: University of Chicago Press, 1990). See in particular chapter 1, "What Is the Problem about Modernity?" 5–44.
8. Henry L. Feingold states the case most directly. "[Auschwitz] was also a mundane extension of the factory system. Rather than producing goods, the raw material was human beings and the end-product was death, so many units per day marked carefully on the manager's production charts. The chimneys, the very symbol of the modern factory system, poured forth acrid smoke, produced by burning human flesh. The brilliantly organized railroad grid of modern Europe carried a new kind of raw material to the factories. . . . Engineers designed the crematoria; managers designed the system of bureaucracy that worked with a zest and efficiency more backward nations would envy. Even the overall plan itself was a reflection of the modern scientific spirit gone awry. What we witnessed was nothing less than a massive scheme of social engineering." Henry L. Feingold, "How Unique Is the Holocaust," in *Genocide: Critical Issues of the Holocaust*, ed. Alex Grobman and Daniel Landes (Los Angeles: Simon Wiesenthal Center, 1983), 399–400.
9. Zygmunt Bauman, *Modernity and the Holocaust* (Ithaca: Cornell University Press, 1989), 17. "At no point of its long and tortuous execution," argues Bauman, "did the Holocaust come in conflict with the principles of rationality. The 'Final Solution' did not clash at any stage with the rational pursuit of efficient, optimal goal-implementation. . . . modern civilization was not the Holocaust's *sufficient* condition; it was, however, most certainly its *necessary* condition" (17, 13).
10. Ibid., 102.
11. Bauman, *Postmodern Ethics*, 8.
12. Zygmunt Bauman, *Postmodernism and Its Discontents* (New York: NYU Press, 1997), 124.
13. Ibid., 203.
14. Bauman, *Life in Fragments*, 191.
15. Dziga Vertov, *Kino-Eye: The Writings of Dziga Vertov*, ed. Annette Michelson, trans. Kevin O'Brien (Berkeley: University of California Press, 1984), 8.
16. Annette Michelson, introduction to *Kino Eye: The Writings of Dziga Vertov*, ed. Annette Michelson, trans. Kevin O'Brien (Berkeley: University of California Press, 1984), xv–lxi.

17. John Grierson, "The E.M.B. Film Unit," in *Grierson on Documentary*, revised and abridged edition, ed. Forsyth Hardy (Berkeley: University of California Press, 1979), 49, 63.

18. Ibid., 41, 48.

19. Brian Winston, "Staatspolitisch Besonders Wertvoll," in *Claiming the Real: The Documentary Film Revisited* (London: British Film Institute, 1995), 74–78.

20. Hans Richter, *The Struggle for the Film: Towards a Socially Responsible Cinema*, ed. Jurgen Romhild, trans. Ben Brewster (New York: St. Martin's Press, 1986), 42–43.

21. Lisa Cartwright, *Screening the Body: Tracing Medicine's Visual Culture* (Minneapolis: University of Minnesota Press, 1995).

22. Fatimah Tobing Rony, *The Third Eye: Race, Cinema, and Ethnographic Spectacle* (Durham, N.C.: Duke University Press, 1996), 4.

23. Bauman, *Life in Fragments*, 221.

24. See the discussion of disavowal in J. Laplanche and J.-B. Pontalis, *The Language of Psycho-Analysis* (New York: W. W. Norton, 1973), 118–21.

25. For further discussion of the idea of epistemological violence regarding traditional documentary film practice, particularly ethnographic filmmaking, see chapter 14, "Domestic Ethnography and the Construction of the 'Other' Self."

26. See in particular André Bazin, "The Ontology of the Photographic Image," in *What Is Cinema*, trans. Hugh Gray (Berkeley: University of California Press, 1967), 9–16.

27. Noël Carroll, "Nonfiction Film and Postmodernist Skepticism," in *Post-theory: Reconstructing Film Studies*, ed. David Bordwell and Noël Carroll (Madison: University of Wisconsin Press, 1996), 285.

28. Ibid., 284.

29. Fredric Jameson, "Video: Surrealism without the Unconscious," in *Postmodernism, or The Cultural Logic of Late Capitalism* (Durham, N.C.: Duke University Press, 1991), 69, 73, 76.

30. See in this regard Maureen Turim, "The Cultural Logic of Video," in *Illuminating Video*, ed. Doug Hall and Sally Jo Fifer (New York: Aperture, 1991), 331–42; Raymond Bellour, "The Images of the World," in *Resolutions: Contemporary Video Practices*, ed. Michael Renov and Erika Suderburg (Minneapolis: University of Minnesota Press, 1996), 149–64; Marita Sturken, "The Politics of Video Memory: Electronic Erasures and Inscriptions," in Renov and Suderburg, *Resolutions*, 1–12; and Erika Suderburg, "The Electronic Corpse: Notes for an Alternative Language of History and Amnesia," in Renov and Suderburg, *Resolutions*, 102–23.

31. Jameson, "Video," 96.

32. Bauman, *Life in Fragments*, 81.

33. Bob Pank, ed., *The Digital Fact Book, Edition 8* (Newbury, U.K.: Quantel, 1996), 60; italics mine.

34. David Throup, *Film in the Digital Age*, edited and with additional material by Bob Pank (Newbury, U.K.: Quantel, 1996), 74.

35. Pank, *The Digital Fact Book*, 13.

36. Throup, *Film in the Digital Age*, 82; italics mine.

37. Ibid., 87; italics mine.

38. Ibid., 98; italics mine.

39. I do not mean to suggest that all modernist *art* necessarily supports the rigid maxims of instrumental rationality that I have linked to the modernist project. Indeed, as I have described earlier, a number of important strands of art making in the modern era (surrealism, suprematism, and literary modernism, to name just a few) actively defined themselves against certainty or science or rationalism as unassailable bulwarks. The digital work to which I now turn is notable for its somewhat paradoxical embrace of scientific technology as a tool to undermine truth as immutable, inevitable, and irreversible. The truths that these digital artists mine are quicksilver, responsive to the touch, reversible at every turn.

40. See chapter 9, "Technology and Ethnographic Dialogue."

41. Gemma Corradi Fiumara, *The Other Side of Language: A Philosophy of Listening*, trans. Charles Lambert (London: Routledge, 1990). See in particular chapter 1, "Towards a Fuller Understanding of *Logos*," 1–17.

42. Daniel Reeves, telephone conversation with author, 26 August 1997.

43. Cited in Bauman, *Life in Fragments*, 66.

44. These ideas are drawn from a 1996 public lecture given by Jim Campbell at New York's Museum of Modern Art, cited in curator Stephen Nowlin's catalog essay for a 1997 exhibition at the Art Center College of Design in Pasadena, California, entitled "Memory/Recollection/Transformation: Reactive Works by Jim Campbell" (n.p.).

45. Cited in Stephen Nowlin's catalog essay for "Memory/Recollection/Transformation: Reactive Works by Jim Campbell" (n.p.).

46. Emmanuel Levinas, "Martin Buber's Thought and Contemporary Judaism," in *Outside the Subject*, trans. Michael B. Smith (Stanford: Stanford University Press, 1994), 15.

9. Technology and Ethnographic Dialogue

1. Louis Althusser, "Philosophy as a Revolutionary Weapon," in *Lenin and Philosophy*, trans. Ben Brewster (New York: Monthly Review Press, 1971), 17.

2. For an exception to this scanting of the community in the emergent discourse of communication technology, see Steven G. Jones, ed., *Cyber Society: Computer-Mediated Communication and Community* (Thousand Oaks, Calif.: Sage Publications, 1995).

3. See, in this regard, Emmanuel Levinas, preface to *Totality and Infinity*, trans. Alphonso Lingis (The Hague: Martinus Nijhoff, 1961), 21: "But violence does not consist so much in injuring and annihilating persons as in interrupting their continuity, making them play roles in which they no longer recognize themselves, making them betray not only their commitments but their own substance, making them carry out actions that will destroy every possibility for action."

4. Emmanuel Levinas, preface to *Outside the Subject*, trans. Michael B. Smith (Stanford: Stanford University Press, 1994), 2–3. A further reference to the human remains to be mentioned, one that bears upon the work of Levinas. In *The Conquest of America: The Question of the Other*, trans. Richard Howard (New York: Harper and Row, 1984), Tzvetan Todorov's monumental critique of the colonization of the Americas in the late fifteenth and sixteenth centuries, two elementary figures of the experience of alterity that impelled the Spanish conquest are identified—one a misguided equalitarianism (i.e., everyone's the same) leading to the projection of one's own values on the Other and thus an aggressive assimilationism; the other the assumption of a fundamentally hierarchical value system in which the Other is devalued or destroyed. In both instances, "What is denied is the existence of a *human* substance truly other, something capable of being not merely an imperfect state of oneself" (42, italics mine). Todorov offers a brilliant and thoroughly convincing case study focusing on a succession of historical figures, among them Columbus, Cortés, and Diego Duran; he demonstrates that the Other has a socially and culturally determined history and that Europe can be understood in the present only through recourse to its colonizing past. Yet on the heels of this historical specificity, Todorov chooses to conclude the book with some proposals for the future, ideas that are deeply influenced by Levinas, whom Todorov calls in a bibliographic note "the philosopher of alterity." He cites Levinas, in all his evanescence: "Our period is not defined by the triumph of technology for technology's sake, as it is not defined by art for art's sake, as it is not defined by nihilism. It is action for a world to come, transcendence of its period—transcendence of self which calls for epiphany of the Other" (250).

5. Stephen Toulmin, *Cosmopolis: The Hidden Agenda of Modernity* (Chicago: University of Chicago Press, 1990), ix. Toulmin's conclusions seem to offer qualified support to those of Levinas, for he argues that the seventeenth century's "pursuit of mathematical exactitude and logical rigor, intellectual certainty and moral purity . . . led both to its most striking technical successes and to its deepest human failures." Toulmin calls for renewed attention to "a practical concern for human life in its concrete detail" as a way to "salvage what is still humanly important" in the project of modernity. Here again we discover the ethicist's concern for "human failures," for the "humanly important" (x–xi).

6. Levinas, *Totality and Infinity*, 43.

7. Emmanuel Levinas, *Otherwise Than Being, or Beyond Essence*, trans. Alphonso Lingis (The Hague: Martinus Nijhoff, 1981), 12.

8. Mark C. Taylor, *Altarity* (Chicago: University of Chicago Press, 1987), 195.

9. Levinas, *Totality and Infinity*, 49.

10. Levinas, *Otherwise Than Being, or Beyond Essence*, 10.

11. The paragraph draws from Alphonso Lingis's introduction, Levinas's preface, and the opening pages of the chapter "Metaphysics and Transcendence," in *Totality and Infinity*, 11–35.

12. Levinas, *Totality and Infinity*, 47.

13. "We name this calling into question of my spontaneity by the presence of the Other ethics" (ibid., 43).

14. Ibid., 46.

15. Ibid., 51.

16. Levinas, *Outside the Subject*, 10, 15.

17. Levinas, *Totality and Infinity*, 305.

18. Ibid., 50.

19. Ibid., 40.

20. David MacDougall, "Beyond Observational Cinema," in *Principles of Visual Anthropology*, ed. Paul Hockings (The Hague: Mouton, 1975), 118.

21. Ibid., 118–19.

22. For a thorough treatment of the modes of documentary exposition, see Bill Nichols, *Represent-*

ing Reality (Bloomington: Indiana University Press, 1991), 32–75; and Nichols, Blurred Boundaries (Bloomington: Indiana University Press, 1994), 92–106.

23. Cited in Martin Buber, On Intersubjectivity and Cultural Creativity, ed. S. N. Eisenstadt (Chicago: University of Chicago Press, 1992), 36–38.
24. Ibid., 39–40.
25. Ibid., 40.
26. Michael Renov, "Video Confessions," in Resolutions: Contemporary Video Practices, ed. Michael Renov and Erika Suderburg (Minneapolis: University of Minnesota Press, 1996), 92, reprinted here as chapter 13.
27. Levinas, Otherwise than Being, or Beyond Essence, 11.
28. Roland Barthes, "Myth Today," in Mythologies, trans. Annette Lavers (New York: Hill and Wang, 1972), 109–59.
29. James W. Carey, Communication as Culture: Essays on Media and Society (New York: Routledge, 1988). In describing Carey's brilliant formulation of the two views of communication, I am drawing upon several chapters, chief among them "A Cultural Approach to Communication" (13–36), "The Mythos of the Electronic Revolution" (113–41), and "Space, Time, and Communications: A Tribute to Harold Innis" (142–72). As Carey so generously notes throughout, his conception is deeply influenced by the work of the late Canadian communication theorist Harold A. Innis, whose most accessible work remains his collection of essays The Bias of Communication (Toronto: University of Toronto Press, 1951).
30. Carey, Communication as Culture, 134.
31. Ibid., 18.
32. The late Harold Innis wrote that "the tragedy of modern culture has arisen as inventions in commercialism have destroyed a sense of time" (The Bias of Communication, 85–86). In this regard, he examined at length the oral cultures of the past such as Greece and its concern for communication by the ear, for example, the Homeric epic, which depended upon a repeated, ritualized telling. (We might add, though Innis does not emphasize this point, that non-Western cultures have generally favored orality.) The papyrus roll, the parchment codex, the printing press, and the linotype machine all facilitated the overthrow of the oral tradition in favor of bureaucratic hierarchy, mercantilism, in short, progress. These technologies made possible a historical shift from the time-based oral culture of the spoken word, a mode geared to listening, to the space-conquering, reproducible species of culture for the eye. And in light of both Levinas and Carey, we might say that the dominant space-binding mode of communication represents a movement toward the transmission view and toward totality.
33. Levinas, Totality and Infinity, 23.
34. On the nontotalizing character of listening in the context of the encounter, see Martin Buber's remarkable account of the "dream of the double cry," in which his dreamed outcry was silently answered. "And then, not from a distance but from the air roundabout me, noiselessly, came the answer. Really it did not come; it was there. It had been there—so I may explain it—even before my cry: there it was, and now, when I laid myself open to it, it let itself be received by me. . . . If I were to report with what I heard it I should have to say 'with every pore of my body'" (On Intersubjectivity and Cultural Creativity, 41–43).
35. In "Video Confessions" (chapter 13), I argue that Wendy Clarke's One on One project, composed of a series of video letters exchanged between prison inmates and those outside, resulted in novel and hybridized relations of the sort I have described here. The difference between the One on One and L.A. Link experiences was the link technology's introduction of a real-time element; interlocutors were able to communicate in the present tense rather than after the fact through the bicycling of tapes. There seem to be crucial differences with regard to the way in which listening and response developed with the two formats. Because the One on One participants, half of whom were incarcerated and frequently given to personal reflection, were able to watch and hear the taped video letters from their "other" many times over, the quality of listening and response was frequently much more refined than was the case with L.A. Link. Another difference was age based, given that the L.A. Link population was under twenty, while the "One on Ones" were undertaken by people ranging in age from twenty to sixty-five.

10. The Address to the Other

1. Emmanuel Levinas, Otherwise than Being, or Beyond Essence, trans. Alphonso Lingis (The Hague: Martinus Nijhoff Publishers, 1981), 87.
2. Hayden White, "The Modernist Event," in The Persistence of History, ed. Vivian Sobchack (New York: Routledge, 1996), 30–32.
3. Dori Laub, M.D., "An Event without a Witness: Truth, Testimony, and Survival," Testimony:

Crises of Witnessing in Literature, Psychoanalysis, and History, by Shoshana Felman and Dori Laub (New York: Routledge, 1992), 75–92.

4. Quoted in White, "The Modernist Event," 30.
5. Jean-François Lyotard, *Heidegger and "the Jews,"* trans. Andreas Michel and Mark S. Roberts (Minneapolis: University of Minnesota Press, 1990), 47.
6. Dori Laub, M.D., "Bearing Witness, or the Vicissitudes of Listening," in *Testimony: Crises of Witnessing in Literature, Psychoanalysis, and History,* by Shoshana Felman and Dori Laub (New York: Routledge, 1992), 64.
7. Ibid., 64–65.
8. Levinas, *Otherwise Than Being, or Beyond Essence,* 119.
9. Laub, "An Event without a Witness," 91.
10. Harold Bloom, foreword to *Zakhor: Jewish History and Jewish Memory,* by Yosef Hayim Yerushalmi (Seattle: University of Washington Press, 1982), xxiii.
11. Levinas, *Otherwise Than Being, or Beyond Essence,* 13.
12. Ibid., 49.
13. Aaron Hass, "Intergenerational Transmission," in *In the Shadow of the Holocaust: The Second Generation* (Cambridge: Cambridge University Press, 1990), 25–50.
14. Levinas, *Otherwise Than Being, or Beyond Essence,* 117.
15. See, in this regard, Yosef Hayim Yerushalmi, *Zakhor: Jewish History and Jewish Memory* (Seattle: University of Washington Press, 1982), 5–26.
16. Martin Buber, *I and Thou,* trans. Walter Kaufman (New York: Simon and Schuster, 1970), 57.
17. Levinas, *Otherwise Than Being, or Beyond Essence,* 116.

11. New Subjectivities

1. Hans Richter, *The Struggle for the Film,* trans. Ben Brewster (New York: St. Martin's Press, 1986), 42–44.
2. Ibid., 43.
3. Joris Ivens, *The Camera and I* (New York: International Publishers, 1969), 26.
4. Dziga Vertov, *Kino-Eye: The Writings of Dziga Vertov,* ed. Annette Michelson (Berkeley: University of California Press, 1984), 7–8.
5. Ibid., 84.
6. See, in particular, Brian Winston, "The Documentary Film as Scientific Inscription," in *Theorizing Documentary,* ed. Michael Renov (New York: Routledge, 1993), 37–57; and Lisa Cartwright, *Screening the Body* (Minneapolis: University of Minnesota Press, 1995).
7. Raymond Williams, "Subjective," in *Keywords: A Vocabulary of Culture and Society* (London: Flamingo, 1976), 308–12.
8. Ibid., 312.
9. Bill Nichols, *Representing Reality: Issues and Concepts in Documentary* (Bloomington: Indiana University Press, 1991), 38–44. Nichols has chosen to update his fourfold typology in his more recent work by adding a fifth category, the performative mode, which corresponds rather closely to what I am terming the "new subjectivity" in documentary film and video. See especially the chapters "Embodied Knowledge and the Politics of Location—an Evocation" and "Performing Documentary," in *Blurred Boundaries: Questions of Meaning in Contemporary Culture,* by Bill Nichols (Bloomington: Indiana University Press, 1994), 1–16, 92–106.
10. Winston, "The Documentary Film," 43.
11. Ibid., 51–52.
12. Stephen Mamber, *Cinema Verite in America: Studies in Uncontrolled Documentary* (Cambridge: MIT Press, 1974), 95.
13. Clifford Geertz, *Local Knowledge: Further Essays in Interpretive Anthropology* (New York: Basic Books, 1983), 4.
14. Stanley Aronowitz, "Reflections on Identity," in his *Dead Artists, Live Theories, and Other Cultural Problems* (New York: Routledge, 1994), 197–98.
15. Quoted in Mick Eaton, "The Production of Cinematic Reality," in *Anthropology—Reality—Cinema: The Films of Jean Rouch,* ed. Mick Eaton (London: BFI, 1979), 51.
16. Quoted in G. Roy Levin, "Jean Rouch," in *Documentary Explorations: Fifteen Interviews with Film-Makers* (Garden City, N.Y.: Doubleday, 1971), 137.
17. Annette Kuhn, *Family Secrets: Acts of Memory and Imagination* (London: Verso, 1995), 4.
18. For an extended analysis of Mekas's place within the documentary tradition, see chapter 4, "*Lost, Lost, Lost:* Mekas as Essayist."
19. Julia Watson, "Unspeakable Differences: The Politics of Gender in Lesbian and Heterosexual Women's Autobiographies," in *De/Colonizing the Subject: The Politics of Gender in Women's Autobiography* (Minneapolis: University of Minnesota Press, 1992), 140.

12. The Electronic Essay

1. "He is troubled by any *image* of himself, suffers when he is named. He finds the perfection of a human relationship in this vacancy of the image: to abolish—in oneself, between oneself and others—*adjectives*; a relationship which adjectivizes is on the side of the image, on the side of domination, of death." Roland Barthes, *Roland Barthes by Roland Barthes,* trans. Richard Howard (New York: Hill and Wang, 1977), 43.

2. Cited in R. Lane Kauffmann, "The Skewed Path: Essaying as Un-methodical Method," *Diogenes* 143 (fall 1988): 66.

3. Pater's statement of the essay's "un-methodical method" serves as the epigraph to Kauffmann's "The Skewed Path," 66; Adorno's pronouncement appears in "The Essay as Form," in *Notes to Literature,* vol. 1, ed. Rolf Tiedemann, trans. Shierry Weber Nicholsen (New York: Columbia University Press, 1991), 13.

4. Georg Lukács, "On the Nature and Form of the Essay," in *Soul and Form,* trans. Anna Bostock (Cambridge: MIT Press, 1974), 18.

5. Reda Bensmaia, *The Barthes Effect: The Essay as Reflective Text,* trans. Pat Fedkiew (Minneapolis: University of Minnesota Press, 1987), 96, 98.

6. "The postmodern would be that which, in the modern, puts forward the unpresentable in presentation itself; that which denies itself the solace of good forms, the consensus of a taste which would make it possible to share collectively the nostalgia for the unattainable; that which searches for new presentations, not in order to enjoy them but in order to impart a stronger sense of the unpresentable. . . . It seems to me that the essay (Montaigne) is postmodern, while the fragment *(The Athaeneum)* is modern." Jean-François Lyotard, *The Postmodern Condition: A Report on Knowledge,* trans. Geoff Bennington and Brian Massumi (Minneapolis: University of Minnesota Press, 1984), 81; Adorno, "The Essay as Form," 18.

7. Adorno, "The Essay as Form," 22.

8. Kauffmann, "The Skewed Path," 68.

9. Adorno, "The Essay as Form," 22.

10. The essay has, since Montaigne, been understood to be judgment "in apprenticeship and on trial." Michel de Montaigne, *Essays,* trans. Donald M. Frame (Stanford: Stanford University Press, 1958), 611. Tobias Wolff has noted of the personal essay that "it doesn't reward authorial discretion, self-effacement, the arts that conceal art. Nor does it reward any of the civic virtues: tact; polish; reasonableness; noble, throat catching sentiment; correct posture." Tobias Wolff, introduction to *Broken Vessels,* by Andre Dubus (Boston: David R. Godine, 1991), xiii.

11. Adorno, "The Essay as Form," 11.

12. Raymond Bellour, "Video Writing," in *Illuminating Video: An Essential Guide to Video Art,* trans. Alison Rowe (San Francisco: Aperture and the Bay Area Video Coalition, 1991), 435.

13. Bill Viola, "An Interview with Bill Viola," by Raymond Bellour, *October* 34 (fall 1985): 100–101.

14. Bellour, "Video Writing," 427.

15. Peggy Phelan, *Unmarked: The Politics of Performance* (New York: Routledge, 1993), 148.

16. Marita Sturken, "Paradox in the Evolution of an Art Form: Great Expectations and the Making of a History," in *Illuminating Video,* 119.

17. Rosalind Krauss, "Video: The Aesthetics of Narcissism," *October* 1 (1976); reprinted in John Hanhardt, ed., *Video Culture* (Rochester, N.Y.: Visual Studies Workshop and Peregrine Smith Books, 1986), 179–80.

18. Montaigne, *Essays,* 821.

19. Ibid., 611, 721.

20. Barthes, *Roland Barthes by Roland Barthes,* 129.

21. Cited in Kauffmann, "The Skewed Path," 74.

22. Roland Barthes, *The Pleasure of the Text,* trans. Richard Miller (New York: Hill and Wang, 1975), 64. Barthes's metaphor of the essayistic text as spider's web occurs earlier in Adorno's *Minima Moralia* (written between 1944 and 1947), but with a crucial and informative difference. For Adorno, the spider's web is a site of textual accretion rather than subjective dissolve: "Properly written texts are like spiders' webs: tight, concentric, transparent, well-spun and firm. They draw into themselves all the creatures of the air. Metaphors flitting hastily through them become their nourishing prey. Subject matter comes winging towards them. The soundness of a conception can be judged by whether it causes one quotation to summon another. Where thought has opened up one cell of reality, it should, without violence by the subject, penetrate the next. It proves its relation to the object as soon as other objects crystallize around it. In the light that it casts on its chosen substance, others begin to glow." Theodor W. Adorno, *Minima Moralia: Reflections from Damaged Life,* trans. E. F. N. Jephcott (London: Verso, 1974), 87. This position is reinforced in the later "The Essay as Form" (1954–1958) in which, for essayistic writing, "the fruitfulness of the thoughts depends on the density of the texture" (13).

23. Viola, interview, 101.
24. Cited in Adorno, "The Essay as Form," 17.
25. Lyotard, *The Postmodern Condition*, 81.
26. Andre Tournon, "Self-Interpretation in Montaigne's *Essais*," *Yale French Studies* 64 (1983): 62.
27. Maureen Turim, "Video Art: Theory for a Future," in *Regarding Television: Critical Approaches—an Anthology*, ed. E. Ann Kaplan (Los Angeles: University Publications of America, 1983), 134.
28. Lukács, "On the Nature and Form of the Essay," 18.
29. Adorno, "The Essay as Form," 13.
30. Slavoj Zizek, "Is There a Cause of the Subject?" in *Supposing the Subject*, ed. Joan Copjec (London: Verso, 1994), 103.
31. Ibid., 102.
32. Ibid., 101.
33. Adorno, *Minima Moralia*, 70–71.

13. Video Confessions

The chapter's first epigraph is cited in Jeremy Tambling, *Confession: Sexuality, Sin, the Subject* (Manchester: Manchester University Press, 1990), 37. Canon 21, "Omnis utrusque sexus," mandated annual confession for the faithful, to be fulfilled before the Easter communion. The place of private confession within church doctrine was the subject of much debate and revision throughout the medieval period.

The second epigraph is drawn from Theodor Reik, *The Compulsion to Confess: On the Psychoanalysis of Crime and Punishment* (New York: Farrar, Straus and Cudahy, 1945), 302. The book is composed of a series of lectures delivered at the Teaching Institute of the Vienna Psychoanalytic Association in 1924; its exhaustive treatment of the subject received the endorsement of Freud himself. (In a letter to Reik, Freud termed the treatise "thoughtful and extremely important.") In Reik's analysis, confession emerges as a functionally complex psychoanalytic term. The inclination to confess is "a modified urge for the expression of the drives," which "are felt or recognized as forbidden" (194–95). Confession produces a "partial gratification" of the repressed thought or act, a kind of emotional relief. While Reik posits a masochistic component to confession (a "need for punishment"), he claims for it another seemingly contradictory function, "the unconscious urge to achieve the loss of love" (208). Reik goes on to analyze the compulsion to confess in its several manifestations: in the fields of criminology and criminal law, religion, myth, art and language, child psychology, and pedagogy.

1. Michel Foucault, "The Confession of the Flesh," in *Power/Knowledge: Selected Interviews and Other Writings, 1972–1977* (New York: Pantheon Books, 1980), 210.
2. Ibid., 211, 215–16.
3. Jeremy Tambling makes the case for a distinction between autobiography, which he takes to be a "self-fashioning," and confession, which of necessity submits itself to the judgment of a higher authority. Despite these differences, however, "the intertwining of the two forms seems important, ultimately, rather than the possibility of attempting to see them as opposites" (Tambling, *Confession*, 9).
4. Michel Foucault, *The History of Sexuality, Volume I: An Introduction*, trans. Robert Hurley (New York: Vintage Books, 1978), 61–62.
5. Peter Dennis Bathory, *Political Theory as Public Confession: The Social and Political Thought of St. Augustine of Hippo* (New Brunswick, N.J.: Transaction Books, 1981), 21.
6. Sigmund Freud, "Transference," in *A General Introduction to Psychoanalysis*, trans. Joan Riviere (New York: Washington Square Press, 1966), 448. Freud notes that the transference can be either affectionate or hostile, can evince faith in the treatment or deep-seated resistance. This is because the analyst becomes an object invested with libido, a process that stands as an absolute requirement for successful treatment.
7. "Even we seekers after knowledge today, we godless anti-metaphysicians still take our fire, too, from the flame lit by a faith that is thousands of years old, that Christian faith which was also the faith of Plato, that God is the truth, that truth is divine.—But what if this should become more and more incredible, if nothing should prove to be divine any more unless it were error, blindness, the lie—if God himself should prove to be our most enduring lie?" Friedrich Nietzsche, *The Gay Science*, trans. Walter Kaufman (New York: Vintage Books, 1974), 283. Lacanian subject construction positions the Other as the source of desire and of meaning. "What I seek in speech is the response of the other. What constitutes me as subject is my queston. In order to be recognized by the other, I utter what was only in view of what will be. In order to find him, I call him by a name that he must assume or refuse in order to reply to me." Jacques Lacan, *Écrits: A Selection*, trans. Alan Sheridan (New York: W. W. Norton, 1977), 86. In Lacanian terms, confes-

sional discourse is always addressed to the other; it is the desiring letter that always arrives at its destination.

8. Foucault, *The History of Sexuality*, 59.

9. Any analysis that constructs the subject's dependency on an external, all-knowing source as separable from the therapeutic effects that accrue from confession clearly misrecognizes the functional dynamic of the confessional act. A sense of unburdening can only occur if one endows the auditor with the power to grant absolution.

10. Peter Brown, *Augustine of Hippo* (Berkeley: University of California Press, 1967), 181.

11. Reik, *Compulsion to Confess*, 250. Philip Woollcett, writing in the *Journal for the Scientific Study of Religion*, concurred with Reik's assessment: "Augustine was the greatest psychologist of his time and probably for many centuries to come" (Bathory, *Political Theory*, 55).

12. Reik, *Compulsion to Confess*, 192.

13. Bathory claims that Augustine developed "a mode of instruction through public confession" (*Political Theory*, 17). He examines Augustine's "therapeutic method," in particular his use of anxiety as a positive rather than negative force. "Anxiety was a necessary part of people's lives, and he offers them the means to face it. In the process, anxiety took on a creative potential in that it could—if properly perceived—challenge people and lead not to paralysis but to an active search for self-realization" (38).

14. Foucault, *History of Sexuality*, 34.

15. William James, *The Varieties of Religious Experience: A Study in Human Nature* (New York: Collier Books, 1961), 360.

16. Norberto Valentini and Clara di Meglio, *Sex and the Confessional*, trans. Melton S. Davis (New York: Stein and Day, 1974), 12, 211.

17. Raymond Williams, *Marxism and Literature* (Oxford: Oxford University Press, 1977), 121–27.

18. Mimi White, *Tele-advising: Therapeutic Discourse in American Television* (Chapel Hill: University of North Carolina Press, 1992), 81, 178.

19. Ibid., 19.

20. "The actual commodity, then, is the ultimate referent of the television discourse." Nick Browne, "The Political Economy of the Television (Super)Text," *Quarterly Review of Film Studies* 9, no. 3 (summer 1984): 181.

21. "The compulsive factor eventually found its representation and objectification in the obligation to confess," says Reik in *The Compulsion to Confess* (300). Mandatory monthly confession after the Council of Trent finds its therapeutic counterpart in the obligatory scheduling of analytic sessions.

22. White, *Tele-advising*, 179. The confessional display can also become the basis for the viewer's own repetition compulsion, as a number of television audience studies have shown.

23. Ibid., 182.

24. Michael Renov, "The Distrust of the Visible: Documentary's Psychoanalytic Encounter," paper presented at "Visible Evidence: Strategies and Practices in Documentary Film and Video," Duke University, September 1993. Techno-analysis refers to the displacement of the analyst by the apparatus itself, resulting in a kind of do-it-yourself psychotherapy. The technology becomes both a site of, and a relay point for, transference.

25. Jean Rouch, quoted in Mick Eaton, "The Production of Cinematic Reality," in *Anthropology—Reality—Cinema: The Films of Jean Rouch*, ed. Mick Eaton (London: BFI, 1979), 51.

26. Spoken by Mekas as narration over images in *Lost, Lost, Lost*. For further discussion of this remarkable film, see chapter 4, "*Lost, Lost, Lost*: Mekas as Essayist."

27. David E. James has written with great insight on the alternative cinemas that emerged in the United States during the 1960s in opposition to the hegemonic or industrial cinema. At issue is a notion of the "mode of cultural production" inspired by Horkheimer and Adorno but considerably qualified by, among other factors, the many "renegade uses" at the point of consumption. David E. James, *Allegories of Cinema: American Film in the Sixties* (Princeton, N.J.: Princeton University Press, 1989), 3–28.

28. Perhaps rather than pointing to the limits of electronic "handcrafting," it would be more accurate to suggest that the artisanal potential for video culture is simply unlike the cinema's, which is organized around tactility (the "feel" of celluloid). The first and legendary video art events of the early 1960s, Paik's and Vostell's, were installations in which the televisual hardware was stripped of its techno–use value and reworked "by hand" to suit the artist's vision. Banks of TV sets became the plastic medium. Video art thus began as a kind of artisanal reflex to the very technology that rendered it possible.

29. A note regarding the title of this section: Long after I had begun to research this essay, which I planned to call "The Electronic Confessional," I chanced upon a book of the same name authored by a husband-and-wife team of writers specializing in sexology, Howard R. Lewis and Martha E. Lewis, *The Electronic Confessional: A Sex Book of the 80's* (New York: M. Evans,

1986). The Lewises had, it seems, developed a computer service called Human Sexuality (HSX, for short), a "videotex" service offering "discussion, information and advice on a wide variety of issues related to sex." The book offers an introduction to the system and its uses for the un-initiated while devoting itself primarily to the reproduction of a selection of HSX queries, entries, and exchanges. One example may serve to illustrate the tone of the book: a married man confesses to a predilection for masturbating while wearing diapers into which he has previously urinated. "My wife and I have 'normal' sex, but I need more sexual release than she does. So I turn to the diaper" (88). Through the services of HSX, the man is informed of a group called the Diaper Pail Fraternity out of Sausalito, California (with a membership of 1,500), with whom he may presumably choose to find fellowship. The book certainly suggested whole new frontiers of confessional discourse for the 1990s. It also convinced me to find another title for this essay.

30. "The emphasis here is on the replication of the historical real, the creation of a second-order reality cut to the measure of our desire—to cheat death, stop time, restore loss." Michael Renov, "Toward a Poetics of Documentary," in *Theorizing Documentary*, ed. Michael Renov (New York: Routledge, 1993), 25.

31. Indeed, the wedding video must delegate the first-person function to the roving or multiple eye of the professional. For a thorough treatment of this video phenomenon, see James M. Moran, "Wedding Video and Its Generation," in *Resolutions: Contemporary Video Practices*, ed. Michael Renov and Erika Suderburg (Minneapolis: University of Minnesota Press, 1996), 360–81.

32. Of course, all confession is spoken in the first person. The distinction I wish to make is between confession that is produced through the intervention of another party who controls enunciation and discourse that is self-activated, subject only to one's own editorial agency.

33. The "interactive mode" is the useful term adopted by Bill Nichols to describe the third of four documentary modes of representation in his *Representing Reality* (Bloomington: Indiana University Press, 1991), 32–75. In comparison to the expository mode, in which arguments are rhetorically developed, frequently via voice-over narration, or the observational mode, which opts for the noninterventionism of American direct cinema, films of the interactive type "stress images of testimony or verbal exchange and images of demonstration. . . . Textual authority shifts toward the social actors recruited. . . . the shift of emphasis [is] from an author-centered voice of authority to a witness-centered voice of testimony" (44, 48).

34. Reik, *Compulsion to Confess*, 210–11.

35. Over a period of many months in the early 1970s, *Carel and Ferd* remained a staple feature at the Video Free America exhibition site in the warehouse district of San Francisco. Local audiences were able to develop a long-term relationship with the unfolding melodrama in the manner of mainstream soaps.

36. Foucault, *History of Sexuality*, 61–62.

37. Hershman's statement is deliciously paradoxical, since she knows her discourse to be a public one, albeit an excruciatingly private public discourse.

38. Here I refer to Reik's analysis of the confessional impulse in which he notes that confession "grants a partial gratification to the repressed wishes and impulses" while also fulfilling the need for punishment. "Actually, we often see symptoms disappear in analysis when needs of this kind, at odds with each other, have found a completely adequate expression in confession" (204).

39. Is it only coincidental that the edifice in which *The Love Tapes* are made is architecturally congruent with the increasingly obsolescent church confessional? The design of each, suited to the containment of a single confessing body, nevertheless provides windowed access to another space that underwrites and authorizes it.

40. I borrow the notion of the mana-word from Roland Barthes: "In an author's lexicon, will there not always be a word-as-mana, a word whose ardent, complex, ineffable, and somehow sacred signification gives the illusion that by this word one might answer for everything? Such a word is neither eccentric nor central; it is motionless and carried, floating, never pigeonholed, always atopic (escaping any topic), at once remainder and supplement, a signifier taking up the place of every signified." For Barthes, that word is *body*. Roland Barthes, *Roland Barthes by Roland Barthes*, trans. Richard Howard (New York: Hill and Wang, 1977), 129.

41. In "The Radio as an Apparatus of Communication," written in 1932, Bertolt Brecht critiqued radio for the singularity of its purpose: as a profit-motivated vehicle for delivering entertainment rather than as a medium of two-way exchange. "But quite apart from the dubiousness of its functions, radio is one-sided when it should be two-. It is purely an apparatus for distribution, for mere sharing out. So here is a positive suggestion: change this apparatus over from distribution to communication. . . . The slightest advance in this direction is bound to succeed far more spectacularly than any performance of a culinary kind. As for the technique that needs to be developed for all such operations, it must follow the prime objective of turning the audience not only into pupils but into teachers." Bertolt Brecht, "The Radio as an Apparatus of

Communication," in *Video Culture*, ed. John Handhardt (Rochester, N.Y.: Visual Studies Workshop Press, 1986), 53–54.

42. Questions of various sorts arise when the tapes of the *One on One* series are exhibited or broadcast. Is there a pact of sorts between the two interlocutors, which the introduction of an audience external to the exchange necessarily breaches? Only recently, three years after the project's completion, as the tapes have begun to be shown in classrooms, at public screenings, and soon on the Los Angeles PBS affiliate, KCET, has public exhibition become an issue. In my own experience of talking about this work and screening it in classes and public venues, I have found that audiences tend to be uneasy with their perceived positioning as voyeurs of exchanged confidences. That the very concept of the *One on One* series was conceived in collaboration with the video workshop participants, all of whom signed releases authorizing future screenings of the work, seems not to dispel the uneasiness. This response is likely connected to a historical tendency in the West in which public forms of confession have been displaced by forms of self-disclosure that are private and protected (such as the "privileged communications" between ourselves and our doctors, lawyers, and priests). The public display of exchanged confessions—when received as "real" rather than fictional and predicated on a one-to-one, reciprocal exchange—strikes some audiences as a violation of principle. It seems to me, however, that the project's fundamental value has always been as a kind of heuristic device, a model for interpersonal communication in a media age. From one point of view, the particulars of any confession are less meaningful than the potentiality of the project as a whole for the creation of human dialogue across a whole series of spatial and cultural disjunctures.

43. Cited in Howard Rosenberg, "*One on One* Is the Best TV Talk You Can't See," *Los Angeles Times*, 8 December 1993, F8.

44. Ibid.

45. Reik, *Compulsion to Confess*, 205.

46. Brecht, "Radio," 53.

47. Reik, *Compulsion to Confess*, 279.

48. John Tagg, *The Burden of Representation* (Amherst: University of Massachusetts Press, 1988), 60–61.

49. Ibid., 63–64.

50. In fact, although the *One on One* tapes were made in conjunction with Clarke's video workshop at Chino and were thus institutionally "legitimate," prison officials had no idea about the particulars of the project. Proposals for future projects of this sort would, in Clarke's opinion, face little chance of acceptance. Personal communication with Wendy Clarke, 19 January 1994.

14. Domestic Ethnography and the Construction of the "Other" Self

1. James Clifford, *The Predicament of Culture: Twentieth Century Ethnography, Literature, and Art* (Cambridge: Harvard University Press, 1988), 34; Johannes Fabian, *Time and the Other: How Anthropology Makes Its Object* (New York: Columbia University Press, 1983), 33.

2. "Desire is desire for the absolutely other. . . . A desire without satisfaction which, precisely, *understands* the remoteness, the alterity, and the exteriority of the other. For Desire this alterity, non-adequate to the idea, has a meaning. It is understood as the alterity of the Other and of the Most-High." Emmanuel Levinas, *Totality and Infinity*, 2d ed., trans. A. Lingis (The Hague: Nijhoff, 1978), 34.

3. Peter Mason, *Deconstructing America: Representations of the Other* (London: Routledge, 1990), 2. The work of Levinas, called by Tzvetan Todorov "the philosopher of alterity," has helped to introduce an increasingly influential perspective in debates surrounding the ethical status of research in the social and human sciences. In a deeply radical gesture, Levinas has suggested that it is Reason itself that has functioned to "neutralize and encompass" the other, translating difference into its own terms in the insatiable pursuit of knowledge. Emmanuel Levinas, *Totality and Infinity*, trans. Alphonso Lingis (The Hague: Martinus Nijhoff, 1961), 43. The Levinasian view does not so much undercut the potential for knowledge in cross-cultural research as relativize its value within a moral universe: "It is not a question of putting knowledge in doubt. The human being clearly allows himself to be treated as an object, and delivers himself to knowledge in the *truth* of perception and the light of the human sciences. But, treated exclusively as an object, man is also mistreated and misconstrued. . . . We are human before being learned, and remain so after having forgotten much." Emmanuel Levinas, *Outside the Subject*, trans. Michael B. Smith (Stanford: Stanford University Press, 1994), 2–3.

4. Trinh T. Minh-ha, "Difference: 'A Special Third World Women Issue,'" *Discourse* 8 (fall–winter 1986–1987): 27, 14, 16.

5. Michael Taussig, *Mimesis and Alterity: A Particular History of the Senses* (New York: Routledge, 1993), xviii, xiii.

6. Stephen A. Tyler, "Post-modern Ethnography," in *Writing Culture: The Poetics and Politics of Ethnography* (Berkeley: University of California Press, 1986), 122–40.

7. George E. Marcus, "Ethnography in the Modern World System," in *Writing Culture: The Poetics and Politics of Ethnography* (Berkeley: University of California Press, 1986), 190–93.

8. Historically, the notion of the "unlearning of privilege" recalls a notable response of feminist theorists to the lure of incrementally shared patriarchal authority and is currently echoed by the growing attention being given indigenous media making around the world. The work of certain progressive scholars becomes a "facilitation" of representation made by and for indigenous peoples.

9. See Clifford Geertz, *Works and Lives: The Anthropologist as Author* (Stanford: Stanford University Press, 1988), 1–24; Hayden White, "Introduction: Tropology, Discourse, and the Modes of Human Consciousness," in *Tropics of Discourse: Essays in Cultural Criticism* (Baltimore: Johns Hopkins University Press, 1978), 1–3.

10. There remains a lacuna that the present commentary cannot adequately address, pertaining to the etiology of the artist's sexual orientation. Given Friedrich's public stance as a lesbian filmmaker, and given the film's inclusion of images alluding to Friedrich's sexuality (mostly water imagery: women showering together, Friedrich bathing alone), the matter of the father's role in shaping the daughter's sexual identity seems to be raised, but only indirectly. Such an elliptical treatment of the topic shrewdly sidesteps diagnostics while remaining consistent with the generally oblique approach to the construal of meaning adopted by the work.

11. Edward Said, *Orientalism* (New York: Pantheon, 1978).

12. Paul Ricoeur, "Universal Civilization and National Cultures," in *History and Truth*, trans. Charles A. Kelbley (Evanston: Northwestern University Press, 1965), 278.

13. Kath Weston, "The Politics of Gay Families," in *Rethinking the Family: Some Feminist Questions*, rev. ed., ed. Barrie Thorne and Marilyn Yalom (Boston: Northeastern University Press, 1992), 137. One proviso is worth adding in this context. The phrase "families we choose" stresses volition, the conscious selection of new family groupings. While it would be wrong to deny that gays and lesbians have indeed begun to "choose" to reinvent the family more aggressively and in greater number, it would be a mistake to focus a discussion of queerness and its interventions solely at the level of consciousness. Such a stance would miss the pertinence of what Judith Butler has called "psychic excess," that which surpasses the domain of the conscious subject in the determination of sexuality. "This psychic excess is precisely what is being systematically denied by the notion of a volitional 'subject' who elects at will which gender and/or sexuality to be at any given time and place. . . . Sexuality may be said to exceed any definitive narrativization. . . . There are no direct expressive or causal lines between sex, gender, gender presentation, sexual practice, fantasy and sexuality. . . . Part of what constitutes sexuality is precisely that which does not appear and that which, to some degree, can never appear." Judith Butler, "Imitation and Gender Insubordination," in *Inside/Out: Lesbian Theories, Gay Theories* (New York: Routledge, 1991), 24–25. All of which is to say that sexuality—gay or straight—eludes volition and the regime of the visible in a most fundamental way.

14. Tamara K. Hareven, "American Families in Transition: Historical Perspectives on Change," in *Family in Transition: Rethinking Marriage, Sexuality, Child Rearing, and Family Organization*, 5th ed., ed. Arlene S. Skolnick and Jerome H. Skolnick (Boston: Little Brown, 1986), 55.

15. The matter of sexualized identifications is a tremendously complex one requiring more qualification than can be undertaken here. As Eve Kosofsky Sedgwick has argued, identifications can be consolidating as well as denegating, structured through a play of idealization and abjection. Sexual identifications can be identifications *with, as,* or *against*. Sedgwick elaborates on the sheer profusion of relations implicit in but one subset, *identifying with*, which she describes as potentially "fraught with intensities of incorporation, diminishment, inflation, threat, loss, reparation, and disavowal." Eve Kosofsky Sedgwick, *Epistemology of the Closet* (Berkeley: University of California Press, 1990), 61. To its credit, *Vintage: Families of Value* allows for the discussion and performance of an astonishing array of identificatory positions and intensities played out among its three sets of siblings. The tape, for the most part, steers clear of etiology, a search for queer sources, opting instead for an interactive on-camera interrogation of family dynamics entailing parents, children, spouses, and lovers as well as siblings. If what emerges is a vision of pluralized queer sexualities in which even siblings are unique in their object choices, fantasies, and preferred practices, this can only be a contribution to the overthrow of the discursive rigidities in which queer subjectivity is still closeted.

16. I am purposely invoking the Derridean notion of undecidability with regard to the determination of identity. Derived from the critical writing of Jacques Derrida, the deconstructive method of textual analysis challenges binary oppositions, first by acknowledging the often unspoken hierarchy through which one term controls the other (race over sexuality, sexuality over race), then by overthrowing that hierarchy and finally displacing it. Jacques Derrida, *Positions*, trans.

Alan Bass (Chicago: University of Chicago Press, 1981), 41–43. In Derrida's work, apparently conflictual categories are often found to inhabit one another, resisting and disorganizing the binary in such a manner as to betray the boundaries of "inside" and "outside." This may well be the case for the queer black/black queer subject as constructed within *Vintage: Families of Value*, in which blackness, queerness, birth order, and family relations play out unevenly though decisively.

17. The reference here is to Bill Nichols's discussion of the several modes of documentary exposition, among them the interactive mode, which "stresses images of testimony or verbal exchange. . . . Textual authority shifts toward the social actors recruited: their comments and responses provide a central part of the film's argument. Various forms of monologue and dialogue (real or apparent) predominate." Bill Nichols, *Representing Reality* (Bloomington: Indiana University Press, 1991), 44. In *Vintage*, Thomas Allen Harris does indeed delegate authority to his interlocutors, who have been quite literally recruited for that task; their experiences supplement his own.

18. Claude Lévi-Strauss, *Tristes Tropiques*, trans. John and Doreen Weightman (New York: Atheneum, 1978), 389.

15. The End of Autobiography or New Beginnings?

1. Elizabeth W. Bruss, "Eye for I: Making and Unmaking Autobiography in Film," in *Autobiography: Essays Theoretical and Critical*, ed. James Olney (Princeton, N.J.: Princeton University Press, 1980), 296.

2. Walter Benjamin, "The Work of Art in the Age of Mechanical Reproduction," in *Illuminations*, trans. Harry Zohn (New York: Schocken Books, 1968), 222.

3. Ibid., 221.

4. Bruss, "Eye for I," 296–97.

5. I am not suggesting that all personal Web pages are, in any meaningful sense, autobiographical or that Web pages conform to the canons of autobiography in the traditional sense. Any serious effort to situate the autobiographical Web site in relation to its literary and cinematic counterparts would require a far more detailed analysis of discursive conditions and aesthetic properties than can be undertaken here. I can only hope to initiate such a discussion. I do so by giving special attention to the unique and rather complicated commodity status of the Web site, which seems to me a point of fundamental contrast with its representational forebears.

6. Noelle Knox, "Internet Merger Mania Is Picking Up," *Buffalo News*, 18 July 1999, 14B.

7. Ibid.

8. Reuters, "Value of Internet Mergers Climbs 22-Fold in First Half," *San Diego Union Tribune*, 27 July 1999, C2.

9. Joseph Menn, "Yahoo's Profit Tops Estimates," *Los Angeles Times*, 8 April 1999, C1.

10. Christopher Parkes, "Disney's go.com Gets Lukewarm Reception," *Financial Times* (London), 13 July 1999, 34.

11. Richard Waters, "NBC Plans to Separate Websites Arm," *Financial Times* (London), 11 May 1999, 29.

12. Jacques Lacan, *Écrits: A Selection*, trans. Alan Sheridan (New York: W. W. Norton, 1977), 153.

13. David E. James, *Power Misses: Essays across (Un)Popular Culture* (London: Verso, 1996), 1–24.

14. Carolyn Marvin, *When Old Technologies Were New: Thinking about Electric Communication in the Late Nineteenth Century* (New York: Oxford University Press, 1988), 5.

15. See in this regard James W. Carey, "Space, Time, and Communications: A Tribute to Harold Innis," in *Communication as Culture: Essays on Media and Society* (New York: Routledge, 1989), 142–72. See also Harold A. Innis, *The Bias of Communication* (Toronto: University of Toronto Press, 1951).

16. Philippe Lejeune, "The Autobiographical Pact," in *On Autobiography*, trans. Katherine Leary (Minneapolis: University of Minnesota Press, 1989), 3–30.

17. See in this regard Hannah Arendt's insightful introduction to Benjamin's *Illuminations*, 1–55.

Publication History

"Early Newsreel: The Construction of a Political Imaginary for the New Left" was originally published in *Afterimage* 14, no. 7 (February 1987). Reprinted with permission from *Afterimage*.

"Warring Images: Stereotype and American Representations of the Japanese, 1941–1991" was originally published in *Media Wars: Then and Now,* a publication of the 1991 Yamagata International Documentary Film Festival for the Pearl Harbor Fiftieth Anniversary, October 1991. Reprinted with permission from the Yamagata International Documentary Film Festival.

"*Lost, Lost, Lost*: Mekas as Essayist" was originally published in David E. James, ed., *To Free the Cinema: Jonas Mekas and the New York Underground* (Princeton: Princeton University Press, 1992), 215–39. Copyright 1992 Princeton University Press. Reprinted by permission of Princeton University Press.

"Charged Vision: The Place of Desire in Documentary Film Theory" was originally published in Swedish as "Ett Fortatat Seende," *Aura* 3, nos. 3–4 (1997).

"The Subject in History: The New Autobiography in Film and Video" was originally published in *Afterimage* 17, no. 1 (February 1989). Reprinted with permission by *Afterimage*.

"Documentary Disavowals and the Digital" was originally published as "Documentary Disavowals, or the Digital, Documentary, and Postmodernity," *Polygraph* 13 (2001).

"New Subjectivities: Documentary and Self-Representation in the Post-verité Age" was originally published in *Documentary Box* 7 (English edition), July 1995. Reprinted with permission by the Yamagata International Documentary Film Festival. This essay was previously reprinted in Diane Waldman and Janet Walker, eds., *Feminism and Documentary* (Minneapolis: University of Minnesota Press, 1999), 84–94.

"Video Confessions" was originally published in Michael Renov and Erika Suderburg, eds., *Resolutions: Contemporary Video Practices* (Minneapolis: University of Minnesota Press, 1996), 78–101.

"Domestic Ethnography and the Construction of the 'Other' Self" was originally published in Jane M. Gaines and Michael Renov, eds., *Collecting Visible Evidence* (Minneapolis: University of Minnesota Press, 1999), 140–55.

Index

Cyberscribes, 236
Cyberscribes I: The New Journalists devoted to "Writing the Story of Your Life," 236

Daley, Richard J., 29, 36–37
Dalí, Salvador, 97
Danish Film Institute, xi
Daughters: fathers and, 219–22
Day after Trinity, The (Else), 120–21
Days of Waiting (Okazaki), 62–63
Death, 123; as negativity, 120; Real and, 121, 124, 125; representation of, 121, 124, 125, 126; society and, 122
December 7 (tract), 65
Deconstruction, 4, 38
Deep Dish TV Network, 66
Defaux, Gerard, 70
Definitions: struggles with, 182
DeGaulle, Charles, 25–26
De Kooning, Willem, 88
Delirium, 23, 100, 219
Delirium (Faber), 224, 225, 226
"Deliver Us from Evil," 54
Democratic National Convention, 17, 21, 23; confrontational events at, 25, 28, 250n30
Depression: domesticity and, 224
De Quincey, 195
Deren, 198
Derrida, Jacques, 79, 108, 118, 266n16; on Abraham/Torok, 40–41; on autobiography/essayistic, 105; conflictual categories of, 287n16; on genres, 251n3; *hermetics* and, 23; on representation/death, 124
Descartes, René, xiv, 132; I/*cogito* and, 110; method of reflection and, 150; subject/object model of, 105
Desire, 100, 103, 219, 265n2
Detective, The: review of, 10
Deus Ex (Brakhage), 82
Dewey, John, 158
DeWitt, John L., 50
Dialogue: ethnographic, 153; meeting and, 151
Diaper Pail Fraternity, 264n29
Diaries, xi, 86, 192, 198, 239; electronic, 115; expansiveness of, 88; taxonomic limits of, 106; video, 156, 177–78
Diaries, Notes, and Sketches (Mekas), 70, 72, 87–88, 111, 198; lessons from, 77, 114; *Lost* and, 112; subjective in, 79
"Diary Film, The" (Mekas), 69
Diary films, 64, 74, 82, 83, 86, 111–15
Diderot, Denis, 31
"Diderot, Brecht, Eisenstein" (Barthes), 31
Diegesis, 18, 23, 25, 28, 35, 38, 95, 98; fictional, 41; history and, 37
Difference, 48, 163, 228
Difference and Pathology (Gilman), 43
Digital Fact Book, The (Quantel), 140
Digital Watch (Campbell): described, 144–45
Di Meglio, Clara, 195
Ding, Loni, 61, 62
Directorial control: erosion of, 224
Discontinuity, 3, 25, 117

Discourse, 15, 71, 106, 118, 194; anthropological, 217; assertiveness of, 142; autobiographical, 179, 191, 218, 235, 241; cinematic, 30; confessional, 195, 198, 200, 204, 215; documentary, 94–95, 121, 148, 152; essayistic, 105, 182, 189; ethical dimension of, 148; historical, 102, 108, 109, 161; incitement to, 195, 214; intensity of, 158, 210; media, 149; nonfictional, 83; philosophical, 99; public, 178, 194; scholarly, 219; scientific, 108; shaping, 226; stereotypical, 45, 48, 54; territorializing, 142
Disney, 52, 234
Displaced persons, 77, 179
Displacement, 95, 179
Dissent, 54, 67–68
Divine: secularization of, 171–74
Documentary, 75, 102, 106, 153, 167; analytic, 11; appeal of, 96, 100; art, xxiii, 83; assertiveness of, 139; historical role of, 135–36; independent, 44; modes of, 97; observational mode of, 152; politicized, 3; roots of, 97; self-confidence of, 131; silent era of, 100–101; standards of, 21–22; theory, 137, 159; tradition, xvii, 147; value, 138
Documentary Box, 171
Documentary detour, 73–85
Documentary disavowals, 136, 137
Documentary films, 74, 82, 85, 99, 103, 121, 176; British, 53; classical styles of, 246n13; development of, 135, 136, 171; ethical questions of, 159; mass projection and, 50–54; movement, 134; reality effect of, 45; socially conscious, 96; state-sponsored, 135; subjectivity in, 130, 178, 260n9; theory, 94; wartime, 53, 54
Documentary impulse, 105, 109
Documentary practice, 22; Bazinian precepts of, 136; community of, 174; ethics and, 157; meanings/effects of, 136; post-verité, xxiii; subjectivity in, 246n13
Documentary spectatorship, 96
Documentary studies, xvi, 133–34, 139, 142, 161; ethics and, 160; Griersonian tradition of, xvii–xviii, 135
Documentation, 111, 216
"Documenting Fictions: Documentary Dimensions of the Fiction Film" (conference), 21
Domestic, the: understanding, 226
Domestic ethnography, xiii, xvii, 223; autobiography and, 218, 228–29; characteristics of, 221; consanguinity/co(i)mplication and, 218; cultural memory and, 226; intersubjective reciprocity and, 219; notion of, 216, 222; self-inscription and, 219; subjectivity and, 219
Domination, xvi, 4, 214
Domino system: transparency of, 140–41
Doolittle, James, 57
Dostoyevsky, Fyodor, 195
Douglas, John, 11, 12, 17
Dower, John W., 45, 46, 57, 250n2; on stereotypes, 47, 49, 50
Dow Jones: Internet Index by, 233
Drama, 21, 33
Drew, Robert, xx–xxi, 174, 175

MICHAEL RENOV is professor of critical studies in the School of Cinema–Television at the University of Southern California. He is author of *Hollywood's Wartime Woman: Representation and Ideology,* editor of *Theorizing Documentary,* and coeditor of *Resolutions: Contemporary Video Practices* (Minnesota, 1996) and *Collecting Visible Evidence* (Minnesota, 1999).

DAT